European Yearbook of International Economic Law

Special Issue

The European Yearbook of International Economic Law (EYIEL) is a Springer-publication in the field of International Economic Law (IEL), a field increasingly emancipating itself from Public International Law scholarship and evolving into a fully-fledged academic discipline in its own right. With the yearbook, editors and publisher make a significant contribution to the development of this "new" discipline and provide an international source of reference of the highest possible quality.

The EYIEL covers all areas of IEL, in particular WTO Law, External Trade Law of major trading countries, important Regional Economic Integration agreements, International Competition Law, International Investment Regulation, International Monetary Law, International Intellectual Property Protection and International Tax Law.

EYIEL publishes articles following a substantive review by the editors and external experts as appropriate.

The editors have published extensively in the field of IEL and European Law alike. They are supported by an international Advisory Board consisting of established scholars of the highest reputation.

The European Yearbook of International Economic Law (EYIEL) is an annual publication in International Economic Law, a field increasingly emancipating itself from Public International Law scholarship and evolving into a fully-fledged academic discipline in its own right. With the yearbook, the editors and publisher intend to make a significant contribution to the development of this "new" discipline and provide an international reference source of the highest possible quality. The EYIEL covers all areas of IEL, in particular WTO Law, External Trade Law for major trading countries, important Regional Economic Integration agreements, International Competition Law, International Investment Regulation, International Monetary Law, International Intellectual Property Protection and International Tax Law. In addition to the regular annual volumes, EYIEL Special Issues routinely address specific current topics in International Economic Law.

Doron Goldbarsht • Louis de Koker
Jamie Ferrill
Editors

The Financial War on Crime and Terrorism

Opportunities and Challenges

Springer

Editors
Doron Goldbarsht
Macquarie University and Financial Integrity Hub (FIH)
Sydney, NSW, Australia

Louis de Koker
La Trobe University and Financial Integrity Hub (FIH)
Melbourne, VIC, Australia

Jamie Ferrill
Charles Sturt University and Financial Integrity Hub (FIH)
Canberra, ACT, Australia

ISSN 2364-8392 ISSN 2364-8406 (electronic)
European Yearbook of International Economic Law
ISSN 2510-6880 ISSN 2510-6899 (electronic)
Special Issue
ISBN 978-3-032-06359-5 ISBN 978-3-032-06360-1 (eBook)
https://doi.org/10.1007/978-3-032-06360-1

This Springer imprint is published by the registered company Springer Nature Switzerland AG
The registered company address is: Gewerbestrasse 11, 6330 Cham, Switzerland

We are deeply grateful to our families for their unwavering support, patience, and encouragement and to the authors for their thoughtful contributions and collegiality throughout the development of this volume.

We also honour the memory of Professor Petrus C. van Duyne, who passed away earlier this year. His pioneering work on organised crime, money laundering, and corruption has left an enduring impact on the field. We are privileged to include his final contribution in this collection.

Contents

Financial Crime Prevention in an Age of Paradox 1
Jamie Ferrill, Louis de Koker, and Doron Goldbarsht

Leadership in the Evolving Landscape of Financial Crime: Navigating AML/CTF Risks and Controls 23
Jamie Ferrill and Rachel Southworth

FATF and the Conundrum of Public-Private Sector Intelligence and Information Sharing 49
Paula Chadderton

Private to Private: The Next Frontier of Financial Intelligence Sharing 75
Doron Goldbarsht and Timothy Goodrick

Network Analytics and Generative Artificial Intelligence: A Hybrid Approach to Money Laundering Detection 99
Milind Tiwari

Illegal Wildlife Trade as a Method of Financing Terrorism 123
Cayle Lupton

Practice to Deceive: A Taxonomy of Money Laundering Deception Based on US and Australian Case Studies 145
Ben Scott

Geopolitics of State Capture: Systemic Corruption as a Professional Service 165
Nicholas Donaldson and Christian Leuprecht

Corrupt Elites and Godfathers in Nigeria: Structural Impunity and the Undermining of Accountability 193
Jackie H. Harvey and Petrus C. van Duyne

Dangerous Play: AML/CTF/CPF Risks in the Gaming Sector 225
Jeffrey Simser

International Arbitration and Money Laundering: Is There an Actual Issue? 245
Robert Walters

The Impact of the Financial Action Task Force (FATF) Standards and Focus: From Effectiveness to Effect 269
Nicholas Morris and Louis de Koker

The Financial War on Crime and Terrorism—Important Research Questions 301
Louis de Koker, Doron Goldbarsht, and Jamie Ferrill

Correction to: Geopolitics of State Capture: Systemic Corruption as a Professional Service C1
Nicholas Donaldson and Christian Leuprecht

Contributors

Paula Chadderton Australia's Department of Foreign Affairs and Trade, Barton, ACT, Australia

Nicholas Donaldson Leiden University, Leiden, The Netherlands

Petrus C. van Duyne, Tilburg, The Netherlands

Jamie Ferrill Charles Sturt University and Financial Integrity Hub (FIH), Canberra, ACT, Australia

Doron Goldbarsht Macquarie University and Financial Integrity Hub (FIH), Sydney, NSW, Australia

Timothy Goodrick KPMG Sydney, Sydney, NSW, Australia

Jackie H. Harvey Newcastle Business School, Northumbria University, Newcastle upon Tyne, UK

Louis de Koker La Trobe University and Financial Integrity Hub (FIH), Melbourne, VIC, Australia,

University of the Western Cape, Bellville, South Africa

Christian Leuprecht Royal Military College of Canada, Kingston, ON, Canada

Cayle Lupton University of Johannesburg, Johannesburg, South Africa

Nicholas Morris La Trobe University, Melbourne, VIC, Australia

Ben Scott Macquarie University and Financial Integrity Hub (FIH), Sydney, NSW, Australia

Jeffrey Simser Royal United Services Institute, London, UK

Rachel Southworth Charles Sturt University, Canberra, ACT, Australia

Milind Tiwari Charles Sturt University, Canberra, ACT, Australia

Robert Walters Victoria University, Melbourne, VIC, Australia

Contributors

Financial Crime Prevention in an Age of Paradox

Jamie Ferrill, Louis de Koker, and Doron Goldbarsht

The fight against money laundering has been energetically introduced and developed into a global enforcement regime. Various economic and financial justifications have been put forward, which are not self-evident. The simple and basic foundation is that ill-gotten profits should not remain in the possession of the criminal. Nevertheless, the cause of fighting money laundering is loaded with arguments about the staggering size and the undermining effects of the crime - money, for which there is no empirical evidence. The arguments concerning the integrity of the financial system, usually taken at face value, proves to be less than coherent. Nevertheless, these (globally) politically accepted arguments prove to be effective in overruling a more careful balancing of legal interests and foundations, like the all-encompassing breadth of the money-laundering approach.

—Petrus van Duyne et al.[1]

[1] van Duyne et al. (2005).

J. Ferrill
Charles Sturt University and Financial Integrity Hub (FIH), Canberra, ACT, Australia
e-mail: jferrill@csu.edu.au

L. de Koker
La Trobe University and Financial Integrity Hub (FIH), Melbourne, VIC, Australia

University of the Western Cape, Bellville, South Africa
e-mail: l.dekoker@latrobe.edu.au

D. Goldbarsht (✉)
Macquarie University and Financial Integrity Hub (FIH), Sydney, NSW, Australia
e-mail: doron.goldbarsht@mq.edu.au

D. Goldbarsht et al. (eds.), *The Financial War on Crime and Terrorism*, European Yearbook of International Economic Law,
https://doi.org/10.1007/978-3-032-06360-1_1

1 Introduction

Financial crimes such as fraud, corruption, and proceeds of crime are embedded in societies globally. These crimes—from money laundering to terrorist financing, sanctions evasion to proliferation financing, corruption to kleptocracy, fraud to tax evasion, and everything in between—manifests in various forms. While the implications of these financial crimes may vary across borders, one thing is true: we—our states, institutors, and indeed ourselves as individuals—are all vulnerable in some way to financial crime abuse.

As a consequence, more than 200 jurisdictions have made commitments to the Financial Action Task Force (FATF), the global intergovernmental anti-money laundering (AML), counter-terrorism financing (CTF), and counter-proliferation financing (CPF) standard-setter, to focus efforts on countering such financial crimes. These include implementing obligations under international treaties addressing money laundering, terrorist financing, and corruption; strengthening risk-based controls across designated sectors such as financial institutions, gaming, real estate, legal, accounting, virtual asset service providers and professional service providers, and addressing risks of new technologies while harnessing the power of innovation. In practice, this entails risk assessment and the implementation of risk-based measures. These measures were initally employed in the context of the War on Drugs, that expanded to the War on Terror and, more generally, into a War on Crime. The leveraging of financial crime measures to enforce sanctions against a growing number of nation states—and their countermeasures to evade the sanctions—added a further geopolitical element to the financial crime framework.

We operate, however, within a complex system where financial crime prevention operates as both solution and catalyst; technological advancement and regulatory innovation creates powerful new detection capabilities while simultaneously providing criminals with more sophisticated tools and attack vectors to exploit. How well do we understand and respond to this systemic paradox?

We agree with van Duyne et al. that many of the key policies and actions are informed by argument rather than empirical evidence. This is illustrated by our fundamental uncertainty about the problem's scope and our responses to that uncertainty. The widely-cited estimate that money laundering represents 2–5% of GDP has never been comprehensively validated, yet forms the bedrock for designing controls, shaping policies, and drafting legislation. The estimates are based on Vito Tanzi's work in the late 1980s,[2] while newer studies have provided updated estimates.[3] Still, the popular 2–5% GDP prevails and seems to dominate scholarship, policy, and practice, often uncritically. This means we are constructing our defences within a framework where enhanced capabilities and enhanced vulnerabilities emerge from the same innovations and where we lack the means to track the impact of our interventions.

[2] Tanzi (1996).

[3] Including Walker (1999); Walker and Unger (2009). Also see Smith (2024).

A case in point is the rise of regulatory technology (RegTech) in AML detection. Digital transformation across the banking sector, for example, has been key to enhancing efficiency and security. Transaction monitoring, risk assessments, know your customer (KYC) and customer due diligence (CDD) procedures, and regulatory reporting are all being transformed by RegTech solutions. Yet the promises of enhanced efficiency in regulatory compliance, automated risk management and detection, real-time monitoring and reporting, and cost reduction have also resulted in a static, pre-2008 crisis approach to regulation and a focus on micro-level problems while remaining blind to systemic, interconnected risks, some of which may cause a financial crisis.[4] The same technological advancement that supposedly represents the greatest opportunity for financial crime prevention also creates unprecedented challenges. This became apparent in the UK's NatWest Bank Fowler Oldfield AML failure.

In 2021, it was revealed that Fowler Oldfield Ltd., a gold-trading business suspected of money laundering, allegedly laundered nearly £400 million between 2012 and 2016 through NatWest. The client deposited £365 million over those 5 years despite having an initial predicted annual turnover of only £15 million, with cash deposits reaching £1.8 million per day at its peak.[5] The bank's technological (and human) failures were staggering: for 8 years, their automated monitoring system mistakenly classified £165 million in cash deposits as cheques, while their fundamental "Security Blanket" monitoring rule, which hadn't been reviewed since 2008, was likely "missing suspicious activity".[6] When automated rules generated too many alerts, staff simply switched them off for 15 months, leaving £90 million in cash deposits virtually unmonitored.[7] Despite initially classifying Fowler Oldfield as high-risk, the bank's own system erroneously downgraded them to low-risk in 2013,[8] and investigators couldn't even access customer risk ratings or business profiles until 2015.

This is not an isolated case.; In 2017, the Commonwealth Bank of Australia (CBA) blamed a 'coding error' in its intelligent deposit-taking ATM system for its failure to file reports on thousands of transactions involving more than AUD 10,000 each.[9] In the Australian federal court ruling, it was alleged that CBA breached AML/CTF laws through failing to adequately monitor high-risk customers and transactions, failing to report over 53,500 threshold transactions totalling AUD 624.7 million on time, failing to provide 149 suspicious matter reports within required

[4] Campbell-Verduyn and Lenglet (2023).

[5] BBC News (2021).

[6] FCA v National Westminster Bank PLC, Agreed Statement of Facts p. 51.

[7] FCA v National Westminster Bank PLC, Agreed Statement of Facts p. 51.

[8] FCA v National Westminster Bank PLC, Agreed Statement of Facts p. 7.

[9] Coyne (2017).

timeframes, and failing to implement proper risk controls for their intelligent deposit taking ATMs over several years, resulting in a AUD 700 million penalty.[10]

Negligence aside, part of the tension here between technology as a challenge and opportunity comes from the idea that, at its essence, the imaginaries of technological possibilities are solutionist. That is, they presume rather than investigate the problems that they are trying to solve.[11] While we do not intend to paint all solutions with this brush, it is indeed endemic of the financial crime space. Without a thorough, accurate understanding of the *problems,* or in many cases the *risks,* our systems cannot be fit for purpose. There is no shortage of cases around the world that demonstrate a lack of congruence between the problems and their constructed 'solutions'.

The convergence of technological revolution, globalisation, and evolving criminal sophistication has created an inflection point. But to understand where we are going, what the problems are we face, we must look to how we got here. This chapter addresses the evolution of financial crime and some of the motivating factors behind how and why institutions address it in certain ways. It sets the background for the book that examines both sides of opportunity-challenge paradox across multiple domains and core patterns found within it.

2 The Historical Context: How We Got Here

The history of the current global financial crime context can be traced back to various points in history[12] but it generally began to take shape in the 1980s with the drafting and adoption of 1988 Convention against Illicit Drugs and Psychotropic Substances.[13] This Convention embedded a finance and asset-focused strategy against drug traffickers and included a number of AML measures. The AML measures were subsequently detailed by the FATF.[14] The 1999 International Convention for the Suppression of the Financing of Terrorism[15] expanded the scope of the measures to the financing of terrorism. The September 11, 2001 attacks on the United States spurred the implementation of that Convention and of the additional terrorist

[10] Federal Court of Australia (2018): Chief Executive Officer of the Australian Transaction Reports and Analysis Centre and Commonwealth Bank of Australia Limited ACN 123123124.

[11] Morozov (2013), page 6.

[12] Including but not limited to The International Opium Commission (Shanghai, February 1909); the Hague Opium Convention of 1912; the US Senate's Kefauver Committee; the US Bank Secrecy Act 1970; the Swiss Due Diligence Agreement 1977; the US Money Laundering Control Act 1986; and so on. For further reading see De Koker and Goldbarsht (2024a) and Moiseienko (2025).

[13] UN Convention against Illicit Traffic in Narcotic Drugs and Psychotropic Substances (opened for signature 20 December 1988, entered into force 11 November 1990) 1582 UNTS 95.

[14] Financial Action Task Force (1990).

[15] International Convention for the Suppression of the Financing of Terrorism, opened for signature 10 January 2000, 2178 UNTS 197.

financing standards adopted by the FATF in 2001.[16] This framework was subsequently broadened to transnational organised crime[17] and corruption.[18]

The FATF Standards were adopted in the context of globalisation. Economically powerful countries, often led by the United States, set global rules that reflected their values and the frameworks in which they wished to conduct business globally. In an era of geopolitical fragmentation the FATF, its functioning and its achievements lend itself to be analysed through a political lens. For purposes of this chapter it is however more relevant to consider the FATF and its financial crime standards in relation to the fast-changing technological background of modern financial services.

Though the FATF's 1990 standards were largely inspired by—and aimed at—the twentieth century financial sector, the FATF was attentive to technology from the start. Tensions between the recognition of the value of technology to advance financial integrity and concerns about the abuse of technology by criminals are woven throughout the FATF's history.

The original Recommendation 25 in 1990, for example, encouraged countries to adopt non-cash payment methods:

> Countries should further encourage in general the development of modern and secure techniques of money management, including increased use of cheques and book entry recording of securities, as a means to encourage the replacement of cash transfers.[19]

This Recommendation was retained as Recommendation 24 in the first revision of the FATF Standards in 1996,[20] but increased use of payment cards and direct deposit of salary checks[21] was added to the list of modern money management techniques. The first part of the sentence was retained in the 2003 revised Recommendations—"Countries should further encourage the development of modern and secure techniques of money management that are less vulnerable to money laundering"—as a part of Recommendation 20, but the specific examples were deleted.[22] The 2012 revised FATF Standards, however, did not contain a similar requirement.[23] The tone of the Standards shifted more to concern about new payment technologies.

Concern about new technologies first appeared as Recommendation 13 in 1996:

---

[16] Financial Action Task Force (2001).

[17] UN Convention against Transnational Organized Crime (opened for signature 12 December 2000, entered into force 29 September 2003) 2225 UNTS 209.

[18] UN Convention against Corruption (adopted 11 December 2003, entered into force 14 December 2005) 2349 UNTS 41.

[19] Financial Action Task Force (1990) Rec 25.

[20] Financial Action Task Force (1996) p. 27.

[21] The spelling of "cheques" changed to the US spelling (checks) in 1996. See Financial Action Task Force (1996) p. 27.

[22] Financial Action Task Force (2003) p 9.

[23] Financial Action Task Force (2012). The same sentiment emerged in 2019 in UNSCR 2462 (2019), when the UN Security Council, acting under Chapter VII of the Charter of the United Nations, called on all States "to enhance the traceability and transparency of financial transactions, in compliance with international law, including international human rights law and humanitarian law, including through (a) Fully exploiting the use of new and emerging financial and regulatory

> Countries should pay special attention to money laundering threats inherent in new or developing technologies that might favour anonymity, and take measures, if needed, to prevent their use in money laundering schemes. [24]

In that year, the FATF's money laundering typology report considered potential challenges linked to new payment technologies, called "cyberpayments":

> A key component of cyberpayments technology is the use of so-called "smart cards," credit-card like devices containing a microchip on which value is encoded. The cards can be read by vending machines or terminals that deduct the amount of each transaction from the total stored value. When the card's value is used up, it may be re-loaded via ATM, telephone, "electronic wallet" or personal computer, or it may be discarded. The term cyberpayments also includes "electronic banking" systems wherein value is held in a personal computer and transferred electronically over the Internet. [25]

Importantly, however, the report stated that "[a]t present, the experts have no evidence to suggest that cyberpayments technologies are being manipulated by criminal interests".[26] It was viewed as a developing risk and therefore experts advised the FATF to be proactive and to work "with the vendors and users of cyberpayments technology to identify vulnerabilities, and to build the appropriate safeguards into system design and operation".[27]

In the 2003 revised Standards, the requirement to pay special attention to any money laundering threats that may arise from new or developing technologies that might favour anonymity was expanded with the explicit requirement that "financial institutions should have policies and procedures in place to address any specific risks associated with nonface to face (sic) business relationships or transactions".[28]

The 2003 Recommendations were expanded in 2012 when a mandatory risk-based approach was introduced in relation to the relevant standards. The current Recommendation 15 requires countries and financial institutions to identify and assess the money laundering or terrorist financing risks that may arise in relation to the development of new products and new business practices, including new delivery mechanisms, and the use of new or developing technologies for both new and pre-existing products.[29] Financial institutions are required to undertake that risk assessment prior to the launch of the new products, business practices or the use of new or developing technologies and to take appropriate measures to manage and mitigate the identified risks.

While the tone of the current Standards is therefore more suspicious of payments technology, the FATF acknowledged the power of RegTech and supervisory

---

technologies to bolster financial inclusion, and to contribute to the effective implementation of AML/CFT measures …".

[24] Financial Action Task Force (1996) p 26.

[25] Financial Action Task Force (1996) pp. 40–41.

[26] Financial Action Task Force (1996) p 41.

[27] Ibid.

[28] Financial Action Task Force (2003) Rec 8.

[29] Financial Action Task Force (2012–2025) Rec 15.

technology (SupTech) in various reports and guidance notes. This reaches back to 2017 when the FATF formally endorsed responsible innovation for AML/CFT in a public statement declaring:

> The FATF strongly supports responsible financial innovation that is in line with the AML/CFT requirements found in the FATF Standards, and will continue to explore the opportunities that new financial and regulatory technologies may present for improving the effective implementation of AML/CFT measures. [30]

As a result, the FATF adopted guidance on digital identities[31] and issued reports, for example on the opportunities and challenges of new technologies for crime combating measures by supervisors, law enforcement and regulated institutions.[32]

The emphasis on the risks of *payment* technologies since 1996 have however had the unintended consequence of increasing the barriers to financial services for vulnerable people, leading to higher risks of financial exclusion. Financial exclusion was recognised by the FATF ministers as a real risk to achieving full implementation of FATF standards.[33] Financial inclusion that mitigates this exclusion integrity risk[34] is best advanced by the responsible use of non face-to-face payments technologies such as mobile money.[35] Since the mid-2000s the design of AML/CTF measures have slowed the pace of financial inclusion in a number of countries, leaving an estimated 1.4 billion people in the cash or informal economy.[36] This unintended consequence of a critical view of payments technology therefore created integrity risks.[37]

In the case of non face-to-face relationships, developments in identification technologies compelled the FATF to revisit its earlier, conservative approach. In 2025, it revised its blanket classification of non face-to-face business relationships transactions as an example of a higher risk transaction and added "where appropriate risk mitigation measures have not been implemented".[38] The FATF also issued new financial inclusion guidance in June 2025[39] and revised its payments transparency standards to support a more proportionate, risk-based approach, including to encourage the responsible use of payments technology to limit the use of cash transfers, as originally envisaged in 1990.[40]

[30] Financial Action Task Force (2017). The FATF position on FinTech and RegTech. https://www.fatf-gafi.org/en/publications/Fatfgeneral/Fatf-position-fintech-regtech.html; FATF (2021) par 19.

[31] Financial Action Task Force (2020).

[32] Financial Action Task Force (2021).

[33] Financial Action Task Force (2012).

[34] Financial Action Task Force (2025a).

[35] See Chatain et al. (2011).

[36] See Financial Action Task Force (2025a) par 30 for 2021 statistics.

[37] See in general Financial Action Task Force (2025a) p. 1.

[38] Financial Action Task Force (2012–2015) INR 10.15.

[39] Financial Action Task Force (2025a).

[40] See Financial Action Task Force (2012–2025) Rec 16 and INR 16, as revised.

In practice, the FATF's attitudes and responses to technology are evolving in response to the changes in technology and the changes in business and social practices driven by new capabilities. The launch of Bitcoin in 2009 has led to a raft of work to assess and address the crime risks posed by virtual assets,[41] including the adoption by the FATF of virtual asset service provider standards in 2018, which were refined in 2019. The implementation of these standards progressed slowly. In 2025, the FATF reported that of the 138 jurisdictions that were assessed for compliance with the FATF standards for virtual assets and virtual asset service providers, 29 countries were assessed as non-compliant; 68 as partially compliant; 40 as largely compliant; and only one jurisdiction was assessed as fully compliant.[42] Even when they are eventually fully implemented, the Standards may have limited impact on criminal use of virtual standards as the FATF measures are focused on service providers and not directly on person-to-person transactions that account for a significant share—if not the majority share—of criminal transactions in the virtual asset context.[43] Ironically, the stellar growth in virtual asset use may have been driven in part by concerns about financial surveillance, introduced by the FATF Standards.

The FATF attitudes to technology are not only impacted by the changes in technology and the changes in societies and business practices in response, but also by the complexity of different understandings of how technology and the related risks and opportunities unfold in different countries and regions globally. The 2025 revisions to FATF's payment messaging transparency rules in Recommendation 16 required two rounds of public consultation and nearly 2 years of discussion.[44] The text that was finally adopted differs markedly from the initial draft as the initial standard-setting ambitions had to adapt to technological and global realities. Further changes and fine-tuning are expected before the full implementation of the new revised Recommendation 16.[45]

The evolution of the global AML/CTF/CPF standards and practices and their response to and interaction with technological innovation provides a lens on challenges in this space. Payment technology that allows for quick, global transactions, RegTech, SupTech, virtual assets, and technology that (should) provide more efficient identification verification are accompanied by the challenges of criminal exploitation, consideration for vulnerable people and financial exclusion, and implementation challenges including how *people* understand risk in the first place. This is a theme that prevails throughout this book as this paradox arises across the wider financial crime prevention landscape.

[41] E.g. Financial Action Task Force (2014).

[42] Financial Action Task Force (2025b) par 5.

[43] De Koker and Goldbarsht (2022) 310.

[44] Financial Action Task Force (2025c) parr 1–7.

[45] Financial Action Task Force (2025c) par 5.

3 The Opportunities/Challenges Framework: Beyond Simple Trade-Offs

Throughout this evolution of financial crime and its prevention in the past decades, we have also seen the evolution of opportunities and challenges. The opportunity to innovatively create effective and efficient regulatory frameworks comes with the challenge of unintended consequences; the opportunities that come with technological capabilities comes with the challenge of overcoming criminal exploitation of technology; opportunities for cross-border collaboration comes with the challenge of privacy concerns and information exchange; opportunities for detection improvements comes with challenges around implementation costs.

Still, underlying these opportunities are uncertainties. For example, the development of the risk-based approach by FATF was not well-informed by evidence when it was adopted as a mandatory element of the FATF standards.[46] With no clear definition of risk, institutional lack of clarity around implementation, and the paradoxical tendency for sophisticated compliance systems to create blind spots rather than eliminate them, regulated entities have faced the challenge of implementing controls on an unstable foundation.

What's more, challenges and opportunities are not mutually exclusive. Rather, they are often manifestations of the same underlying phenomena. For example, in Australia in 2023–2024, 381,758 suspicious matter reports (SMRs) were submitted to AUSTRAC;[47]in the UK, 827,048 suspicious activity reports (SARs) were submitted to the National Crime Agency between April 2023 and March 2024;[48] in the United States, 3.8 million SARs were submitted to the Financial Crimes Enforcement Network (FinCEN)[49] in the 2024 financial year. On the one hand, the ability to usefully analyse and disseminate intelligence from this volume of reports is limited.[50] On the other hand, the sheer number of reports drives technological and AI development to prioritise the high-value intelligence. While information overload can paralyse the system, it also necessitates smarter analytical tools.

To complicate it further, these statistics could lead to questions around *why* so many suspicious reports (SARs/SMRs/STRs)[51] are submitted in the first place. We have to ask if the system is designed in the most effective way. With an already questionable risk-based approach guiding the suspicious reporting principle, the added abstraction of 'suspicion' renders the system dubious.

The developments of our anti-financial crime processes and practices are experienced differently across actors as well. That is, one stakeholder's opportunity can be

---

[46] De Koker and Goldbarsht (2024b).

[47] AUSTRAC (2024) p. 6.

[48] National Crime Agency (2024).

[49] FinCEN (2024).

[50] Leuprecht and Ferrill (2023).

[51] We will refer to SARs throughout for clarity, however we also acknowledge the use of SMR and suspicious transaction report (STR) terminology based on the jurisdiction.

a challenge for another. This creates interdependencies where solving one problem can exacerbate another. Returning to RegTech, Chainalysis illustrates the central paradox: born from cryptocurrency's promise of financial freedom, it now serves as the very surveillance infrastructure that makes crypto both institutionally acceptable and fundamentally less private. For financial institutions, Chainalysis offers the confidence to accept crypto clients at the cost of expensive licensing fees. For regulators and law enforcement, it provides borderless transaction tracing without cumbersome mutual legal assistance treaties (MLATs), at the cost of depending on private infrastructure they don't control. Meanwhile, for both criminals and legitimate users of cryptocurrency, formerly anonymous transactions are now traceable; both may resultantly be pushed towards privacy coins and mixing services (more likely the criminals), but legitimate users are provided the added legitimacy that enables institutional adoption. The *Bitcoin Fog* case, which saw Roman Sterlingov found guilty of "operating among the longest-running and most prolific bitcoin money laundering services on the darknet"[52] is a clear example of this—and one where Chainalysis was legitimised in a court itself.[53]

Another layer of the paradox is the temporal dimension. That is, we need to consider not only the binary of short-term costs vs long-term benefits, but also that time can transform opportunities into challenges or obligations, as well as innovation into infrastructure. This is not a philosophical contemplation, but rather a practical planning challenge in itself. SARs serve as another useful example here. Introduced vis-à-vis currency transaction reporting/unusual transaction reports required by the Bank Secrecy Act 1970 in the United States, transaction reporting was intended as a 'preventative' AML measure[54] or an opportunity to provide intelligence on suspected money laundering activity. But what began as a mechanism for financial transparency has paradoxically created opacity through volume. The very abundance of reports makes it difficult to identify actual threats due to the structural limits on their analysis.[55] The reasons for this volume are complex themselves; from varying understandings of risk and suspicion, to defensive reporting due to industry enforcement actions. Of course there is also the issue of criminals capitalising on this and quickly learning how to avoid being 'suspicious'. That said, we need to consider the longitudinal effects of our current solutions.

While a simple cost-benefit analysis is straightforward, it often misses the complexity. That is, we are presented with a false binary. The concepts explored throughout this book do not present as 'either or' fallacies, but rather carefully balance the nuances of challenges and opportunities. In doing so, several core patterns emerge in our systems beyond the binary. In turn, the human factor, technology,

[52] United States Department of Justice (2024), "Jury Finds Russian-Swedish Operator of 'Bitcoin Fog' Guilty of Running the Darknet Cryptocurrency Mixer".

[53] Chainalysis (2024), "Bitcoin Fog Case Confirms Chainalysis Analytics is Reliable and Admissible in Court".

[54] Moiseienko (2025).

[55] Simser (2023).

globalisation, and industry connectivity emerge as core patterns that reflect the challenge/opportunity paradox in action.

4 Core Patterns

Innovations in AML/CTF compliance continue to advance rapidly, offering new opportunities to strengthen the global financial system. While we focus on technicalities like SARs and RegTech solutions, these tools operate within a broader ecosystem shaped by human behaviour, technological evolution, globalisation, and industry connectivity. These macro forces don't just provide context, rather they fundamentally determine whether our technical solutions succeed or fail.

The first and perhaps most fundamental of these forces is the human factor. In many ways, people remain both the greatest asset and the greatest vulnerability: people decide how to design and implement AML/CTF compliance programs; they decide what technologies to adopt and how to implement them; and they shape organisational cultures. People, however, are biased and fallible and can be criminals themselves.

The book demonstrates this duality throughout, particularly in the chapters by Ferrill and Southworth, Harvey and van Duyne, Chadderton, and Goldbarsht and Goodrick. Across multiple domains, organisational and cultural dynamics are seen as having significant implications for anti-financial crime efforts: leadership deficiencies reduce compliance to performative gestures, cultural hierarchies enable elite impunity, institutional mistrust creates exploitable information gaps, and risk-averse behaviours prioritise individual liability concerns over collective security imperatives. These patterns demonstrate that technical regulatory frameworks often fail when human and organisational factors—such as cultural deference, intersectoral suspicion, and institutional self-preservation—create vulnerabilities that sophisticated criminal networks readily exploit.

Even our most sophisticated technological solutions ultimately depend on human judgement and input: analysts must interpret risk scores generated by AI; compliance officers decide whether to file a SAR; relationship managers may choose to look the other way. As the NatWest case illustrated, years of technological investment can be undone by a single human's decision to trust rather than verify. The human factor is not merely another risk to be managed; it is the medium through which all other risks manifest. As a former HSBC employee stated during the fallout of the FinCEN files leak: "You can't get a man to believe in something when a salary depends on him not believing it. That's the biggest challenge you have in this industry".[56]

We are in an era of rapid technological evolution. But the technological thread woven through these chapters reveals an uncomfortable truth: we seem to be stuck

[56] Woodman (2020), ICIJ Report.

in a recursive loop where our solutions tend to generate new problems. Whether it is AI creating both detection capabilities and algorithmic blind spots as Tiwari explores, or automation simultaneously enhancing efficiency while degrading human judgment as we saw in the CBA and NatWest cases, technology is not purely instrumental. Instead, it reshapes the very landscape of financial crime, ensuring that the idea that the 'good guys' can win remains perpetually out of reach.

The theme of globalisation also keeps the 'win' out of reach. But it goes beyond this. Interconnectedness creates both opportunities and vulnerabilities. It is how we deal with those vulnerabilities that matters. An example of this can be seen in relation to correspondent banking. Correspondent banking relationships enable banks to facilitate payments to recipients in countries where the bank has no physical presence. Along with being able to provide services to multinational corporations, it also provides developing countries with links to the global financial system. However, in the past decade, the total number of correspondent banking relationships has shrunk by about 30%.[57] This withdrawal is largely driven by banks' fear of regulatory penalties, the desire to 'de-risk' and the avoidance of relationships rendered unprofitable, often due to high compliance costs.[58]In turn, populations find themselves cut off from legitimate financial services, driving transactions into informal channels that are harder to monitor and regulate. The irony is unmistakable: in attempting to reduce their exposure to financial crime risk, banks have created systems where that very risk flourishes unchecked.[59] In this case, connection creates vulnerability but risk mitigation resulting in disconnection creates greater vulnerability, while the criminals we seek to exclude are often the most adept at navigating the gaps we create.

The issue of cross-border collaboration versus jurisdictional complexity also plays a role. While the imperative for international cooperation grows stronger as financial crimes transcend borders with increasing complexity, the practical challenges of aligning legal frameworks, cultural contexts, and institutional barriers present challenges. For one, countries must balance their commitment to global security cooperation with the protection of sensitive intelligence sources, methods, and indeed national interests. But any drive towards a standardised approach confronts the reality of varying legal systems, regulatory systems, and varying levels of institutional maturity across jurisdictions.

These factors present an asymmetry; one that disadvantages legitimate participants in the war against financial crime. Criminal networks operate with disregard for jurisdictional boundaries, privacy laws/protections, and informational sharing protocols. At the same time, investigators, intelligence bodies, and law enforcement, are bound by elements like Multilateral Assistance Treaties (MLATs), diplomatic protocols, and regulatory frameworks that tend to impede timely action. In

[57] Davies (2023), Reserve Bank of Australia bulletin.

[58] Davies (2023), Reserve Bank of Australia bulletin.

[59] De Koker and Casanovas (2024).

turn, criminals have an operational advantage that lies in their freedom from the ethical and legal constraints that govern those trying to stop them.

Despite the challenges associated with cross-border (and indeed domestic) information sharing, there is a broad consensus across the AML/CTF community that collaboration is key in the fight against financial crime.[60] As we see particularly across the chapters by Lupton, Simser, Donaldson and Leuprecht, and Walters, there are complex issues surrounding jurisdictional challenges. Financial crime largely operates through the exploitation of jurisdictional fragmentation, where regulatory arbitrage enables illicit actors to navigate between different legal frameworks to avoid detection and enforcement.[61] At the same time, economic globalisation has fundamentally transformed issues like localised corruption and criminal enterprises into transnational networks, facilitated by professional intermediaries who leverage regulatory asymmetries and legal gaps between jurisdictions.[62] These dynamics reveal a tension between established principles of confidentiality, sovereignty, and dispute resolution mechanisms, and the emerging imperative for transparency and cross-border cooperation in combating financial crime.[63] The resulting pattern demonstrates how traditional regulatory frameworks, designed for discrete national contexts, struggle to address the increasingly sophisticated and mobile nature of modern illicit financial flows.

Finally, the book reveals that interconnectivity transcends industry or even conceptual boundaries. Whether examining AI challenges in gaming (Simser) or international arbitration (Walter), tracking illicit wildlife trade and terrorism financing (Lupton) or shell company networks (Tiwari), the same deceptive practices and strategic imperatives emerge across disparate sectors. This shared vulnerability creates both common targets for exploitation and parallel laboratories for innovation.

Yet we systematically underutilise this interconnectedness. The regulated entity landscape suffers from insufficient cross-sector knowledge sharing, forcing each industry—and in many cases countries—to repeatedly confront similar challenges around privacy, technology, risk, and geopolitics rather than building upon collective wisdom. Our fragmented approach risks wasting resources and perpetuating avoidable failures.

The solution lies in recognising that our common challenges represent our greatest strategic advantage. By fostering deliberate cross-industry collaboration and systematically sharing proven solutions, we transform individual vulnerabilities into collective strength. The very interconnectivity that creates shared risks can become the foundation for shared resilience. This is a common message throughout the book, for it is ultimately an effort to address how we can transform vulnerabilities into strengths. Considering the human factor, technological innovation,

[60] AUSTRAC (2025); Financial Action Task Force (2022); Public Safety Canada (2025).

[61] Khan et al. (2025).

[62] Cooley and Sharman (2017).

[63] De Koker and Goldbarsht (2024b).

globalisation, and indeed interconnectivity, the book brings together a collection of our known challenges and proposed solutions to that end.

5 The Collection

The chapters in this book, all double-blind peer reviewed, provide a critical examination of the landscape of financial crime. In doing so, it exposes the vulnerabilities of the global financial system and offers innovative solutions to strengthen our controls and combat illicit activities. The collection addresses the urgent problem of increasingly sophisticated financial crimes, fuelled by rapid technological advancements, human fallibility, globalisation, and regulatory gaps, which threaten the stability of economies and the integrity of societies worldwide.

Examining the role of leadership and culture in institutional AML/CTF compliance programs, Jamie Ferrill and Rachel Southworth navigate the complexities of a constantly shifting regulatory landscape. Their chapter, *Leadership in the Evolving Landscape of Financial Crime: Navigating AML/CTF Risks And Controls* (Ferrill and Southworth 2025) utilises contemporary leadership theories to assess the impact of strategic leadership on financial crime risk management. In turn, they propose a model for measuring program effectiveness and bolstering compliance capabilities. Through case study analysis, the chapter exposes leadership and cultural challenges that result in regulatory breaches, underscoring the necessity of adaptive and ethical principles. Ultimately, it presents a framework for enhanced financial crime control, advocating for the implementation of culturally aware and adaptable leadership strategies to effectively address the evolving AML/CTF environment.

In her chapter *FATF and the Conundrum of Public-Private Sector Intelligence and Information Sharing* (Chadderton 2025), Paula Chadderton analyses the efficacy of public-private sector information sharing in combating sophisticated financial crimes and transnational organised crime activities. In doing so, she addresses the discord between international instruments and national implementation. She examines the evolution of support for such initiatives within key agreements like the Vienna, Palermo, and Cybercrime Conventions, alongside FATF standards, while acknowledging historical reservations regarding private sector engagement. The chapter investigates the practical involvement of FATF with the private sector, highlighting persistent biases that impede robust information sharing. Paula contends that the increasing complexity of transnational organised crime necessitates overcoming these historical barriers to enhance public-private collaboration in AML/CTF/CPF efforts.

In *Private to Private: The Next Frontier of Financial Intelligence Sharing* (Goldbarsht and Goodrick 2025), Doron Goldbarsht and Timothy Goodrick examine the legal and operational challenges of private-to-private data sharing among financial institutions for enhanced AML/CTF efforts, using the Bank of Tokyo case as an example of information-sharing limitations. They analyse the constraints imposed by national legislation like the *Privacy Act* 1988 (Cth) and the *AML/CTF*

Act, contrasting them with FATF recommendations for cross-border collaboration. The research investigates the development of secure legal and governance frameworks, platform mechanisms, and key participant identification to facilitate effective data exchange. The chapter works to define the "why, what, and where" of private-to-private information sharing, contributing to improved detection and prevention of transnational financial crimes.

In his chapter *Network Analytics and Generative Artificial Intelligence: A Hybrid Approach to Money Laundering Detection* (Tiwari 2025), Milind Tiwari explores the integration of graph databases and generative artificial intelligence, specifically large language models, to revolutionise money laundering detection. The chapter examines how graph databases uncover relationships within illicit networks, while generative artificial intelligence enables real-time mapping and actionable insights from these complex connections. By visualising and interpreting illicit networks with greater accuracy, this integration aims to foster a more agile and proactive AML infrastructure. The chapter also addresses challenges including data bias, ethical implications, and the necessity of interdisciplinary collaboration, to ensure the responsible and effective deployment of these technological innovations in combating financial crime.

In *Illegal Wildlife Trade as a Method of Financing Terrorism* (Lupton 2025), Cayle Lupton examines the contentious link between the illegal wildlife trade and terrorism financing. He addresses widely accepted claims, particularly regarding Al-Shabaab's alleged involvement in the ivory trade. While acknowledging the 2015 RUSI report that debunked specific claims based on weak evidence, the chapter posits that the illegal wildlife trade remains a viable, though under-researched, avenue for terrorist financing. It emphasises the need for a proactive and contextual approach to combating terrorism financing, advocating for a deeper understanding of the financial flows associated with the illegal wildlife trade, especially in regions like Africa, where the threat to the financial ecosystem is unique.

To address the evolving role of deception within money laundering, Ben Scott examines its legal foundations and practical manifestations over the past 25 years. *Practice to Deceive: A Taxonomy of Money Laundering Deception Based on US and Australian Case Studies* (Scott 2025) begins with a review of the criminal law of money laundering in key common law jurisdictions, focusing on legislative and judicial interpretations of deception. Utilising a taxonomy of deception, the chapter dissects prominent money laundering cases, including Liberty Reserve, the Russian Laundromat, Toronto Dominion Bank, and the 2023 Singaporean cases, to illustrate prevalent deceptive practices. Finally, it identifies and assesses the impact of technological, financial, legal, and political enablers on the evolution of money laundering, highlighting how these factors have shaped deceptive strategies in the modern era.

In their chapter *Geopolitical Implications of Embedded Corruption in Global Capital Markets: The Professional Brokers Who Enable the Transnational Illicit Political Economy of Systematic State Capture* (Donaldson and Leuprecht 2025), Nicholas Donaldson and Christian Leuprecht address state capture as a globalised and transnational process, examining how private interests subvert public institutions through systemic legal failures. It critiques the inadequacy of current regulatory frameworks and law enforcement strategies, highlighting the legal vacuum that facilitates state capture and the limitations of existing legal regimes, such as AML/CTF, in addressing its complexity. The chapter emphasises the failure to hold intermediaries accountable and proposes targeted domestic and international reforms to enhance identification, prosecution, and enforcement. However, it also acknowledges the inherent challenges posed by politicisation and the collusive nature of state capture, which threaten to undermine reform efforts.

In a similar vein, Jackie Harvey and the late Petrus C van Duyne write on *Corrupt Elites and Godfathers in Nigeria: Structural Impunity and the Undermining of Accountability* (Harvey and van Duyne 2025). They examine the pervasive nature of corruption within Nigeria's fragile democracy, analysing the social-historical context of elite corruption and its impact on national wealth distribution. The chapter examines the phenomenon of "godfatherism", where wealthy political patrons influence the appointment of "godsons" to high positions, leading to rigged elections and compromised decision-making. It argues that established norms and hierarchical deference protect these powerful elites, effectively placing them above the law. The chapter concludes that greater transparency in decision-making processes is essential to challenge this entrenched system of corruption.

Offering a useful conceptualisation of risk, Jeffrey Simser explores the significant AML/CTF risks inherent in the gaming industry, highlighting its susceptibility to financial crime. In *Dangerous Play: AML/CTF/CPF Risks in the Gaming Sector* (Simser 2025), a range of money laundering techniques within the gaming sector are explored, from basic structuring to more complex schemes. The chapter analyses regulatory frameworks, using Canada as a case study, and contextualises its findings through real-world examples, including UNODC's report on casinos and human trafficking, RUSI's findings on gaming and North Korean proliferation financing, the Crown Casino scandal in Australia, and the Wynn Casino prosecution in California. Finally, it explores emerging challenges, such as the implications of AI and quantum computing, for the future of AML/CTF in the gaming industry.

In his chapter, Robert Walters questions: *International Arbitration and Money Laundering: Is there an Actual Issue?* (Walters 2025). He examines the potential for money laundering to occur within international commercial arbitration, despite its confidential nature. The chapter offers analysis of relevant international and national laws, including those of the United National Commission on International Trade Law to the former, and the national laws of Australia, India, United Kingdom, United States, and the European Union to the latter to assess if they adequately address money laundering risks and if updates are needed to better equip arbitrators to handle such issues. The chapter also explores the role of technology in detecting money laundering within arbitration and the challenges arbitrators face in balancing confidentiality with their legal and ethical obligations to report potential criminal activity. Ultimately, it aims to provide guidance on how to effectively manage money laundering risks in international commercial arbitration.

Nicholas Morris and Louis de Koker examine *The Impact of the Financial Action Task Force (FATF) Standards and Focus: From Effectiveness to Effect* (Morris and de Koker 2025), offering a critical assessment of the FATF's regulatory architecture and its real consequences. They dissect the mechanics of peer reviews, greylisting, and blacklisting processes, moving beyond procedural analysis to interrogate their substantive impact on global financial crime prevention. Offering an examination of the FATF's intermediate and high-level outcomes which effectiveness is measured against, the chapter reveals a disconnect: these FATF compliance activities show little correlation with actual effectiveness scores or meaningful improvements in governance and crime prevention. This finding exposes a paradox within the current system: heightened regulatory activity does not necessarily translate into enhanced security outcomes. The chapter then points to a critical shift required for the fifth round of mutual evaluations: redirecting political will toward ensuring robust implementation of FATF standards within wealthier economies. This reorientation becomes essential as resource constraints and capacity limitations continue to disproportionately burden low-income countries, creating an uneven global landscape where compliance expectations exceed practical capabilities.

The concluding chapter, *Crime and Terrorism: Important Research Questions* by de Koker, Goldbarsht, and Ferrill draws parallels between military warfare and the war on financial crime, examining how the framing of organised crime and terrorism as "wars" have influenced the development of financial crime control measures from their development in the 1970s/1980s to the twenty-first century. The chapter examines the intersection of geopolitical fragmentation and proliferation financing through the lens of sanctions and blacklisting regimes, revealing how governments have enlisted regulated institutions in financial warfare without necessarily providing the resources needed to make these measures effective. The chapter paves a way forward, suggesting a Financial Integrity Harm Index, along with five key research questions to take away.

6 Synthesis

The chapters within this book are united by several critical commonalities. Foremost among these is their shared focus on risk, examined from a multitude of perspectives. Risk, arguably one of the most significant yet frequently misunderstood concepts in the realm of anti-financial crime efforts, lies at the very heart of the emergent problems explored. Indeed, the conceptualisation of these issues as risks is foundational to their inclusion and analysis within this book. Second, they all rely on evidence. Every chapter in this book has carefully examined case law, extant scholarship, policy, case studies, industry reporting, and/or statistics. The evidence has been thoughtfully integrated into analysis and discussion, offering grounded perspectives. Third, the chapters are all forward looking. They propose a multitude of innovative solutions, based on evidence, that consider the temporal nature of such solutions. Fourth, nearly every chapter highlights the inadequacy of our traditional frameworks. Around the globe, the differing challenges become the ties that connect us. Finally, every chapter recognises that financial crime is not merely a technical problem to be solved, but a complex adaptive system where human behaviour, technological innovation, globalisation, regulatory frameworks, and institutional norms intersect, often creating the very vulnerabilities they were designed to prevent.

Importantly, together, the chapters in this book address adaptation; specifically, how institutions, regulations, professionals, and even research must evolve. One of the common threads is that collaboration and innovation are imperative. To the former, in a globalised world where our financial systems are more connected than ever, we cannot operate in siloes if we want to stand any chance of designing more suitable financial crime regimes. To the latter, we cannot think in static terms. While criminals innovate without constraint, bound by neither law nor ethics, we must match their creativity within our legal frameworks, transforming regulatory boundaries into an opportunity for innovation. Of course, in an era of powerful tools and persistent vulnerabilities, the role of ethics becomes an increasingly important touchpoint.

The reality is, institutions have bottom lines, states have sovereignty concerns and national interests, regulators have political pressures, and society has competing values. Success isn't about finding a perfect equilibrium but about navigating these competing imperatives while maintaining forward momentum against financial crime.

7 Conclusion

Returning to the quote that opened this chapter: How can strategies and solutions be meaningfully proposed without first understanding the full extent of the problem? The chapters of this book attempt to address some of the known gaps. By acknowledging and carefully balancing challenges and opportunities, we are afforded greater insight into the state of financial crime in the twenty-first century. Arguably, the paradox is inevitable; yet, we are better placed to offer well-informed solutions by thoroughly examining the paradox itself, while understanding that our incomplete knowledge is not a barrier to action, but rather the very foundation upon which adaptive and resilient strategies must be built.

We are living in very uncertain times, which adds a layer of complexity and necessity for thought leadership in policymaking, research, industry practice, and the overall financial crime regime. This thought leadership necessarily means we must break free from unfounded, politically accepted conclusions, but rather base our actions on evidence and carefully balanced considerations. This may be idealist given that interests and agendas invariably range from state to individual levels, but we must endeavour to strike this balance for the sake of society. Ultimately, as stated at the beginning of this chapter, our states, institutors, ourselves as individuals are vulnerable to financial crime abuse, and the more efficiently and effectively we can work towards mitigating that vulnerability, the better.

References

AUSTRAC (2024) Submission to the senate legal & constitutional affairs legislation committee inquiry into anti-money laundering and counter terrorism financing amendment bill. https://www.aph.gov.au/DocumentStore.ashx?id=f3933309-e57c-423d-9e40-f8b4ce717ad0&subId=768286

AUSTRAC (2025) Partners. https://www.austrac.gov.au/partners

BBC News (2021) NatWest faces fine over money laundering failings. https://www.bbc.com/news/business-58826491

Campbell-Verduyn M, Lenglet M (2023) Imaginary failure: RegTech in finance. New Polit. Econ. 28(3):468–482. https://doi.org/10.1080/13563467.2022.2140795

Chadderton P (2025) FATF and the conundrum of public-private sector intelligence and information sharing. In: Goldbarsht D, de Koker L, Ferrill J (eds) The financial war on crime and terrorism: opportunities and challenges. Springer, Cham

Chatain P-L, Christen B, Dannaoui N, De Koker L, Noor SMW, Zerzan, A (2011) Protecting mobile money against financial crimes: global policy challenges and solutions directions in development. World Bank. https://documents.worldbank.org/en/publication/documents-reports/documentdetail/854951468337169489

Cooley A, Sharman JC (2017) Transnational corruption and the globalized individual. Perspect Polit 15(3):732–753

Coyne A (2017) CBA blames coding error for alleged money laundering. itnews. https://www.itnews.com.au/news/cba-blames-coding-error-for-alleged-money-laundering-470233

De Koker L, Casanovas P (2024) 'De-risking', de-banking and denials of bank services: an over-compliance dilemma? In: Goldbarsht D, de Koker L (eds) Financial crime, law and governance. Ius Gentium: comparative perspectives on law and justice, vol 116. Springer, Cham. https://doi.org/10.1007/978-3-031-59547-9_3

De Koker L, Goldbarsht D (2022) Financial technologies and financial crime: key developments and areas for future research. In: Goldbarsht D, De Koker L (eds) Financial technology and the law. Law, governance and technology series, vol 47. Springer, Cham. https://doi.org/10.1007/978-3-030-88036-1_13

De Koker L, Goldbarsht D (2024a) Towards a global approach to combating financial crime. In: Financial crime, law and governance. Ius Gentium: comparative perspectives on law and justice, vol 116. Springer, pp 1–20

De Koker L, Goldbarsht D (2024b) FATF's risk-based approach: has the pendulum swung too far? In: Financial crime and the law: identifying and mitigating risks. Springer, pp 247–262

Donaldson N, Leuprecht C (2025) Geopolitical implications of embedded corruption in global capital markets: the professional brokers who enable the transnational illicit political economy of systematic state capture. In: Goldbarsht D, de Koker L, Ferrill J (eds) The financial war on crime and terrorism: opportunities and challenges. Springer, Cham

Federal Court of Australia (2018) Chief Executive Officer of the Australian transaction reports and Analysis Centre v Commonwealth Bank of Australia Limited FCA 930

Ferrill J, Southworth R (2025) Leadership in the evolving landscape of financial crime: navigating AML/CTF risks and controls. In: Goldbarsht D, de Koker L, Ferrill J (eds) The financial war on crime and terrorism: opportunities and challenges. Springer, Cham

Financial Action Task Force (1990) The forty recommendations of the financial action task force on money laundering. https://www.fatf-gafi.org/content/dam/fatf-gafi/recommendations/FATF%20Recommendations%201990.pdf

Financial Action Task Force (1996) Annual report 1995–1996. https://www.fatf-gafi.org/content/dam/fatf-gafi/annual-reports/1995%201996%20ENG.pdf

Financial Action Task Force (2001) Eight special recommendations on terrorist financing. https://www.fatf-gafi.org/content/dam/fatf-gafi/annual-reports/2001%202002%20ENG.pdf

Financial Action Task Force (2003) FATF forty recommendations. https://www.fatf-gafi.org/content/dam/fatf-gafi/recommendations/FATF%20Standards%20-%2040%20Recommendations%20rc.pdf.coredownload.pdf

Financial Action Task Force (2012) Declaration of the Ministers and representatives of the Financial Action Task Force. https://www.fatf-gafi.org/en/publications/Fatfgeneral/Ministersrenewthemandateofthefinancialactiontaskforceuntil2020.html
Financial Action Task Force (2012–2025) International standards on combating money laundering and the financing of terrorism & proliferation: the FATF recommendations. https://www.fatf-gafi.org/en/publications/Fatfrecommendations/Fatf-recommendations.html
Financial Action Task Force (2014) FATF report: virtual currencies - key definitions and potential AML/CFT risks. https://www.fatf-gafi.org/content/dam/fatf-gafi/reports/Virtual-currency-key-definitions-and-potential-aml-cft-risks.pdf
Financial Action Task Force (2017) The FATF position on FinTech and RegTech. https://www.fatf-gafi.org/en/publications/Fatfgeneral/Fatf-position-fintech-regtech.html
Financial Action Task Force (2020) Guidance on digital identity. https://www.fatf-gafi.org/publications/documents/digital-identity-guidance.html
Financial Action Task Force (2021) Opportunities and challenges of new technologies for AML/CFT. https://www.fatf-gafi.org/publications/fatfrecommendations/documents/opportunities-challenges-newtechnologies-aml-cft.html
Financial Action Task Force (2022) Partnering in the fight against financial crime: data protection, technology and private sector information sharing. https://www.fatf-gafi.org/en/publications/digitaltransformation/partnering-in-the-fight-against-financial-crime.html
Financial Action Task Force (2025a) Guidance on financial inclusion and anti-money laundering and terrorist financing measures. https://www.fatf-gafi.org/content/fatf-gafi/en/publications/Financialinclusionandnpoissues/guidancefinancial-inclusion-aml-tf-measures.html
Financial Action Task Force (2025b) Targeted update on implementation of the FATF standards on virtual assets/VASPs. https://www.fatf-gafi.org/content/fatf-gafi/en/publications/Fatfrecommendations/targeted-update-virtualassets-vasps-2025.html
Financial Action Task Force (2025c) Explanatory note for revised R.16. https://www.fatf-gafi.org/content/dam/fatf-gafi/recommendations/Explanatory%20note%20for%20revised%20R.16.pdf.coredownload.pdf
FinCEN (2024) Suspicious activity report statistics (SAR stats). https://www.fincen.gov/reports/sar-stats
Goldbarsht D, Goodrick T (2025) Private to private: the next frontier of financial intelligence sharing. In: Goldbarsht D, de Koker L, Ferrill J (eds) The financial war on crime and terrorism: opportunities and challenges. Springer, Cham
Harvey J, van Duyne P (2025) Corrupt elites and godfathers in Nigeria: structural impunity and the undermining of accountability. In: Goldbarsht D, de Koker L, Ferrill J (eds) The financial war on crime and terrorism: opportunities and challenges. Springer, Cham
Khan A, Jillani MAHS, Ullah M, Khan M (2025) Regulatory strategies for combatting money laundering in the era of digital trade. J Money Laund Control 28(2):408–423
Leuprecht C, Ferrill J (2023) Dirty money: financial crime in Canada. McGill-Queen's Press, Kingston
Lupton C (2025) Illegal wildlife trade as a method of financing terrorism. In: Goldbarsht D, de Koker L, Ferrill J (eds) The financial war on crime and terrorism: opportunities and challenges. Springer, Cham
Moiseienko A (2025) Doing business with criminals: between exclusion and surveillance. Cambridge University Press
Morozov E (2013) To save everything, click here: the folly of technological solutionism. PublicAffairs
Morris N, de Koker L (2025) The impact of the Financial Action Task Force (FATF) standards and focus: from effectiveness to effect. In: Goldbarsht D, de Koker L, Ferrill J (eds) The financial war on crime and terrorism: opportunities and challenges. Springer, Cham
National Crime Agency (2024) SARs annual report. https://www.nationalcrimeagency.gov.uk/who-we-are/publications/747-sars-annual-report-2024/file

Public Safety Canada (2025) Combatting money laundering. https://www.publicsafety.gc.ca/cnt/trnsprnc/brfng-mtrls/prlmntry-bndrs/20200621/041/index-en.aspx
Scott B (2025) Practice to deceive: a taxonomy of money laundering deception based on US and Australian case studies. In: Goldbarsht D, de Koker L, Ferrill J (eds) The financial war on crime and terrorism: opportunities and challenges. Springer, Cham
Simser J (2023) Responses to money laundering and Canadian intergovernmental affairs. In: Leuprecht C, Ferrill J (eds) Dirty money: financial crime in Canada. McGill-Queen's University Press, Kingston
Simser J (2025) Dangerous play: AML/CTF/CPF risks in the gaming sector. In: Goldbarsht D, de Koker L, Ferrill J (eds) The financial war on crime and terrorism: opportunities and challenges. Springer, Cham
Smith R (2024) Estimating the costs of serious and organised crime in Australia, 2022–23. Statistical Report no. 50. Canberra: Australian Institute of Criminology. https://doi.org/10.52922/sr77796
Tanzi V (1996) Money laundering and the international financial system working paper WP/96/55. IMF. https://doi.org/10.5089/9781451847598.001
Tiwari M (2025) Network analytics and generative artificial intelligence: a hybrid approach to money laundering detection. In: Goldbarsht D, de Koker L, Ferrill J (eds) The financial war on crime and terrorism: opportunities and challenges. Springer, Cham
United Nations Security Council (2019) UNSCR 2462, Adopted by the Security Council at its 8496th meeting, on 28 March 2019. https://docs.un.org/en/S/RES/2462(2019)
United States Department of Justice (2024) Jury finds Russian-Swedish operator of 'Bitcoin Fog' guilty of running the darknet cryptocurrency mixer. https://www.justice.gov/usao-dc/pr/jury-finds-russian-swedish-operator-bitcoin-fog-guilty-running-darknet-cryptocurrency
van Duyne PC, Groenhuijsen MS, Schudelaro AAP (2005) Balancing financial threats and legal interests in money-laundering policy. Crime Law Soc Chang 43(2):117–147. https://doi.org/10.1007/s10611-005-5984-1
Walker J (1999) How big is global money laundering? J Money Laund Control 3(1):25–37
Walker J, Unger B (2009) Measuring global money laundering: the Walker gravity model. Review of Law & Economics 5(2):821–853
Walters R (2025) International arbitration and money laundering: is there an actual issue? In: Goldbarsht D, de Koker L, Ferrill J (eds) The financial war on crime and terrorism: opportunities and challenges. Springer, Cham
Woodman S (2020) HSBC moved vast sums of dirty money after paying record laundering fine. https://www.icij.org/investigations/fincen-files/hsbc-moved-vast-sums-of-dirty-money-after-paying-record-laundering-fine/

Dr. Jamie Ferrill is a Senior Lecturer of Financial Crime Studies at the Australian Graduate School of Policing and Security, Charles Sturt University and a research fellow with the Financial Integrity Hub (FIH). Before transitioning to academia, she gained nearly a decade of experience in law enforcement, serving with the Canadian federal government. Jamie's research addresses threats to national and economic security, with a particular interest in the intersection of financial crime with border governance frameworks, international cooperation, and organisational effectiveness. Jamie has been a visiting fellow at the Academy of International Affairs NRW and the Border Policy Research Institute, and she is a fellow of the Financial Integrity Hub, the Institute of Intergovernmental Relations at Queen's University, and Borders in Globalization at the University of Victoria. Her latest book is titled Dirty Money: Financial Crime in Canada (McGill-Queen's University Press).

Prof. Louis de Koker is a Professor of Law at La Trobe Law School, Australia and an advisory board member of the Financial Integrity Hub (FIH). His financial crime research focuses on managing the relationship between financial inclusion and anti-money laundering and counter terrorist financing objectives. He has undertaken various university research engagements with the bodies such as the World Bank and the Asian Development Bank and has worked closely with the DC-based Consultative Group to Assist the Poor (CGAP) and with the Financial Integrity Working Group of the Alliance for Financial Inclusion (AFI). This work extended to a range of developing countries including Ghana, Indonesia, Kenya, Kyrgyzstan, Malaysia, Namibia, Nigeria, Uganda, the Ukraine and Palau. His publications have been cited in publications and research papers of international bodies such as the World Bank, the Basel Committee on Banking Supervision, and the International Labour Organization. Louis is also an Extraordinary Professor of Law at the University of the Western Cape, South Africa.

Dr. Doron Goldbarsht LLB, LLM, (HUJI), PHD (UNSW) is an Associate Professor at Macquarie Law School, the Academic Head of the Graduate Certificate in Financial Integrity Law and the Founder and Director of the Financial Integrity Hub (FIH). With over 20 years of expertise in anti-money laundering (AML) and counterterrorist financing (CTF), he has co-edited several books on financial crime and compliance, including Financial Crime and the Law: Identifying and Mitigating Risks (Springer 2024) and Financial Technology and the Law: Combating Financial Crime (Springer, 2022). Certified as a lawyer in both Israel and Australia, Doron also provides expert opinions to government and private sector in litigation, advising on financial crime and regulatory matters.

Leadership in the Evolving Landscape of Financial Crime: Navigating AML/CTF Risks and Controls

Jamie Ferrill and Rachel Southworth

Abstract The global Anti-Money Laundering and Counter-Terrorism Financing (AML/CTF) control landscape is characterised by continuous evolution, driven by diverse and shifting regulatory frameworks, societal expectations, emerging threats, and interpretations of risk. This chapter investigates the critical role of leadership in navigating this complex environment in an institutional setting, offering theoretical insights and practical outcomes for improving financial crime risk assessment and strategic response.

Drawing on contemporary leadership scholarship and practice, the chapter explores how leadership can influence financial crime risk management practices, specifically in maintaining effective AML/CTF compliance programs. The authors present the need for a measure of "effectiveness" and propose a model to illustrate the tangible benefits of strategic leadership for financial crime prevention, including the implementation of risk assessment frameworks that enhance compliance capabilities.

The chapter further explores the influence of organisational culture, arguing that a culture aligned with adaptive and ethical principles is essential for effective AML/CTF risk management initiatives. It highlights how leaders can cultivate such a culture to meet evolving regulatory demands and societal pressures. Additionally, the analysis offers practical guidance on fostering environments that are receptive to innovation as well as proactive regulatory compliance.

To ground these insights in real-world challenges, the chapter examines a high-profile case, offering a critical analysis of leadership and cultural missteps that resulted in regulatory breaches, organisational fallout, and an increased risk of financial crime. This case study serves as a cautionary tale, providing lessons on

J. Ferrill (✉)
Charles Sturt University and Financial Integrity Hub (FIH), Canberra, ACT, Australia
e-mail: jferrill@csu.edu.au

R. Southworth
Charles Sturt University, Canberra, ACT, Australia

D. Goldbarsht et al. (eds.), *The Financial War on Crime and Terrorism*, European Yearbook of International Economic Law,
https://doi.org/10.1007/978-3-032-06360-1_2

what can go wrong and how ineffectiveness leading to such failures can be mitigated through improved leadership and cultural strategies.

Ultimately, this chapter bridges academic literature with practical implications, proposing a framework for leaders and policymakers to enhance financial crime control and prevention efforts. It calls for a rethinking of traditional leadership models and a greater emphasis on the application of adaptive, culturally aware strategies to keep pace with the evolving AML/CTF risk and control landscape.

1 Introduction

Recurring financial scandals and record-breaking regulatory fines are evidence that ineffective and/or non-compliant anti-money laundering (AML) and counter-terrorist financing (CTF) compliance programs present significant risks (operational, regulatory, legal and reputational) to financial institutions worldwide. Despite research into technical controls, systems, and regulatory frameworks, there remains a critical gap in understanding the human and social-organisational dynamics that contribute to these persistent failures. Billions of dollars are invested annually in financial crime systems and controls by the regulated sector, including transaction monitoring systems and compliance processes. Still, the underlying factors that drive the effectiveness of financial crime risk management and compliance remain understudied, particularly in relation to organisational culture and leadership. This chapter investigates the critical role of leadership in navigating complex AML/CTF compliance programs in regulated institutions, offering theoretical insights and practical outcomes for improving financial crime governance and oversight, risk assessment and strategic response.

Decades of research into leadership have told us it is an important factor in attaining organisational goals. In today's world, ensuring an effective AML/CTF compliance program is necessary and important for any regulated entity's operations. Whilst there is a breadth of practitioner material across regulated sectors—primarily financial institutions—on the significant roles of "compliance culture", "senior management responsibility", and "tone from the top", the role and impact of leaders and leadership has been neglected. Compounding this, there has also been minimal academic attention on the role that "leadership" plays in the financial crime control landscape, and virtually no academic attention solely on leadership and AML/CTF compliance. This chapter aims to fill this gap by exploring the critical role of leadership in financial crime risk management, particularly when implementing AML/CTF compliance programs. Importantly, we must distinguish our use of the terms "leaders" versus "leadership". For clarity, we refer to leaders as the individuals who establish direction and inspire change, and to leadership as the broader processes of vision-setting, alignment, and motivation that drive those changes.[1] In other words, people (leaders) and outcomes (leadership).

[1] Kotter (1999), p. 16–17.

First, to establish a foundational understanding, we introduce a theoretical construct for effectiveness in AML/CTF compliance, emphasising the concept and importance of leadership. We define effectiveness in this context as a comprehensive approach encompassing: (1) the interpretation of financial crime risk; (2) the application of a robust control framework to manage that risk through prevention, detection, and disruption; and (3) the efficient reporting of suspected illicit activity to the Financial Intelligence Unit (FIU). Building upon this understanding of effectiveness, we then propose a theoretical construct that emphasises the pivotal role of leadership in achieving these outcomes. Specifically, we argue that leadership should be analysed as a causal factor, alongside culture, when evaluating the robustness of an institution's internal AML/CTF risk and control infrastructure. To test this theoretical construct, we explore a case study of leadership and AML/CTF compliance program 'ineffectiveness', highlighting that the construct of leadership has been underexplored as a causal factor to successes or failures in compliance with both national AML/CTF regulations and international standards. Finally, the chapter offers reflections on how we can address what is meant by the term "leadership" in a practical setting and circumstances in which "leaders" are deemed and/or perceived as accountable for these failings.

2 Background of the AML/CTF Landscape: What Is Effectiveness?

Measuring the "effectiveness" of AML/CTF compliance at a global, national, and institutional level is challenging. At the global level, the Financial Action Task Force (FATF) evaluate the "effectiveness" of compliance against specific "outcome" measures.[2] That is, effectiveness is determined by the extent to which the defined set of outcomes are being achieved by a country.[3] However, the effectiveness, and how to measure effectiveness, of the FATF recommendations has been called into question[4]; despite claiming to be outcome-oriented, the framework primarily measures outputs and activities that may have been incorrectly labelled as outcomes. This misclassification has hindered the proper evaluation of AML policies' true impact and effectiveness[5] creating a gap in connecting discourse on AML/CTF with action taken by agencies and actors within the money laundering and terrorism financing control landscape.

The effectiveness of the FATF and its standards is dependent on the effectiveness of the measures employed by regulated institutions within states.[6] At the national

[2] FATF (2013).

[3] FATF (2013).

[4] De Koker (2022), p. 265–267; Levi et al. (2018), p. 307–328.

[5] Pol (2018), p. 215–230.

[6] Pol (2018), p. 215–230.

level, theoretically, this can be measured by the extent to which states are achieving the defined sets of outcomes provided by the FATF. However, the veracity of the data behind this effectiveness measure is questionable.[7] Still, the key standard for evaluating effectiveness is the ability to detect and prevent serious crime by monitoring financial flows, with the ultimate goal of reducing the social and economic harm caused by profit-driven criminal activities.[8] Success should logically be measured against these crime reduction goals. Yet, notably, no metrics were established to assess whether an AML/CTF compliance program actually prevented or reduced crime. This adds to the contentious point that at the state and institutional level, it is possible to estimate what AML/CTF policies cost, but almost impossible to quantify their benefits.[9]

By the time an AML/CTF compliance program is implemented in an institution, multiple layers of influence—representing multiple layers of leadership—have already shaped its foundation. While the FATF recommendations provide the ideological and conceptual framework, the actual interpretation of AML/CTF risk and implementation of AML/CTF control frameworks are constructed by various stakeholders' interests and agendas which can also be influenced by political, environmental and social conditions. Jurisdictional authorities adapt the FATF principles to their national context, often reflecting their specific concerns and political priorities. Industry players further interpret these requirements through the lens of their operational realities and commercial interests.

Figure 1 illustrates the relationship between leadership and compliance activities, highlighting how the concept of "effectiveness" is multifaceted and depends on the scope of measurement at different levels, from the macro (i.e., global and national level) to micro (i.e., the level of a regulated entity). While each level has its own measures of effectiveness, they are interconnected. We can also distinguish between the effectiveness of global standards and regulation and the effectiveness of the application of those standards and regulations.

In theory, there may be ineffective recommendations and regulations that are implemented and compliant, but this may not result in effective outcomes for crime prevention and control. The effectiveness of national strategies therefore depends on the effectiveness of regulations, which in turn relies on the effectiveness of private sector compliance; the latter being the focus of this chapter. The complex interplay between ideology and stakeholder interests ultimately determines how leadership at the institutional level must navigate the implementation and ongoing management of AML/CTF risk and control frameworks, to ensure the effectiveness of their AML/CTF compliance program.

---

7 Levi et al. (2018), p. 307–328.

8 Pol (2020), p. 73–94.

9 Unger et al. (2014); Zoppei (2015), p. 130–148.

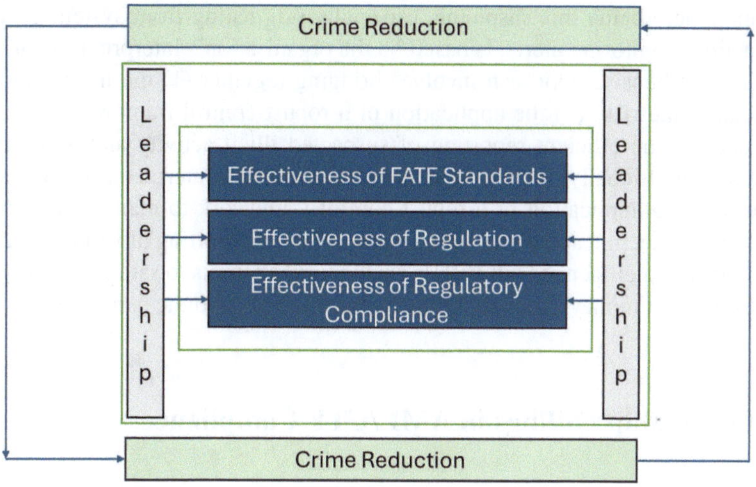

Fig. 1 Measurements of effectiveness and relationship to leadership and crime reduction. Authors' own work

3 Leadership and Effectiveness in AML/CTF Risk and Controls

To connect leadership and AML/CTF compliance program effectiveness, we turn to what "effectiveness" means at the institutional level and the challenges in measuring this construct. A foundational distinction exists between effectiveness and compliance, but their relationship requires careful examination. Accepting that application of a risk-based approach (RBA) for money laundering and terrorism financing risk management is not a "zero failure" approach,[10] we argue strategic leadership in regulated entity firms is essential to ensure that compliance activities truly contribute to AML/CTF compliance program effectiveness. We also highlight how leaders that follow a strategic leadership approach, where the organisation has a shared goal to achieve compliance, can contribute significantly to the effectiveness of regulatory compliance.

So how do we mobilise the construct of effectiveness to usefully analyse the role of leadership? If we address effectiveness in an institution as contributing to crime-reduction goals, it is rather hard to quantify. That is, we can never establish a baseline, or account for undetected crime. Whilst there have been attempts to quantify the costs of compliance for regulated entities there is no data to compare the costs for each firm against the number of convictions for money laundering or predicate offences, for example. Even scarcer is comparative data on crime prevention. If we address effectiveness as successfully adhering to compliance activities, it arguably can become a tick-box exercise. For example, institutions must report suspicion; the

[10] FATF (2014), p. 6.

challenge here being this suspicion, especially originating from system generated transaction monitoring alerts, is based on the organisation's interpretation of risk.

A comprehensive approach involves bringing together (1) the interpretation of financial crime risk, (2) the application of a robust control framework to manage risk, and (3) the efficient reporting of suspected illicit activity and/or suspicious matters. Definitionally, then, effectiveness is about the interpretation of financial crime risk and application of a robust control framework to manage that risk via prevention, detection and disruption, and the efficient reporting of valid suspicion to the Financial Intelligence Unit (FIU). This in turn, attempts to safeguard the institution from illicit money flows and aims to protect the economic community.

4 Leadership Failings in AML/CTF Compliance

Globally, there have been many examples of ineffective AML/CTF compliance involving some form of leadership and/or cultural weakness. An early example of corporate governance failings that can be attributed to weaknesses in, and in this case unethical, leadership practice is the case of Bank of Credit and Commerce International (BCCI). In July 1991, BCCI ceased operating following a significant fraud and money laundering scandal.[11] More recently, in 2020, Swedbank was fined 4 billion crowns (approximately €350 million) by the Swedish regulator, Finansinspektionen, for "serious deficiencies in its work to combat money laundering".[12] Media outlets can be quick to respond to perceived and/or reported leadership failings, often focusing on the failures and the criminal liability (where relevant) of the most Senior Executive—the Chief Executive Officer (CEO). The global headlines included "Swedbank's leadership ignored money laundering risks as suspicious transactions worth $37bn flowed through the bank"[13] and "Former Swedbank CEO Bonnesen sentenced to prison in money laundering case"[14], while the former CEO Birgitte Bonneson was found guilty of gross fraud and sentenced to 15 months in prison.

In 2021, NatWest Bank in the UK was convicted for failing to prevent money laundering and fined £264.8 million for breaches of AML regulations by the Financial Conduct Authority (FCA).[15] The media was quick to highlight the role of multiple executives amongst these failings, announcing that "NatWest Claws Back Bonuses from Ex-Staff Over Laundering Penalty".[16] NatWest Bank is quoted as stating "we recognise that the senior executive committees drive the firm's culture

[11] ICA (2016).

[12] Finansinspektionen (2020).

[13] RegTech Analyst (2020).

[14] Reuters (2024).

[15] FCA (2021).

[16] Bloomberg (2024).

and sets its strategy, so it is appropriate that the colleagues in role when the failures occurred are impacted in the same way that the 2021 population were".[17]

Also in 2021, Deutsche Bank was fined for commodities fraud and violations to the Foreign Corrupt Practices Act (FCPA) by the US Department of Justice (DoJ) and Securities Exchange Commission (SEC). The bank agreed to pay over $130 million in a settlement involving claims of bribery and market manipulation. Whilst not AML/CTF specific, the bank's culture was cited as lacking an emphasis on strong compliance which was later exacerbated by the 2023 consent order and $186 million fine imposed by the Federal Reserve for AML and Sanctions failings dating back to 2015. The media also reported how "Deutsche Bank CEO Christian Sewing could be held criminally responsible for his bank's activities".[18]

In 2022 Danske Bank was fined 2 billion USD by the US DoJ for compliance breaches involving high-risk customers in the Baltic region—a case study that we will review in this chapter. Headlines included "Ousted Dankse Bank CEO faces nearly $400 million lawsuit tied to historic money laundering scandal"[19] and "Scandal at Dankse Bank explained: a striking saga of lousy governance".[20]

In 2024, the US Financial Crimes Enforcement Network (FinCEN) assessed a 1.3 billion USD penalty against TD Bank for multiple violations of AML law, in addition to the US DoJ 1.8 billion USD penalty. In the consent order, it emerged that "TD Bank's senior management and directors did not provide sufficiently strong, explicit, and visible support and commitment to the AML program"[21] and "this lack of commitment was evident in the prioritisation of cost-saving measures over compliance, leading to underinvestment in AML resources and technology".[22] The media were quick to highlight "TD Bank Governance Failure: Where was the Board?"[23] and "The high price of negligence: Inside TD Bank's record fine".[24]

So how do institutions find themselves in these situations and what is the role of leaders—the CEO, the Board and Senior Executive Management—and *leadership* to ensure effective regulatory compliance? While we acknowledge that the FATF recommendations and their manifestation at the state and institutional level are imperfect, there is an obligation, enforced by regulations, to at least *try* to implement effective controls to manage money laundering and terrorism financing risk.

Previously, we addressed what effectiveness means when it comes to compliance and AML/CTF compliance programs, now we can turn to the role of leadership in that effectiveness model. At the time of writing, there have been no published studies on the concept of leadership and its role in constructing and maintaining

[17] Bloomberg (2024).

[18] Forbes (2020).

[19] ACFCS (2020).

[20] Corporate Governance Institute (n.d.).

[21] FinCEN Consent Order, p. 61.

[22] FinCEN Consent Order, p. 63.

[23] Boardroom Metrics (n.d.).

[24] ICA (2025).

effective AML/CTF compliance programs in institutions. While adjacent issues including board influence on risk management[25], director liability in the context of AML/CTF obligations,[26] corporate governance practices related to bank performance,[27] national leadership of AML efforts,[28] and the role of leadership in mitigating employee fraud[29] have been explored, we know very little about the link between leadership and AML/CTF compliance program effectiveness in institutions. This is despite decades of scholarship on leadership and its implications in organisational settings,[30] specifically in financial institutions,[31] and a growing body of institution-focused AML/CTF,[32] including those that focus on the level of private sector actors and/or the compliance officer.[33]

The very way leadership has been studied or approached has led to this gap. That is, we know much less about how leaders make organisations effective than how leaders are perceived,[34] as is evidenced in the media reporting relating to regulatory failures. AML/CTF compliance programs within regulated entities are just one measure of effectiveness. There are of course exceptions to this noted gap; Kaiser et al. (2008) propose conceptualising leadership and evaluating leaders in terms of the performance of the team or organisation for which they are responsible, while Nauman et al. (2022) explore the influence of leadership on team performance.[35] While team performance and outcomes are indeed important factors, we tend to overlook the role leaders and leadership play in ensuring an institutional-wide program, such as the AML/CTF compliance program, is effective. To measure this relationship and ultimately the effectiveness of leadership in regulated entities we must also analyse the layers of leadership beneath the role of the Board and the CEO. That is, the middle layers of "senior leadership" across the organisation; those responsible for ownership of financial crime risks in their respective business areas, and the critical roles with delegated responsibility for managing financial crime compliance: the Money Laundering Reporting Officer (MLRO) or AML/CTF Officer.

The link between leadership and AML/CTF program compliance is not transactional, nor is it binary. Rather it involves an ecosystem of human and technical components throughout various levels of and beyond the organisation. The relationship between leadership and effectiveness hinges on how leaders are perceived, how

---

[25] Aebi et al. (2012), p. 3213–3226.

[26] Goldbarsht (2025), p. 1–17.

[27] Beltratti and Stulz (2012), p. 1–17.

[28] Bociga et al. (2024), p. 1–20.

[29] Said et al. (2018), p. 907–922.

[30] Bolden (2011), p. 251–269; Bryman (2013); Conger and Kanungo (1998); Yukl (2006).

[31] Ali et al. (2015), p. 161–169; Haddon et al. (2015), p. 612–627; Tuffour et al. (2019), p. 543–560.

[32] Dorn and Levi (2008), p. 91–110; Goldbarsht (2025), p. 1–17; Sathye and Islam (2011), p. 169–182; Sciurba (2018), p. 222–235.

[33] Favarel-Garrigues et al. (2008), p. 1–19; Harvey (2004), p. 333–346; Tsingou (2018), p. 191–205; Verhage (2011).

[34] Dinh et al. (2014), p. 36–62.

[35] Kaiser et al. (2008), p. 36–62; Nauman et al. (2022), p. 17–32.

leadership interacts with organisational processes, the effects of leadership, and the importance of events.[36] That is, we consider leadership at the person, dyadic, group, organisational, and event level.[37] At the person level, individual leaders, such as Board Members, the CEO, Business Executives and the MLRO or AML/CTF Officer, influence risk appetite and risk management decisioning. At the dyadic level, the relationship between regulators and financial institutions determines the effectiveness of compliance strategies.[38] At the group and organisational level, leaders establish governance structures that guide AML/CTF compliance program responses, systems, and controls for example implemented and maintained by the business and/or Financial Crime Operations teams. Finally, at the event level, leaders and leadership responses to major enforcement actions or regulatory changes shape industry-wide standards and perceptions of compliance.

This discussion raises questions about what leadership means in the first place. Not a term to be taken for granted, the construct of leadership has evolved significantly, shifting from trait-based theories to situational contingencies and, ultimately, distributed models.[39] It now transcends individual agency, functioning as a dynamic force for change that encompasses a complex interplay of influence within organisational structures, reflecting both historical shifts in conceptualisation and a contemporary understanding of its collective and context-dependent nature.[40] In an institution, the relationship between leadership and AML/CTF program compliance necessitates not only individual leader responsibility, at the CEO level for example, but also the cultivation of a distributed, adaptable approach that fosters a culture of compliance and proactively responds to evolving risks. In this, these factors work to ensure the AML/CTF compliance program's success is embedded throughout the organisation, by a team of leaders and "followers", rather than reliant on a single individual. Ergo, the importance of addressing the *culture* that emerges throughout the organisation.

5 Organisational Culture and Leadership

> *Effective organizations require both tactical and strategic thinking as well as culture building by its leaders.*[41]

The phrase *culture of compliance* is referenced throughout this chapter. This can usefully be understood through the lens of *risk culture*, specifically focusing on how employees perceive the priority given to compliance. This includes their

---

[36] Dinh et al. (2014), p.36–62.

[37] Gardner et al. (2024), p. 139–164.

[38] Dansereau (1995), p. 479–490.

[39] Iszatt-White and Saunders (2020).

[40] Dinh et al. (2014), p. 36–62.

[41] Bass and Avolio (1993), p. 112.

perceptions of the compliance-related practices and behaviours that are expected, valued, and supported within the organisation.[42] In a similar vein, organisational compliance culture reflects the individual firm's approach to regulation, encompassing its values, attitudes, and practices regarding compliance.[43] Whether at the personal or organisational level, the significance of the corporate or organisational environment is crucial.[44]

Importantly here, the behaviour and communication of leaders significantly influence the culture of compliance within financial institutions, as employees look to leaders for cues on the importance of risk management versus profit generation.[45] We acknowledge these competing priorities, however, in the scope of effective AML/CTF compliance programs, a culture that embraces compliance and *why* it is important is arguably driven by a "tone from the top".[46] To effectively manage evolving financial crime risks, leaders must cultivate an organisational culture—the shared values and beliefs of a certain group[47]—that is both adaptive and ethical, enabling their institutions to respond to changing regulatory demands and societal pressures.

At the same time, leadership and culture do not exist in vacuums; they influence and are influenced by each other.[48] While top-down leadership and its influence on culture has been established, the flip side of the coin is the idea that culture shapes how decision-makers view the world, what they consider important, how they behave, and how they evaluate the potential pros and cons of different compliance functions, or applications of systems and controls. As KPMG identified in their 2016 report *Building a strong AML culture: Seven building blocks to help you measure and improve your AML culture*, "while poor AML culture has been identified as a common cause of AML/CFT failings; a strong AML culture can help to reduce the risk of shortcomings, identify compliance issues early and lead to more efficient compliance solutions".[49]

5.1 A Model of Leadership

In this section (Fig. 2) we present a model of leadership, applicable for regulated entities, to show how strategic leadership and compliance culture can interact with, and have implications for, the key functional outputs (or organisational concepts) of governance and oversight and the effective execution of system and control frameworks for AML/CTF program compliance Fig. 2.

---

[42] Sheedy et al. (2017), p. 101–116.

[43] Alfon (1997), p. 16–22; Burdon and Sorour (2020), p. 47–80.

[44] Teichmann and Wittmann (2024), p. 226–232.

[45] Sheedy et al. (2019).

[46] Lail et al. (2015), p. 25–37.

[47] Schein (2010).

[48] Bass and Avolio (1993), p. 112–121.

[49] KPMG (2016), p. 3.

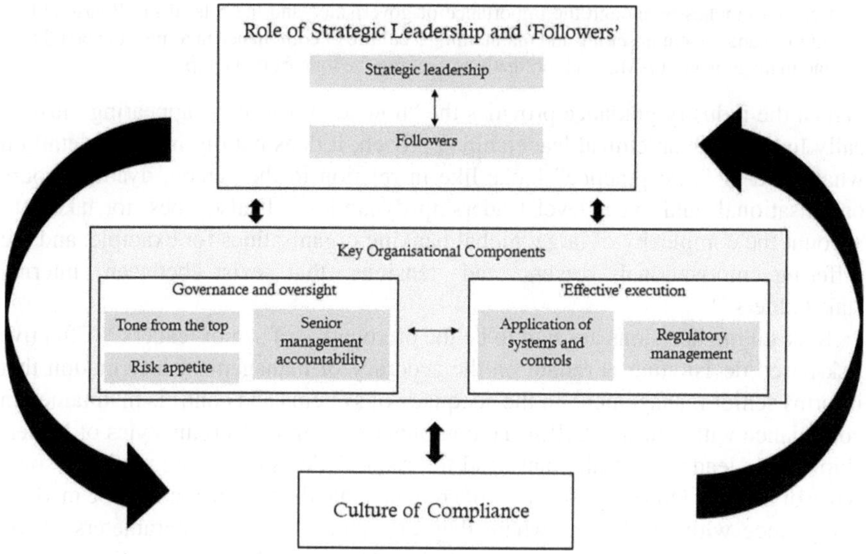

Fig. 2 A model of effective AML/CTF program compliance. Authors' own work

5.2 Governance and Oversight

5.2.1 "Tone from the Top" and "Senior Management Accountability"

In line with FATF standards and the principles of Basel Compliance, it is a regulatory requirement to have adequate governance and oversight of financial crime risk, including money laundering and terrorism financing risk. The Australian financial regulator and FIU, the Australian Transaction Reports and Analysis Centre (AUSTRAC) defines effective AML/CTF governance as (1) clear responsibilities for board and senior management for oversight of AML/CTF compliance; (2) a comprehensive money laundering and terrorism financing risk assessment; (3) documented AML/CTF programs and procedures, and (4) a dedicated AML/CTF compliance officer to oversee AML/CTF compliance.[50] Industry guidance is clear in its expectations of the responsibilities of the Board and Senior Management responsibilities as well as the Compliance Officer, with checklists available on the regulator's website and a video advising firms on how to build a strong AML/CTF compliance culture.

To illustrate, the former CEO of AUSTRAC, Nicole Rose, stated at an Association of Certified Anti-Money Laundering Specialists (ACAMS) conference in June 2022:

[50] AUSTRAC (2025).

> I cannot emphasise enough the importance of governance and the role of the Board and senior management in setting and maintaining a culture of compliance in terms of oversight and management of AML/CTF obligations - setting the tone from the top.[51]

Whilst the industry guidance provides the "how to" for leaders, appearing intrinsically linked with an ethical leadership approach, it does not dig into any detail on what good or "best practice" looks like in relation to the person, dyadic, group, organisational, and event level leadership dynamics.[52] It also does not take into account the complexity of large, global banking organisations for example, and the differing motivational drivers and tensions that exist between internal stakeholders.[53]

Risk-taking decisions are said to be the prerogative of senior leaders.[54] Effective risk-based decisioning is reliant on the accuracy of management information that informs senior management on the adequacy of systems and controls maintained in compliance with a firm's AML/CTF compliance program. Certain styles of leadership and/or leadership traits may lead to "riskier" decisions being made by some types of leaders. However, the principle remains that those decisions can be made in compliance with regulations where they are made within the parameters of the established risk appetite and are supported by documented evidence in line with the firm's risk assessment. This is the premise of the RBA in terms of managing financial crime risk, including money laundering and terrorism financing risk.

Board experience, expertise in regulatory compliance matters, and experience of the regulatory environment[55] are deemed critical for regulatory success, especially where senior management are held accountable—in some countries with criminal liability—for AML/CTF regulatory compliance. A Board and Senior Executive team that relies solely on the MLRO or AML/CTF Officer may not be able to ask the "right" questions and challenge metrics and decision making in the same way that a Line 3 Audit team will not be able to effectively test the adequacy of systems and controls without the requisite experience and expertise. In some jurisdictions, such as the United Kingdom and the United States, MLROs can face criminal prosecution for failure to report suspicious activity, negligence or wilful misconduct.[56] This emphasises the need for experienced and skilled staff in this position. In the UK, for example, it is also a requirement that the MLRO is an approved person: that is, they are deemed "fit and proper" to perform a control function.[57] This level of testing does not exist in all countries. Australia, for example, "fit and proper" has

[51] AUSTRAC (2022).

[52] Gardner et al. (2024), p. 139–164.

[53] Southworth (2013); Southworth and Levi (2024), p. 101–121.

[54] Sheedy et al. (2019).

[55] Clifford Chance (2017).

[56] See Proceeds of Crime Act 2002 (United Kingdom); Bank Secrecy Act 1970 (United States); and Uniting and Strengthening America by Providing Appropriate Tools Required to Intercept and Obstruct Terrorism (USA PATRIOT) Act (2001) (United States).

[57] FCA (2025).

been an absent requirement from AUSTRAC for the AML/CTF Officer role, presenting a risk that some holders of these roles have not had or do not have the qualification nor capability to perform this function in line with industry expectations. If these AML/CTF Officers are also not supported by a senior management team with experience of the regulatory environment and that can challenge appropriately, there is a risk that financial crime risk, including AML/CTF risk, cannot be or has not been managed effectively.[58] There is a growing need for global qualifications and formal training to strengthen technical expertise in these roles, not only to ensure effective compliance outcomes, but to prevent defensive, risk-averse practices that can lead to unpragmatic outcomes and negative customer impact. To achieve effective financial crime risk management, Financial crime compliance, and the MLRO/AML/CTF Officer should be viewed as strategic partners in decision making.

5.2.2 Risk Appetite

As part of the RBA to AML/CTF risk management, there is an expectation that firms will define their money laundering and terrorism financing risk appetite, often via a risk appetite statement (RAS) that is approved by the Board. This sets the parameters that the firm will operate within and is the basis for, and a potential output from, the enterprise-wide risk assessment. The RAS defines who the firm will or won't do business with.

Whilst there is usually a zero tolerance for sanctions and terrorist financing, zero-tolerance for money laundering requires knowledge and evidence that a crime has taken place.[59] Setting the risk appetite sets the tone from the top of what will and will not be tolerated within the organisation and is the basis for setting clear rules and goals within the organisation for all staff to adhere to. Effective strategic leadership would embed a compliance culture that measures adherence to these rules and goals, with key risk indicators (KRIs) to flag rule slippage or where goals are at risk, and a performance measurement framework to hold senior leaders to account. Ineffective leadership would be the lack of a Board approved RAS and/or a lack of adherence to the RAS.

---

[58] This is changing in Australia with AML/CTF Act (2006) reforms due to be implemented in 2026, as AUSTRAC state "the new framework emphasises the role of governing bodies and senior management in overseeing ML/TF/PF risk and AML/CTF compliance and taking reasonable steps to comply with AML/CTF obligations. It is now an explicit requirement to appoint a fit and proper AML/CTF compliance officer responsible for implementing the AML/CTF program". (AUSTRAC 2025).

[59] Southworth and Levi (2024), p. 101–121.

5.3 *Effective Execution*

5.3.1 Application of Systems and Controls

Effective execution of the AML/CTF compliance program involves embedding and maintaining an infratructure of systems and controls to manage the risks identified via the risk assessment process. This is a constantly evolving process as the interpretation and measurement of risks change. Systems and controls can include and relate to: customer due diligence (CDD), onboarding, and enhanced due diligence measures; customer screening; transaction monitoring and system testing; and suspicious matter or activity reporting. The adequacy of systems and controls is measured via a range of practices including control self-assessments, quality control testing, assurance reviews and internal audit.

The extent to which leaders and leadership influence the "effectiveness" of systems and controls in place requires further study. Southworth and Levi (2024) outline operational challenges and variations of application of the RBA to financial crime risk management by banks. Two of the operational challenges include the multiple actors involved in business decision making within banks, and the inability to measure or even conceptualise "effectiveness" meaningfully.

5.3.2 Regulatory Management

Often overlooked in assessing compliance is an organisation's leadership capability to manage the regulatory relationship and expectations, with attitudes towards regulators being central to this dynamic. For example, a firm may be technically compliant but exhibit a poor attitude toward compliance, only meeting minimal requirements and showing limited concern for corporate social responsibility. Some organisations may excel at "playing the game" with effective showmanship, presenting a facade of compliance to regulators. Others may genuinely believe they are doing the right thing, while their compliance record reveals a different story. Internal tensions between leaders with differing commitments to compliance (often the MLRO or AML/CTF Officer versus business-driven leaders) can also hinder regulatory engagement. Simply put, following rules (compliance) does not guarantee desired outcomes (effectiveness), and perceived performance may not reflect actual compliance or genuine effectiveness. Whilst regulatory management is not critical to the implementation and maintenance of the AML/CTF compliance program, it is arguably a critical factor for its effectiveness. It ensures the regulator is informed and engaged, especially in relation to mandatory or voluntary disclosures of self-identified issues (dependent on the jurisdiction).

The concepts of strategic leadership and culture of compliance interact with the key organisational concepts covered by governance and oversight and effective execution. To put this model into practice and assess the interaction, we can review a case of ineffectiveness in AML/CTF compliance programs. This ineffectiveness is reflected in the Danske Bank case.

6 Case Study: Failure in Leadership and Cultural Missteps

The Danske Bank case is one of the largest money laundering scandals involving a bank in recent years.[60] The 2018 *Report on the Non-Resident Portfolio* at Danske Bank's Estonian Branch details the investigation and findings related to the branch, focusing on AML and accountability issues.[61] In doing so, it exposes issues around leadership, particularly in the context of accountability and the actions taken by the Board of Directors, the Chairman, and the CEO of Danske Bank, as well as branch leadership.

For context, Danske Bank's acquisition of Sampo Bank's Estonian branch in 2006 exposed a critical lack of oversight and risk management, particularly concerning the non-resident portfolio.[62] Despite repeated warnings from both internal parties and external parties including Estonian, Russian, and Danish regulators about inadequate KYC protocols and suspicious transactions, Danske Bank failed to address these concerns effectively.[63] Internal communications were flawed, and a culture evidently prioritising profit over compliance allowed the Estonian branch to become a conduit for illicit funds, ultimately resulting in a massive money laundering scandal.

Danske Bank's leadership and cultural failures led to extensive financial crime compliance breaches and regulatory violations, ultimately resulting in severe consequences. The bank was forced to close its Estonian branch, employees were arrested, share prices plummeted, and the CEO resigned. The bank also faced heightened financial crime risks, exemplified by over €200 billion in suspicious transactions.[64] These failures also triggered substantial legal repercussions. Danske Bank was subjected to penalties, settlements, and criminal forfeiture in several jurisdictions across Europe and the United States, including a 2 billion USD fine imposed by the US DoJ in 2022 after pleading guilty to conspiracy to commit bank fraud.[65] The systemic AML failings also resulted in regulatory enforcement in other jurisdictions including, Denmark, France, and Estonia.[66] Applying the model of effectiveness from Fig. 2, we can review what led to such catastrophic regulatory failings at

[60] Chapter by Donaldson and Leuprecht (2025) in this book provide more insights on the case, specifically the role of globalisation and state capture.

[61] Bruun and Hjejle (2018).

[62] Bruun and Hjejle (2018), p. 40.

[63] Minto and Rasmussen (2022).

[64] Bjerregaard and Kirchmaier (2019).

[65] US Department of Justice (2022).

[66] In 2023, Dankse was also fined $4.4 million by the Norwegian Financial Supervisory Authority for market manipulation.

Dankse Bank. With the construct of leadership extending beyond the acts of one person, (i.e., the “leader”) in this case the CEO, Thomas Borgen, we can explore the multitude of leadership dynamics at play and the associated failings. Again, the focus is on how strategic leadership and compliance culture interact and have implications for the key functional outputs (or organisational concepts) of governance and oversight and effective execution for systems and controls for AML/CTF compliance.

In the Danske Bank case, these considerations comprise key functional outputs of governance in terms of Board and Executive oversight, the frameworks and motivations for decision making, and the impact of these on the management of financial crime risk(s). In terms of effective execution, we can explore the need for the implementation of the three lines of defence model and actioning the recommendations from internal audit findings, as well as appropriate management of conflict of interests (profit maximisation versus adequate risk management), reporting, effective whistleblowing programmes, and the regulatory relationship. This is, of course, all representing a dynamic interplay between strategic leadership and a culture of compliance.

6.1 Leaders, Followers, and Culture

It is evident that there was a complete breakdown in all three lines of defence at Danske Bank, indicating a lack of strong leadership in establishing a culture of compliance and accountability.[67] In other words, it is the role of governing bodies and senior management to define the organisation’s goals, create its strategic plans, and implement the risk management structures that oversee the three lines of defence.

The breakdown in communication and transparency was also driven by ineffective leadership. Senior leaders failed to ensure robust and transparent communication and reporting lines, particularly between the Estonian branch and the Group level.[68] This lack of communication hindered effective oversight and contributed to the persistence of AML failings. Further, communication between the Estonian branch and Group functions, including Compliance and AML, Legal, Executive, and the Board, was often incomplete.[69] The lack of initiative from the team in effectively communicating critical information and concerns undoubtedly contributed to the failings. Finally, 42 employees and agents were identified in facilitating suspicious activities.[70] It is well documented that ethical leadership temperaments

[67] Bruun and Hjejle (2018).

[68] Bruun and Hjejle (2018).

[69] Bruun and Hjejle (2018).

[70] Bruun and Hjejle (2018).

stimulate ethical culture of the organisation.[71] This case is a clear demonstration of what can happen when an appropriate culture is not tempered by management. Ultimately, the Danske Bank scandal resulted in ten former employees of the Estonian branch being arrested and the resignation of the CEO, Thomas Borgen, and Chairman of the Board of Directors, Ole Anderson.

When we consider that culture is about the shared values and beliefs of a certain group,[72] it is apparent that that the culture at Danske Bank's Estonian branch was maladaptive to principles of risk management and compliance.[73] Executives ignored rumours and whistleblowing, and in turn created a culture of impunity. The culture of acceptance, conducive to risk-taking, undoubtedly contributed to the demise of the Estonian branch.[74] These can be further understood through an exploration of the key functional outputs.

6.2 Key Organisational Components: Governance and Oversight

The Estonian branch of Danske Bank had a high risk appetite, particularly concerning non-resident customers.[75] This risk appetite was not adequately managed or mitigated by strategic leadership, leading to significant AML breaches. The report notes that

> [t]he Estonian FSA... inserted additional text when reviewing the minutes [of a meeting with the branch]...however they pointed out that from the FSA perspective, risk appetite in Estonian Danske A/S looks above average comparing with the Estonian banking sector in general".[76]

It also notes,

> [t]he relatively big concentration of the business relationships from risk countries in Branch is not accidental and that "the same risk patterns" had been identified by the Estonian FSA during its inspections in 2007 and 2009.[77]

This suggests that the Estonian branch operated with a higher risk appetite than other banks in Estonia, especially regarding non-resident customers.

Despite the damning findings, the report found that the CEO, Board of Directors, nor the Audit Committee breached any legal obligations related to the Estonian branch. However, it notes that the CEO could have done more, particularly in

[71] Ullah et al. (2022), p. 99–119.

[72] Schein (2010).

[73] Logan (2019).

[74] Gottschalk (2023), p. 307–328.

[75] Bruun and Hjejle (2018).

[76] Bruun and Hjejle (2018), p. 47.

[77] Bruun and Hjejle (2018), p. 44.

ensuring the information provided by management was scrutinized and challenged via the Board. As per the report:

> In our view, Thomas Borgen could have taken a more active role in setting the overall standard and direction by making sure that relevant issues were thoroughly debated, that investigation results were properly documented, that presentations and materials were adequately reflected in minutes, etc.[78]

Along with the notes on the CEO, the report clearly outlines the role of the Board:

> The Board of Directors is entrusted with the overall and strategic management of Danske Bank. The Board of Directors must ensure proper governance, which includes determining the bank's risk profile, laying down policies for how the bank must control its significant activities and risks related thereto and assessing whether the Executive Board performs its duties appropriately, pursuant to sections 70 and 71 of the Financial Business Act and the Executive Order on Management and Control of Banks, etc.[79]

Danske assigned blame to poor communication between the executive board of the bank in Copenhagen and corrupt management in the bank's Estonian branch. However, it was a clear lack of accountability at the Group level and the Branch level that led to these disconnects. The priorities of the Group are questionable, however, given that in 2013, Danske's head office had no person responsible for AML, as required by Danish law, until November. What's more, the bank had a separate IT platform with computer systems designed and programmed in software that the headquarters did not understand.

Together, these findings demonstrate a perfect storm in terms of risk appetite, tone from the top, and senior management accountability. A breakdown in these factors, driven by ineffective leadership and its accompanying (lack of) culture of compliance consistent across the organisation, were clear contributors to the scandal. These factors are accompanied by the application of (in this case inadequate) risk-based systems and controls, and the management of regulatory relationships: referred to as "effective" execution.

6.3 Key Organisational Components: "Effective" Execution

Alongside the governance and oversight factors, the (in)"effective" execution—the application of systems and controls and regulatory management—further contributed to the Danske Bank downfall. As per the report,

> AML procedures at the Estonian branch involving the Non-Resident Portfolio had been manifestly insufficient and inadequate. It was also realised that all control functions (or lines of defence) had failed, both within the branch and at Group level. This included business functions as well as Group Compliance & AML and Group Internal Audit.[80]

---

[78] Bruun and Hjejle (2018), p. 85.

[79] Bruun and Hjejle (2018), p. 79.

[80] Bruun and Hjejle (2018), p. 7.

This control function failure was primarily based on the Branch's lack of knowledge about customers, including beneficial owners and their source of funds (i.e., CDD), insufficient and manual screening of customers and payments, and a lack of response to suspicious customers and transactions.[81] The reports point to Danske failing to report suspicious activities, noting that risks were underestimated. Compounding this, some customer information was written in only Estonian or Russian, creating a linguistic barrier between the Estonian branch and the Group; another example of over-dependence on local management resulting in struggles to control non-resident accounts.[82]

In terms of risk, the case brings into stark relief the lack of compliance with the recommendations of regulatory bodies assessing risk. In a 2007 inspection by the Estonian Financial Supervisory Authority (FSA), it was revealed that routine practices with respect to KYC have "not been fully in compliance with the requirements stipulated in valid legal acts and international standards" and that "the Bank has underestimated potential risks, associated with providing services to legal entities registered in a low-tax area and undue compliance with relevant procedure rules".[83] The branch management was aware of the Estonian FSA's concerns, but they did not take sufficient action to address these concerns.

The Estonian FSA issued an instruction ordering the bank to comply with its recommendations, but the bank failed to do so. In 2012 and 2013, the Danish FSA followed up on concerns around the non-resident portfolios as the Estonian branch and were provided comforting, yet incorrect, information about the bank's AML procedures. What's more, news from the Estonian FSA and internal auditors was not escalated in true transparency to the Board.[84] These examples not only highlight the failure of leadership within the branch, but also at the Group level. In this case, leadership of the branch as well as Group level senior leadership did not manage the relationship with regulators effectively, instead presenting a facade of compliance to regulators. The result was a culture of *non*compliance. It is clear that branch management was more concerned with procedures than with identifying actual risk.[85] Even so, they fell short on the requirements of procedures.

We have established that in an institution, the relationship between leadership and AML/CTF program compliance necessitates not only individual responsibility, but also the cultivation of a distributed, adaptable approach that fosters a culture of compliance and proactively responds to evolving risks. In our model, strategic leadership involves setting the tone for a culture of compliance and ethical conduct, which, when combined with effective execution of policies and procedures, ensures sound governance and oversight, ultimately leading to organisational success and

---

[81] Bruun and Hjejle (2018).

[82] Milne and Winter (2018).

[83] Bruun and Hjejle (2018), p. 40.

[84] Bruun and Hjejle (2018).

[85] Danske Bank (2018).

the prevention of misconduct. The Danske Bank case is the antithesis of this, demonstrating the catastrophe that can ensue when these factors break down.

7 Discussion and Future Directions

The Danske Bank case is not unique. Numerous financial institutions, casinos, cryptocurrency exchanges, and other regulated entities worldwide have been implicated in ineffective AML/CTF compliance practices, falling short of regulatory expectations. Regardless of the sophistication of the technology implemented in institutions, the detail included in compliance programs, or the legislative requirements, if the human element—that is, leadership—is ineffective, AML/CTF compliance is bound to fail. Institutions require effective leadership that fosters, or results in, a culture of compliance. It is of course more nuanced than this, however at its core, we posit that the human-organisational element is central.

This extends to all areas where decision-making around risk is involved. For example, while outside of the scope of this chapter, leadership decision-making around de-risking (i.e., exiting segments of high-risk customers potentially suspected of money laundering). This can have a negative impact for the effectiveness of crime control at a national level where displacement of the suspicious activity may go undetected by other industries or firms, resulting in an ineffective result for law enforcement. Here, tensions may exist between risk management and personal liability at the leadership level and effective compliance programs in accordance with regulatory requirements, versus the overall effectiveness of crime prevention, detection and disruption.

Our conceptual model, with its key organisational components (functional outputs), helps understand decision-making in risk management. While we showed how ignoring these components can lead to ineffective compliance, our main goal is to highlight how leadership can use them to achieve the opposite. Effective leadership strengthens effective execution and governance and oversight, fostering a culture of compliance. This, in turn, reinforces effective leadership, creating a cycle that promotes continuous improvement.

Ultimately, it is difficult to judge how well AML/CTF compliance measures are working overall. This is because there is no single global standard for how regulated businesses should measure their own compliance. Further, it is not clear how these measures reduce financial crime risks, and how they help prevent, detect, and stop crime. This makes it challenging for policymakers to assess the overall effectiveness of AML/CTF efforts. Still, we can add to this conversation by interrogating key factors that may contribute.

Looking ahead, this chapter opens new questions about measuring effectiveness, training leaders in financial crime risk management and compliance, and structuring regulatory frameworks to encourage true effectiveness. The theoretical and practical implications of the model we have proposed are significant. We move beyond traditional views of leadership effectiveness to understand how leadership contributes to effective—or ineffective—AML/CTF compliance programs. Practically, this means rethinking how we assess leadership and effectiveness in AML/CTF compliance programs. Technical compliance alone isn't enough. We need leaders who create cultures of genuine compliance, and we need to think about what effectiveness—in both the AML/CTF compliance and leadership realms—really means. At the centre of this is the idea that we need to foster organisations that assist in the war on financial crime while navigating complex and imperfect regulatory requirements (as well as commercial priorities).

8 Conclusion

As technology advances, regulatory regimes shift, and the threats posed by financial criminals evolve, regulated entities are under more pressure than ever to safeguard themselves and contribute to the global war on financial crime. With a growing focus on what can be accomplished with technology and efficiency in organisations, we cannot lose sight on the fact that the human element is fundamental to the success of any initiative. For example, advanced software that can complete risk assessments will not be successful if factors such as governance and oversight and effective execution are not considered in the wider organisational context. That is, without a culture of compliance that proactively responds to evolving risks and understands *why* compliance is necessary, any technical advancements are all for naught. On the flip side, it takes effective leadership in the first place to source and champion appropriate and innovative software and its deployment, and to make informed decisions on the risk-based approach. Again, factors that go hand in hand in a cycle of continuous improvement.

We operate in uncertain times, but one thing remains certain; effective leadership is a necessity for effective AML/CTF compliance. This chapter highlights that there is more to be done to research the human and social-organisational dynamics of leadership and culture that impact, and are intrinsically linked to, the output from AML/CTF compliance programs. This chapter paves the way for future research into what "effectiveness" looks like as well as opportunity to analyse further case studies of ineffectiveness *and* effectiveness. With further research linking effective leadership to effective AML/CTF compliance there is hope for a brighter future for regulated entities and agencies and actors within the broader AML/CTF control landscape to manage and mitigate money laundering and terrorist financing risk.

References

ACFCS (2020) Ousted Dankse Bank CEO faces nearly $400 million lawsuit tied to historic money laundering scandal. https://www.acfcs.org/ousted-danske-bank-ceo-faces-nearly-400-million-lawsuit-tied-to-historic-money-laundering-scandal

Aebi V, Sabato G, Schmid M (2012) Risk management, corporate governance, and bank performance in the financial crisis. J Bank Financ 36(12):3213–3226

Alfon I (1997) Cost-benefit analysis and compliance culture. J Financ Regul Compliance 5(1):16–22

Ali NM, Jangga R, Ismail M, Kamal SNM, Ali MN (2015) Influence of leadership styles in creating quality work culture. Procedia Econ Finance 31:161–169

AUSTRAC (2022) ACAMS Conference. https://www.austrac.gov.au/news-and-media/our-recent-work/austrac-ceo-nicole-rose-speaking-notes-acams-2nd-annual-aml-anti-financial-crime-conference-australasia

AUSTRAC (2025) AML/CTF reform. https://www.austrac.gov.au/about-us/amlctf-reform

Bank Secrecy Act (1970) United States of America. https://www.fincen.gov/resources/statutes-and-regulations/bank-secrecy-act

Bass BM, Avolio BJ (1993) Transformational leadership and organizational culture. Public Adm Q 17(1):112–121

Beltratti A, Stulz RM (2012) The credit crisis around the globe: why did some banks perform better? J Financ Econ 105(1):1–17

Bjerregaard E, Kirchmaier T (2019) The Danske Bank money laundering scandal: a case study. Copenhagen Business School, CBS. https://doi.org/10.2139/ssrn.3446636

Bloomberg (2024) NatWest Claws back bonuses from ex-staff over laundering penalty. https://www.bloomberg.com/news/articles/2024-02-16/natwest-claws-back-bonuses-from-ex-staff-over-laundering-penalty?embedded-checkout=true

Boardroom Metrics (n.d.) TD Bank governance failure: where was the board? https://www.boardroommetrics.com/blog/td-bank-governance-failure-where-was-the-board-20241031.htm

Bociga D, Lord N, Bellotti E (2024) Dare to share: information and intelligence sharing within the UK's anti-money laundering regime. Polic Soc:1–20

Bolden R (2011) Distributed leadership in organizations: a review of theory and research. Int J Manag Rev 13(3):251–269

Bruun & Hjejle (2018) Report on the non-resident portfolio at Danske Bank's Estonian Branch. Law firm Bruun Hjejle, Copenhagen, Denmark

Bryman A (2013) Leadership and organizations (RLE: Organizations). Routledge

Burdon WM, Sorour MK (2020) Institutional theory and evolution of 'a legitimate' compliance culture: the case of the UK financial service sector. J Bus Ethics 162:47–80

Clifford Chance (2017) Banking executive accountability regimes. https://treasury.gov.au/sites/default/files/2019-03/c2017-t228532-Clifford-Chance.pdf

Conger JA, Kanungo RN (1998) Charismatic leadership in organizations. Sage Publications

Corporate Governance Institute (n.d.) Scandal at Danske Bank explained: a striking saga of lousy governance. https://www.thecorporategovernanceinstitute.com/insights/news-analysis/scandal-at-danske-a-striking-saga-of-lousy-governance/#:~:text=The%20scandal%20at%20Danske%20Bank,watchdog%20probes%20and%20international%20condemnation

Dansereau F (1995) A dyadic approach to leadership: creating and nurturing this approach under fire. Leadersh Q 6(4):479–490

Danske Bank (2018) Findings of the investigations relating to Danske Bank's branch in Estonia. https://danskebank.com/news-and-insights/news-archive/press-releases/2018/pr19092018

De Koker L (2022) Editorial: regulatory impact assessment: towards a better approach for the FATF. J Money Laund Control 25(2):265–267

Dinh JE, Lord RG, Gardner WL, Meuser JD, Liden RC, Hu J (2014) Leadership theory and research in the new millennium: current theoretical trends and changing perspectives. Leadersh Q 25(1):36–62

Donaldson N, Leuprecht C (2025) Geopolitical implications of embedded corruption in global capital markets: the professional brokers who enable the transnational illicit political economy of systematic state capture. In: Goldbarsht D, de Koker L, Ferrill J (eds) The financial war on crime and terrorism: opportunities and challenges. Springer, Cham

Dorn N, Levi M (2008) East meets West in anti-money laundering and anti-terrorist finance: policy dialogue and differentiation on security, the timber trade and 'alternative' banking. Asian J Criminol 3:91–110
FATF (2013) International standards on combating money laundering and the financing of terrorism and proliferation - the FATF recommendations. https://www.fatf-gafi.org/en/publications/Fatfrecommendations/Fatf-recommendations.html
FATF (2014) Guidance for a risk-based approach: the banking sector. https://www.fatf-gafi.org/en/publications/Fatfrecommendations/Risk-based-approach-banking-sector.html
Favarel-Garrigues G, Godefroy T, Lascoumes P (2008) Sentinels in the banking industry: private actors and the fight against money laundering in France. Br J Criminol 48(1):1–19
FCA (2021) NatWest sentenced for AML failings. https://www.fca.org.uk/news/press-releases/natwest-fined-264.8million-anti-money-laundering-failures#:~:text=National%20Westminster%20Bank%20Plc%20(NatWest,%2C%20today%20said%3A%20'%E2%80%A6
FCA (2025) Approved Persons. https://www.fca.org.uk/firms/approved-persons
Finansinspektionen (2020) Swedbank fined for AML deficiencies. https://www.fi.se/en/published/sanctions/financial-firms/2020/swedbank-receives-a-warning-and-an-administrative-fine-of-sek-four-billion/
Forbes (2020) Deutsche Bank CEO could be held criminally responsible for bank's activities. https://www.forbes.com/sites/jackkelly/2020/10/05/deutsche-bank-ceo-christian-sewing-could-be-held-criminally-responsible-for-his-banks-activities/
Gardner WL, Hanna AA, Noghani F, Cogliser CC (2024) Leadership emergence: answering the "how" and "why" questions by considering levels of analysis and form of emergence. Annu Rev Organ Psych Organ Behav 11(1):139–164
Goldbarsht D (2025) Adapting director liability to modern AML/CTF compliance: risks and regulatory implications in Australia. Curr Issues Crim Just 37(2):228–244
Gottschalk P (2023) Reducing financial crime convenience for sustainable finance. A case study of Danske Bank in Estonia. In: Dion M (ed) Sustainable finance and financial crime. Springer International Publishing, pp 307–328
Haddon A, Loughlin C, McNally C (2015) Leadership in a time of financial crisis: what do we want from our leaders? Leadersh Organ Dev J 36(5):612–627
Harvey J (2004) Compliance and reporting issues arising for financial institutions from money laundering regulations: a preliminary cost benefit study. J Money Laund Control 7(4):333–346
ICA (2016) The BCCI scandal. https://www.int-comp.org/insight/the-bcci-scandal/
ICA (2025) The high price of negligence: inside td bank's record fine. https://www.int-comp.org/insight/the-high-price-of-negligence-inside-td-banks-record-fine/
Iszatt-White M, Saunders C (2020) Leadership. Oxford University Press
Kaiser RB, Hogan R, Craig SB (2008) Leadership and the fate of organizations. Am Psychol 63(2):96–110
Kotter J (1999) Change leadership. Exec Excell 16(4):16–17
KPMG (2016) Building a strong aml culture. Seven building blocks to help you measure and improve your AML culture. https://kpmg.com/bs/en/home/insights/2016/04/building-strong-anti-money-laundering-culture.html
Lail B, MacGregor J, Stuebs M, Thomasson T (2015) The influence of regulatory approach on tone at the top. J Bus Ethics 126(1):25–37
Levi M, Reuter P, Halliday T (2018) Can the AML system be evaluated without better data? Crime Law Soc Chang 69(2):307–328
Logan B (2019) The case of Danske Bank and money laundering. Seven Pillars Institute for Global Finance and Ethics. https://sevenpillarsinstitute.org/the-case-of-danske-bank-and-money-laundering/
Milne R, Winter D (2018, December 19) Danske: anatomy of a money laundering scandal. Financial Times. https://www.ft.com/content/519ad6ae-bcd8-11e8-94b2-17176fbf93f5
Minto J, Rasmussen C (2022) Danske Bank: a case study in AML failure. Thomson Reuters

Nauman S, Bhatti SH, Imam H, Khan MS (2022) How servant leadership drives project team performance through collaborative culture and knowledge sharing. Proj Manag J 53(1):17–32
Pol R (2018) Anti-money laundering effectiveness: assessing outcomes or ticking boxes? J Money Laund Control 21(2):215–230
Pol RF (2020) Anti-money laundering: the world's least effective policy experiment? Together, we can fix it. Policy Design Pract 3(1):73–94
Proceeds of Crime Act (2002) United Kingdom https://www.legislation.gov.uk/ukpga/2002/29/contents
RegTech Analyst (2020) Swedbank's leadership ignored money laundering risks. https://fintech.global/2020/03/25/swedbanks-leadership-ignored-money-laundering-risks-as-suspicious-transactions-worth-e37bn-flowed-through-the-bank-probe-reveals/
Reuters (2024) Former Swedbank CEO Bonnesen sentenced to prison in money laundering case. https://www.reuters.com/world/europe/former-swedbank-ceo-bonnesen-sentenced-prison-over-handling-money-laundering-2024-09-10/
Said J, Omar N, Rafidi M, Syed Yusof SN (2018) Are organizational factors more prevailing than individual factors in mitigating employee fraud? J Financ Crime 25(3):907–922
Sathye M, Islam J (2011) Adopting a risk-based approach to AMLCTF compliance: the Australian case. J Financ Crime 18(2):169–182
Schein EH (2010) Organizational culture and leadership, vol 2. John Wiley & Sons
Sciurba M (2018) The heart of know your customer requirements: the discriminatory effect of AML and CTF policies in times of counter-terrorism in the UK. Eur J Crime Crim Law Crim Justice 26(3):222–235
Sheedy E, Zhang L, Tam KCH (2019) Incentives and culture in risk compliance. J Bank Financ 107:105611
Sheedy EA, Griffin B, Barbour JP (2017) A framework and measure for examining risk climate in financial institutions. J Bus Psychol 32(1):101–116
Southworth R (2013) Financial crime control: risk, regulation and the role(s) of the UK banking sector. PhD thesis. Cardiff University
Southworth R, Levi M (2024) Application of the risk-based approach (RBA) for financial crime risk management by banks. In: Financial crime and the law: identifying and mitigating risks. Springer, pp 101–121
Teichmann FMJ, Wittmann C (2024) Compliance cultures and the role of financial incentives. J Financ Crime 31(1):226–232
Tsingou E (2018) New governors on the block: the rise of anti-money laundering professionals. Crime Law Soc Chang 69(2):191–205
Tuffour JK, Gali AM, Tuffour MK (2019) Managerial leadership style and employee commitment: evidence from the financial sector. Glob Bus Rev 23(3):543–560
Ullah I, Hameed RM, Kayani NZ, Fazal Y (2022) CEO ethical leadership and corporate social responsibility: examining the mediating role of organizational ethical culture and intellectual capital. J Manag Organ 28(1):99–119
Unger B, Ferwerda J, van den Broek M, Deleanu I (2014) The economic and legal effectiveness of the European Union's anti-money laundering policy. In: The economic and legal effectiveness of the European Union's anti-money laundering policy. Edward Elgar Publishing
Uniting and Strengthening America by Providing Appropriate Tools Required to Intercept and Obstruct Terrorism (USA PATRIOT) Act (2001) United States of America. https://www.congress.gov/107/plaws/publ56/PLAW-107publ56.pdf
US Department of Justice (2022) Danske Bank pleads guilty to fraud on U.S. banks in multi-billion dollar scheme to access the U.S. financial system. https://www.justice.gov/archives/opa/pr/danske-bank-pleads-guilty-fraud-us-banks-multi-billion-dollar-scheme-access-us-financial
Verhage A (2011) The anti money laundering complex and the compliance industry. Routledge
Yukl G (2006) Leadership in organizations, 9th edn. Pearson Education India
Zoppei V (2015) Money laundering: a new perspective in assessing the effectiveness of the AML regime. Eur Rev Organ Crime 2(1):130–148

Dr. Jamie Ferrill is a Senior Lecturer of Financial Crime Studies at the Australian Graduate School of Policing and Security, Charles Sturt University and a research fellow with the Financial Integrity Hub (FIH). Before transitioning to academia, she gained nearly a decade of experience in law enforcement, serving with the Canadian federal government. Jamie's research addresses threats to national and economic security, with a particular interest in the intersection of financial crime with border governance frameworks, international cooperation, and organisational effectiveness. Jamie has been a visiting fellow at the Academy of International Affairs NRW and the Border Policy Research Institute, and she is a fellow of the Financial Integrity Hub, the Institute of Intergovernmental Relations at Queen's University, and Borders in Globalization at the University of Victoria. Her latest book is titled Dirty Money: Financial Crime in Canada (McGill-Queen's University Press).

Dr. Rachel Southworth has a Ph.D. in 'Financial Crime Control: Risk, Regulation and the Role of the UK Banking Sector' from Cardiff University, Wales. Rachel is an Adjunct Lecturer at Charles Sturt University, Australia, where she specialises in leadership and strategic thinking in financial crime control. Rachel has worked internationally in a range of Financial Crime Compliance, Risk and Operations positions for major financial institutions in Australia, Hong Kong and the UK. Prior to working in the banking sector, Rachel has also worked in various policy roles, with the UK Regulator, the Financial Services Authority (now Financial Conduct Authority); the UK Treasury in Financial Crime Policy; and Surrey Police in Policing Policy. Rachel is alumni of the London School of Economics and Political Science (LSE) where she was awarded her MSc in Criminal Justice Policy and BSc in Sociology.

FATF and the Conundrum of Public-Private Sector Intelligence and Information Sharing

Paula Chadderton

Abstract Concerns at the international, regional, and national levels about the increasing sophistication of financial crime and the strategies transnational organised crime groups use to launder money have led to increased interest in exploring innovative initiatives that optimise available information and resources. Public-private sector information sharing initiatives have been seen as a useful mechanism for optimising resources, garnering new insights on financial information and intelligence and improving reporting on financial crimes and transnational organised crime activities. However, a tension exists between the international community's encouragement of greater public-private sector information and intelligence sharing on financial crime issues, and the extent to which international instruments (including the Financial Action Task Force (FATF) Standards) actually support that sharing. This tension has caused some commentators to doubt the effectiveness of anti-money laundering, counter-terrorism financing, and counter-proliferation financing (AML/CTF/CPF) frameworks in enabling public and private sector entities to identify, mitigate, and prevent their financial crime risks.

In its current form, the FATF Standards' focus is on providing financial intelligence units and law enforcement agencies with the information they need to identify, investigate, and prosecute financial crimes. This focus, however, effectively discounts the private sector's role need for information and intelligence from diverse sources to fruitfully contribute to AML/CTF/CPF efforts.

The increasing complexity of the evolving criminal environment warrants that the FATF reconsider its position and provide a clear, demonstrable basis for public-private sector information sharing. Moreover, the FATF must also consider granting the private sector a more active position in FATF activities. Implementing these reforms would not only recognise the importance of public-private sector collaboration in combatting financial crime, they would also offer the prospect of optimising the financial intelligence and information holdings of both the public and private sectors to the benefit of those sectors and the broader community.

P. Chadderton (✉)
Department of Foreign Affairs and Trade, Barton, ACT, Australia

D. Goldbarsht et al. (eds.), *The Financial War on Crime and Terrorism*, European Yearbook of International Economic Law,
https://doi.org/10.1007/978-3-032-06360-1_3

1 Introduction

Concerns at the international, regional and national levels about the increasing sophistication of financial crime, and other transnational organised crime activities, have led to increased interest in exploring innovative information sharing initiatives that optimise information and resources. The Financial Action Task Force (FATF), for example, has asserted that 'effective information sharing is one of the cornerstones of a well-functioning anti-money laundering/counter-terrorist financing (AML/CTF) framework.'[1] Within the FATF Standards, information and intelligence concepts play a key role.

Although frequently interchanged, data, information and intelligence refer to distinct concepts. *Data* consists of raw numbers, text, and simple observations that have not been analysed or interpreted to give meaning.[2] In the FATF Standards, data includes transaction amounts, account names and details, and SWIFT codes. *Information* compiles, manipulates, organises, and analyses data from multiple sources to provide meaning, context, and purpose that expands the recipient's knowledge of a subject or issue.[3] It is this *knowledge* that connects data and information to intelligence.[4] Notwithstanding the absence of agreement on what *intelligence* comprises,[5] scholars generally agree that intelligence is a process that transforms information into a form that informs and enhances decision-making or other activities (whether covert, defensive, or offensive). This process transforms 'otherwise innocuous information' into a tool that can give insights into the capabilities, intentions, strengths, and weaknesses of adversaries, competitors, and partners, and be used against them.[6] In the context of AML/CTF and counter-proliferation financing (CPF) efforts, public and private sector entities use intelligence to identify, investigate, and report criminal activities, as well as take preventative action to protect individuals, businesses, and the community from the harmful effects of criminal activities.

Against this backdrop, information sharing partnerships with diverse entities (government, private sector, and civil society organisations) have been recognised and accepted at national and international levels, as key to combatting evolving criminal threats.[7] Among these partnerships, public-private sector intelligence and information sharing initiatives are seen as a useful mechanism for harnessing extant skills and resources (including technology), garnering new insights, and improved

[1] FATF (2016–17), p. 6.

[2] Ratcliffe (2016), p. 71.

[3] Brown (2018), p. 2 and Standards Australia and Standards New Zealand (2012), p. 15.

[4] Ratcliffe (2016), p. 72 discussing Davenport and Prusak.

[5] Warner (2019), p. 4.

[6] Chadderton (2025) and Commonwealth of Australia (2020), vol 1, p. 156.

[7] Chadderton and Norton (2019). For a discussion on private-to-private information sharing, see Goldbarsht and Goodrick (2025) in this book.

reporting on financial crimes, including money laundering, terrorism financing, and proliferation financing (ML/TF/PF).

Notwithstanding the FATF's recognition of the importance of constructive relations between governments, the private sector, civil society, and other interested stakeholders in maintaining the integrity of the financial system,[8] the extent to which the FATF has supported public-private sector information and intelligence sharing is nascent, if not questionable. Barriers in the FATF framework constrain the extent to which the public and private sectors may share or exchange intelligence and information in practice.

As a result, a tension exists between the FATF and the international community's encouragement for public-private sector information sharing initiatives focussed on financial crimes and the extent to which they are actually supported by international instruments (including the FATF Standards), and consequently national laws.

This tension has caused some commentators to doubt the overall effectiveness of the FATF's AML/CTF/CPF framework in enabling public and private sector entities to identify, mitigate, and prevent their financial crime risks.[9] It has also resulted in questions on whether that framework remains appropriate to confronting the ML/TF/PF risks that public and private sector entities now face, particularly given the increasing sophistication of organised crime groups' typologies and activities.[10]

This chapter considers these issues by examining how public-private sector information sharing is supported under the FATF Standards. It also considers whether the current construction of those Standards is sufficient to support such sharing and offers recommendations on how it may be improved.

After introducing key components of the FATF and its AML/CTF/CPF framework (in Sect. 2), the FATF Standards are examined in terms of their treatment of information and intelligence sharing and collaboration between the public and private sectors from the perspectives of risk awareness, prevention and reporting, and extant information sharing mechanisms (Sect. 3). Notwithstanding the recognised benefits of expanded public-private sector information sharing in combating financial crime, it is not without its risks. Section 4 outlines the key barriers and risks of greater public-private sector information sharing and offers suggestions on how to mitigate those risks.

Section 5 contends that in their current form the FATF Standards' primary role is to provide financial intelligence units (FIUs) and law enforcement agencies with the information they need to identify, investigate and prosecute ML/TF/PF-related crimes. As such, the Standards discount the private sector's role in AML/CTF/CPF efforts and consequently its need for information and intelligence. However, in an increasingly complex criminal environment, the FATF must reconsider this position and therefore how the FATF Standards provide for public-private sector information sharing.

[8] Financial Action Task Force (FATF) (2019b), p. 8.

[9] Turkington (2019) ; Vlcek (2018).

[10] Financial Action Task Force (FATF) (2007), Pieth and Aiolfi (2003) and Aiolfi and Bauer (2012).

2 FATF and its Standards

2.1 Financial Action Task Force

In 1989, the G-7 instigated a task force as a pilot project to tackle the drug trade's use of the international financial system to launder the proceeds of the trade.[11] Since then, the FATF and its Standards (comprising the FATF 40 Recommendations, their Interpretative Notes and applicable definitions)[12] have arguably become an influential force in global AML/CTF/CPF efforts. Under its Mandate, the FATF seeks to:

> protect the financial system and the broader economy from the threats of money laundering and the financing of terrorism and proliferation, thereby strengthening financial sector integrity and contributing to safety and security.[13]

The FATF's AML/CTF framework seeks to create a globally consistent legal, regulatory, and operational approach aimed at maintaining the integrity of the financial system and preventing exploitable weaknesses in jurisdictions' AML/CTF/CPF regimes.[14]

Under its mandate, the FATF is responsible for: developing and publishing reports on ML/TF/PF risks, trends, typologies, and best practice; promoting and evaluating members' implementation and compliance with the FATF Standards; and overseeing FATF-Style Regional Bodies (FSRBs).[15] Beyond its members, the FATF's Mandate also extends to engaging and consulting with the private sector and civil society on the FATF's work to 'foster transparency and dialogue towards more effective implementation of the FATF Standards.'[16] With this in mind, the FATF's Ministers have emphasised the importance of 'effective sharing of information—domestically, across borders and with the private sector in a timely and secure manner' in their efforts to combat ML/TF/PF.[17]

At the date of writing, the FATF comprised 40 members (38 jurisdictions and two regional organisations), accounting for approximately 85% of global GDP and 59% of the global population.[18] In addition, 31 international and regional organisations are associate members or observers of the FATF.[19]

---

[11] G-7 Group of Nations (G-7) (1989), para 53; Turkington (2019) and Financial Action Task Force (FATF) (2014), p. 2.

[12] Through the *International Standards on combating money laundering and terrorism financing* (FATF Standards) and the FATF Recommendations.

[13] Financial Action Task Force (FATF) (2019a).

[14] FATF (2023b), p. 7.

[15] Ibid.

[16] Ibid., p. 5, para (i).

[17] Ibid., p. 2, para 13.

[18] The FATF suspended the Russian Federation's membership on 24 February 2023, Financial Action Task Force (FATF) (2024c); Financial Action Task Force (2024g); Financial Action Task Force (n.d.).

[19] Financial Action Task Force (FATF) (2022) p. 9.

Separately, over 190 jurisdictions are members of an FSRB.[20] FSRBs promote the FATF Standards and are critical to ensuring the AML/CTF/CPF regulatory consistency of their members. FSRB member jurisdictions commit to implement the FATF Standards. They also agree to a mutual evaluation, or peer review, of their AML/CTF/CPF regimes that assesses technical compliance and effectiveness.[21] In terms of private sector participation, no private sector organisations or industry associations are FATF or FSRB members in any capacity at the date of writing.

2.2 *FATF Standards*

The FATF Standards apply a multi-pronged approach to AML/CTF/CPF that is structured around six core objectives: (a) identify ML/TF/PF risks; (b) criminalise ML/TF/PF offences, and pursue offenders; (c) implement regulatory and supervisory measures by establishing FIUs; (d) empower competent authorities with investigative, enforcement, and supervisory powers and responsibilities; (e) obligate financial institutions and designated non-financial businesses and professionals (DNFBPs) to apply preventative measures (customer due diligence), and report specified or suspicious transactions (for example, international transfers, transactions exceeding a specified threshold or that satisfy other requirements); and (f) engage in international cooperation, including by exchanging information, or making and facilitating mutual legal assistance and extradition requests.

2.3 *Immediate Outcomes (IOs)*

Eleven Immediate Outcomes (IOs) complement the FATF Standards by measuring how effectively a jurisdiction implements its AML/CTF/CPF regime and achieves the intended results. Critically, the intersection between the FATF Recommendations technical compliance components and the IOs complicate information sharing requirements. This is evident in the IOs' differing characterisations of information sharing between public sector agencies and between the public and private sectors. Under the IOs, public sector agencies' information sharing is assessed as 'mandatory', whereas public-private sector information sharing is optional. Consequently, the IOs implicitly prioritise information sharing between public sector agencies, and thus reduce the primacy afforded to public-private sector information-sharing. As a result, the IOs' characterisation of public-private sector information sharing

[20] According to FATF, in 2022, 75% of FATF members are also members or observers of one or more FSRBs, these include Australia, China, Germany and Indonesia, Financial Action Task Force (FATF) (2022) and Financial Action Task Force (FATF) (2024c).

[21] Financial Action Task Force (FATF) (2023c), p. 8; Financial Action Task Force (FATF) (2024d); Financial Action Task Force (FATF) (2022), p. 9; Reimer (2024) and Nance (2018).

reduces jurisdictions' willingness to instigate cross-sector information sharing initiatives, notwithstanding their benefit in combatting financial crimes and organised crime activities.

2.4 Role of the FIU under the FATF Standards

Consistent with international agreements including the 1988 *United Nations Convention against Illicit Traffic in Narcotic Drugs and Psychotropic Substances* (Vienna Convention)[22] and the 2000 *United Nations Convention against Transnational Organized Crime* (Palermo Convention),[23] FATF Recommendation 29 requires jurisdictions to establish an FIU.

FIUs serve as national centres for the receipt and analysis of: (a) suspicious transaction reports, and other prescribed transaction reports derived from private sector entities; and (b) other information relevant to ML/TF and associated predicate offences.[24] Under Recommendation 29 FIUs should also be empowered to obtain 'additional information from reporting entities.'[25]

In its present form, an FIU's role is that of an information and intelligence repository for the sole use of public sector agencies and international counterparts, including international and regional organisations such as Interpol, Europol and the Egmont Group of FIUs.[26] Recommendation 29, however, is silent on its support for FIUs' dissemination of financial information and intelligence to private sector entities or industry associations, such as the Wolfsberg Group.[27] This is notwithstanding the value of that information to private sector efforts in identifying, reporting, and

[22] United Nations (1988).

[23] United Nations (2000).

[24] Financial Action Task Force (FATF) (2024d).

[25] Financial Action Task Force (FATF) (2024d), p. 24.

[26] Financial Action Task Force (FATF) (2024d), p. 24. The Egmont Group of FIUs is an international organisation comprising 177 members (at the date of writing). It actively supports FIU-FIU cooperation and hosts a secure platform (known as the Egmont Secure Web) through which FIUs can securely exchange financial information and intelligence. FIU members agree to: exchange information in accordance with the Egmont Group's Principles; disseminate information spontaneously and on request to other FIUs; and maintain the confidentiality of information exchanged, Egmont Group (n.d.) and Egmont Group (2013).

[27] At the date of writing, the Wolfsberg Group is an association of 12 major, global financial institutions from the private banking sector. Established in 2000 in response to concerns about the integrity of the financial services industry, it promotes frameworks and guidance on combatting financial crime risks in private banking. To address concerns about the misuse of the banking system for money laundering purposes, the Wolfsberg Group issued the *Wolfsberg Anti-Money Laundering Principles* in 2000. These Principles provided a common framework on customer due diligence and Know Your Customer (or KYC) rules. Wolfsberg Group members comprise a significant portion of the global market the significance of this agreement cannot be underestimated. However, the Group's influence in shaping AML/CTF policies is most evident in its success in persuading FATF to apply a risk-based approach, instead of a rule-based approach, in the FATF

preventing financial crime-related activities, or the sector's 'gatekeeper' responsibilities.

As this Chapter demonstrates, the current construction of the FATF Standards is based on the premise that the private sector's role is to provide FIUs and law enforcement agencies with the data, information, and intelligence they need to identify, investigate and prosecute investigate ML/TF/PF activities and crimes. In contrast, the FATF Standards do not countenance that the private sector also requires information to identify and prevent ML/TF/PF risks.[28] The FATF Standards' simplicity is therefore at odds with the increasingly complex world of financial crime[29]

Moreover, while the FATF Standards *proscribe* unidirectional information sharing between the private sector and their FIU, they *support*, if not encourage, two-way information sharing between FIUs and their counterparts for AML/CTF/CPF purposes. As a result, the FATF Recommendations provide limited opportunities for the private sector to receive information from law enforcement agencies and FIUs or exchange information with them. In restricting information sharing, the FATF Standards arguably hinder public and private sector efforts to combat financial crime and minimise its risks.

2.5 Information and Intelligence Sharing and the FATF Standards

The present construction of the FATF Standards is therefore surprising, if not contradictory, to the FATF's position that the private sector has 'a shared responsibility' in identifying and preventing ML/TF/PF-related crimes, and maintaining the financial system's integrity. As the FATF-recognised first line of defence in preventing financial crimes and criminals' misuse of the financial system,[30] limited endorsement of public-private sector interactions in the FATF Standards impedes public and private sector efforts to identify financial crime-related activities.

The consequence of this situation is that financial services entities—whether banks, insurance institutions, remittance providers, or DNFBPs—are impeded in performing their 'gatekeeper' responsibilities and in identifying and reporting suspicious transactions and activities. Moreover, without access to a broad range of intelligence and information on emerging financial crime trends and typologies (from public, private and open sources), financial services entities are arguably inhibited in preventing criminals using financial services and products for nefarious

Recommendations, The Wolfsberg Group (n.d.), Pieth (2007), Aiolfi and Bauer (2012) and Imobersteg Harvey (2019), p. 50–1.

[28] Financial Action Task Force (FATF) (2022), p. 5–6.

[29] Turkington (2019), 'The Effectiveness of Private Sector Engagement in International Financial Crime Countermeasures', p. 68, footnote 56, discussing Johnson (2003), p. 127, 130.

[30] Financial Action Task Force (FATF) (2024b).

purposes. As Pontes et al. (2022) reflect, referencing Kang (2018): 'regulators require FIs [financial institutions] to share information in their possession, leaving FIs [financial institutions] to search for suspicious activity "in the dark".'[31]

In response to calls from the private sector for greater feedback from FIUs and AML/CTF/CPF regulators for information, FATF issued its *Consolidated FATF Standards on Information Sharing* (Consolidated Standards), in 2016.[32] Although a useful compilation, the Consolidated Standards offered few suggestions for practically implementing public-private sector information sharing measures. The following year (2017), the FATF issued its *Guidance on Private Sector Information Sharing* but sidestepped the issue of public-private sector information sharing and instead concentrated on information sharing between private sector entities.[33]

As transnational organised crime groups increasingly exploit the cyber-enabled environment to threaten the security of nations, communities and individuals, the FATF Standards' restrictions on information sharing between the public and private sectors significantly hinder mitigation and prevention efforts and need urgent review.

Having introduced the key components of the FATF and its AML/CTF/CPF framework, and their relevance to information sharing, Sect. 3 turns to examine how the FATF Standards treat information and intelligence sharing and collaboration between the public and private sectors.

3 The FATF Standards and Public-Private Sector Information and Intelligence Sharing

In their present form, the FATF Standards are designed to serve four information objectives, being to:

(a) support FIUs in their role as national centres for the receipt and analysis of financial information and intelligence;
(b) provide FIUs, law enforcement and intelligence agencies with information and intelligence to advance investigations and prosecutions;
(c) provide a mechanism for financial services entities to report specified and suspicious transactions and activities; and
(d) enable financial services entities to identify, mitigate and manage the AML/CTF/CPF vulnerabilities of their services and products.

As a result, the FATF Standards prioritise mechanisms that support cooperation and information exchanges between public sector agencies and their counterparts, not

[31] Pontes et al. (2022), p. 404 referring to Kang (2018).

[32] Financial Action Task Force (FATF) (2016–17).

[33] FATF's guidance did, however, acknowledge that information-sharing was relevant to 25 of the 40 FATF Recommendations, and impacted seven of the 11 immediate outcomes used to assess the effectiveness of AML/CTF regimes, Financial Action Task Force (FATF) (2016–17) and Maxwell and Artingsall (2017), p. 9.

between the public and private sectors.[34] Consequently, public-private sector information sharing is not an objective of the FATF Standards, and forms only a minor consideration in the Standards.

This section considers how the FATF Standards provide for public-private sector information sharing and the barriers to that sharing from the perspectives of: (a) enhancing risk awareness; (b) the restrictions surrounding suspicious activity reports (SARs) in the FATF Standards; (c) the construction of mechanisms in the FATF Standards for public-private sector information sharing, including outreach activities; and (d) FATF's involvement of the private sector in its activities.

3.1 Enhancing Risk Awareness

Enhancing understanding of ML/TF/PF-related risks is at the core of the FATF Standards. By understanding ML/TF/PF risks, public and private sector entities can be positioned to take an informed approach to mitigating, managing and preventing them. For this reason, successfully implementing FATF Recommendation 1 (and its relevant IOs) has consequential implications for the remaining Recommendations found in the FATF Standards. However, as presently drafted, this risk-focussed Recommendation provides only limited support for public-private sector information and intelligence sharing, notwithstanding its importance to enabling both sectors to augment their knowledge of ML/TF/PF risks and vulnerabilities.

As currently framed, FATF Recommendation 1 (together with Recommendation 2) explicitly provides for information sharing and cooperation between public sector agencies, but it is silent on public-private sector information sharing. This absence of explicit endorsement for public-private sector collaboration is compounded by the assessment criteria found in IO1. Under IO1, effectiveness is assessed in terms of collaboration and information sharing between competent authorities and government agencies. Collaboration and information sharing with private sector entities[35] is only considered in terms of whether they *contribute* to the development of risk assessments, and only as an ancillary, not definitive, assessment element.[36] The FATF's position, as articulated in IO1, therefore reinforces the notion that AML/CTF/CPF risk assessments are matters for public sector agencies, with limited involvement of the private sector—irrespective of the harm ML/TF/PF risks pose to both sectors. The FATF's stance also appears inconsistent with its guidance on managing ML/TF/PF risks.

[34] Financial Action Task Force (FATF) (2016–17), p. 11–12 discussing Interpretative Note to FATF Recommendation 25.

[35] Such as financial institutions and designated non-financial businesses and professions (DNFBPs). Under FATF Recommendation 22, DNFBPs include: casinos, real estate agents; dealers in precious metals and stones; lawyers, notaries, other independent legal professions and accountants; and trust and company service providers.

[36] Financial Action Task Force (FATF) (2024e), p. 121, para 6.

3.2 FATF Guidance

In its 2024 guidance on ML/TF/PF risks, the FATF acknowledged that impediments to public-private sector information sharing were a challenge in managing those risks.[37] The FATF specifically encouraged public sector agencies to engage with non-governmental entities, and in particular the private sector, at all stages of the risk assessment development process: from data collection and analysis to outreach fora.[38] In the FATF's view, by sharing 'frontline' experiences, the private sector could offer invaluable insights that inform data and challenge assumptions. Consequently, public-private sector information sharing could enable the development of a 'more comprehensive and nuanced understanding of the risk landscape.'[39] Public-private partnerships were also highlighted in the FATF's guidance as a useful vehicle for overcoming information silos and promoting a shared understanding of ML/TF/PF risks and vulnerabilities.[40]

While the FATF's encouragement of public-private sector information sharing and collaboration is welcomed, FATF Recommendation 1 and IO1 arguably overlook or discount the concept of sharing information with the private sector for AML/CTF risk assessment purposes. Consequently, until FATF Recommendation 1 and IO1 specifically provide for this, and include it as an assessable criterion, information sharing impediments will remain.

Given the importance of risk assessments to the FATF Standards, and to public and private sector entities' operations in mitigating, managing and preventing ML/TF/PF risks and vulnerabilities, this situation could have significant consequences.

To address this situation, two recommendations are offered. Firstly, FATF Recommendation 1 and IO1 must be amended to support greater information sharing between the public, private and non-governmental sectors, and to include such collaboration as a measurable assessment criterion. Retaining the current incongruity between FATF Recommendation 1 and IO1 has the potentially to inhibit the accurate identification and mitigation of ML/TF risks and impede the private sector in fulfilling its 'shared responsibility'[41] under the FATF Standards of identifying and preventing ML/TF/PF risks.

Secondly, greater alignment is also needed between the FATF Standards and its guidance on risk assessment issues, together with specific endorsement for information and intelligence sharing between the public and private sectors. Without such endorsement, such sharing will be attributed a lower priority by both sectors.

By articulating clearly defined parameters on public-private sector information sharing in the FATF Standards and FATF's guidance materials, the FATF will provide a demonstrable basis for information sharing between those sectors that

---

[37] Financial Action Task Force (FATF) (2024a).

[38] Financial Action Task Force (FATF) (2024a).

[39] Financial Action Task Force (FATF) (2024a), p. 27.

[40] Financial Action Task Force (FATF) (2024a), p. 27.

[41] Financial Action Task Force (FATF) (2022), p. 5–6.

supports the development of a shared view of ML/TF/PF risks and vulnerabilities. In an increasingly complex world, adopting these recommendations would significantly demonstrate FATF's support for enhanced public-private sector information sharing. Without such endorsement, the value of existing public-private sector collaboration may be reduced.

3.3 Preventing ML/TF/PF Activities and Tipping Off

FATF Recommendations 9-23 (together with IOs 3, 4 and 10) impose a range of reporting and regulatory obligations on financial service entities, which States must supervise and enforce. These preventative measures aim to reduce, if not counteract, the private sector's vulnerability to misuse for ML/TF/PF activities. That said, these measures are also unidirectional. While financial services entities must submit reports about suspicious and specified transaction, and other customer information, to FIUs, law enforcement agencies and other government agencies, financial services entities are largely restricted limited, and if not prohibited, from sharing with each other information.

For financial services entities, it is the prohibitions surrounding suspicious action reports (SARs, also known as suspicious transaction reports (STRs) or suspicious matter reports (SMRs)) that have had a chilling effect on information sharing. Section 3.4 considers these issues and their impact on public-private sector information sharing and offers suggestions for improving the FATF Standards and their treatment of SARs that enhance financial service entities' efforts to prevent financial crime.

3.4 Tipping Off

Under FATF Recommendation 20, financial services entities must report transactions suspected to be linked to ML/TF/PF activities and other nefarious activities to their FIU. For FIUs and law enforcement agencies, SARs are a key tool that provide actionable intelligence on those involved in the broader criminal enterprises that facilitate money laundering and other financial crimes.[42] SARs are also a highly valued information source for public-private sector information sharing initiatives targeting financial crimes. However, the value of SAR-derived information, and its potential to empower the financial services sector to take preventative action against financial crime is reduced by FATF Recommendation 21. Under that Recommendation, financial services entities are largely prohibited from disclosing

[42] Morgan (2024) and Menz (2024).

('tipping off') that they have submitted a SAR to avoid inadvertently alerting the customer.[43]

Tipping off was originally introduced to prevent potential suspects being made aware (or 'tipped off') that they were under suspicion, thus compromising an actual or ongoing investigation.[44] However, the unintended consequences of the 'tipping off' prohibition have been threefold. Firstly, financial services entities have been discouraged from sharing *any* information with other financial services entities on ML/TF/PF-related issues.[45] This overlooks the financial crime prevention benefits that could result from private sector entities sharing information about suspicious accounts of customers, and from supporting financial institutions in their role as gatekeepers against financial crime. Secondly, financial services entities have been discouraged from having *any* further contact with the customer to confirm the character of their transactions, resulting in over-reporting and impacting the quality of SARs.[46] Thirdly, the 'tipping off' prohibition has not prevented criminals from moving their business between banks, knowing that financial services entities cannot warn each other.

That the prohibition is considered a source of tension between the public and private sectors is also noteworthy. Although valued by law enforcement agencies, the financial services sector considers the prohibitions and limitations on disclosing SARs combined with the cost associated with AML/CTF compliance to be burdens with limited benefit. This situation is only compounded by the private sector's limited involvement in the original negotiations that introduced the tipping off provision.[47]

Although some countries, including the US, have introduced legislation enabling multiple private sector entities to author and report SARs, and to discuss customers' suspicious activities, a specific inclusion in the FATF Standards permitting greater information sharing of SAR-related information in specified circumstances could reduce duplicate efforts, thereby optimising resources and enhancing collaboration between public and private sector entities.[48]

---

[43] Financial Action Task Force (FATF) (2016–17) discussing Interpretative Note to FATF Recommendation 20.

[44] Financial Action Task Force (FATF) (2013), p. 59, Ball et al. (2020), and Menz (2024).

[45] Chadderton and Norton (2019).

[46] Menz (2024).

[47] Turkington (2019).

[48] Lormel (2012), Maxwell (2022) and US Treasury and Financial Crimes Enforcement Network (2020).

4 Mechanisms in the FATF Standards that Support Public Sector Information-Sharing with Financial Service Entities

4.1 Unidirectional Sharing of Information

As discussed earlier in this chapter, the FATF Standards provide limited support for two-way information sharing between the public and private sectors. Instead, as currently framed, the Standards reinforce a unidirectional approach to information sharing. This occurs in two ways. First, from private sector entities to FIUs (and law enforcement agencies) in compliance with their transaction reporting and SAR obligations. Second, from FIUs (and law enforcement agencies) to private sector entities to assist the latter to comply with their AML/CTF/CPF obligations. As a result, the opportunity for the sectors to share or exchange information is not specifically endorsed in the FATF Standards. This situation arguably promotes (or reinforces) unidirectional, rather than two-way, information-sharing or exchange.

For example, FATF Recommendation 19 requires countries to advise financial institutions of concerns about the weaknesses in other countries' AML/CTF regimes.[49] Such advice aims to support financial institutions and other financial services providers in applying enhanced due diligence measures appropriate to the risks associated with dealing with high-risk jurisdictions. Similarly, FATF Recommendation 34 requires public sector agencies to establish guidelines and provide feedback that will assist financial institutions to detect and report suspicious transactions, and thus combat ML/TF/PF activities.

The unidirectional approach employed by FATF Recommendations 19 and 34 concentrates on public sector agencies providing advice to private sector entities. As such, the Recommendations do not accommodate the possibility of a two-way dialogue between public and private sector entities on ML/TF/PF trends and typologies. Therefore, beyond the mechanisms available to report SARs, the FATF Recommendations do not provide a basis for the private sector to inform public sector agencies on how private sector entities manage and mitigate ML/TF/PF-related risks, or to obtain private sector views on emerging financial crime trends.

The current framing of the FATF Standards overlooks the opportunity for FIUs and law enforcement agencies to learn from the experiences of financial services entities in combatting ML/TF/PF and other financial crimes. The Standards' current construction also discounts the potential for knowledge transfer between financial services entities and FIUs about the strategies that entities have used to mitigate and manage their financial crime risks and vulnerabilities. As a result, the FATF Standards do not optimise public or private sector entities' knowledge about financial crime activities, typologies, and trends. Consequently, public and private sector entities' information and intelligence holdings and other resources, are treated sub-optimally. In an environment where resources, whether information, human or

[49] Financial Action Task Force (FATF) (2016–17), p. 19.

capital, are limited, it is critical that the FATF Standards provide the basis for the public and private sectors to maximise the value and benefits of expanded information and intelligence sharing.

Against this backdrop, greater endorsement in the FATF Standards for information sharing practices between the public and private sectors would achieve four outcomes. First, it would encourage the public and private sectors to share and exchange information from the trove of information and intelligence available to those sectors. Second, endorsement in the FATF Standards and inclusion as an assessable criteria in the IOs would also support the development of information and intelligence sharing initiatives targeting ML/TF/PF and other financial crime activities. Third, clear support would also encourage knowledge transfer between those sectors, and provide a basis for each sector to learn from the other's experiences in combating financial crime. Fourth, it could assist to overcome historical concerns about potential misuse or use for competitive advantage of information shared by law enforcement and government agencies with the private sector.

4.2 Outreach Activities

The FATF Standards also provide few mechanisms to support outreach activities and other information sharing initiatives between the public and non-governmental sectors, whether private sector entities or not-for-profit organisations (NPOs). In this respect, it is only the interpretative note to FATF Recommendation 8 (on NPOs) that explicitly provides for information sharing through outreach activities between public sector agencies and NPOs.[50] According to the FATF, information sharing in these circumstances is critical to addressing NPOs' TF vulnerabilities. As the FATF explains:

> Information sharing is a key element of prevention and detection of TF abuse of NPOs. Fostering an environment of trust in which information on particular NPOs of concern for TF or related issues can easily be made available to oversight bodies or government authorities from the public and from the NPO sector itself is key.[51]

While the FATF's support for outreach activities concerning NPOs is welcomed, it is unclear why the FATF Standards do not similarly provide for outreach activities and other information sharing initiatives in respect of other financial services entities, including DNFBPs.

This lacuna in the FATF Standards overlooks an invaluable opportunity to disseminate and exchange information and intelligence on financial crime risks, trends,

[50] It is also noted that the FATF's Methodology also assesses compliance with FATF Recommendation 8, including outreach activities, as part of its technical compliance and effectiveness evaluations, Financial Action Task Force (FATF) (2024e).

[51] For example, non-profit organisations (NPOs) or DNFBPs, Financial Action Task Force (FATF) (2023a), p. 25 para 71.

and typologies. It also overlooks another method for FIUs to encourage greater compliance with AML/CTF/CPF obligations, including reporting on suspicious activities. The absence of overt support for outreach activities and fora involving FIUs, other public sector agencies and private sector entities also appears at odds with expanded interest, internationally, in public-private sector information sharing (discussed earlier in this chapter).

To address this issue, the FATF should review its Standards and other guidance material to demonstrate its support for outreach activities, whether with NPOs, financial services entities, or DNFBPs. Clarity on these issues would also confirm FATF's support for cross-sector information sharing initiatives.

4.3 Involvement of the Private Sector in FATF Activities

> Without the private sector, the FATF mandate to tackle money laundering and the financing of terrorism and proliferation could not be achieved. The private sector is at the forefront of the fight against financial crimes. In this fight, public authorities and private sector play on the same team.[52]

The lacuna in the FATF Standards concerning outreach activities with the private sector is consistent with the FATF's approach to private sector participation in general, notwithstanding the FATF's statements on that sector's importance to AML/CTF/CPF efforts. However, contemporary international precedent does exist that would support expanded involvement of the private sector in FATF activities and endorsement of public-private sector information sharing initiatives.

Although the FATF has increasingly consulted the private sector on updates to the FATF Standards[53] and has acknowledged the importance of deepening public private sector collaboration, it remains hesitant to involving the private sector in all FATF activities. This situation arguably reflects historical mistrust between the public and private sectors concerning the perceived trustworthiness of the latter.[54]

While the FATF has hosted annual consultative fora with the private sector since 2010,[55] private sector representatives continue to be excluded from the FATF's plenary meetings (even as observers).[56] In contrast, the FATF has recently invited NPOs

---

[52] Financial Action Task Force (2025b).

[53] See for example, Financial Action Task Force (FATF) (2025a).

[54] Chadderton and Norton (2019), p. 26 and 38–39, and de Oliveira et al. (2016), p. 5.

[55] For examples of early private sector consultative fora, see: Financial Action Task Force (FATF) (2015) and Financial Action Task Force (FATF) (2016). After a pause in 2020–2022 due to the COVID-19 pandemic, FATF has held Private Sector Consultative fora annually, for example: Financial Action Task Force (FATF) (2023c), Financial Action Task Force (FATF) (2024f) and Financial Action Task Force (FATF) (2025b). FATF has also held for a with FinTech and RegTech providers to discuss financial innovation techniques including the use of data mining, artificial intelligence and machine learning, Ferreira (2025), p. 117.

[56] Jakobi (2018), p. 183–4.

to its meetings as observers. As a result, other than the FATF's annual private sector fora, there is little demonstrable evidence of reforms to support FATF's claim that it actively supports public-private sector information sharing.

While greater involvement of the private sector in the FATF's activities and other FATF-hosted information sharing initiatives could support the sector in fulfilling its 'gatekeeper' role, any expanded involvement is not without its risks and will require careful balancing. However, given the complexities of the evolving criminal environment, the FATF must consider this issue sooner rather than later. With this in mind, it is contended that the FATF consider granting select private sector entities and representative associations a more active position in its activities, in acknowledgement of the sector's critical role in combatting financial crime.

By adopting this position in its activities and Standards, the FATF would also ensure that it aligns with other contemporary international agreements. These include the 2003 *United Nations Convention against Corruption* (2003 UN Convention against Corruption)[57] and the 2024 *United Nations Convention against Cybercrime* (2024 UN Convention against Cybercrime)[58] which include provisions supporting measures promoting cooperation between law enforcement agencies and the private sector.[59] Article 39 of the 2003 UN Convention against Corruption, for example, specifically encourages cooperation between investigatory and prosecuting agencies and private sector entities, in particular financial institutions, in investigating and prosecuting offences related to corruption.

Building on this, the 2024 UN Convention against Cybercrime includes a specific provision on exchange of information (Article 55). Under that provision, State Parties must 'consider' consulting experts from public and private sectors (together with NGOs, civil society and academia) on cybercrime trends as part of efforts to prevent and combat such crimes.[60] In this respect, the Convention arguably adopts a holistic approach to collaboration on preventing and combatting cybercrime involving the public and private sectors, together with NGOs, civil society, and academia.[61]

Against this backdrop, a strategy that combines expanded involvement of the private sector (together with civil society and NGOs) in the FATF's activities and endorsement in the FATF Standards for public-private sector information sharing would provide a cogent basis for enhancing knowledge of financial crime trends and typologies. Such a strategy also offers the potential to deepen public and private sector cooperation in combatting financial crime. That said, an increase in information sharing will be accompanied by an increased risk that information will not be appropriately protected. Consequently, strategies that manage and mitigate key risks are therefore critical to protecting the information holdings of public and private sector entities.

---

[57] United Nations (2003).

[58] United Nations (2024).

[59] See for example, United Nations (2003), Article 12, and United Nations (2024), Article 53.

[60] United Nations (2024), Articles 55(3)–(4) and (6).

[61] United Nations (2024), Article 54(6).

5 Information-Sharing Barriers and Risks, and Strategies to Mitigate Them

Notwithstanding the recognised benefits of public-private sector information sharing in optimising data, 'connecting the dots' and overcoming silos,[62] risks do arise in greater information-sharing. While legal barriers—including those found in the FATF Standards discussed throughout this Chapter—can inhibit information sharing, other operational (technological), political and cultural barriers can impede and potentially exacerbate risks. This section explores key information sharing risks that impact public-private sector information sharing and offers suggestions on how to mitigate them.

5.1 Sensitive and Confidential Information

Protecting sensitive and confidential information in public-private sector information sharing initiatives is critical to maintaining trust in public and private institutions. The impact of a privacy breach or information leakage cannot be underestimated, and risks reducing trust in institutions and could threaten the integrity of the information.[63] Further, such risks have the potential to reveal the investigation methods used by law enforcement agencies.[64] Although these risks exist irrespective of public-private sector information sharing initiatives and could arise through unauthorised access to information by a 'trusted insider' or 'external hacker', information sharing initiatives have the potential to exacerbate such risks.

To mitigate against these risks, protocols governing how partners in public-private sector information sharing initiatives store, handle, manage, and protect the information must be established. In this respect, protocols are critical to preventing and identifying instances of unauthorised access or misuse of data and information. Moreover, by articulating how partners will respond in the event of an information leakage or breach it is suggested that information protocols will also have a deterrence value.

[62] Brown (2018), p. 3, National Commission on Terrorist Attacks upon the United States (2004), Schmidt (2024), p. 81, Chadderton and Norton (2019), Maxwell and Artingsall (2017).

[63] Schmidt (2024), p. 81.

[64] Ibid, p. 13.

5.2 Technological and Operational Barriers

From a technological perspective, differing data or information standards and formats have the potential to be an information sharing barrier and a risk. If information is difficult to share or requires manual processes to access, upload, or analyse, it is less likely that such information will be shared (by originators) or used (by recipients). As a result, the value of that information in identifying potential trends and typologies will not be realised. Moreover, it could lead to the development of multiple, incomplete and inaccurate sources of information rather than 'a single source of truth'.[65] To avoid this situation developing, common interoperability (technical) standards governing how information is shared and in what format are important to enabling public-private information sharing initiatives to optimise their information or data holdings to their fullest extent.

Similarly, complex information sharing practices may result in information sharing being considered a burden, and reduce the willingness to share information with others, whether within the same organisation or sector, or with another organisation or sector.[66] These operational barriers risk reinforcing information silos,[67] inhibiting how and the extent to which information is used, and causing it to be used sub-optimally. Moreover, a lack of awareness of the information available on a particular issue or person of interest, or training on how to access or use that information optimally,[68] may similarly impact on how and the extent that information is used.

In the context of financial crime investigations, reduced information sharing between the public and private sectors may result in financial crimes or typologies being identified with less expediency resulting in greater harms ensuing to individuals, businesses and society more broadly.

5.3 Political Barriers

From a political perspective, support and encouragement for information sharing practices at all levels, or a willingness to accommodate them are key to sustaining information sharing.[69] Moreover, a willingness of senior leadership to make the changes needed to facilitate information sharing is arguably essential to maintaining the longevity of such practices. Without such support, information-sharing initiatives whether between or within the public and private sectors may falter or their objectives remain unrealised.[70] That said, Chadderton and Norton's 2019 study also

---

65 Brown (2018), p. 6.

66 Chadderton and Norton (2019), OECD (2017), p. 29.

67 Ibid.

68 Ibid.

69 Ibid, Chadderton and Norton (2019).

70 Chadderton and Norton (2019), p. 14.

notes that support from middle-level managers is also critical to successfully implementing information sharing practices. To engender support at all levels, developing practices in which information sharing is simplified or considered part of 'business as usual' are important as is recognition of the benefits of information sharing to all parties involved.[71]

5.4 Cultural Barriers

Beyond legal, political, and operational barriers, cultural barriers also have the potential to inhibit information sharing and pose risks. In his 2018 study, Brown (2018) identified eight cultural issues that could inhibit information sharing. These included inter-agency competition, distrust, mutuality (reciprocity), secrecy and competence (or fear of embarrassment), ego (desire to control or withhold information), and an ethos based on 'need to know' rather than 'need to share'.[72]

As risks, these cultural barriers—if allowed to flourish—could significantly impact how information is used and the extent to which it is optimised in efforts to identify, mitigate and prevent financial crimes. In the context of information sharing between the public and private sectors, the effect of such barriers includes reduced information flows that limit opportunities to synthesise information. Moreover, cultural impediments could allow information silos to fester within and between organisations that thwart opportunities for organisations to identify criminal networks or 'connect the dots' to detect emerging trends in financial crime typologies. To mitigate against the emergence of such cultural barriers, public-private sector information sharing initiatives (whether public-private partnerships, forums, or information exchanges) offer opportunities to overcome barriers by deepening understanding and awareness of information holdings (relevant to law enforcement agencies investigations) and emerging financial trends and typologies (relevant to both sectors).

When viewed cumulatively, the barriers discussed above have the potential to become risks that impede both the public and private sector's efforts to combat financial crime.

For private sector entities, these information barriers can inhibit entities in accurately identifying and therefore reporting and preventing suspicious activities. However, when viewed alongside legislative restrictions such as tipping off (discussed earlier in this Chapter) such barriers also have the potential to result in misidentification of financial activities.[73] That is, without the opportunity to share information, activities considered genuine could be mischaracterised as nefarious, and reported as suspicious transactions; conversely, transactions considered nefari-

[71] Chadderton and Norton (2019).

[72] Brown (2018), p. 5. See also Chadderton (2025), p. 399–400 discussing Schneider and Hurst (2008) who also listed as information-sharing barriers issues including resources, jurisdictional (national sovereignty), trust, and differing mandates, p. 373.

[73] Chadderton (2025), p. 400.

ous could be categorised as genuine, and not reported. For public sector agencies, information barriers can result in 'information uncertainty, inaccuracy and a duplication of analytical and operational efforts.'[74] Transactions (mis)identified and reported as suspicious (by financial services entities) could divert public and private sector resources away from pursuing other evidence or investigation channels. In turn, reducing the resources available to public and private sector entities to take action to prevent financial crime harms and protect communities. It is at this juncture where the current framing of the FATF Standards needs to be reconsidered.

6 Conclusion

This chapter has demonstrated that the FATF Standards are currently framed to support FIUs and law enforcement agencies' engagement with other public sector agencies but are silent on the sharing of information between public and private sector entities. Without a clear, specific basis empowering the sharing of financial information and intelligence, the Standards have largely overlooked financial services entities' need for information to identify, report, and prevent financial crimes. While the FATF contends it values public-private sector information sharing and collaboration, the value its Standards—and therefore governments—place on that sharing is arguably questionable.

To address this situation, amending and aligning the FATF Standards, IOs and FATF's guidance materials to provide a clear, demonstrable basis for public-private sector information and intelligence sharing is recommended. By articulating clearly defined parameters on such sharing, the FATF will provide strong endorsement for information sharing initiatives and support the development of a shared view of ML/TF/PF risks and vulnerabilities. Without such endorsement, public-private sector information sharing will be attributed a lower priority by both public and private sector entities, irrespective of its benefits.

This chapter also examined the unintended consequences of the tipping off prohibition on SARs in FATF Recommendation 21. While designed to prevent the inadvertent alerting of customers suspected of involvement in financial crime, the tipping off prohibition has unintentionally discouraged all information sharing between financial services entities, irrespective of its potential to prevent further criminal activities. To address this anomaly, the FATF should consider amending Recommendation 21 to allow SAR-related information to be shared in a broader range of circumstances, subject to appropriate safeguards. Such amendments would enable private sector entities to take an informed approach to preventing financial crime that could assist the sector, FIUs and law enforcement agencies, and the broader community.

[74] Ibid, p. 402–3 discussing Parliamentary Joint Committee on Law Enforcement (2013), p. 38–9 para [4.31]–[4.37] and Rickards (2016), p. 96.

It was also demonstrated that the construction of the FATF Standards largely favours (or reinforces) unidirectional, rather than two-way, information sharing. As a result, the FATF Standards do not specifically provide for the sectors to share or exchange information, although the FATF has indicated its support for this. This posture overlooks the opportunity for FIUs and law enforcement agencies to learn from financial services entities' experiences in combatting financial crime and thereby optimise existing information and intelligence holdings.

To address this, it is recommended that the FATF Standards provide a definitive basis for the public and private sectors to maximise the benefits of expanded information and intelligence sharing on financial crime issues. Greater endorsement in the FATF Standards for information sharing practices between the public and private sectors would achieve three outcomes. First, it would encourage the public and private sectors to share and exchange information from the trove of information and intelligence available to those sectors. Second, endorsement in the FATF Standards and inclusion as an assessable criterion in the IOs would support the development of information and intelligence sharing initiatives within and between the public and private sectors targeting ML/TF/PF and other financial crime activities. Third, it would encourage expanded knowledge transfer on financial crime issues between the public and private sectors.

The FATF Standards provide few mechanisms to support outreach activities and other information sharing initiatives between the public and non-governmental sectors, whether private sector entities or NPOs. To that end, while FATF Recommendation 8 specifically provides for outreach activities with NPOs, the FATF Standards do not contain a similar provision for outreach activities with financial services entities or DNFBPs. Given the importance of outreach fora for promoting AML/CTF/CPF compliance efforts, and in informing private sector entities of emerging trends and typologies in financial crime, amending the FATF Standards and guidance to provide specifically for outreach activities in respect of financial services entities and DNFBPs is recommended.

Although the FATF has increasingly involved the private sector in FATF activities, including seeking the sector's views on proposed reforms, there is little demonstrable evidence of reforms to support FATF's claim that it supports actively public-private sector information sharing or engagement. In contrast, the 2003 UN Convention against Corruption and, recently adopted, 2024 UN Convention against Cybercrime both contain provisions supporting private sector cooperation and engagement.

To ensure that the FATF's approach aligns with other international Conventions in which the private sector is a key stakeholder, it should consider granting select private sector entities or industry associations a more active position in its activities. In addition to aligning with other international agreements, adopting this approach would acknowledge the private sector's critical role and lay the foundations for improved public-private sector collaboration and cooperation in efforts to combat financial crime.

Notwithstanding the potential benefits of greater public-private sector information sharing, information barriers and risks need to appropriately manage and safeguarded sensitive and confidential information and thereby ensure confidence in public and private institutions maintained.

In an era typified by rapidly evolving criminal interests, optimising public and private sector information and intelligence holdings, knowledge and resources are, now more than ever, critical to efforts to combat financial crime.

References

Aiolfi G, Bauer H-P (2012) The Wolfsberg Group. In: Pieth M (ed) Collective action: innovative strategies to prevent corruption. Basel Institute on Governance. https://baselgovernance.org/sites/default/files/2019-02/the-wolfsberg-group.pdf

Ball K, Canhoto A, Daniel E, Dibb S, Meadows M, Spiller K (2020) Organizational tensions arising from mandatory data exchange between the private and public sector: the case of financial services. Technol Forecast Soc Change 155. https://doi.org/10.1016/j.techfore.2020.119996

Brown R (2018) Understanding law enforcement information sharing for criminal intelligence purposes. Trends and Issues in crime and criminal justice, 566 (December 2018). Australian Institute of Criminology, Canberra

Chadderton P (2025) Take a look at what I just found! Anti-money laundering and public and private sector information and intelligence sharing in Australia. PhD thesis, La Trobe University, Victoria, Australia

Chadderton P, Norton S (2019) Public-private partnerships to disrupt financial crime: an exploratory study of Australia's Fintel Alliance, SIWP 2017–0003. SWIFT Institute, London

Commonwealth of Australia (2020) Comprehensive review of the legal framework of the National Intelligence Community by Mr Dennis Richardson AC. Commonwealth of Australia, Canberra

Egmont Group (2013) Principles for information exchange between financial intelligence units (Updated 15 April 2023). https://egmontgroup.org/wp-content/uploads/2022/07/2.-Principles-Information-Exchange-With-Glossary_April2023.pdf. Accessed 24 May 2025

Egmont Group (n.d.) About the Egmont Group. https://egmontgroup.org/about/. Accessed 10 Mar 2025

Ferreira I (2025) The legal status of the financial action task force in the international legal system. Brill/Nijhoff, Leiden

Financial Action Task Force (FATF) (2007) Guidance on the risk-based approach to combating money laundering and terrorist financing - high level principles and procedures. Financial Action Task Force (FATF), Paris

Financial Action Task Force (FATF) (2013) International standards on combating money laundering and the financing of terrorism & proliferation – the FATF Recommendations (February 2012). Financial Action Task Force (FATF)/Organisation for Economic Cooperation and Development (OECD), Paris

Financial Action Task Force (FATF) (2014) FATF: 25 years and beyond. Financial Action Task Force (FATF)/Organisation for Economic Cooperation and Development (OECD), Paris

Financial Action Task Force (FATF) (2015) The Financial Action Task Force leads renewed global effort to counter terrorist financing. https://www.fatf-gafi.org/en/publications/Fatfgeneral/Fatf-leads-renewed-global-effort-to-counter-terrorist-financing.html. Accessed 10 Mar 2025

Financial Action Task Force (FATF) (2016) AML/CFT and public-private sector partnership. https://www.fatf-gafi.org/content/fatf-gafi/en/publications/Fatfgeneral/Public-private-sector-partnership.html. Accessed 10 Mar 2025

Financial Action Task Force (FATF) (2016–17) Consolidated FATF standards on information sharing (Updated November 2017). Financial Action Task Force (FATF)/Organisation for Economic Cooperation and Development (OECD), Paris

Financial Action Task Force (FATF) (2019a) Financial Action Task Force mandate. Financial Action Task Force (FATF), Washington, DC
Financial Action Task Force (FATF) (2019b) International standards on combating money laundering and the financing of Terrorism & Proliferation, the FATF Recommendations. Financial Action Task Force, Paris
Financial Action Task Force (FATF) (2022) Report on the state of effectiveness and compliance with the FATF standards. Financial Action Task Force, Paris
Financial Action Task Force (FATF) (2023a) Best practices - combating the terrorist financing abuse of non-profit organisations. https://www.fatf-gafi.org/content/fatf-gafi/en/publications/Financialinclusionandnpoissues/Bpp-combating-abuse-npo.html. Accessed 24 May 2025
Financial Action Task Force (FATF) (2023b) International standards on combating money laundering and the financing of terrorism and proliferation. FATF/OECD, Paris
Financial Action Task Force (FATF) (2023c) Private sector consultative forum, May 2023. https://www.fatf-gafi.org/en/publications/Fatfgeneral/PSCF-May-2023.html. Accessed 10 Mar 2025
Financial Action Task Force (FATF) (2024a) FATF guidance - money laundering national risk assessment guidance. Financial Action Task Force, Paris
Financial Action Task Force (FATF) (2024b) FATF report – horizontal review of gatekeepers' technical compliance related to corruption, July 2024. FATF/OECD, Paris
Financial Action Task Force (FATF) (2024c) Frequently asked questions – membership. https://www.fatf-gafi.org/en/pages/frequently-asked-questions.html#tabs-36503a8663-item-cacccf71cf-tab. Accessed 10 Mar 2025
Financial Action Task Force (FATF) (2024d) International standards on combating money laundering and the financing of terrorism and proliferation - the FATF Recommendations (Updated November 2023). Financial Action Task Force, Paris
Financial Action Task Force (FATF) (2024e) Methodology for assessing technical compliance with the FATF recommendations and the effectiveness of AML/CTF/CPF systems. FATF/OECD, Paris
Financial Action Task Force (FATF) (2024f) Private sector consultative forum, April 2024. https://www.fatf-gafi.org/en/publications/Fatfgeneral/private-sector-consultative-forum-April-2024.html. Accessed 10 Mar 2025
Financial Action Task Force (FATF) (2024g) Which jurisdictions are members of the FATF? https://www.fatf-gafi.org/en/pages/frequently-asked-questions.html#tabs-36503a8663-item-cacccf71cf-tab. Accessed 10 Mar 2025
Financial Action Task Force (FATF) (2025a) FATF plenary – press conference – February 2025. https://www.fatf-gafi.org/en/publications/Fatfgeneral/outcomes-fatf-plenary-february-2025.html. Accessed 15 Mar 2025
Financial Action Task Force (FATF) (2025b) Private Sector Collaborative Forum reinforces importance of public-private collaboration in the fight against financial crime (27 March 2025). https://www.fatf-gafi.org/en/publications/Fatfgeneral/pscf-march-2025.html. Accessed 24 May 2025
Financial Action Task Force (FATF) (n.d.) FATF - Countries - About the FATF. https://www.fatf-gafi.org/en/countries/fatf.html. Accessed 10 Mar 2025
G-7 Group of Nations (G-7) (1989) Economic declaration. G-7 Group of Nations (G-7), Paris
Goldbarsht D, Goodrick T (2025) Private to private: the next frontier of financial intelligence sharing. In: Goldbarsht D, de Koker L, Ferrill J (eds) The financial war on crime and terrorism: opportunities and challenges. Springer, Cham
Imobersteg Harvey A (2019) Anti-money laundering and counter-terrorism financing law and policy: showcasing Australia. Brill Nijhoff, Leiden
Jakobi A (2018) Governing illicit finance in transnational security spaces: the FATF and anti-money laundering. Crime Law Soc Chang 69(2):173–190
Johnson J (2003) How will the financial services sector respond to the Financial Action Task Force's increased customer due diligence requirements? J Int Bank Regul 5(2):127–145

Kang S (2018) Rethinking the global anti-money laundering regulations to deter corruption. Int Comp Law Q 67(3):695–720. https://doi.org/10.1017/S0020589318000106

Lormel D (2012) Section 314(B) information sharing revisited. https://www.acamstoday.org/section-314b-information-sharing-revisited/. Accessed 10 Mar 2025

Maxwell N (2022) Financial intelligence sharing (FFIS) a survey and policy discussion paper: lessons in private-private financial information sharing to detect and disrupt crime. Royal United Services Institute (RUSI), London

Maxwell N, Artingsall D (2017) The role of financial information-sharing partnerships in the disruption of crime. Royal United Services Institute (RUSI), London

Menz M (2024) It is best to say nothing at all – suspicious activity reporting in the financial services sector. J Financ Crime. https://doi.org/10.1108/JFC-04-2023-0090

Morgan A (2024) Money laundering and the harm from organised crime: results from a data linkage study. Australian Institute of Criminology, Canberra

Nance M (2018) The regime that FATF built: an introduction to the financial action task force. Crime Law Soc Change 69(2):109–129. https://doi.org/10.1007/s10611-017-9747-6

National Commission on Terrorist Attacks upon the United States (2004) The 9/11 Commission report: final report of the National Commission on Terrorist Attacks upon the United States (9/11 Commission report). Norton

OECD (2017) Effective inter-agency co-operation in fighting tax crimes and other financial crimes, 3rd edn. OECD Publishing, Paris

de Oliveira I, Keatinge T, Stickings A (2016) Building trust and tackling risks in the global effort to tackle financial crime, RUSI occasional paper, October 2016. Royal United Services Institute (RUSI), London

Parliamentary Joint Committee on Law Enforcement (2013) Inquiry into the gathering and use of criminal intelligence (May 2013). Parliament of Australia, Canberra

Pieth M (2007) Chapter 9: The Wolfsberg process. In: Muller W, Kalin C, Godsworth J (eds) Anti-money laundering: international law and practice. John Wiley & Sons, Chichester

Pieth M, Aiolfi G (2003) The private sector becomes active: the Wolfsberg process. J Financ Crime 10(4):359–365

Pontes R, Lewis N, McFarlane P, Craig P (2022) Anti-money laundering in the United Kingdom: new directions for a more effective regime. J Money Laund Control 25(2):401–413. https://doi.org/10.1108/JMLC-04-2021-0041

Ratcliffe J (2016) Intelligence-led policing. Routledge, Milton Park

Reimer S (2024) Weaponisation of the FATF standards - a guide for global civil society. Royal United Services Institute (RUSI), London

Rickards C (2016) What are the barriers to gathering and sharing organised crime intelligence: an Australian perspective. Eur Rev Organ Crime 3(1):78–104

Schmidt A (2024) Impacts of money laundering and terrorism financing: final report. Australian Institute of Criminology, Canberra. https://doi.org/10.52922/sp77543

Schneider S, Hurst C (2008) Obstacles to an integrated, joint forces approach to organized crime enforcement: a Canadian case study. Policing 31(3):359–379

Standards Australia and Standards New Zealand (2012) Information and documentation - Principles and functional requirements for records in electronic office environments (Part 1: Overview and statement of principles). AS/NZS ISO 16175:1:2012. Sydney, Australia

The Wolfsberg Group (n.d.) About us. https://wolfsberg-group.org/about. Accessed 10 Mar 2025

Turkington M (2019) The effectiveness of private sector engagement in international financial crime countermeasures. PhD thesis, La Trobe University, Victoria, Australia

United Nations (1988) United Nations convention against illicit traffic in narcotic drugs and psychotropic substances. Opened for signature 20 December 1988, 1582 UNTS 95 (entered into force 11 November 1990)

United Nations (2000) United Nations convention against transnational organized crime. Opened for signature 15 November 2000, 2225 UNTS 209 (entered into force 29 September 2003)

United Nations (2003) United Nations convention against corruption. Opened for signature 31 October 2003, 2349 UNTS 41 (entered into force 14 December 2005)
United Nations (2024) United Nations convention against cybercrime. Opened for signature 24 December 2024 (not yet in force)
US Treasury and Financial Crimes Enforcement Network (2020) FinCEN's 314(B) fact sheet. US Government, Washington
Vlcek W (2018) Global financial governance and the informal: limits to the regulation of money Crime Law and Social Change 69(2): 249–264 . https://doi.org/10.1007/s10611-017-9754-7
Warner M (2019) Chapter 1: Wanted: a definition of intelligence. In: Andrew C, Aldrich R, Wark W (eds) Secret intelligence. Routledge, London

Paula Chadderton holds a PhD from La Trobe Law School (Australia). She is an Assistant Director in Australia's Department of Foreign Affairs and Trade. Paula's research interests concern intelligence and information sharing between the public and private sectors targeting financial crime, with a specific focus on money laundering, terrorism financing and transnational organised crime activities. Paula has also worked as a lawyer and legislative counsel in a range of Australia government agencies including the Australian Transaction Reports and Analysis Centre (AUSTRAC), Department of Home Affairs, Department of the Prime Minister and Cabinet, and Australian Federal Police, specialising in advising on financial crime issues, statutory interpretation and legislative drafting. Paula is admitted as a legal practitioner to the Supreme Court of the Australian Capital Territory and High Court of Australia.

Private to Private: The Next Frontier of Financial Intelligence Sharing

Doron Goldbarsht and Timothy Goodrick

Abstract Efforts to counter financial crime have increasingly relied on Public-Private Partnerships (PPPs) to facilitate intelligence sharing between law enforcement and the financial sector. While these arrangements have improved coordination and contributed to the disruption of illicit financial activity, they remain limited by their dependence on public-sector initiation and oversight. This chapter argues that Private-to-Private (P2P) information sharing represents a necessary next step in the evolution of financial crime prevention frameworks. Drawing on global regulatory developments and practical case studies, the chapter explores the potential for P2P mechanisms to close existing intelligence gaps, enabling earlier detection and disruption of criminal networks. It critically evaluates two dominant models of P2P information exchange, highlighting the legal, technical, and governance challenges they present. Ultimately, the chapter calls for the development of trust-based, accountable systems of intra-sector collaboration, capable of enhancing the effectiveness and efficiency of global anti-money laundering and counter-terrorism financing regimes.

The author(s) would like to thank the anonymous reviewers for their insightful and constructive feedback, which significantly improved the quality of this chapter.

D. Goldbarsht
Macquarie University and Financial Integrity Hub (FIH), Sydney, NSW, Australia
e-mail: doron.goldbarsht@mq.edu.au

T. Goodrick (✉)
KPMG Sydney, Sydney, NSW, Australia
e-mail: tgoodrick1@kpmg.com.au

D. Goldbarsht et al. (eds.), *The Financial War on Crime and Terrorism*, European Yearbook of International Economic Law,
https://doi.org/10.1007/978-3-032-06360-1_4

1 Introduction

Over the past 10 years, jurisdictions have enhanced their ability to detect and disrupt financial crime by leveraging Public Private Partnerships (PPPs) to enhance information sharing. However, the financial intelligence shared within PPPs is only providing a partial picture. Private to Private (P2P) information sharing has the capacity to complete that picture. This chapter argues that P2P information sharing is the next frontier in the fight against financial crime. While there are significant benefits, there are a number of key challenges to implement effective P2P information sharing, and the models adopted by different jurisdictions are critical to overcoming these challenges.

The nature of financial transactions, facilitated by greater global technological, economic, and geographical integration, continues to create significant opportunities for financial inclusion and borderless commerce.[1] However, the speed and breadth of these opportunities also present an escalating global challenge in the detection and prevention of money laundering (ML), terrorism financing (TF), and other financial crimes. Law enforcement agencies worldwide are increasingly confronting criminal actors who exploit this seamless connectivity to commit financial crimes on both local and global scales. The rapidly evolving nature of these crimes, coupled with the growing complexity and sophistication of financial transactions and technologies, highlights the need for enhanced collaboration. Sharing information and expertise, as well as pooling resources, can significantly bolster investigations into financial crime, strengthen detection and interception efforts, and, ultimately, promote global financial integrity.

PPPs are increasingly recognised as a vital tool for addressing the challenges of financial crime,[2] driven by an understanding of the limitations inherent in relying solely on financial institutions to comply fully with legal obligations, conduct adequate due diligence to disrupt and deter criminal activity, and ensure that law enforcement can identify and act on all instances of potentially criminal conduct.[3]

Since 2015, PPPs information sharing partnerships have evolved from a novel concept to a foundational element in combating financial crime within liberal democracies. The UK piloted the Joint Money Laundering Intelligence Task Force (JMLIT) in 2015, formally establishing it in April 2016. Canada followed in 2016 with its first partnership initiative under the "Project Protect" framework, and Australia launched the Fintel Alliance in March 2017. Other notable initiatives include the establishment of the Singapore Anti-Money Laundering and Countering the Financing of Terrorism Industry Partnership (ACIP) in April 2017, the Netherlands Terrorist Financing Taskforce (NL-TFTF) in July 2017, the New Zealand Financial Crime Prevention Network (NZ-FCPN) in December 2017, the Netherlands Fintell Alliance (FA-NL) in October 2018, the Netherlands Serious

[1] Goldbarsht and de Koker (2022).

[2] Turkington (2020), p. 282.

[3] Ibid.

Crime Taskforce (NL-SCTF) in August 2019 and the South African Anti Money-Laundering Integrated Task Force (SAMLIT) in December 2019. These partnerships reflect a global shift toward collaborative approaches to financial crime detection and prevention.[4]

While the AML/CTF regime aims for regulated entities to identify and report suspicions of criminal activity within their operations, achieving this goal is often fraught with practical challenges, particularly in the absence of partnership frameworks. Regulated entities frequently struggle to detect potential criminality without sufficient guidance from public agencies regarding patterns, trends, and specific entities under investigation.[5]

While PPPs are a significant step forward[6], there is an opportunity to enhance efforts to combat financial crime through P2P information sharing. This chapter will assert the value of P2P information sharing and explore how it can be effectively implemented. Starting with the global regime, the chapter provides the context in which P2P operates within the international standards. The analysis will explore the potential and realised benefits of P2P collaboration including enhanced detection and disruption and greater operational efficiency. However, implementing an effective P2P model is challenging and requires jurisdictions to overcome a number of legal, supervisory, technological and data challenges. This chapter will explore these challenges by outlining the two common global models. It will conclude with observations to further enhance the facilitation of P2P information sharing and its role in combating financial crime.

2 The Global Regime

The Financial Action Taskforce (FATF), an intergovernmental organisation established in 1989 by the G7 countries, sets the global standard for anti-money laundering (AML), counter-terrorist financing (CTF), counter-proliferation financing (CPF) and other threats to the integrity of the international financial system.[7] As part of its framework, the FATF emphasises that "effective information-sharing is [a] cornerstone of a well-functioning AML/CFT framework".[8] In fact, the FATF has long recognised the importance of information sharing, incorporating it into several recommendations.[9] Recommendation 2 emphasises the role of authorities in addressing barriers to information sharing and aligning AML/CFT with data protection

[4] For the full global development up until 2020, see Nick J. Maxwell (2021), p. 35.

[5] Ibid, p. 34.

[6] As discussed in the chapter by Chadderton (2025) in this book.

[7] Goldbarsht (2017), p 127.

[8] FATF (2021), p. 10.

[9] Financial Action Task Force, *International Standards on Combating Money Laundering and the Financing of Terrorism and Proliferation: The FATF Recommendations.*

requirements. Recommendation 18 requires financial groups to share information, including suspicious matter reports (SMRs) and related data, for customer due diligence (CDD) and ML/TF risk management, while recommendation 21 permits the disclosure of SMRs within group-wide risk management frameworks. However, while these standards support sharing within financial groups, they do not extend to broader private-to-private information sharing, leaving a significant gap unaddressed.[10]

The FATF has recognised the challenges, highlighting that a single financial institution only has a partial view of a transaction which is an information gap that criminals exploit.[11] P2P information sharing has the opportunity to close this gap by pooling together information from multiple financial institutions to provide a more accurate view when determining whether a transaction is suspicious.[12] Cross-border information sharing not only enhances investigative and preventative efforts but also provides critical support to countries with weaker institutional capacities.[13]

In 2016, the FATF released a supplement to its Recommendations titled *The Consolidated FATF Standards on Information Sharing* ('Consolidated Standards').[14] By consolidating this guidance, the FATF aimed to help private entities better align their efforts with its effectiveness metrics for AML/CTF programs. The *Consolidated Standards* provide detailed guidance on how the private sector should manage and share information across several key areas, including correspondent banking, wire transfers, reliance on third parties during the CDD process, the implementation of group-wide AML/CTF programs, and safeguarding against the misuse of non-profit organisations for terrorist purposes.

In 2017, the FATF issued supplementary non-binding guidance on *Private Sector Information Sharing* (PSIS), expanding on its general recommendations and highlighting the benefits within a P2P context. This guidance addressed gaps in earlier recommendations, advocating for information sharing both within the same institution—domestically and internationally—and between unrelated institutions.[15] While reliance solely on FIUs and law enforcement often results in a legally defensive strategy focused on sanctions compliance rather than leveraging timely, actionable intelligence for crime prevention and detection.[16] The FATF's guidance suggests that broader P2P sharing could significantly improve outcomes in combating illicit financial activity.[17] The FATF outlined benefits on both macro and micro levels. At the macro level, information sharing contributes to greater financial system integrity and provides a comprehensive view of evolving risks, trends, and financial crime

[10] FATF (2021), p. 8.

[11] FATF (2022), p. 3.

[12] Ibid, p. 10.

[13] Financial Action Task Force (2017), p. 10.

[14] Financial Action Task Force (2016–2017).

[15] Financial Action Task Force (2017).

[16] Murr et al. (2023), p. 61.

[17] Ibid.

typologies.[18] On a more granular level, P2P sharing enhances the detection, prevention, and enforcement of financial crimes, offering a proactive approach to identifying threats.[19]

The potential benefits reported by the FATF may also include greater awareness of blind spots through pooled knowledge,[20] prevention of criminal arbitrage (differences in legal systems, regulatory frameworks, or enforcement levels) across national financial systems,[21] and the potential to share information that allows for faster response than what regulators might provide over the current approach of centralising detection response.[22] Leveraging of private sector resources to address transnational and scaling issues may also provide benefits to smaller institutions more susceptible to exploits of AML/CTF controls,[23] due to fewer resources to keep up with the speed of criminal groups' methods.

In 2022, the FATF issued additional non-binding guidance on *Partnering in the Fight Against Financial Crime: Data Protection, Technology and Private Sector Information Sharing*. This chapter is intended to help jurisdictions strike an appropriate balance of combatting money laundering and terrorism financing through P2P information sharing initiatives while ensuring that data protection and privacy is protected.[24] The FATF reiterated the potential benefits of P2P initiatives but noted that this must in accordance with data protection and privacy rules.

3 Potential Benefits of Private-to-Private Information Sharing

Professional money launderers are often adept at opening and managing multiple accounts across various financial institutions.[25] However, the traditional approach to detecting financial crime relies on individual financial institutions analysing their own business data in isolation, limiting their visibility into broader criminal networks. This fragmented approach, based on partial financial data, poses challenges in effectively identifying suspicious activity.[26] This fragmentation is exploited by criminal groups that seek to circumvent detection by undertaking financial activity across multiple institutions.

---

[18] Ibid, p. 2.

[19] Ibid, p. 12.

[20] Financial Action Task Force (2017), p. 38.

[21] Ibid, p. 22.

[22] Murr et al. (2023), p. 61.

[23] Ibid, p. 55.

[24] Financial Action Task Force (2022), p. 3.

[25] Financial Action Task Force 2018.

[26] Nick J. Maxwell (2021), p. 115.

P2P information sharing is a scalable and effective means of addressing this gap, offering the potential to uncover previously unknown risks and enabling consistent preventive actions to block illicit funds from entering the financial system. Complementing this, PPPs information sharing remains critical for addressing threats already known to law enforcement, creating a holistic framework to combat economic crime more convincingly.

P2P information sharing also provides an opportunity to reduce false positives by creating a more holistic view of risk.[27] Access to additional data may support financial institutions to make more accurate decisions when determining whether a customer or transaction is suspicious as further information can provide explanations to discount investigations.[28] This provides higher quality financial intelligence to the FIU and competent authorities to enhance their risk-based approach in the investigation and disruption of financial crime.

3.1 Enhanced Detection and Disruption of Financial Crime

The first gap in P2P information-sharing is in correspondent banking.[29] This relationship involves one financial institution providing services to another, often acting as a 'middleman' to facilitate services between sending and receiving institutions, particularly when one of the institutions lacks a physical presence in the other's country. Correspondent banking accounts for approximately 50% of global cross-border money flows, and due to the complexity and opacity of these institutions, they are vulnerable to exploitation by criminal actors who seek to use these weak systems to launder illicit funds.[30] Efficient P2P information-sharing in this context would ensure that respondent banks have conducted proper CDD on their customers, with the correspondent bank facilitating access to relevant information. Exchange between the institutions should occur to verify that this requirement is met, thereby mitigating the risks of financial crime.[31]

To the extent that information should be exchanged between respondent and correspondent banks, both parties should ensure open sharing, control, and retention of relevant data (including beneficial ownership and the details of natural persons involved in the transactions), where such information is pertinent to the prevention of ML and TF. Where any of the entities party to the transaction are companies, recommendations on the depth of information to be obtained and shared are specific. These include a list of company directors and any nominee directors, proof of

[27] Financial Action Task Force (2022), *Partnering in the Fight Against Financial Crime: Data Protection, Technology and Private Sector Information Sharing*.

[28] RUSI (2024), p. 15.

[29] Ibid, p. 16.

[30] Basel Institute of Governance (2022), p. 10.

[31] Financial Action Task Force (2017), p. 18.

incorporation, legal form[32] that should also be kept and shared.[33] Where trusts are involved, their usual opacity is offset by recommendations to collect and share information on the trustees, assets held by the trust, and any service providers or regulated agents working with the trusts. In addition to collecting and sharing information, it is essential that both respondent and correspondent institutions have current and timely access to this information when needed, and that competent authorities can easily access it as well. The quality of information is also recommended to be both current, and regularly updated, in aid of preventative measures.

The rate of crime committed through wire transfer is challenging to accurately measure, as many of these crimes go unreported, or are detected only after significant delays or revelation of systemic issues of lapses or absence of Know Your Customer (KYC) controls. There is a need for information sharing and retention between institutions during wire transfer operations throughout the entirety of the payment chain.[34] The FATF Standards highlight vulnerabilities in information sharing and retention between originating and beneficiary institutions; respectively, those sending and receiving wire transfers for customers.

The FATF offers guidance on P2P sharing where institutions have relied upon third parties to perform KYC measures.[35] These parties may be based domestically or internationally, and part of the same group, or part of another institution. The *Consolidated Standards* recommend that the requesting institution takes adequate steps to satisfy itself that the due diligence performed is sufficient, performed by a regulated, supervised, and monitored entity, and that it has strong measures in place for CDD standards and record-keeping requirements. At this point, P2P information sharing becomes necessary as part of the requesting entity's responsibility to monitor the accuracy and quality of the documentation collected by the third party, as well as the timeliness of any required response.

Among the benefits of P2P, its ability to address the speed and complexity of cross-border financial crime schemes stands out. P2P information sharing serves as an additional layer of connectivity, enhancing detection and prevention efforts and ultimately strengthening global efforts against financial crime.[36] This additional source of real-time information-sharing enhances the detection and disruption of financial crime, complementing traditional information flows that are often triangulated between competent authorities and private organisations. Conversely, barriers to such sharing can significantly undermine effectiveness, creating opportunities for criminal networks to exploit gaps in communication and coordination.[37]

Recognising this, prevention systems must evolve to mirror the interconnected nature of financial crime itself. As financial crimes operate as a 'network', so too

[32] Financial Action Task Force (2017), p. 12.
[33] Ibid, p. 8.
[34] Ibid, p. 13.
[35] Financial Action Task Force (2017), p. 14.
[36] Hardouin (2009), p. 204.
[37] Murr et al. (2023), p. 53.

should the systems of prevention; to further develop this network of prevention, private entities can be sources of information as FIUs and public authorities currently are.[38] That is, as well as being recipients of intelligence and trends necessary to develop preventative efforts, private institutions may become additional sources of near real-time intelligence between each other and for FIUs. Benefits to the broader financial system are an additional point that the PSIS outlays, turning the focus to the promotion of transparency in financial systems in general, as an expectation and best practice.[39] Such improvements could enhance transparency and build trust within individual institutions, reducing fraud, corruption, and regulatory violations while strengthening risk management. More broadly, these institutional improvements may contribute to greater financial system stability nationwide. This enhanced stability could improve a country's international reputation and access to capital, potentially enabling greater financial inclusion in traditionally higher-risk markets.[40] Though the correlation of strong economies to banking transparency alone would be simplistic, those adhering to high standards for AML/CTF prevention, accompanied by a strong reputation for banking transparency, tend to be more advanced economies with high GDP.[41]

A key benefit of P2P information to enhance the detection of suspected criminal activity. This can be realized in two ways depending on the model of P2P information sharing:

First, where transaction data is pooled from multiple financial institutions, it allows analysis to take place to detect previously unidentified suspicious activity. Financial institutions only see part of the overall picture when assessing whether transactions or transactions are suspicious and may struggle to identify a complex suspicious transaction pattern or network.[42] Additional information or transactions from other institutions can provide a more accurate and comprehensive picture and reduce fragmentation. In particular, the ability to analyse data on a network basis from multiple financial institutions will be more effective at detecting suspicious activity that spans across the financial sector.[43]

Second, where targeted information sharing takes place on either one-on-one or one-on-many basis, it allows financial institutions to commence an investigation to determine if they face similar risks. This can include the sharing of information on transactions and customers that institutions have identified as suspicious. The sharing of this information on a targeted basis allows other institutions to take a targeted approach to their investigation to identify previously unidentified risks.

[38] Financial Action Task Force (2017), p. 2.

[39] Ibid.

[40] Murr et al. (2023), p. 54.

[41] Thony (2007), p. 13.

[42] FATF (2022), p. 7.

[43] Westmore et al. (2022), p. 14.

As the fight against financial crime has evolved and PPPs have expanded, an opportunity remains for P2P information sharing, a frontier that has yet to be fully realised in combating financial crime.

3.2 Greater Operational Efficiency

At a practical level, P2P information sharing across borders and entities can lead to improved assessments of customer and geographical risks, and better identification of risk exposure at an enterprise level due to onboarding of the same customer by multiple entities, filling in gaps that may occur in customer profiles over time.[44] Operationally, this may result in more accurate risk profiles and internal risk management mitigation strategies at a global level. This would be facilitated by additional access to the entirety of the customers activities across different products such as banking, insurance, commodities, and so on, allowing for further segmentation of enterprise risk management measures.[45] Similarly, sharing of account information may lead to more effective due diligence and monitoring, with more complete information on transaction patterns. That is, monitoring efforts would be based on a broader set of data for the same customer and would presumably be more accurate in detecting suspicious transactions, as abnormal activities across the customer's entire financial profile would be visible.[46] This broader data set available through a consolidated screening approach, coupled with increasing advances in data science analytics and capacity available to institutions, may assist in the identification of better internal controls and improve decision-making at the point of decisions to report suspicious transactions.[47]

At present, the volume of SMRs is growing at over 11% per year across some major markets.[48] However, this growth in reporting is largely inefficient, with an estimated 80–90% of SMRs to FIUs ineffective and not useful to law enforcement actions.[49] A broader dataset has the potential to refine monitoring efforts and reduce false positives by allowing institutions to make more accurate decisions when determining suspicion, and in real-time.[50] P2P information sharing, particularly with awareness of SMRs lodged, can leverage this information to support more informed and effective decision-making, and improved reporting[51].

---

[44] Financial Action Task Force (2017), p. 9.

[45] Ibid.

[46] Ibid, p. 11.

[47] RUSI (2017), p. 8.

[48] Ibid, p. 7.

[49] Goldbarsht (2022), p. 21. For reducing false positives and improving the identification of true positives by incorporating AI in AML procedures, see: Goldbarsht (2023), p. 5.

[50] Jean-Francois Thony (2007), p. 13.

[51] Thus, providing opportunities to face the challenges highlighted in the chapter by Ferrill et al. (2025) in this book.

This P2P initiative provides FIUs and competent authorities with higher quality financial intelligence which allows them to be more effective in the investigation and disruption of financial crime, and strategic analysis of financial crime threats. In turn, it enables authorities to enhance their risk-based approach by targeted their efforts at an operational level, and providing more accurate insights at a strategic level.

3.3 Positive Impact on De-Risking

Where P2P sharing is outside of the same financial group, similar benefits to those outlined above will apply. Another benefit is that institutions currently terminate customer relationships when they complete information needed to assess customers or transactions and cannot manage the associated individual or country risks. Better information sharing could prevent these terminations. Avoiding this scenario where termination may not be necessary can positively impact the trend of de-risking,[52] which can lead to financial exclusion. De-risking refers to the practice of institutions reducing their risk by ceasing to deal with products, markets, sectors or customers perceived as higher risk, or an exit from correspondent banking in the region entirely.[53] AML/CFT measures are a common driver of de-risking.[54] The result is limiting access to banking and financial services for legitimate individuals and companies, and may disproportionately impact developing nations, compounding economic problems and stunting legitimate attempts at growth, and sometimes driving transactions to less traceable means, which may often be counterintuitive to efforts to improve monitoring for money laundering and terrorism financing.[55]

The PSIS has provided examples of P2P information sharing that could go beyond current FATF rules, focusing on how the private sector may be leveraged to disrupt networks more broadly when information is pooled. The PSIS reports that some jurisdictions have created an alerts system of customers who have been refused or exited from any institution due to ML/TF concerns, preventing arbitrage.[56] The system has also been used to consolidate information on customers' transactions overall, thwarting attempts to avoid detection by structuring payments across different institutions at the same time.[57] Such information would not be available without P2P collaboration.

[52] Murr et al. (2023), p. 53.

[53] Ibid.

[54] Ibid, p. 54.

[55] Ibid.

[56] Financial Action Task Force (2016–2017), p. 22.

[57] Ibid.

The potential benefits must be balanced against the risk of targeted de-risking based on information shared between financial institutions. There is a risk that targeted sharing of information by one institution to another could lead to the termination of business relationships with customers identified in the information. For example, where one institution terminates the business relationship with a customer and informs another institution that it is aware has a relationship with the customer, this may lead to termination if a blanket approach is applied.

Clearly the potential benefits have been explored by the FATF across the *Consolidated Guidelines*, and the practical means to achieving these have been offered in the PSIS. These benefits underscore the critical role of P2P information-sharing in advancing global efforts against financial crime while fostering a more resilient and inclusive financial system.

4 Models to Implementing Private-to-Private Information Sharing

The risks and issues associated with P2P information sharing include those arising from data privacy,[58] banking secrecy, and fair competition legislation,[59] both within and across jurisdictions. Additional challenges involve operationalisation difficulties stemming from technological limitations, data collection formats, and the lack of systems integration.[60]

While the benefits of promoting and facilitating P2P information sharing are widely acknowledged in both theory and practice, the implementation of such networks faces significant legal, operational, and supervisory challenges. These challenges are critical to overcome to design and implement an effective regime for P2P information sharing to combat money laundering and terrorism financing.

The way in which jurisdictions overcome these challenges depends on the model adopted for P2P information sharing. This chapter explores two of the most common models available to jurisdictions to consider and analyses the challenges of each.

[58] Japanese bank Mitsubishi UFJ Financial Group ('MUFG') was recently fined for sharing information within its securities firms and its own branches outside of Japan. Japan has 'firewall' legislation that prohibits the sharing of non-public information between banking units, preventing violation of client confidentiality provisions. See Gamut and Sekiguchi (2024).

[59] European Court of Justice recently ruled that the sporadic sharing of information between 14 Portuguese banks was inherently harmful to competition, even without harmful effects having materialised. Banco BPN, Banco Bilbao, Banco Português and Others v Autoridade de Concorrência (Antitrust Authority) (2024).

[60] Financial Action Task Force (2017), p. 4.

4.1 P2P Model Options

There are multiple ways in which jurisdictions can establish a model for P2P information sharing to combat money laundering and terrorism financing. As jurisdictions design and implement an effective P2P information sharing network, it is important that the model is appropriate for their jurisdiction. In its review of data protection and private sector information sharing, the FATF recognised that the different models for P2P will involve different data protection and privacy considerations with pre-suspicion sharing generally being subject to stricter limitations.[61]

To consider we have seen that there are broadly two models to consider when establishing P2P information sharing (Table 1).[62] These two models are explored in more detail below.

4.2 P2P Model Analysis

4.2.1 P2P Model 1. Pooling Transaction Data

Under this model, transaction data is pooled together from multiple financial institutions that is de-personalised or encrypted for analysis to detect criminal activity. There is typically a limited number of institutions involved with a specific data set that is maintained in a centralised platform to allow the application of analytical

Table 1 Models to consider when establishing P2P information sharing

Model	P2P Model 1. Pooling transaction data	P2P Model 2. Targeted information sharing
Summary	Pooling transaction data from multiple financial institutions that is de-personalised or encrypted for analysis to detect criminal activity.	Targeted sharing of information between institutions during or after an investigation has taken place on either a one-to-one or one-to-many basis.
Participants	Limited number of institutions involved with a specific data set.	Potential for a wide range of participating institutions and collaborative investigations.
Information shared	Transaction data that is subject to encryption or pseudonymization	Investigative information subject to data security requirements
Role of Government	Central role subject to the model	Government oversight and monitoring
Platform/ Mechanism	Centralized platform for analysis	Decentralized which may include a gateway
Examples	Netherlands, Singapore	Netherlands

[61] FATF (2022) at 19.

[62] FATF (2022) at 19.

tools. In this model, the platform may be governed and operated by a centralised body which has authority, with enduring funding. It may be only feasible for limited number of institutions with a specified data set. The Netherlands have sought to establish P2P information sharing models that pool transaction data for a limited number of institutions (see below).

This model allows for the identification of previously unknown threats through advanced analytics of large data sets. In particular, it may increase the detection of complex ML/TF schemes where traditional rules are not effective. Critical to its success are the tools required for data encryption or pseudonymisation, as well as for analysing the potentially large dataset.

There is also the opportunity to allow institutions to reduce false positives by focusing on targeted data.[63] However, this also brings a risk of additional operational burden for institutions where they are required to investigate alerts from the centralised platform in addition to their traditional transaction monitoring system.

This model allows for the detection of suspicious activity that can only be identified by pooling data from multiple institutions, but it presents a risk of increased operational burden for institutions if no relief is provided and efforts are duplicated.

4.2.2 P2P Model 2. Targeted Information Sharing

Targeted sharing of information between institutions takes place on either a one-to-one or one-to-many basis. Information may be shared directly from one institution to another, or through a secure gateway, and participation may occur on a voluntary basis.

This provides the opportunity for a wide range of participating institutions and collaborative investigations which may produce higher quality financial intelligence for investigation and confiscation. This may reduce the operational burden for financial institutions by investigating higher quality information and enhance the risk-based approach for the FIU through higher quality SMRs.

Jurisdictions will need to consider appropriate requirements to ensure that institutions that participate in the model have the appropriate controls in place, and a supervisory mechanism to support and monitor compliance.

Information security is also critical to ensure that information initially provided by the financial institution is accurate and complete, and that it is treated appropriately by the receiving institution. This can involve direct sharing of information on a bilateral or multilateral basis, with requirements placed on the security of communications, or alternatively, sharing through a supporting platform or gateway.

The role of governments is critical in terms of enabling the P2P information sharing and oversight and monitoring to ensure appropriate controls are in place. For example, this may require government funding to establish a platform or secure gateway as well as additional resources are also required for the supervisory body.

[63] Goldbarsht (2022).

Given that information is shared on customers posing a higher risk, a critical component is ensuring that cases are treated on a case-by-case basis to mitigate the risk of de-banking.

Several jurisdictions offer models to implement P2P information-sharing frameworks, detailing strategies to address these challenges, which are outlined below.

4.3 Case Studies

There are multiple variations that jurisdictions may consider when adopting the appropriate model that is appropriate for their jurisdiction. To further consider the P2P models available, we have identified three examples below.

4.3.1 The United States' Model of Information-Sharing

The United States FinCEN is a government agency operating under the Department of the Treasury, tasked with combating financial crimes, which includes ML/TF, and other illicit financial activities.[64] FinCEN's PPPs are part of its regular operations, notably working with Fintech companies in recent past to harness knowledge on the evolving risk ML/TF and fraud committed through cryptocurrencies.

However, The *Uniting and Strengthening America by Providing Appropriate Tools Required to Intercept and Obstruct Terrorism* (*Patriot Act*) also allows for financial institutions, upon providing notice to the United States Department of the Treasury, to share information with one another, in recognition of this supporting in the more effective identification and reporting activities related to AML/CTF efforts.[65] The initiative is voluntary, but FinCEN has been vocal in urging private institutions to participate in such efforts. Section 314(b) is designed specifically with some of the earlier discussed benefits in mind and provides a safe harbour for companies that utilise it. That is, additional information on customers and transactions that may be indicative of money laundering or terrorism financing, including accounts and individuals that are periphery to main transactors.[66] Ultimately, FinCEN and the U.S. Treasury's guidance aligns with the FATF *Consolidated Principles* in supporting that such information sharing will allow for better tracing activities, especially when related to complex, layered webs and in cases of financial arbitrage. The scheme also recognises that this sharing will build out a better and more accurate picture of customers' activities where AML/CTF is involved, thereby supporting better decision making, and risk management.

[64] Wright and Meier (2021), p. 55.

[65] U.S. Treasury (2020), p. 3.

[66] Ibid, p. 4.

FinCEN also predicts that SMRs would be more accurate and likely to yield enforcement results than if information is not shared.[67] Section 314(b) does not require a completed transaction and can be invoked with an attempted transaction. Provided some of these and other requirements are met, the information that can be shared in reliance on Section 314(b) may include personally identifiable information.[68] Furthermore, the type of information, for example IP addresses, video footage, or written information, and how it can be shared, are not subject to limitations within Section 314(b). To participate in such sharing, registration with FinCEN is required to express interest, and submissions are reviewed, acknowledged, and approved if appropriate. To share information, the receiving party must also be registered through this means. The intent of these controls is to ensure the confidentiality and security of information shared, and that the information shared be governed by standards relating to its utility and end use of detecting financial crimes.[69] FinCEN runs successful engagement with private institutions under s 314(a) of the *Patriot Act*, where it acts as the facilitator and host of relationships between institutions (but this is representative of PPP information sharing, still requiring the public sector as an intermediary).[70] Section 314(b) would enable private institutions to interact directly with each other.

Despite circulars and guidance available that apparently address some key challenges, complexities remain. Concerns about privacy and legal risks associated with actioning Section 314(b) exist. Institutions are sensitive about protection of their customers' personal and financial information, which may lead to lost trust and other reputation issues that affect business.[71] The inadvertent violation of customer privacy legislation in the U.S. (*Gramm-Leach-Bliley* Act) or the General Data Protection Regulation ('GDPR')[72] where European customers are concerned, may deter participation in the scheme. Although 'good faith' participation is covered in Section 314(b) legislation, residual legal concerns around over-sharing or misinterpretation of the protections provided, may also lead to underuse. An added complexity will be where customers or transactions are cross-border, and a lack of familiarity with the privacy legislation in the customer's domicile location, or indeed that they may conflict with local legislation, or each other (for example where information is required to stay within national borders).[73]

One privacy concern that has been addressed by the FinCEN Section 314(b) arrangements is the creation of specific, secure channels administered by FinCEN itself, that financial institution participants can use to communicate with each other,

[67] Ibid, p. 3.

[68] Ibid.

[69] RUSI (2017), p. 15.

[70] Financial Action Task Force (2017), p. 4.

[71] Wright and Meier (2021), p. 61.

[72] Regulation (EEC) No 2016/679 The General Data Protection Regulation.

[73] Financial Action Task Force (2017), p. 4; Panagiotis Chatzidiannis et al. (2023), p. 9.

avoiding or at least mitigating potential data breaches.[74] While concerns remain on the perceived legal 'grey area' on what can be shared specifically, the method of sharing is one that could be applied to other arrangements.

Participation in the scheme in the U.S. may also raise operational concerns. Incorporating additional sources of information could lead to the misallocation of human resources or necessitate increased resources to follow up on leads and respond to new or additional information requests.[75] For smaller institutions, that may have resource constraints, these competing priorities could lower the participation rate. An additional hurdle is the lack of standardisation in reporting practices, mainly in the quality, content, timeliness and formats in which information should be shared.[76] Adding to these challenges, Section 314(b) provides no incentives for participation. While it does not penalise non-participation as regular reporting obligations do, there are no consequences for not engaging in Section 314(b). When weighing this against the possibility of additional resources and legal burdens, the incentives to participate actively may be lessened.

4.3.2 Singapore's Model of Information-Sharing

In 2024, the Monetary Authority of Singapore (MAS) launched a P2P information sharing initiative by establishing a secure digital platform.[77] This Collaborative Sharing of Money Laundering/Terrorism Financing (ML/TF) Information & Cases (COSMIC), provides a platform for the six major commercial banks to share pre-STR and post-STR information.

Singapore identified a weakness in its AML/CFT regime: the inability of financial institutions to alert each other to unusual activity in their customers' accounts. It identified that criminals exploited what it termed "information silos" by using multiple accounts across financial institutions and by moving from one institution to another to avoid detection.[78]

COSMIC establishes a legal and operational framework for participants to share customer information, risk analysis, and transaction data to assess suspicion and warn of potentially suspicious activity.[79] The sharing of information is voluntary, although the FATF reported that MAS is considering making sharing mandatory in higher risk situations after the initial phase.[80]

[74] Financial Action Task Force (2017), p. 40.

[75] Ibid, p. 5.

[76] Michael Levi et al. (2018), p. 308.

[77] https://www.mas.gov.sg/news/media-releases/2024/mas-launches-cosmic-platform

[78] Explanatory Brief for Financial Services and Markets (Amendment) Bill 2023 at paragraph 2–3.

[79] FATF (2022), p. 22.

[80] Ibid.

Information can be shared among participants in a number of ways:[81] (1) information may be requested from other institutions that are linked where more information is required to determine a suspicion, (2) institutions may provide risk information on a customer to other institutions where there is a greater risk if the customer being involved in illicit activity; and (3) institutions should place an alert on a customer where it has identified suspicious activity and terminated the relationship.

Privacy concerns for financial institutions, are overcome by specific legislation relating to sharing of customer information between financial institutions for the purposes of combating ML/TF through amendments to the Financial Services and Markets Act.[82] The amendments provide statutory protection from civil liability for participants in respect of their disclosure of information in COSMIC, provided that the disclosure was made with reasonable care and in good faith, and in accordance with the disclosure thresholds.[83]

The introduction of COSMIC also came with specific obligations placed on participants by amending its Notice 626 Prevention of Money Laundering and Countering the Financing of Terrorism and supporting guidelines. Participants are required to incorporate information from COSMIC as part of AML/CFT controls, including how information obtained through COSMIC is taken into account as part of the AML/CFT program.[84] Participants are also required to ensure that information is accurate and complete, that records are properly maintained, and that appropriate information security measures are in place.[85]

While this is a positive start, the initiative only covers a limited set of commercial banks. Although limited information on COSMIC's success is available thus far, the operational concerns of P2P information-sharing regarding differences in consistency and integration of reporting across private institutions, has had steps taken towards improvement facilitated by COSMIC.[86]

4.3.3 The Netherlands Experience in Information-Sharing

Lastly, the Netherlands' experience provides some insights into the challenges associated with the roles of supervisors: the designated persons responsible for reporting money laundering, terrorism financing, and other risks of financial crime to

[81] Ibid, p. 23.

[82] For details see the Explanatory Brief for Financial Services and Markets (Amendment) Bill 2023 at https://www.mas.gov.sg/news/speeches/2023/explanatory-brief-for-financial-services-and-markets-amendment-bill

[83] Explanatory Brief for Financial Services and Markets (Amendment) Bill 2023 at paragraph 10.

[84] MAS consultation paper at 8, https://www.mas.gov.sg/-/media/mas-media-library/regulation/anti-money-laundering/cosmic/consultation-paper-on-notice-relating-to-fi-fi-information-sharing-for-amlcft.pdf

[85] Ibid, p. 12.

[86] Ministry of Finance (2024), p. 27.

competent authorities within the jurisdiction. In the Netherlands, financial institutions collaborate closely with the country's FIU and central reporting point for AML/CFT.[87] This FIU is embedded within the Netherlands' police force, and is an autonomous entity, reporting directly to the Minister of Justice and Security. The relevant legislation, the *Dutch Money Laundering and Terrorism Financing (Prevention) Act* ('WWFT'), places responsibility for monitoring and reporting suspicious transactions linked to money laundering, terrorism financing, and other financial crimes, to the entities registering or processing potentially suspicious transactions.[88] These include but are not limited to banks, virtual asset service providers, accountants, gambling companies, payment service providers and Fintech participants, and casinos.

These supervisors are seen as the first line of defence in the Netherlands' system and tasked with a 'gatekeeper' role against ML/TF, and similar crimes. The analysis of transactions is managed by the FIU. In general, the system is characterised by a strong balance of responsibility held by the private sector.[89] At one stage, this was a point of contention. Financial institutions complained about the significant investment required and onerous supervisory responsibilities, which they felt were not matched by corresponding value from the FIU. Institutions expected the FIU to develop better tools and risk mitigation resources for supervisors and institutions, and to make better use of the vast amount of intelligence it received.[90] In turn, such opacity led to concerns raised about the lack of transparency around the FIU's day-to-day operations, the possible lack of oversight, and its use of information received from obligated.[91]

To aid this, several P2P information sharing initiatives arose. The Fintell Alliance ('TFA') in Netherlands[92] was developed in 2022 as a partnership between the FIU and the 6 largest retail banks. The FIU is involved in its operation. In this alliance, bank representatives and the FIU work at the same physical location, and all of the FIU's taskforce and active investigations are supported by interventions passed down from the banks' representatives to these banks' operations. In turn this directs the institutions' efforts in prevention, detection, and intervention of live and emerging issues. Institutions are able to legally and confidentially share sensitive information, including knowledge of terrorism financing, subject data, modus operandi, and typologies.[93] The effort has improved public confidence in the FIU's functioning[94] and use of information.

---

[87] KPMG Advisory (2023), p. 21.

[88] Ibid, p. 7.

[89] Ibid, p. 28.

[90] Ibid.

[91] Ibid, p. 66.

[92] Ibid, p. 67.

[93] Ibid, p. 8.

[94] Ibid, p. 37.

As a completely P2P information sharing group without the facilitation of government entities, 5 Dutch banks known as the network 'Transaction Monitoring Netherlands' (TMNL) have been carrying out information-sharing, performing joint transaction monitoring since 2020 and looking at unusual patterns across different banks and monitoring potentially criminal money flows between banks.[95]

At the time of writing, however, the initiative is beginning to be wound down after the European Directive 2024/1620[96] came into effect in June 2024. This legislation establishes a European Union-wide AML/CTF Authority. The legislation does not yet address P2P sharing explicitly but does propose an EU-wide source of data where information on individuals will be made available to specific persons on request. It is not yet clear if this access refers to legal persons such as financial institutions, persons in the employ of the state or FIUs, or some other configuration. Considering its stated intentions of facilitating sharing across the members states, watching the EU Directive evolve to see what level of sharing is allowed and how the application of the GDPR may differ within this context will be critical for further learning that can be applied elsewhere.

5 Observations

The risks and challenges of P2P information sharing in AML/CTF are significant, arising from issues of data privacy, banking secrecy, fair competition, and operational hurdles such as technological limitations and lack of systems integration. While the theoretical and practical benefits of P2P frameworks are widely acknowledged, their implementation remains complex due to legal, operational, and supervisory barriers.

The United States' model, led by FinCEN under Section 314(b) of the Patriot Act, encourages voluntary information sharing among financial institutions with safe harbour protections. However, legal uncertainties, privacy concerns, and resource constraints limit participation.

The Netherlands' model of information sharing focuses on collaboration through the Fintell Alliance, which brings together public and private institutions to share intelligence and develop joint responses to combat financial crime, particularly by leveraging secure data-sharing channels and technology-driven solutions to overcome privacy and operational challenges. These models highlight diverse approaches to mitigating legal and operational challenges, emphasising secure communication channels, regulatory alignment, and collaborative frameworks as key to effective P2P information-sharing.

---

95 Transaction Monitoring Netherlands (Web Page). https://tmnl.nl/en/article/transaction-monitoring-netherlands-adapts-its-working-method-to-new-european-legislation/.

96 Council Directive (2024/1640).

There are a range of key considerations when establishing an appropriate P2P information sharing model, including: the information that is to be shared, which may include transaction data, investigation or suspicious matter data, or KYC information, and whether the information is to be encrypted or de-personalised; participants in the P2P model, which may be a narrow scope of a handful of financial institutions or alternatively a wide range of institutions involved; the role of the regulator, which may include bilateral info sharing or alternatively government sitting at the heart of the model managing the end to end under a government agency or specifically created entity; the platform used in and operational framework for P2P information sharing, may include a secure sharing network for targeted information sharing or a standalone platform for pooling transaction data to apply data analytics; the legal framework, including for the appropriate management of tipping off, data protection and privacy and the sharing of information to provide a sound framework for institutions to share information; the supervisory framework, including nominating an appropriate supervisor and establishing an effective supervisory model to ensure that information is shared in accordance with legal requirements.

6 Conclusions and Recommendations

The current state of knowledge and shared examples of P2P information sharing is sparse, despite evidence that detection, investigation, and enforcement against money laundering, terrorism financing, and other forms of financial crime would benefit from the utility, speed, and depth of information that financial institutions could share directly. The FATF and other bodies have been clear on these benefits and have taken steps to facilitate P2P sharing by way of advice through additional publications, and through sharing case studies of countries that have put these models into practice in some form.

This chapter has explored several potential benefits, both those posited by the FATF and those directly observed through practical implementation. The benefits for individual financial institutions include improved risk assessments both at an enterprise level and also at a customer profile level, which are better indicators for action and mitigation, considering that a broader dataset of customer activity is taken into account. Private institutions will also benefit from improved internal controls due to better knowledge of crime typologies and schemes, and more accurate monitoring capabilities. This accuracy comes from access to broader datasets that track customer behaviour more realistically across multiple institutions, as well as better understanding of system-wide vulnerabilities beyond the institution's direct control.

At a broader, country-level, we have seen that FIUs, and by extension nations, will also benefit from the flow-on effects of institutions' improved risk assessments based on richer information. This is particularly important considering that current SAR reporting often results in ineffective enforcement actions and detection outcomes. As accuracy increases, de-risking by way of exit and divestment from certain countries due to an excess of risk adversity of financial institutions may decrease. In turn, financial inclusion may be better promoted, further driving citizens of these countries to use conventional, traceable forms of financial operations. Also at a country level, and at a societal level, real-time data sharing that avoids the lapse in regulatory response or no response at all, may mean improved detection and enforcement particularly in terrorism financial, where time is a critical element.

While some evidence of implementation was discussed across the United States, Singapore, and the Netherlands, several of these models were facilitated in some manner by the public system. As such, they provide little insight into how the barriers to participation can be overcome, and how private institutions might hold such initiatives autonomously, within the bounds of the law and privacy considerations, and with technical proficiency. The legal, ethical, and regulatory concerns explored in this chapter support both the reluctance of institutions to participate in such initiatives where not required legally, and as such result in few examples that can be explored. Furthermore, the models discussed provide general insights, but do not look at cross-border sharing. All occur within the same jurisdiction, which is opposed to the very nature of ML/TF. Irrespective of its future form, further research into these barriers to participation, a more in-depth examination of how these challenges have been or could be addressed, and an analysis of models that may be applied across jurisdictions will be valuable, for the reasons outlined.

References

Banco BPN, Banco Bilbao, Banco Português and Others v Autoridade de Concorrência (Antitrust Authority) (Court of Justice of the European Union, C-298/22, ECLI:EU:2024:638, 29 July 2024)

Basel Institute of Governance (2022) Annual report

Chadderton P (2025) FATF and the conundrum of public-private sector intelligence and information sharing. In: Goldbarsht D, de Koker L, Ferrill J (eds) The financial war on crime and terrorism: opportunities and challenges. Springer, Cham

Chatzidiannis P et al (2023) Privacy-enhancing technologies for financial data sharing. arXiv. https://doi.org/10.48550/arXiv.2306.10200

Council Directive 2024/1640 of the European Parliament and of the council of 31 May 2024 on the mechanisms to be put in place by Member States for the prevention of the use of the financial system for the purposes of money laundering or terrorist financing [2024] OJ L 2024/1624

Ferrill J, de Koker L, Goldbarsht D (2025) Financial crime prevention in an age of paradox. In: Goldbarsht D, de Koker L, Ferrill J (eds) The financial war on crime and terrorism: opportunities and challenges. Springer, Cham

FATF (2016–2017) Consolidated FATF Standards on Information Sharing, FATF, Paris, updated November 2017

FATF (2017) Guidance on private sector information sharing, FATF, Paris www.fatfgafi.org/publications/fatfrecommendations/documents/guidance-information-sharing.html

Financial Action Task Force (2018) Professional money laundering

Financial Action Task Force (2021) Stocktake on data pooling, collaborative analytics and data protection. FATF, Paris. https://www.fatf-gafi.org/publications/digitaltransformation/documents/data-pooling-collaborativeanalytics-data-protection.html

Financial Action Task Force (2022) Partnering in the fight against financial crime: data protection, technology and private sector information sharing. FATF, Paris. https://www.fatf-gafi.org/en/publications/Digitaltransformation/Partnering-in-the-fight-against-financial-crime.html
Gamut T, Sekiguchi Y (7 June 2024) MUFG Bank, brokerages face possible penalty for sharing client information. Nikkei Aşia. https://asia.nikkei.com/Business/Finance/MUFG-bank-brokerages-face-possible-penalty-for-sharing-client-info
Goldbarsht D (2017) Who's the legislator anyway? How the FATF's global norms reshape Australian counter terrorist financing laws. Fed Law Rev 45(1):127–151. https://doi.org/10.1177/0067205X1704500106. (Original work published 2017)
Goldbarsht D (2022) Artificial intelligence and financial integrity: the case of anti-money laundering. J Bank Finance Law Pract 33(1):21
Goldbarsht D (2023) Leveraging AI to mitigate money laundering risks in the banking system. In: Bednarz Z, Zalnieriute M (eds) Money, power, and AI: automated banks and automated states. Cambridge University Press, pp 51–69
Goldbarsht D, de Koker L (2022) From paper money to digital assets: financial technology and the risks of criminal abuse. In: Goldbarsht D, de Koker L (eds) Financial technology and the law. Law, governance and technology series, vol 47. Springer, Cham
Hardouin P (2009) Banks, governance and public-private partnership in preventing and confronting organised crime, corruption, and terrorism financing. J Financ Crime 16(2):204
KPMG Advisory N.V. (2023) Joined forces: towards a more effective and efficient fulfilment of the gatekeeper role in the Netherlands (Report 2023)
Levi M, Reuter P, Halliday T (2018) Can the AML system be evaluated without better data? Crime Law Soc Change 69(2):308
Maxwell NJ (2021) FFIS briefing paper – Canada in context
Ministry of Finance (2024) National anti-money laundering strategy Singapore (Report, 2024)
Murr A, Donovan T, Yee Man Y (2023) The role of the private sector in detecting and disrupting terrorist financing activities. In: El Khoury C (ed) Countering the financing of terrorism: good practice to enhance effectivenesss. International Monetary Fund Publication Services
Royal United Services Institute (2017) The role of financial information-sharing partnerships in the disruption of crime
Royal United Services Institute (2024) The case for national policy-makers to unleash the potential of payments infrastructure to identify economic crime risk. https://www.future-fis.com/uploads/3/7/9/4/3794525/ffis_-_payments_policy_discussion_paper_1_-_unleashing_the_potential_of_payments_infrastructure_to_identify_economic_crime_risk.pdf
Thony J-F (2007) Use of information exchange in criminal matters to combating money laundering and financing of terrorism. In: Working together: improving regulatory cooperation and information exchange. International Monetary Fund Publication Services
Turkington M (2020) Compliance, effectiveness, and the rise of the public-private partnership. J Money Laund Control 23(2):282
U.S. Treasury (2020) FinCEN Section 314 (b) information sheet (Report, 2020)
Westmore K, Miller S, Frost J, Foltean D (2022) *Enabling Cross-Sector Data-Sharing to Better Prevent and Detect Scams*, RUSI Conference Report, September 2022.
Wright A, Meier S (2021) Analysing FinCEN's proposed regulation relating to AML and KYC Laws. Conference paper, 25th Financial Cryptography Conference 2021, FC 2021 International Workshops

Dr. Doron Goldbarsht , LLB, LLM (HUJI), PHD (UNSW) is an Associate Professor at Macquarie Law School, the Academic Head of the Graduate Certificate in Financial Integrity Law and the Founder and Director of the Financial Integrity Hub (FIH). With over 20 years of expertise in anti-money laundering (AML) and counterterrorist financing (CTF), he has co-edited several books on financial crime and compliance, including Financial Crime and the Law: Identifying and Mitigating Risks (Springer 2024) and Financial Technology and the Law: Combating Financial

Crime (Springer, 2022). Certified as a lawyer in both Israel and Australia, Doron also provides expert opinions to government and private sector in litigation, advising on financial crime and regulatory matters.

Timothy Goodrick is a Partner in KPMG's Financial Crime practice, specialising in leading projects to design and implement effective systems to combat financial crime, with a particular focus on financial crime transformation. Prior to his current role, Tim spent 5 years with the Financial Action Task Force (FATF) in France and South Korea, most recently serving as the Acting Director at the FATF's Training and Research Institute. Before joining the FATF, Tim held the position of Director of Financial Crime at the Australian Attorney-General's Department (2007–2012) and previously worked at AUSTRAC in policy and compliance. He has represented Australia and the FATF at various international fora including the OECD, United Nations, Asia-Pacific Group (APG), Eurasian Group (EAG), Inter Governmental Action Group against Money Laundering in West Africa (GIABA), Action Group against Money Laundering in Central Africa (GABAC), and the Basel Institute.

Network Analytics and Generative Artificial Intelligence: A Hybrid Approach to Money Laundering Detection

Milind Tiwari

Abstract This chapter focuses on the potential integration of graph databases and generative artificial intelligence (GenAI), such as large language models (LLMs), for enhancement of anti-money laundering (AML) detection efforts. The explored methodology is primarily conceptual, outlining a framework for how these technological advancements could be combined, rather than detailing currently deployed systems. The methodology involves focusing on the growing role of LLMs in regulatory compliance and graph databases in uncovering money laundering schemes, thus paving the way for supporting an agile and proactive AML infrastructure. Graph databases facilitate investigators to identify hidden relationships within a network of illicit entities, exposing hidden relationships across entities. By leveraging the capabilities of GenAI, organisations could potentially map these complex relationships between entities in real-time and draw actionable insights. Moreover, such an integration would allow AML practitioners to visualise, interpret, and disrupt illicit networks with unprecedented precision. The integration, while offering enormous opportunity, underscores the importance of addressing challenges including data biases, ethical considerations, and the need for interdisciplinary collaboration to fully utilise capabilities of technological innovations in combatting financial crime.

1 Introduction

Money laundering involves giving illicit funds a legitimate appearance. According to the United Nations Office on Drugs and Crime (UNODC) 2000 Convention, it involves the conversion or transfer of an asset while knowingly concealing the

M. Tiwari (✉)
Australian Graduate School of Policing and Security, Charles Sturt University, Canberra, ACT, Australia
e-mail: mtiwari@csu.edu.au

D. Goldbarsht et al. (eds.), *The Financial War on Crime and Terrorism*, European Yearbook of International Economic Law,
https://doi.org/10.1007/978-3-032-06360-1_5

criminal source or aiding the criminal involved in committing the crime.[1] The objective is to obscure the nature and origin of the illicit income generated and integrate it into the financial system without drawing attention from tax authorities or law enforcement agencies.[2] In addition to traditional underground activities such as cybercrime, corruption, and drug trafficking, quasi-legal activities, including the concealment of income from public authorities (e.g., tax evasion), contribute to the shadow economy and money laundering.[3]

Traditionally, the process of money laundering was classified into three stages, namely, placement, layering and integration.[4] Placement, the initial stage, involves introduction of funds generated from illicit sources into the financial system. It is at this stage that the criminal proceeds are most vulnerable to detection. Common methods comprise of depositing money in small amounts into bank accounts (a process sometimes referred to as "smurfing" or "structuring") or purchase of goods which can be easily resold. Following placement, layering seeks to obscure the origin of such illicit funds through a web of transactions. This can be accomplished by the transfer of funds in related accounts or across jurisdictions, converting cash into other monetary instruments, investment in real estate or other such legitimate business, or into financial securities. The final stage in the process, integration, reintroduces the laundered funds into the economy through normal business operations or seemingly legitimate transactions, making it difficult to distinguish between the legitimately derived and the laundered income. However, while this three-stage model may still hold some value for understanding sophisticated schemes, the analysis has been criticised for being overly simplistic and not universally applicable.[5]

Various organisations have provided estimates to direct attention towards the scale of money laundering globally.[6] For example, the International Monetary Fund (IMF) has estimated that money laundering ranges between 2% and 5% of the world's annual gross domestic product (GDP), equating to around USD 1.5 trillion.[7] Similarly, the Australian Transaction Reports and Analysis Centre (AUSTRAC) in 2011 reported the level of money laundering to be between AUD 10 and AUD 15 billion per annum.[8] By 2020, it was estimated that, after five rounds of international flows in 2014, the amount of money being laundered was estimated to be 3% of global GDP or USD 2.3 trillion.[9] The magnitude of the problem is demonstrated by high-profile cases such as the "Troika Laundromat", uncovered by the Organized

[1] UNODC (2004) United Nations convention against transnational organized crime and the protocols thereto.

[2] Compin (2008), p. 591–602.

[3] Schneider (2010), p. 473–486; Schneider and Windischbauer (2008), p. 387–404.

[4] Buchanan (2004), p. 115–127.

[5] Cassella (2018), p. 494–497.

[6] However, as in the chapter by Ferrill et al. (2025) in this book, these numbers are disputable.

[7] FATF (2012).

[8] Singh and Best (2019).

[9] Ferwerda et al. (2020), p. 18552.

Crime and Corruption Reporting Project (OCCRP), involving the movement of billions of US dollars of illicit Russian funds to offshore companies.[10] Additionally, between 2010 and 2014, shell companies incorporated in the United Kingdom have been identified to be associated with laundering GBP 80 billion of stolen money.[11] Money laundering poses a significant threat to the global economy, with its proceeds often utilised to fund further criminal activities and undermining the integrity of financial systems worldwide.

Going back a step, the Financial Action Task Force (FATF) was formed in 1989 by The Group of Seven (G7). Initially focused on combatting money laundering, the FATF expanded its scope by defining money laundering to include proceeds derived from other illicit sources such as bribery and fraud, embezzlement, illegal arms sales, and insider trading. Over time, to curb this growing problem, its mandate has been regularly widened to include activities such as combatting the financing of terrorism.[12] The FATF continues to serve as a vanguard in combatting money laundering by providing critical guidance to governmental bodies worldwide. However, it is widely acknowledged that in the current economic environment, regulators are struggling to stay ahead of fraudulent schemes, and financial institutions are being challenged to ensure that they identify and stop criminal activities while serving legitimate customers effectively and efficiently.[13] The issue is compounded by the sophistication of money launderers who continuously adapt their methods to exploit vulnerabilities in the financial system.[14]

These challenges can be attributed to the fact that money laundering occurs via the exploitation of networks of disguised relationships, making it challenging and time-consuming to untangle the networks.[15] These networks include various methods of placing money, its movement between actors in the financial system, and the organisational entities and their owners involved in the process. Shell companies, in particular, frequently play a transitory role to receive and distribute money within these networks.[16]

While shell companies have legitimate uses such as facilitating reverse mergers, serving as holding companies, or for protecting small entrepreneurs from bankruptcy risks, they have also become instruments for laundering dirty money.[17] Shell companies enable illicit funds to appear legitimate while concealing the identity of true beneficial owners. As a result, they have become popular tools for illicit arms dealers, drug cartels, corrupt politicians, terrorists, and cyber-criminals.[18] The ease

[10] OCCRP (2019).

[11] Cowdock (2017).

[12] Unger (2013), p. 658–676.

[13] Pol (2018a), p. 215–230; Pol (2018b), p. 294–308; Ray (2015).

[14] Unger (2013), p. 658–676.

[15] Tiwari et al. (2023), p. 474–487; Tiwari et al. (2025), p. 100123.

[16] Findley et al. (2013), p. 657–693; Singh (2010), p. 459–484.

[17] Floros and Sapp (2011).

[18] Nougayrède (2019).

of establishing these entities, the trans-nationality involved, and minimal compliance with the FATF standards have posed significant challenge for law enforcement authorities in countering crime and corruption.[19]

Therefore, it is critical to detect shell companies that are employed to launder the proceeds of illicit activities. The continuously evolving regulatory landscape, coupled with numerous instances of money laundering violations, has highlighted the need for improved technological solutions in managing anti-money laundering efforts.[20] An improvement in data analytics attributed to technological innovations would assist investigators to focus more on suspicious activities and less on false positives.[21] For instance, the representation of data in the form of graphs (i.e., networks of nodes and edges representing entities and their connections) would establish the presence, if any, of a relational structure between entities (e.g., individuals, companies, accounts), and graph computations can provide a stronger relational inductive bias.[22] Such a visualisation of relational structures facilitates the identification of patterns and anomalies that might otherwise be obscured in tabular data. Graph analysis, in conjunction with the use of large language models (LLMs), may enable investigators to effortlessly infer ownership and relationships, such as common or joint ownership of businesses; this may mean prompt detection of illicit shells.

Subsequently, this chapter explores the potential of integrating graph databases with generative artificial intelligence (GenAI), including LLMs, to enhance anti-money laundering (AML) detection efforts. Acknowledging the challenges posed by limited data science application, this work demonstrates how proactive AML infrastructure could analyse hidden relationships between illicit entities to stay ahead of actors using these entities for illicit purposes. The contribution of this chapter is twofold: first, it demonstrates the potential of incorporating graph databases and GenAI for gaining insights in complex financial networks; second, it emphasises the need for interdisciplinary collaboration, to ensure responsible and effective application of these technologies in combatting financial crime. Such an integration would facilitate AML practitioners and investigators in detecting, visualising, and disrupting illicit networks more effectively, thus improving responses to combat money laundering. Key takeaways associated with the benefits and challenges of this integrated approach will be highlighted throughout the analysis.

The rest of the chapter is structured as follows: the next section provides an overview of GenAI and LLMs, followed by a discussion on using graph databases in conjunction with LLMs. Subsequently, an explanation into the data utilised and the graph database schema adopted for analysis is provided. This is followed by an analysis of the results, a discussion, and finally, the conclusion.

---

[19] Findley et al. (2015), p. 146–161; Martini et al. (2019).

[20] Ray (2015).

[21] Newman (2007), p. 31–34.

[22] Battaglia et al. (2018); Schweitzer et al. (2009), p. 422.

2 GenAI and LLMs

In an age of digital innovation, the increasing prominence of artificial intelligence (AI) acts as a key factor in transforming numerous industries. Within this context, GenAI, that employs machine learning, neural networks, and other related techniques to create new content, has garnered significant attention. Its application ranges from generating text, images, and music,[23] with a continuous advancement in its functionalities. For instance, LLMs which started off as generating text,[24] are evolving into multimodal models capable of creating videos and analysing images. Some examples of these include Gemini (Google) and ChatGPT (OpenAI). While these models are forecasted to contribute significantly to global GDP and productivity, their significance in the context of this chapter lies in their analytical capabilities rather than their economic impact.[25]

LLMs, in particular, have exhibited significant potential in numerous natural language processing tasks. This can be attributed to these models relying on corpus of text databases and self-supervising, pre-trained technology to tackle complex problems by predicting what word is likely to follow in a sequence of words. The more extensive training they have through data, the better they become in anticipating what is to follow. Consequently, they are extensively utilised for tasks such as to converse, find information, generate content, or organise data. By automating complex tasks, these models are likely to have profound implications for businesses and society, thus enhancing productivity and efficiency.[26]

As a result, their application has become widespread across sectors, such as banking, e-commerce, and tourism.[27] For instance, in the field of food science and technology, LLMs, such as the Generative Pre-Trained (GPT) series have gained traction owing to their ability to perform data analysis and interpretation.[28] They are valuable for predictive analytics, facilitating the detection of contaminants and assessment of food safety risks by exploring past datasets and reports.[29] This represents a shift towards the use of computational analytics in place of traditional microbiological and chemical testing methods, thus transforming LLMs into a critical tool in pre-emptive risk identification.

The banking and financial services sector, a critical interface for businesses, consumers, and organisations, generates large volumes of data. This data-intensive environment presents numerous opportunities for leveraging AI, especially in AML and compliance. Financial institutions are increasingly exposed to money laundering risks and are already exploring and, in some cases, deploying AI models to

[23] Ooi et al. (2023).

[24] Dwivedi et al. (2023).

[25] Nishant et al. (2020), p. 102104.

[26] Nishant et al. (2020), p. 102104.

[27] Peruchini et al. (2024).

[28] Ma et al. (2024).

[29] Wang et al. (2022), p. 416–434.

tackle this risk and associated compliance burdens. One notable example is Swedbank, which has employed generative adversarial neural networks to prevent fraud and money laundering.[30]

Similarly, these models can be leveraged to develop sophisticated investment strategies for optimum portfolio returns by accounting for numerous factors, such as asset allocation, market conditions, and risk tolerance. For instance, BloombergGPT, a model trained on a variety of data, has been developed to provide financial services.[31] The integration of these models facilitates an improvement in customer services while reducing costs and risks. Furthermore, they can streamline time-consuming and repetitive tasks, facilitate staff training, and allow workforce to focus on innovative and strategic initiatives. This leads to increased accuracy, efficiency, and productivity.

These are just some applications of these models; they have broader applications, including adherence to regulations by parsing, analysing, and extracting insights from regulatory texts, thus aiding organisations in compliance with evolving regulatory standards. Furthermore, they can process information from numerous sources for identifying inconsistencies indicative of wrongdoing.[32] However, like with any development, there are challenges: their effective application depends upon addressing issues such as data biases, ownership, misinformation, and ethical use.[33] At times, these models generate responses which may be misleading: a tendency that has been referred to as AI hallucination. Consequently, efforts are being made to address this, including incorporation of GPT capabilities with external online sources.[34] Despite such advances, concerns associated with accountability, fairness, and transparency are still major concerns that need to be addressed. Moreover, there is a need for collaboration between AI experts, relevant experts from different fields such as criminologists, investigators, and other industry practitioners to harness the full potential of LLMs and overcome its vulnerabilities.

From a financial crime perspective, these models provide the opportunities to understand patterns of fraud and other financial crimes via identification of anomalies in transactional data.[35] It becomes important to leverage upon the benefits of LLMs to detect and prevent suspicious activities given the prevailing vulnerabilities of financial institutions to be exploited for wrongdoing. Given the growth in arguments supporting the use of model-based approaches against rule-based approaches,[36] the aforementioned example of Swedbank's reported use of generative adversarial

[30] Newman (2007), p. 31–34; Ray (2015).

[31] Mogaji et al. (2021), p. 101711.

[32] Ooi et al. (2023).

[33] See the chapter by Walters (2025) in this book for more on the challenges associated with the application of AI.

[34] Piktus (2023), p. 465–466.

[35] Ooi et al. (2023).

[36] Van Vlasselaer et al. (2017), p. 3090–3110.

neural networks serves as an illustration. Motivated by this, the present work outlines an approach utilising a combination of graph databases and LLMs.

3 Graph Databases and LLMs

A network can be understood as a specific type of relational structure linking persons, objects, or events. The elements constituting this network are called actors or nodes, while the connections between these nodes in a network are described as relationships.[37] For example, the graph data model in Neo4J consists of nodes (referring to actors or entities), relationships (connections between nodes), properties (attributes describing nodes and relationships), and labels (naming conventions adopted for nodes and relationships).[38]

Recently, there has been a growing interest in identifying economic networks in trade and products, and even in detecting fraudulent companies.[39] For this purpose, graph analysis techniques have proven useful for identifying suspicious individuals, assessing existing network relationships, identifying unusual changes, analysing geospatial dispersions, and recognising anomalous network structure, all while handling a large volume of data efficiently.[40] Moreover, the ability to visualise dynamic and complex datasets as graphs facilitate users to gain a comprehensive overview, filter, select, and investigate network details. Graph database technologies further enhance the management of interrelated and densely connected datasets by enabling development of predictive models and recognition of patterns through traversal queries.[41] They utilise graph models to store, manage, and update relationships and data with free and flexible schemas.[42]

Building on prior research, the works of Tiwari et al. (2023, 2025) have advanced the development of models for detecting illicit shell companies by analysing network of entities engaged in unlawful activities.[43] Neo4J, a graph database platform, was employed to construct graphs from the data collected. This platform employs a query language called 'cypher', which offers flexibility in setting up the data model. Neo4J's features, such as online transaction processing on graph data (OLTP) and graph analytics, enable users to assess hidden relationships in the data and draw conclusions accordingly.[44] These works extend the idea of developing a detection

[37] Fitina et al. (2010), p. 1.

[38] Miller (2013); Van Bruggen (2014).

[39] Barabási and Albert (1999), p. 509; Pacini et al. (2016), p. A42-A65; Schweitzer et al. (2009), p. 422; Vitali et al. (2011), p. e25995.

[40] Liu et al. (2016), p. 33–46.

[41] Miller (2013).

[42] Huang and Dong (2013).

[43] Tiwari et al. (2023), p. 474–487; Tiwari et al. (2025), p. 100123.

[44] Van Bruggen (2014).

system for various kinds of fraudulent activities,[45] focusing specifically on shell companies involved in illicit operations. Within these networks, firms may exert influence over other firms through direct or indirect relationships that span multiple jurisdictions, thus making it critical to analyse these complex networks to uncover the structures of control and understand its broader implications.

With the advent of GenAI and the advances made, LLMs have demonstrated potential in handling graph-structured data tasks. Their ability to process and interpret such data continues to be an area of active research. LLMs can interact with how graph data is structured to perform tasks related to both structural and semantic understanding.[46] Structural understanding tasks include identifying significant nodes, calculating centrality metrics,[47] and determining diameters,[48] while semantic understanding tasks comprise of knowledge graph question answering,[49] node classification, and graph classification.[50] One such semantic understanding task that can be performed by LLMs is generation of graph query language, such as cypher in the case of Neo4J, enabling users to extract information pertaining to graph databases.

However, there are challenges associated with understanding graph-structured data for query generation. For instance, graph data is unorganised and complex; it consists of nodes representing entities or concepts, and edges expressing relationships between them. This makes it difficult for LLMs to directly handle graph data. Moreover, there is a wide range of graph-related tasks, and each task requires different approaches and prompting techniques. Finally, LLMs typically handle text-based input, whereas graph data requires conversion to a suitable format. Therefore, LLMs need to understand the relationships between entities and attributes to formulate accurate queries,[51] requiring graph data to be converted into a graph description language (GDL) that LLMs can understand. One such example of adapting LLMs to specific graph database scenarios is that of Liang et al. (2024) who demonstrated the integration of graph database information with LLMs.[52] The authors, acknowledging that different LLMs exhibit varying performance in cypher query generation,[53] concluded that performance of these models is improved when provided with relevant graph database schema which informs the generation of appropriate GQL.

The following section outlines the data used and the schema adopted for importing the data on graph database, namely Neo4J, consistent with the works of Tiwari

---

[45] Bangcharoensap et al. (2015); Battaglia et al. (2018); Van Vlasselaer et al. (2017), p. 3090–3110.

[46] Guo et al. (2023).

[47] Diviák et al. (2019), p. 274–297; Malinick et al. (2013), p. 148–158; Marsden (2002), p. 407–422; Salavati et al. (2019), p. 36–45; Chung et al. (1994), p. 351–387.

[48] Munir and Aldini (2024).

[49] Huang et al. (2019), p. 105–113; Zhang et al. (2018), p. 31.

[50] Bhagat et al. (2011), p. 115–148.

[51] Guo et al. (2023); Munir and Aldini (2024).

[52] Liang et al. (2024).

[53] Liang et al. (2024); Munir and Aldini (2024).

et al. (2023, 2025).[54] Appendix 1 includes the codes for importing the data on the graph database platform. These codes were also used to inform OpenAI's ChatGPT-4o model of the database schema, enabling it to generate additional cypher queries for investigating the dataset.

4 Data and Methodology

The information on the entities used for analysis in this chapter were utilised in the 2017 report called "Hiding in Plain Sight: How UK Companies are used to Launder Corrupt Wealth"[55] as well as in the works of Tiwari et al. (2023, 2025).[56] These entities were used as corporate veils to launder illicit funds and hide the real beneficial owners. While some entities were established to facilitate a wide range of illicit activities, laundering of funds was the central theme for all the entities. Subsequently, the development of the property graph database model incorporated a wide range of information from publicly available data sources, such as OpenCorporates, EveryPolitician, OpenSanctions, UK Companies House Disqualified Directors, and the Financial Secrecy Index.

The information considered for the development of property graph database model included variables such as company status, incorporation date, dissolution date, availability of previous company names, number of previous company names, tenure of company previous names, registered company address, instances of change in registered address, number of previous addresses, tenure of previous addresses, industry codes of the companies, change in latest available cash balances, current assets, current liabilities and fixed assets of companies, total number of executives for each company, and other basic details including their nationality. Finally, information on the ultimate beneficial owners was also considered.

The rationale for considering such a comprehensive set of variables is as follows:

- Previous Name: Entities change their names for legitimate reasons; however, at times, it can also be linked to criminal activities. It may indicate past association with illicit activities, and this approach is consistent with the findings of Lee and Palstra (2018), who suggest that frequent name changes of entities should raise red flags and warrant further investigation.[57]
- Company Status: The focus on whether the company is still in operation or has been dissolved is to comprehend whether an entity was dissolved after undertaking its illicit purpose or whether it continued to operate afterward. This is consistent with Ravenda et al., who stated that mafia-controlled firms (MCFs) are often

[54] Tiwari et al. (2023), p. 474–487; Tiwari et al. (2025), p. 100123.

[55] Cowdock (2017).

[56] Tiwari et al. (2023), p. 474–487; Tiwari et al. (2025), p. 100123.

[57] Lee and Palstra (2018).

liquidated once the purpose of such entities is accomplished to prevent detection from authorities.[58]

- Period of Operation: The lifespan of an entity, defined as the period between incorporation and dissolution dates, can provide insights into whether an entity was used for carrying out illegitimate activities. This hypothesis aligns with Ravenda et al. (2015), who concluded that Mafia-controlled firms (MCFs) are likely to have shorter lifespans as they are often liquidated once the purpose of such entities is accomplished to prevent detection from authorities.[59]
- Nationality of Directors: The integration of corporate governance variables, such as nationality of directors, helps to determine if there exists a trend or pattern between the corporate structure of illicit entities from the ones being used for legitimate purposes. The choice of this variable is motivated by Lee and Palstra (2018), who found that high-profile money-laundering scandals involved people from specific regions.[60] The academic literature has extensively linked corporate governance characteristics, such as board structure, to misconduct.[61] However, sophisticated corporate governance variables are less applicable here due to limited data availability.
- Appointment of Directors: The information about the number of companies in which directors hold executive positions could be a useful indicator of suspicious activity. It is presumed that an executive holding appointment in five or more companies should raise suspicion, as managing multiple entities effectively is unlikely. This aligns with the assertion of Lee and Palstra (2018) who state that such cases may involve nominee directors acting on behalf of true owners.[62]
- Ultimate Ownership Information (Person of Significant Control Information—PSC Information): Entities that provide information about the ultimate beneficial owners are considered relatively safer than those that do not. This aligns with the findings of Singh who states that shell companies established for illicit purposes often obscure their true ownership.[63] Lee and Palstra (2018) also emphasised that entities established for illicit purposes avoid disclosing information about true beneficial owners by resorting to methods including declaration that a company has no beneficial owners, using an ineligible foreign company as a beneficial owner, and using circular ownership structures or nominees.[64]
- Financial Statement Information: The incorporation of variables related to financial statement information to distinguish between legitimate and illicit entities is

[58] Ravenda et al. (2018).

[59] Ravenda et al. (2018).

[60] Lee and Palstra (2018).

[61] Chapple et al. (2018), p. 222–242; Holtz and Sarlo Neto (2014), p. 255–266; Ndofor et al. (2015), p. 1774–1797.

[62] Lee and Palstra (2018).

[63] Singh (2010), p. 459–484.

[64] Lee and Palstra (2018).

consistent with Ravenda et al. (2015).[65] They utilised a logistic regression model for classification of MCFs from non MCFs using various financial variables. Furthermore, within variables depicting the financial position, considering information on both assets and the availability of cash is consistent with the work of Floros and Sapp (2011) and Singh (2010), who noted that shell companies are likely to be less capital-intensive and have lower total assets because of the absence of a real business operations.[66]

Figure 1 provides an overview of the methodology utilised for this chapter. It illustrates how publicly available information from diverse sources is collated, which is then imported into the Neo4J graph database platform. It provides an opportunity, based on human expertise, to explore the dataset and uncover insights. However, the cypher queries employed to import the dataset on graph database platforms, such as Neo4J, can be used to inform LLMs, such as ChatGPT 4o and DeekSeep R1, about the graph database structure, facilitating the generation of additional investigative queries. The combination of human expertise and LLMs provides an additional layer of inquiry into the dataset, enhancing the investigation of hidden relationships within illicit networks of entities. Additionally, this approach opens future opportunities to generate additional graph algorithm scores which can be used to refine

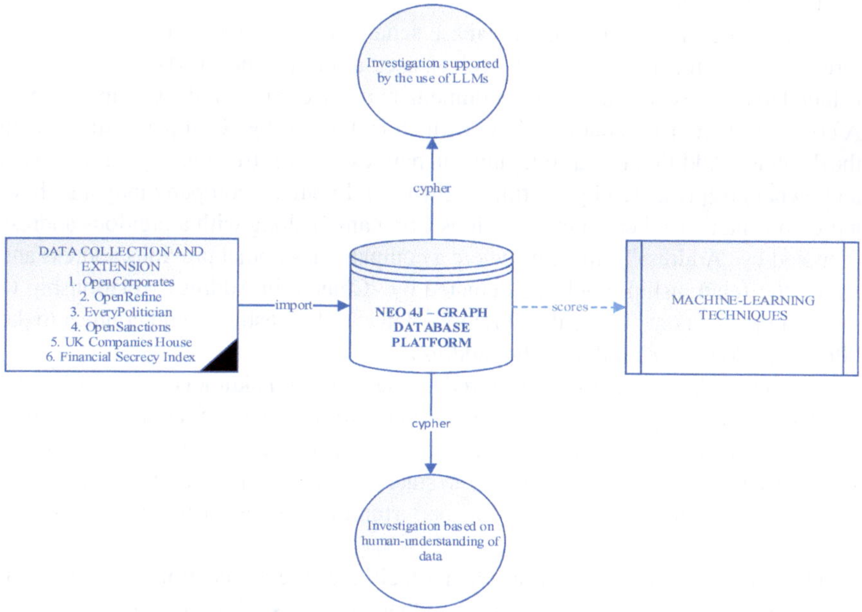

Fig. 1 Overview of methodology

65 Ravenda et al. (2015), p. 23–39.

66 Floros and Sapp (2011), p. 850–867; Singh (2010), p. 459–484.

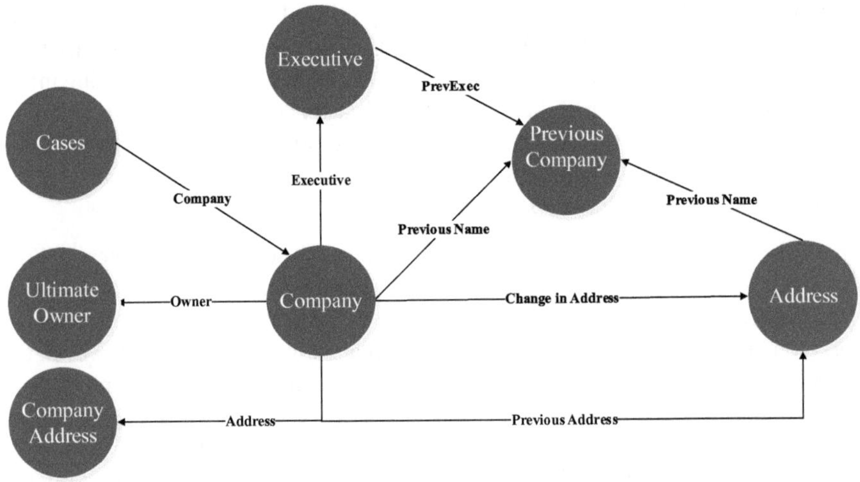

Fig. 2 Database schema for the data model, which is consistent with prior research of Tiwari et al. (2023, 2025)

classification models, improving their accuracy and effectiveness in developing better detection models.

Figure 2 describes the graph database schema of how the data has been structured in Neo4J for investigation as well as used to inform the LLMs. The root node is labelled as "Cases", and it has an immediate connection with the Company node. A company is registered at an address which is denoted by "Company Address" in the database. Additionally, a company will have executives (denoted by "Executive") and owners (represented by "Ultimate Owner"). Finally, a company may also have a previous name (indicated by "Previous Company") along with a previous address (denoted by "Address"). In cases where a company has both a previous address and name, the relationship would be depicted by "Change in Address" relationship to the "Company" node, while the "PreviousName" relationship would connect to the "Previous Company" at that earlier address.

This network construction is inspired by the views of Fakhraei et al. (2015), who emphasise that integrating the multi-relational nature of networks enhances predictive performance.[67] Furthermore, the network construction is consistent with the views of Drakopoulos et al. (2015), who state that graph databases not only act as a means for graph storage but offer opportunities to perform graph analytics techniques.[68]

The above-described database schema facilitates the application of graph algorithms on the dataset and to draw insights that are discussed in the next section.

[67] Fakhraei et al. (2015), p. 1769–1778.

[68] Drakopoulos et al. (2015).

5 Results: Uncovering Relational Insights and the Role of LLMs

The utilisation of graph database platforms, such as Neo4J, facilitates a detailed examination of the network of illicit entities implicated in money laundering schemes and allows for an examination of critical links within such networks. The insights gained by identifying links between entities in these illicit networks can assist investigative journalists and compliance professionals in disrupting the flow of dirty money. The central hypothesis underpinning such an analysis is that entities in these networks have hidden links, which can be identified using a graph database to store and analyse publicly available data. For example, in line with the views of Van Bruggen (2014) and Memon and Wiil (2014) on the effectiveness of GQL such as cypher, Neo4J was used to examine networks in data leaks, such as the Panama Papers and Paradise Papers.[69] Investigative journalists employed it to identify hidden patterns.[70] Similarly, graph analysis has been employed by Liu et al. (2016) to detect suspicious activities in large health-care datasets.[71]

For the dataset analysed in this chapter, which is based on publicly available information concerning entities previously identified in money laundering schemes,[72] a range of cypher queries was executed to extract pertinent information and illustrate the capabilities of graph analysis.

- *Disclosure of beneficial ownership:* On querying the database to find companies with ultimate beneficial owners, it was revealed that only 51 in the dataset disclosed such beneficial ownership information. Lack of information disclosure can be suspicious suggesting the need for further investigation.[73]
- *Common addresses:* Querying the dataset for the number of companies located at a postal address identified instances of multiple entities sharing the same address, with one address hosting 16 entities.
- *Patterns of executive appointments:* Analysing the dataset to determine the number of executive appointments held by a director from a particular nationality uncovered one individual serving as a director in 139 entities, while another held directorship positions in 610 entities, suggesting the need for further investigation.

Furthermore, this chapter explored the potential of leveraging LLMs, such as ChatGPT 4o and DeepSeek R1,[74] to enhance the depth and effectiveness of such investigations. By providing the database schema to these LLMs, new investigative

[69] Van Bruggen (2014); Memon and Wiil (2014), p. 107–114.

[70] International Consortium of Investigative Journalists (n.d.); Kubzansky (2018); Obermayer et al. (2016).

[71] Liu et al. (2016), p. 33–46.

[72] Cowdock (2017); Tiwari et al. (2023), p. 474–487; Tiwari et al. (2025), p. 100123.

[73] Lee and Palstra (2018); Singh (2010), p. 459–484.

[74] Guo et al. (2025).

cypher queries were generated, exhibiting an augmented approach to data exploration. This integration, in line with the works of Guo et al. (2023) and Munir and Aldini (2024), offers potential to come up with new queries to investigate the dataset.[75]

Examples of insights gained through LLM-generated queries include:

- *Entities with high executive counts:* Upon querying with an LLM-suggested query, it was identified that one of the entities in the dataset had 32 executives.
- *Pathfinding between entities:* The combination of human expertise with LLMs, offers opportunities to run pathfinding algorithms between entities within the network. The shortest path algorithm was executed to extract the shortest path between a given pair of entities. For instance, Fig. 3, exhibits the traversal of relationships in the graph network to draw out the shortest path among two entities in the network, Companies BL and ME. This visualisation highlights how graph databases can quickly reveal indirect connections that might not be obvious otherwise.

Figure 4, outlines the generation of cypher queries upon introducing the database schema to a LLM model, DeepSeek R1 in this case, using GQL. It outlines the critical need for integration of LLMs with human expertise enhance the effectiveness of investigations.

These results, while derived from a specific dataset of known illicit entities, serve to demonstrate the analytical power of graph databases and the potential augmentation offered by LLMs. The ability to visualise complex relationships, identify outliers, such as directors with high number of appointments, and uncover hidden connections, such as through shared addresses, are key takeaways from this analytical approach. The generation of novel queries by LLMs further suggests a pathway to more dynamic and comprehensive investigations, especially for users who may not be experts with programming languages.

6 Discussion

The findings presented underscore the persistent challenge posed by the global proliferation of shell companies and their role in facilitating corruption, money laundering, and tax evasion.[76] While there has been a progress in the implementation of intergovernmental measures, such as implementation of cross-border information sharing and beneficial ownership registries, these measures face challenges including resistance from certain jurisdictions, variable enforcement on part of national regulators and law enforcement agencies, and issues pertaining to data quality

[75] Guo et al. (2023); Munir and Aldini (2024).

[76] Findley et al. (2013), p. 657–693; Nougayrède (2019).

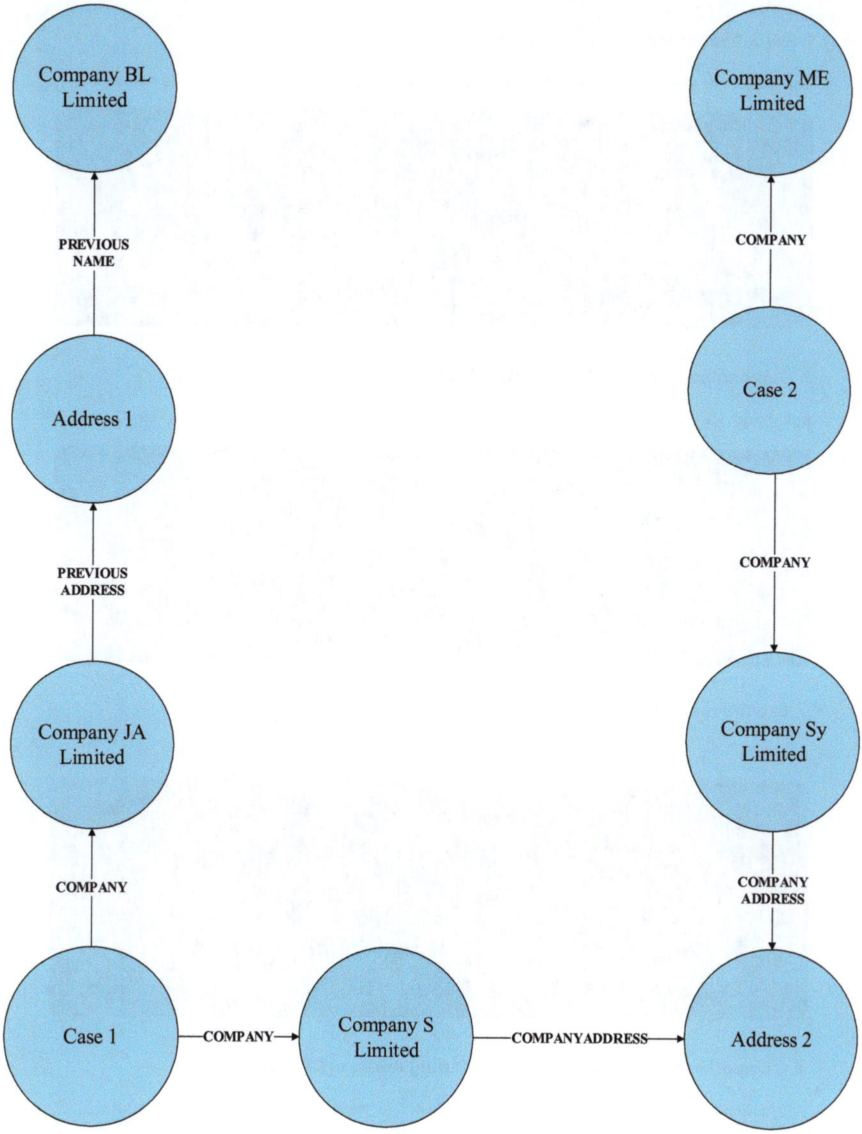

Fig. 3 Shortest path between Companies BL and ME

1. Executives Linked to Previous Addresses

Scenario: Find executives who were active during the tenure of a company's previous address.

```cypher
MATCH (c:Company)-[:PREVIOUSADDRESS]->(a:Address)-[]->(p:PreviousCompany)
WHERE c.companypreviousnames <> "NA"
WITH c, p
MATCH (c)-[:EXECUTIVE]->(e:Executive)
WHERE e.tenureend <> "NA" AND
      e.tenurestart >= p.StartofTenure AND e.tenureend <= p.EndofTenure
MERGE (e)-[:PREVEXEC]->(p)
RETURN c, e, p;
```

2. Companies with Executives Active During Previous Names

Scenario: Identify executives who were active during a company's previous name tenure.

```cypher
MATCH (c:Company)-[:PREVIOUSNAME]->(p:PreviousCompany)
WHERE c.companypreviousnames <> "NA"
WITH c, p
MATCH (c)-[:EXECUTIVE]->(e:Executive)
WHERE e.tenureend <> "NA" AND
      e.tenurestart >= p.StartofTenure AND e.tenureend <= p.EndofTenure
MERGE (e)-[:PREVEXEC]->(p)
RETURN c, e, p;
```

3. Executives Linked to Multiple Previous Addresses

Scenario: Find executives associated with multiple previous addresses of a company.

```cypher
MATCH (c:Company)-[:PREVIOUSADDRESS]->(a:Address)-[]->(p:PreviousCompany)
WHERE c.companypreviousnames <> "NA"
WITH c, p, a
MATCH (c)-[:EXECUTIVE]->(e:Executive)
WHERE e.tenureend <> "NA" AND
      e.tenurestart >= p.StartofTenure AND e.tenureend <= p.EndofTenure
WITH e, COLLECT(DISTINCT a) AS Addresses
WHERE SIZE(Addresses) > 1
RETURN e, Addresses;
```

4. Companies with Executives Active During Address Changes

Scenario: Find companies where executives were active during a change in registered address.

```cypher
MATCH (c:Company)-[:CHANGEINREGISTEREDADDRESS]->(a:Address)
WITH c, a
MATCH (c)-[:EXECUTIVE]->(e:Executive)
WHERE e.tenureend <> "NA" AND
      e.tenurestart <= a.endtenure AND e.tenureend >= a.starttenure
MERGE (e)-[:ACTIVE_DURING_ADDRESS_CHANGE]->(a)
RETURN c, e, a;
```

Fig. 4 Sample Cypher queries generated using DeepSeek R1

maintained by local authorities.[77] The problems are exacerbated further by lack of resources to conduct necessary due diligence, instances of non-compliance on part of corporate service providers,[78] and the questions around the effectiveness of AML regulations in achieving the desired objectives.[79] Consequently, the identification and investigation of networks of entities involved in illicit activities remains crucial.

Graph database platforms have proven their significance through their application by the International Consortium of Investigative Journalists (ICIJ) for mapping complex financial transactions and detecting irregularities. These efforts have been crucial in uncovering crimes as exemplified by the renowned investigations of the "Panama Papers" and the "Paradise Papers". Since the inception of the investigations in 2016, graph technology has facilitated recovery of over USD 1.2 billion in fines and back taxes.[80] Another instance of the use of graph technology is its adoption by the company Dun and Bradstreet, who use graph technology to accelerate clients' compliance with company ownership checks.

In line with the views of Becerra-Fernandez et al. (2000), Eifrem (2019), and Hawking et al. (2005), the use of graph database platforms provides value for multiple stakeholders due to their ability to represent large volumes of complex network data into graphs.[81] For investigative journalists and compliance professionals, such platforms provide an opportunity to organise data on corporate entities, facilitating the identification of hidden connections and the deterrence of money laundering activities. For corporate registries and incorporation services, this chapter outlines an approach for importing data into graph database platforms, thereby strengthening the first line of defence against financial crime. Finally, for academics, the use of graph databases offers opportunities for incorporating analysis to conduct further research.

Additionally, the use of LLMs, such as ChatGPT 4o and DeepSeek R1, in conjunction with graph database platforms, such as Neo4J, further provides an opportunity to enhance investigative methodologies. By introducing database schemas to LLMs, they can generate sophisticated cypher queries to further aid identification of hidden patterns and connections within datasets. Such integrations not only facilitate investigators to explore the datasets more effectively but also democratise access to advanced analytical tools for individuals lacking expertise in data science. Moreover, in line with the views of Shan et al. (2024), the use of LLMs could also facilitate the construction of better graphs by leveraging their abundant knowledge and reasoning capabilities.[82]

The key arguments stemming from this exploration are twofold. First, graph databases provide a powerful and intuitive mechanism to model and analyse the

---

[77] Nougayrède (2019).

[78] Findley et al. (2013), p. 657–693; Findley et al. (2015), p. 146–161.

[79] Pol (2018a), p. 215–230; Pol (2018b), p. 294–308.

[80] Dalby and Wilson-Chapman (2019); Romera and Gallego (2018).

[81] Becerra-Fernandez et al. (2000), p. 39–41; Eifrem (2019), p. 6–8; Hawking et al. (2005), p. 83.

[82] Shan et al. (2024).

complex, interconnected data prevalent in money laundering schemes. Their ability to reveal hidden relationships, shared entities, and complex patterns provides a significant advantage over traditional methods that are ineffective with relational data. Second, the integration of GenAI, particularly LLMs, offer a promising avenue for augmenting these capabilities. LLMs can assist in understanding the data architecture, thus assisting in query generation, potentially uncovering lines of inquiry that a human investigator might have overlooked and can make sophisticated graph analysis accessible to a broader range of users. Such synergy facilitates a more dynamic and potentially more exhaustive examination of suspicious networks.

However, there are important challenges and considerations that need to be acknowledged. The success of LLMs in producing precise and meaningful graph queries depends on the clarity and completeness of the underlying schema, as well as the model's understanding of the domain.[83] The quality of data is critical: incomplete or inaccurate data will result in unreliable results, regardless of the tools used. Ethical considerations, including data privacy and the potential for bias in AI algorithms, must be proactively addressed.[84] Furthermore, the 'black box' nature of AI models continue to make it difficult to understand the reasoning behind their outputs, which is critical aspect of investigations resulting in legal or regulatory action.

The objective of this chapter is not to outline multiple graph query construction or evaluate model performances but to emphasise the potential of such integration. Such investigative approaches can be critical in aiding individuals lacking data science expertise while also supporting novel mechanisms for investigating datasets. This chapter lays the groundwork for future research by highlighting the potential of integrating graph database platforms with LLMs to analyse networks of illicit entities. This becomes particularly important keeping in mind the views of Rodriguez and Shinavier (2010), who have highlighted that multiple relationship types can complicate design of network algorithms.[85] Such complex designs can be addressed by the use of graph query languages. Furthermore, such an integration provides opportunity to come up with simulations of alternative network topologies to yield meaningful insights.

7 Conclusion and Future Directions

This chapter has examined the hypothetical integration of graph analytics and GenAI, particularly LLMs, as a hybrid approach to improve the detection of money laundering. The key takeaway lies in acknowledging the potential of this combination for uncovering complex illicit financial networks by visualising relationships, identifying anomalies, and augmenting investigative capabilities. Graph databases

[83] Liang et al. (2024).

[84] Nishant et al. (2020), p. 102104.

[85] Rodriguez and Shinavier (2010), p. 29–41.

enhance the modelling and querying of interconnected data, while LLMs offer a novel way to interact with these databases, thus improving the scope of inquiry.

The analysis, illustrated using a dataset of known illicit entities, explores how graph queries can reveal critical red flags such as lack of information on beneficial ownership disclosure, shared addresses among multiple companies, and directors holding many executive appointments. Furthermore, the introduction of LLMs to generate cypher queries demonstrate a pathway to democratise advanced data analysis and uncover new avenues for investigation.

Despite the potential, the application of such a hybrid approach is not without challenges. These include ensuring data quality and completeness, addressing the ethical considerations associated with the use of LLMs, managing the complexity of LLM integration with graph databases, and the continuing need for human expertise and oversight to ensure the reliability of LLM-generated queries and the obtained results.

Looking ahead, future research can direct attention on several key areas:

- Development of robust and standardised methodologies for integration of LLMs with graph databases for AML, including improvement in prompt engineering techniques and validation frameworks for LLM-generated queries.
- Investigating the scalability of hybrid approach for real-world, large-scale financial datasets.
- Exploring the use of LLMs not only for query generation but also for interpretation of graph patterns, summarising findings, and even generation of reports for investigators.
- Addressing the "explainability" of AI-driven insights to ensure findings are reliable.
- Fostering interdisciplinary collaboration between relevant stakeholders, such as AML practitioners, data scientists, and legal experts to ensure responsible development and deployment of these technologies.

In conclusion, while still in its exploration stage for many applications, the synergistic combination of graph analytics and GenAI provides a new frontier in the fight against money laundering. By facilitating a more nuanced understanding of complex financial networks and enabling advanced analytical techniques more accessible, this hybrid approach could significantly enhance the capabilities of financial institutions and regulatory bodies to detect, investigate, and disrupt illicit financial flows. However, realising this potential will need a concerted effort to address technical, ethical, and practical challenges.

References

Bangcharoensap P, Kobayashi H, Shimizu N, Yamauchi S, Murata T (2015) Two step graph-based semi-supervised learning for online auction fraud detection. In: Machine learning and knowledge discovery in databases. Springer, Cham

Barabási AL, Albert R (1999) Emergence of scaling in random networks. Science 286:509–512. https://doi.org/10.1126/science.286.5439.509

Battaglia PW, Hamrick JB, Bapst V, Sanchez-Gonzalez A, Zambaldi V, Malinowski M, Tacchetti A, Raposo D, Santoro A, Faulkner R, Gulcehre C, Song F, Ballard A, Gilmer J, Dahl G, Vaswani A, Allen K, Nash C, Langston V, Pascanu R (2018) Relational inductive biases, deep learning, and graph networks. arXiv e-prints. https://ui.adsabs.harvard.edu/abs/2018arXiv180601261B. Accessed 1 June 2018

Becerra-Fernandez I, Murphy KE, Simon SJ (2000) Enterprise resource planning: integrating ERP in the business school curriculum. Commun ACM 43:39–41. https://doi.org/10.1145/332051.332066

Bhagat S, Cormode G, Muthukrishnan S (2011) Node classification in social networks. In: Aggarwal CC (ed) Social network data analytics. Springer, pp 115–148. https://doi.org/10.1007/978-1-4419-8462-3_5

Buchanan B (2004) Money laundering—a global obstacle. Res Int Bus Financ 18:115–127. https://doi.org/10.1016/j.ribaf.2004.02.001

Cassella SD (2018) Toward a new model of money laundering: is the "placement, layering, integration" model obsolete? J Money Laund Control 21:494–497. https://doi.org/10.1108/JMLC-09-2017-0045

Chapple L, Dunstan K, Truong TP (2018) Corporate governance and management earnings forecast behaviour: evidence from a low private litigation environment. Pac Account Rev 30:222–242. https://doi.org/10.1108/PAR-09-2016-0081

Chung FRK, Graham RL, Saks ME (1994) Dynamic search in graphs. In: Discrete algorithms and complexity. Academic Press, pp 351–387

Compin F (2008) The role of accounting in money laundering and money dirtying. Crit Perspect Account 19:591–602. https://doi.org/10.1016/j.cpa.2007.01.001

Cowdock B (2017) Hiding in plain sight: how UK companies are used to launder corrupt wealth. http://www.transparency.org.uk/publications/hiding-in-plain-sight/#.WwInj3eFO70

Dalby D, Wilson-Chapman A (2019) Panama papers helps recover more than $1.2 billion around the world. https://www.icij.org/investigations/panama-papers/panama-papers-helps-recover-more-than-1-2-billion-around-the-world/

Diviák T, Dijkstra JK, Snijders TAB (2019) Structure, multiplexity, and centrality in a corruption network: the Czech Rath affair. Trends Organ Crime 22:274–297. https://doi.org/10.1007/s12117-018-9334-y

Drakopoulos G, Baroutiadi A, Megalooikonomou V (2015) Higher order graph centrality measures for Neo4j. In: 2015 6th international conference on information, intelligence, systems and applications (IISA). IEEE

Dwivedi YK, Kshetri N, Hughes L, Slade EL, Jeyaraj A, Kar AK, Baabdullah AM, Koohang A, Raghavan V, Ahuja M, Albanna H, Albashrawi MA, Al-Busaidi AS, Balakrishnan J, Barlette Y, Basu S, Bose I, Brooks L, Buhalis D, Wright R (2023) "So what if ChatGPT wrote it?" Multidisciplinary perspectives on opportunities, challenges and implications of generative conversational AI for research, practice and policy. Int J Inf Manag 71:102642. https://doi.org/10.1016/j.ijinfomgt.2023.102642

Eifrem E (2019) How graph technology can map patterns to mitigate money-laundering risk. Comput Fraud Secur 2019(10):6–8. https://doi.org/10.1016/S1361-3723(19)30105-8

Fakhraei S, Foulds J, Shashanka M, Getoor L (2015) Collective spammer detection in evolving multi-relational social networks. In: KDD '15: Proceedings of the 21th ACM SIGKDD international conference on knowledge discovery and data mining. Association for Computing Machinery, pp 1769–1778

FATF (2012) The FATF recommendations: international standards on combating money laundering and the financing of terrorism & proliferation. https://www.fatf-gafi.org/en/topics/fatf-recommendations.html. Accessed 15 Jan 2025

Ferrill J, de Koker L, Goldbarsht D (2025) Financial crime prevention in an age of paradox. In: Goldbarsht D, de Koker L, Ferrill J (eds) The financial war on crime and terrorism: opportunities and challenges. Springer, Cham

Ferwerda J, van Saase A, Unger B, Getzner M (2020) Estimating money laundering flows with a gravity model-based simulation. Sci Rep 10:18552. https://doi.org/10.1038/s41598-020-75653-x

Findley MG, Nielson DL, Sharman JC (2013) Using field experiments in international relations: a randomized study of anonymous incorporation. Int Organ 67:657–693. https://doi.org/10.1017/S0020818313000271

Findley MG, Nielson DL, Sharman JC (2015) Causes of noncompliance with international law: a field experiment on anonymous incorporation. Am J Polit Sci 59:146–161. https://doi.org/10.1111/ajps.12141

Fitina L, Imbal J, Uiari V, Murki N, Goodyear E (2010) An application of minimum spanning trees to travel planning. Contemp PNG Stud 12:1

Floros IV, Sapp TRA (2011) Shell games: on the value of shell companies. J Corp Finance 17:850–867. https://doi.org/10.1016/j.jcorpfin.2011.03.004

Guo D, Yang D, Zhang H, Song J, Zhang R, Xu R, Zhu Q, Ma S, Wang P, Bi X (2025) DeepSeek-R1: incentivizing reasoning capability in LLMs via reinforcement learning. arXiv preprint. https://doi.org/10.48550/arXiv.2501.12948

Guo J, Du L, Liu H, Zhou M, He X, Han S (2023) GPT4graph: can large language models understand graph structured data? An empirical evaluation and benchmarking. arXiv preprint. https://doi.org/10.48550/arXiv.2305.15066

Hawking P, McCarthy B, Stein A (2005) Integrating ERP's second wave into higher education curriculum. PACIS 2005 Proceedings, paper 83. https://aisel.aisnet.org/pacis2005/83/

Holtz L, Sarlo Neto A (2014) Effects of Board of Directors' characteristics on the quality of accounting information in Brazil. Revista Contabilidade & Finanças 25:255–266. https://doi.org/10.1590/1808-057x201412010

Huang H, Dong Z (2013) Research on architecture and query performance based on distributed graph database neo4j. In: 2013 3rd international conference on consumer electronics, communications and networks. IEEE

Huang X, Zhang J, Li D, Li P (2019) Knowledge graph embedding based question answering. In: Proceedings of the twelfth ACM international conference on web search and data mining. ACM, pp 105–113

International Consortium of Investigative Journalists (n.d.) ICIJ offshore leaks database. https://offshoreleaks.icij.org/

Kubzansky C (2018) Nine essential tools from ICIJ's data journalists and programmers. ICIJ: International Consortium of Investigative Journalists

Lee A, Palstra N (2018) The companies we keep: what the UK's open data register actually tells us about company ownership. https://www.globalwitness.org/en/press-releases/groundbreaking-analysis-owners-uk-companies-uncovers-serious-money-laundering-risks/

Liang Y, Tan K, Xie T, Tao W, Wang S, Lan Y, Qian W (2024) Aligning large language models to a domain-specific graph database for NL2GQL. In: Proceedings of the 33rd ACM international conference on information and knowledge management, Boise, ID, USA. ACM. https://doi.org/10.1145/3627673.3679713

Liu J, Bier E, Wilson A, Guerra-Gomez JA, Honda T, Sricharan K, Gilpin L, Davies D (2016) Graph analysis for detecting fraud, waste, and abuse in healthcare data. AI Mag 37:33–46

Ma P, Tsai S, He Y, Jia X, Zhen D, Yu N, Wang Q, Ahuja JKC, Wei CI (2024) Large language models in food science: innovations, applications, and future. Trends Food Sci Technol 148:104488. https://doi.org/10.1016/j.tifs.2024.104488

Malinick TE, Tindall DB, Diani M (2013) Network centrality and social movement media coverage: a two-mode network analytic approach. Soc Networks 35:148–158. https://doi.org/10.1016/j.socnet.2011.10.005

Marsden PV (2002) Egocentric and sociocentric measures of network centrality. Soc Networks 24:407–422. https://doi.org/10.1016/S0378-8733(02)00016-3

Martini M, Constantino F, France G (2019) Who is behind the wheel? Fixing the global standards on company ownership. Transparency International

Memon BR, Wiil UK (2014) Predicting links in multi-relational networks. Institute of Electrical and Electronics Engineers, pp 107–114

Miller JJ (2013) Graph database applications and concepts with Neo4j. In: Proceedings of the Southern Association for Information Systems Conference, Atlanta, GA, USA. AISEL

Mogaji E, Balakrishnan J, Nwoba AC, Nguyen NP (2021) Emerging-market consumers' interactions with banking chatbots. Telematics Inform 65:101711. https://doi.org/10.1016/j.tele.2021.101711

Munir S, Aldini A (2024) Towards evaluating large language models for graph query generation. arXiv preprint arXiv:2411.08449

Ndofor H, Wesley C, Priem R (2015) Providing CEOs with opportunities to cheat: the effects of complexity-based information asymmetries on financial reporting fraud. J Manag 41:1774–1797. https://doi.org/10.1177/0149206312471395

Newman L (2007) Making the most of anti-money laundering systems. J Superann Manag 1:31–34

Nishant R, Kennedy M, Corbett J (2020) Artificial intelligence for sustainability: challenges, opportunities, and a research agenda. Int J Inf Manag 53:102104. https://doi.org/10.1016/j.ijinfomgt.2020.102104

Nougayrède D (2019) After the Panama papers: a private law critique of Shell companies. Int Lawyer 51

Obermayer B, Ryle G, Guevara MW, Hudson M, Bernstein J, Fitzgibbon W, Cabra M, Hamilton M, Obermaier F, Chittum R (2016) Giant leak of offshore financial records exposes global array of crime and corruption. https://www.icij.org/investigations/panama-papers/20160403-panama-papers-global-overview/

OCCRP (2019) The Troika Laundromat. https://www.occrp.org/en/troikalaundromat/

Ooi KB, Tan GWH, Al-Emran M, Al-Sharafi MA, Capatina A, Chakraborty A, Dwivedi YK, Huang TL, Kar AK, Lee VH, Loh XM, Micu A, Mikalef P, Mogaji E, Pandey N, Raman R, Rana NP, Sarker P, Sharma A, Wong LW (2023) The potential of generative artificial intelligence across disciplines: perspectives and future directions. J Comput Inf Syst. https://doi.org/10.1080/08874417.2023.2261010

Pacini CJ, Sinclair DT, Hopwood WS (2016) Domestic asset tracing: identifying, locating and freezing stolen and hidden assets. J Forensic Account Res 1:A42–A65

Peruchini M, da Silva GM, Teixeira JM (2024) Between artificial intelligence and customer experience: a literature review on the intersection. Discov Artif Intell 4:4. https://doi.org/10.1007/s44163-024-00105-8

Piktus A (2023) Online tools help large language models to solve problems through reasoning. Nature 618:465–466. https://doi.org/10.1038/d41586-023-01411-4

Pol R (2018a) Anti-money laundering effectiveness: assessing outcomes or ticking boxes? J Money Laund Control 21:215–230. https://doi.org/10.1108/JMLC-07-2017-0029

Pol R (2018b) Uncomfortable truths? ML=BS and AML= BS2. J Financ Crime 25:294–308. https://doi.org/10.1108/JFC-08-2017-0071

Ravenda D, Argilés-Bosch JM, Valencia-Silva MM (2015) Detection model of legally registered mafia firms in Italy. Eur Manag Rev 12:23–39. https://doi.org/10.1111/emre.12039

Ravenda D, Valencia-Silva MM, Argiles-Bosch JM, García-Blandón J (2018) Money laundering through the strategic management of accounting transactions. Crit Perspect Account. https://doi.org/10.1016/j.cpa.2018.08.003

Ray A (2015) Emerging solutions in anti-money laundering technology. http://celent.com/reports/emerging-solutions-anti-money-laundering-technology

Rodriguez MA, Shinavier J (2010) Exposing multi-relational networks to single-relational network analysis algorithms. J Informetr 4:29–41. https://doi.org/10.1016/j.joi.2009.06.004

Romera P, Gallego CS (2018) How ICIJ deals with massive data leaks like the Panama Papers and Paradise Papers. https://www.icij.org/blog/2018/07/how-icij-deals-with-massive-data-leaks-like-the-panama-papers-and-paradise-papers/

Salavati C, Abdollahpouri A, Manbari Z (2019) Ranking nodes in complex networks based on local structure and improving closeness centrality. Neurocomputing 336:36–45. https://doi.org/10.1016/j.neucom.2018.04.086
Schneider F (2010) Turnover of organized crime and money laundering: some preliminary empirical findings. Public Choice 144:473–486. https://doi.org/10.1007/s11127-010-9676-8
Schneider F, Windischbauer U (2008) Money laundering: some facts. Eur J Law Econ 26:387–404. https://doi.org/10.1007/s10657-008-9070-x
Schweitzer F, Fagiolo G, Sornette D, Vega-Redondo F, Vespignani A, White DR (2009) Economic networks: the new challenges. Science 325:422. https://doi.org/10.1126/science.1173644
Shan R, Lin J, Zhu C, Chen B, Zhu M, Zhang K, Zhu J, Tang R, Yu Y, Zhang W (2024) An automatic graph construction framework based on large language models for recommendation. arXiv preprint arXiv:2412.18241
Singh D (2010) Incorporating with fraudulent intentions: a study of various differentiating attributes of shell companies in India. J Financ Crime 17:459–484. https://doi.org/10.1108/13590791011082805
Singh K, Best P (2019) Anti-money laundering: using data visualization to identify suspicious activity. Int J Account Inf Syst. https://doi.org/10.1016/j.accinf.2019.06.001
Tiwari M, Ferrill J, Mehrotra V (2023) Using graph database platforms to fight money laundering: advocating large scale adoption. J Money Laund Control 26:474–487. https://doi.org/10.1108/JMLC-03-2022-0047
Tiwari M, Gepp A, Kumar K (2025) Using data analytics to distinguish legitimate and illegitimate shell companies. J Econom Criminol 7:100123. https://doi.org/10.1016/j.jeconc.2024.100123
Unger B (2013) Can money laundering decrease? Public Finance Rev 41:658–676. https://doi.org/10.1177/1091142113483353
UNODC (2004) United nations convention against transnational organized crime and the protocols thereto
Van Bruggen R (2014) Learning Neo4j. Packt Publishing Ltd
Van Vlasselaer V, Eliassi-Rad T, Akoglu L, Snoeck M, Baesens B (2017) GOTCHA! Network-based fraud detection for social security fraud. Manag Sci 63:3090–3110. https://doi.org/10.1287/mnsc.2016.2489
Vitali S, Glattfelder JB, Battiston S (2011) The network of global corporate control. PLoS One 6:e25995
Walters R (2025) International arbitration and money laundering: is there an actual issue? In: Goldbarsht D, de Koker L, Ferrill J (eds) The financial war on crime and terrorism: opportunities and challenges. Springer, Cham
Wang X, Bouzembrak Y, Lansink AO, Van Der Fels-Klerx HJ (2022) Application of machine learning to the monitoring and prediction of food safety: a review. Compr Rev Food Sci Food Saf 21:416–434. https://doi.org/10.1111/1541-4337.12868
Zhang J, Hu X, Zhang Z, An X, Zhao M, Li X (2018) Weakly-supervised discovery of visual pattern configurations. Adv Neural Inf Proces Syst 31

Dr. Milind Tiwari is a Senior Lecturer in Financial Crime Studies at the Australian Graduate School of Policing and Security, Charles Sturt University. Milind has an extensive experience in AML investigations pertaining to customer due diligence, enhanced customer due diligence, and transaction monitoring, among others, and has worked for Big 4, namely, KPMG, EY, and Deloitte, in India and Australia. Milind holds a PhD in money laundering from Bond University (Australia), a Master of Science in Finance from University of Manchester (UK), and a Bachelor of Business Administration from Christ University (India). Additionally, he is a Certified Fraud Examiner (CFE) and a Certified Anti-Money Laundering Specialist (CAMS). As a financial crime academic and researcher, Milind's work focuses on various facets associated with money laundering, including a focus on technological advancement in undertaking and detecting it.

Illegal Wildlife Trade as a Method of Financing Terrorism

Cayle Lupton

Abstract The economic, societal, and environmental harm associated with the illegal wildlife trade (IWT) is well-documented and uncontroversial. The same, however, is not true of the connection between IWT and terrorism, since early claims in point were supported by weak, unverifiable evidence. In recent times, however, several authoritative sources have referred to a limited use of IWT in the financing of terrorism. Despite these pronouncements, there remains a notable gap in the academic literature on the terrorism financing-IWT nexus. This chapter seeks to illustrate the potential of IWT to develop into a prolific terrorism financing method. The chapter concludes that to effectively address the terrorism financing-IWT nexus and terrorism in general, an integrated approach, involving multiple stakeholders, is essential.

1 Introduction

The past two decades have witnessed persistent patterns of terrorist activity worldwide.[1] On the African continent, terrorist groups inflict a high level of fear, violence, and destruction on innocent civilian populations. The most noteworthy of these terrorist groups are the Janjaweed (Sudan), the Lord's Resistance Army (Democratic

[1] Institute for Economics and Peace (2025).

Gratitude is hereby extended to the anonymous interviewees whose insights and perspectives shaped the analysis of the aspects under consideration. They hail from various environments, including AML/CTF, regulatory compliance and wildlife conservation. I am also grateful to the anonymous reviewers for their constructive comments.

C. Lupton (✉)
University of Johannesburg, Johannesburg, South Africa
e-mail: clupton@uj.ac.za

D. Goldbarsht et al. (eds.), *The Financial War on Crime and Terrorism*, European Yearbook of International Economic Law,
https://doi.org/10.1007/978-3-032-06360-1_6

Republic of the Congo, the Central African Republic and South Sudan), Boko Haram (Nigeria) and Al-Shabaab (Somalia, Kenya, Ethiopia and, more recently, Mozambique).[2] The proliferation of terrorist activities in Africa and beyond continues to undermine international peace and security as well as compromise the stability of the international financial system.[3]

Unified in their response to the threat of terrorism, the United Nations (UN) and the Financial Action Task Force (FATF) call for the adoption of domestic anti-terrorism laws that are intended to disenable terrorists from perpetrating their activities by, *inter alia*, preventing them from accessing funding and financial resources.[4] However, the success of counter terrorism financing (CTF) legal frameworks is not readily clear, particularly since terrorists have been known to make use of a variety of financing methods which may or may not fall under the scope of the relevant laws.[5] Moreover, terrorism financing methods may involve the exploitation of legitimate activities[6] or the commission of illegitimate (or criminal) activities,[7] with funds often moving through formal (regulated) and informal (under-regulated) channels.[8]

Of the many possible terrorism financing methods, the illegal wildlife trade (IWT)[9] has emerged most controversially. The main problem is that early claims in favour of a terrorism financing-IWT nexus were mostly advanced spuriously and without proper evidence.[10] This is especially true in relation to Al-Shabaab and the Lord's Resistance Army which allegedly generated substantial proceeds from trafficking in ivory. These claims, however, were later debunked by Maguire and Haenlein (2015), who effectively conclude that the claims amount to a misrepresentation of poaching in Africa and, consequently, that the true IWT role players went

[2] FATF (2016); GIABA (2020); Financial Intelligence Centre (2024), p. 4. Note that the Al-Shabaab terrorist group in Mozambique is seemingly unrelated to its counterpart in East Africa. Though, both groups embrace the jihadist movement.

[3] UNSC CTED (2022), p. 5.

[4] UNSC Resolution 2462 (2019), paras 6–8; FATF (2012–2023), p. 13.

[5] GIABA (2020). In this context, 'relevant laws' also include anti-money laundering (AML) laws and regulations. The FATF is the leading international institution on the combatting of money laundering, terrorism financing, and the financing of the proliferation of weapons of mass destruction. It is well-known for setting global standards or recommendations for its members to implement domestically. See FATF (2012–2023).

[6] Such as donations and crowdfunding.

[7] This includes kidnapping for ransom, extortion, the illicit trade and trafficking in cultural property, human trafficking, drug trafficking and the illicit trade in small weapons.

[8] Byrne et al. (2022), p. 252.

[9] The term refers to activities associated with the sale of protected wildlife, including both animals and plants or derivatives thereof, that is in contravention of international or domestic law. See Mozer and Prost (2023), p. 1.

[10] Maguire and Haenlein (2015).

unpunished.[11] Duffy (2022) added that framing IWT as a security threat was a convenient way for conservation role players to tap into bigger resources at the international level.[12]

These studies do, however, concede that instances of a terrorism financing-IWT nexus are conceivable. In particular, Maguire and Haenlein (2015) explain that interviewees in Kenya 'reported knowledge of very small [ivory] quantities crossing the border from their own monitoring' and that this was 'piecemeal evidence of potential small-scale movement of ivory at the very most'.[13] Major AML/CTF role players have made similar statements. In its 2020 report titled *Assessment of Counter Terrorist Financing Capacities in West Africa*, the Inter-Governmental Action Group Against Money Laundering in West Africa (GIABA)[14] states that Cote d'Ivoire is at risk 'of increasing illicit transnational trafficking in arms, smuggling and trafficking of protected species such as Ivory, which could constitute sources of TF'.[15] In the same year, the FATF published its report titled *Money Laundering and the Illegal Wildlife Trade*, which does not address the links between IWT and terrorism financing 'as current evidence suggests that this is not yet a widespread typology'.[16] By reflecting a cautious approach as to the scale of such linkages, the FATF's statement acknowledges the likelihood that terrorist groups are engaging in IWT for terrorism financing purposes. The FATF's statement has since been cited authoritatively by the Counter-Terrorism Committee of the UN.[17] Despite these pronouncements, there remains a notable gap in academic literature on the terrorism financing-IWT nexus.

This chapter seeks to illustrate the potential of IWT to develop into a prolific terrorism financing method. Its primary contribution is to position IWT as a high-risk vulnerability for terrorism financing that requires proactive intervention. The focus in this regard is on Africa. To this end, the chapter begins with an overview of the terrorism landscape in Africa, including known and suspected terrorism financing methods, with a particular focus on Al-Shabaab and Boko Haram. This is followed by an analysis of the factors that contribute to the appeal of IWT for terrorism financing. The chapter concludes that to effectively address the terrorism financing-IWT nexus and terrorism in general, an integrated approach, involving multiple stakeholders, is essential.

---

[11] Maguire and Haenlein (2015). This study was published under the auspices of the Royal United Services Institute for Defence and Security Studies (RUSI), the United Kingdom's leading independent think-tank on international defence and security.

[12] Duffy (2022), pp. 23–44.

[13] Maguire and Haenlein (2015), p. 22.

[14] GIABA is a FATF-style Regional Body that promotes policies to protect member states against threats to their respective financial systems.

[15] GIABA (2020), p. 34.

[16] FATF (2020), p. 11. See also FATF (2016), p. 23.

[17] UNSC CTED (2022), p. 8.

2 Terrorism in Africa

A definition of the concept of 'terrorism' has escaped universal acceptance. Many definitions have been proffered over the years, but they tend to emphasise different factors and raise competing views, often leading to controversy and uncertainty.[18] It is, nevertheless, a fact that acts of terror generally cause fear and destruction, including loss of life. It is against this background that the likes of Al-Shabaab, the Lord's Resistance Army and Boko Haram are regarded universally as terrorist groups, even though the groups may differ in their purposes and objectives.[19] African terrorist groups invariably feature in major terrorism studies and explorations.[20]

There are many interrelated factors encouraging terrorism in Africa: the proliferation of arms and the ease with which foreign arms suppliers and trainers can be engaged; the perception of a lack of legitimacy of the ruling government; political instability; poverty; illiteracy; unemployment; porous borders; distrust in judicial institutions; and, finally, corruption.[21] While these factors are typically informed by state failure, historical disenfranchisement and poor socio-economic conditions, they are exploited by terrorist groups to advance their own purposes and objectives.[22] This is particularly true of Al-Shabaab and Boko Haram.

Al-Shabaab[23] is a Somalia-based terrorist group operating in the East African region. Born out of its role as the youth militia of the Islamic Courts Union (ICU), an organisation comprising insurgent groups which controlled approximately half of Southern Somalia in the early 2000s, Al-Shabaab emerged around 2006 as an established jihadist organisation with military bases located in remote areas in close proximity to local villages.[24] Having pledged allegiance to al-Qaeda in 2012, Al-Shabaab's main goal is the removal of Western and other foreign influences and ideologies in Somalia, and in Africa as a whole, with a view to inculcating the widespread embodiment of the jihadist movement.[25] To this end, Al-Shabaab has wreaked havoc in Somalia through the use of a wide range of extreme measures, including kidnappings, bombings, random mass shootings, and death threats, effectively leaving the country devoid of any real government, hampering peacekeeping initiatives and contributing to a devastating humanitarian crisis.[26]

[18] Bekele (2021), p. 628.

[19] For an assessment of the definitions of 'terrorism' that have been proffered at the international level, see Bekele (2021), pp. 619–628.

[20] See e.g. Mentan (2017); Reeve and Pelter (2014); Solomon (2013).

[21] Mentan (2017), p. ix; Solomon (2013), pp. 33–34.

[22] Solomon (2013), p. 34; Gow et al. (2013), p. 7.

[23] Its full Arabic name is *Harakat al-Shabaab al-Mujahideen*.

[24] Gilroy (2024). Simply put, the Jihadist movement entails a rejection of any knowledge, system or rule which is not aligned to the principles of Islam.

[25] Ali (2008), p. 3.

[26] Abioye (2019), p. 13.

More recently, the group has extended its operations to neighbouring countries, particularly Kenya, apparently in response to the role that Kenya plays in assisting the African Union (AU) and Western allies to combat Al-Shabaab. In this regard, the African Union Mission Support and Stabilisation Mission in Somalia (AUSSOM), which includes Kenyan and Ethiopian military forces, was established to support the Somalian government in combatting Al-Shabaab. AUSSOM replaced the AU Transition Mission in Somalia (ATMIS) with effect from 1 January 2025.[27] ATMIS operated under the auspices of the AU and UN until the end of 2024. The mandate of AUSSOM substantively mirrors that of ATMIS.

Al-Shabaab has perpetrated numerous raids and bombing incidents in Kenya, targeting bus terminals, churches, military convoys, hotels, and other places of gathering.[28] The attacks at the Westgate Mall and Garissa University College especially generated widespread media coverage. During September 2013, the Westgate mall in Nairobi endured an attack that lasted several hours and left at least 67 people dead. In April 2015, Garissa University College in the northeastern province of Kenya endured an attack that left more than 100 people (of mostly Christian faith) dead.[29] These attacks, coupled with several other more recent terrorist activities,[30] are indicative of the escalating threat Al-Shabaab poses to Kenya and the broader East African region.

The known funding sources of Al-Shabaab include extortion; so-called 'zakat tax';[31] influential businesspeople; looting; donations from sympathisers; illegal trafficking in charcoal and people; and the smuggling of sugar.[32] These activities have been categorised by regional authorities and the FATF as forming part of a broader pattern of terrorist financing that takes advantage of weak border controls and informal financial systems.[33] Notably, Al-Shabaab's involvement in the illicit charcoal trade has generated tens of millions of dollars annually, often laundered through cross-border trade routes. This suggests a strong relationship with customs and border officials operating along the relevant trade routes, characterised by bribery and corruption. The FATF has also identified the group's integration into local taxation systems and extortion rackets in areas under its control as key means to sustain operational capacities and finance attacks, especially in Kenya.[34]

In West Africa, Boko Haram dominates the terrorism conversation. Officially known as *Jamā'at Ahl as-Sunnah lid-Da'wah wa'l-Jihād*, Boko Haram is a Nigeria-based jihadist group that seeks to overthrow the current Nigerian government and

27 ATMIS (2025).

28 Abioye (2019), p. 13.

29 Cannon (2016).

30 See ACLED (2023).

31 This tax system is enforced through systematic intimidation and violence. Individuals or community leaders who refuse to pay zakat demands run the risk of assassination.

32 US Department of Treasury (2023).

33 FATF (2016), p. 1.

34 FATF (2016), p. 10.

replace it with a regime based on Islamic law.[35] The group first emerged in north-eastern Nigeria, one of the least developed regions in the country, and then rapidly expanded to other parts of the country as well as neighbouring states. Boko Haram is believed to have existed as early as the mid-1990s though under different names, most notably the Nigerian Taliban, Yusufiyyah sect (after its founder, namely, Muhammad Yusuf), and now Boko Haram.[36] Over time it has evolved to become one of the deadliest terrorist groups in the world.[37]

Over the past two decades, Boko Haram has committed a plethora of terrorist attacks in northern and central Nigeria. Following the death of its founder in 2009, the apparatus and measures used in its attacks have varied significantly, giving rise to unpredictability and, in turn, extreme levels of destruction, loss, and fear. Notable terrorist activities include a deadly attack against a UN compound in Abuja in 2011, which left scores dead; the abduction in 2014 of over 200 girls from a government school in Borno State, where the girls had gathered to write a national exam; and, finally, the targeting of places of worship, with no discrimination towards religion or ethnicity, and other gatherings.[38] Between 2011 and 2023, Boko Haram was responsible for thousands of deaths in Nigeria, Cameroon, Chad and Niger, with the vast majority of deaths having occurred in Nigeria.[39]

Multiple known and suspected terrorism financing methods in the West African region, including Nigeria, have been documented by the FATF. These include: extortion; robberies and looting; cattle/livestock rustling; donations; abuse of non-profit organisations; local businesses/commercial enterprises; kidnapping for ransom; drug trafficking; and trafficking in weapons, persons, and ivory.[40] The FATF reports that several authorities have referred to the involvement of armed groups in IWT, both at the poaching and trafficking levels.[41] GIABA confirms that Boko Haram frequently raises funds through these means, and highlights particular concern over the group's exploitation of regional informal value transfer systems, such as Hawala, which operate outside the regulated banking sector.[42] Boko Haram has also been linked to regional organised crime syndicates, enabling access to funds through drug and arms trafficking. Importantly, the abuse of charitable organisations and front companies in Nigeria and the Lake Chad Basin for the purpose of laundering terrorist proceeds is a growing area of focus for Nigerian CTF strategies.[43]

To combat Boko Haram, the Multinational Joint Task Force (MNJTF) against Boko Haram was established in 2015 as a transnational initiative in the countries

[35] FATF (2016), p. 5.

[36] Azumah (2015), pp. 33–40.

[37] GIABA (2020), p. 46.

[38] Abioye (2019), p. 16.

[39] Statista (2024).

[40] FATF (2016), pp. 10–26.

[41] FATF (2016), p. 23.

[42] For more information on Hawala, see Sect. 3.5 below.

[43] See generally GIABA (2020).

around the Lake Chad area affected by the activities of the group. The countries involved include Niger, Chad, Cameroon and, to some degree, Benin. The AU endorses the MNJTF mission to effect coordination of military operations at an inter-state level, conduct border patrols, stop the flow of arms and assist in bringing justice to those responsible for the crimes.[44] Though under-resourced, the MNJTF has recorded some success, orchestrating the release of hostages (especially the Chibok girls), the destruction of Boko Haram training camps, confiscation and destruction of arms and ammunition belonging to the group, and the liberation of certain territories.[45] Yet, Boko Haram remains agile and resilient in the face of MNJTF initiatives.

This overview of terrorism in Africa, particularly the evolving financing mechanisms of Al-Shabaab and Boko Haram, serves as necessary background to the ensuing analysis of the factors that contribute to the appeal of IWT for terrorism financing. The financing dimension is critical to understanding not only the terrorist groups' longevity and regional reach, but also their adaptability in securing funds from both licit and illicit sources within certain areas.

3 Factors that Contribute to the Appeal of IWT for Terrorism Financing

3.1 Introductory Remarks

Africa represents a remarkable display of biodiversity and ecological, cultural, and economic significance, exemplified by phenomena such as the so-called 'big five' (which refers to lions, rhinos, elephants, buffalos, and leopards), the great migration of wildebeest and the apex predator dynamics of lion populations. It is, however, the very majesty of African wildlife that render them vulnerable to exploitation. As indicated above, IWT refers to activities associated with the sale of protected wildlife, including poaching, transporting and trafficking, that is in contravention of international or domestic law. African countries are typically regarded as source and transit jurisdictions for purposes of poaching and trafficking.[46] Given the growing demand for African wildlife and wildlife parts in especially Asia, IWT has progressively developed into one of the most sophisticated and profitable criminal enterprises the world over.[47] As a result, IWT is widely recognised as an organised crime

[44] AU (2024).

[45] Zabala (2023).

[46] SAMLIT (2021), p. 8.

[47] Sullivan and Weerd (2021), p. 9.

under domestic legal frameworks.[48] It has had a profound economic, societal, and environmental impact on the African continent.[49]

The question of the susceptibility of IWT to terrorism financing can broadly be analysed with reference to five factors: (1) profitability; (2) proximity to poachers and wildlife; (3) porous borders; (4) reliance on cash and informal payment systems; and (5) AML/CTF considerations. These five factors are inextricably linked and collectively demonstrate the susceptibility of IWT to terrorism financing.

3.2 *Profitability*

The demand for wildlife and wildlife products (such as elephant ivory, rhino horn, and pangolin scales) is driven by a variety of factors, most notably the perceived medicinal value of wildlife products, social status, and the desire to own exotic pets. Despite the meaningful work of conservationists, the United Nations Office on Drugs and Crime (UNODC) and other wildlife advocates in addressing the overexploitation of wildlife, the demand—especially in Asia—continues to rise.[50] At the time of writing, illicit proceeds generated from IWT are estimated to be in the range of USD 7–23 billion per annum, making it one of the most profitable illicit activities worldwide.[51]

In 2014, Lawson and Vines quoted the street value of ivory to be as high as USD 2205/kg in Beijing.[52] They also contend that rhino horn could fetch up to USD 66139/kg on the Chinese black market. Derived from these figures, the averages of USD 2000/kg for ivory and USD 65000/kg for rhino horn formed the basis of the Eastern and Southern Africa Anti Money Laundering Group's (ESAAMLG)[53] calculation of the street value 'lost' to countries from which ivory and rhino horn had been illegally procured over a specific period of time.[54] An average weight of 6 kg per pair of tusks was assumed and for rhino horns, the average weight assumed was 5 kg. Against this background, Table 1 contains statistics on the estimated value of elephant ivory and rhino horn lost to South Africa between 2011 and 2015.

It would be fair to assume that these figures have increased since 2014.[55]

[48] See e.g. South African Government (2023), pp. 21–23.

[49] ESAAMLG (2016), p. 6; World Bank Group (2019), pp. 12–13.

[50] MacFarlane et al. (2022).

[51] OECD (2019), p. 16; FATF (2020), p. 13.

[52] Lawson and Vines (2014), p. viii.

[53] ESAAMLG is a FATF-style Regional Body focused on, as the name suggests, Eastern and Southern Africa.

[54] ESAAMLG (2016), p. 31.

[55] Rhino horn and elephant tusk prices fluctuate depending on various factors such as whether horns and tusks are from harvested stock or poached animals, and the quality of the finished product once it is processed. Price is also influenced by financial factors during the trafficking process, which include labour expenses and resources at the source level, packing and transport fees, as well as clearance fees along the supply chain. See Wildlife Justice Commission (2022), p. 126.

Table 1 Estimated value of elephant ivory and rhino horn lost to South Africa between 2011 and 2015, ESAAMLG (2016), p. 32

Year	Ivory weight (kg)	Rhino horn (kg)	USD value lost (street value)	USD value lost (official)
2011	12	2240	24,000	144,480,000
2012	–	3340	217,100,000	220,440,000
2013	24	5020	326,300,000	343,870,000
2014	–	6075	394,875,000	N/F/A
2015	–	5115	332,475,000	N/F/A

It stands to reason that the potential to generate significant profits from wildlife crimes may serve as an enticing opportunity for criminals, including terrorist groups, to become involved in IWT. These high margins allow terrorist groups to sustain activities on a low-risk basis, especially in comparison to the high-risk, heavily monitored domains of drug or arms trafficking. Moreover, profits generated from IWT may not only be co-mingled with funds from other activities to obfuscate their illicit origin but also moved through formal and informal channels to enable the financing of terrorist activity. This includes the use of cash and alternative (unregulated) payment systems, both of which are explored in more detail in Sect. 3.5 below.

3.3 *Proximity to Poachers and Wildlife*

In Africa, national parks, game reserves and other protected areas are invariably far removed from cities and urban areas. Instead, they are usually located in underdeveloped areas, near rural communities where high levels of poverty, illiteracy, and unemployment abound. Members of rural communities are often persuaded to participate in IWT activities. They typically become involved as poachers. As poachers, they are required to locate, kill, and, if necessary, remove the relevant wildlife parts (for example, tusks or horns)—commonly known as the 'collection' stage of the IWT process.[56] The South African Anti-Money Laundering Integrated Task Force (SAMLIT) provides insight into the profile of a typical poacher in South Africa:

> Poachers make relatively high returns for their illegal activity but are the lowest paid in the entire value chain, despite the high risks involved. At this level, poverty is a major driver for wildlife crime, with poachers poorly educated, and living in poor communities, unable to sustain and support their families. Social pressure exists to join gangs and gang members'

[56] Nanima (2016), p. 225.

> lifestyles become aspirational. These individuals tend to operate within the reserves and are solicited to assist in sourcing products. Syndicates have been known to offer loans to poachers for their families, luring them in and allowing them to accumulate debt to sustain their loyalty.[57]

Although these statements are made in relation to South Africa, other African countries share similar experiences.

Poachers are generally not involved in the trafficking operation. They may, however, also be responsible for transporting wildlife or wildlife parts from the protected area to a national receiver who acts as a middleman between the poacher and trafficker. The middleman then delivers the wildlife or wildlife parts to the trafficker, creating distance between the trafficker and the predicate offence.[58] Transportation represents the second stage of the IWT process.[59] The third stage entails the distribution, and oftentimes the processing, of the wildlife or wildlife parts and is typically facilitated in a different country by higher echelons in the value chain.

From the discussion above on terrorism it is apparent that military bases and training operations are usually located in remote areas where rural communities reside. With poachers near wildlife parks and games reserves, terrorist groups may decide to engage with poachers or facilitate poaching themselves. The fact that rural communities rely strongly on cash and are knowledgeable on alternative payment systems may serve as further motivation for terrorist groups to engage with poachers. Against this background, a key consideration is whether proximate areas have sufficient wildlife populations to render wildlife crime viable for terrorist groups. Al-Shabaab serves as an important case study in this regard. Maguire and Haenlein (2015) convincingly rebut the alleged Al-Shabaab-ivory nexus—which has been endorsed, categorically, by international media outlets and US government officials—by raising several valuable arguments. One of those arguments concerns the long-time disappearance of Somalian elephant populations and the particularly low number of elephants in proximate areas of northeast Kenya.[60] While appreciating the rationality of this argument in this specific case, it may not be applicable in all cases. A good example is where a terrorist group extends its footprint to areas with sufficient wildlife populations. Or, where a terrorist group engages in correspondent terrorism financing, meaning that it partners with an affiliate in a different region with sufficient wildlife populations. The essential point is that each case must be evaluated on its own merits.

---

[57] SAMLIT (2021), p. 12.

[58] ESAAMLG (2016), p. 36.

[59] Nanima (2019), p. 2.

[60] Maguire and Haenlein (2015), p. 14.

3.4 *Porous Borders*

Porous borders are common in Eastern, Western, and Southern Africa. Terrorist groups and criminals alike exploit porous borders to engage in cross-border illicit activities. Commenting on the CTF capacities and trends in Burkina Faso, Cote d'Ivoire, Mali, Niger, and Nigeria (West Africa), GIABA reports as follows:

> Meanwhile, there exist continuous land borders connecting the five countries studied and parts of the vast border areas are porous and under-patrolled and sometimes overlapping. These border areas also have under-governed spaces with numerous unofficial access points often exploited by terrorists for illicit cross-border trafficking that aid their activities.[61]

Factors contributing to porous borders in Africa include corruption among border officials, deficient border infrastructure, difficulty in monitoring movement across borders, and the potential for instability due to easy movement of armed groups, often exacerbated by complex geographical terrains and weak border controls.[62]

Porous borders enable cross-border trafficking and the smuggling of wildlife and wildlife parts. Since terrorist groups have been known to regularly cross over into neighbouring countries or proximate regions to carry out their agendas, wildlife parts could easily be trafficked or smuggled in cross-border terrorist operations. Beyond the logistical vulnerabilities, the free movement of terrorist groups into neighbouring countries also presents financial vulnerabilities: it perpetuates the continued reliance on established cross-border financial networks,[63] promotes opportunities to diversify revenue streams along the trade corridor and in neighbouring countries, and, importantly, enables terrorist groups to sustain their activities.

While the factors discussed above (profitability, proximity to poachers and wildlife, and porous borders) make IWT appealing for terrorism financing, it must be noted that especially the use of sophisticated, unregulated financing arrangements in IWT activities is consistent with patterns of terrorism financing in Africa.

3.5 *Reliance on Cash and Informal Payment Systems*

In the IWT value chain, payments are made periodically to enable the next steps. Payment methods are determined by various factors. In addition to risk aversion by the parties involved, financial exclusion[64] is a major factor in this regard.[65] Many

---

[61] GIABA (2020), p. 10.

[62] Obah-Akpowoghaha et al. (2020).

[63] including the use of informal taxation and protection rackets on smuggling corridors to extract revenue from illegal traders dealing in wildlife.

[64] As explored further in the chapter by Chadderton (2025) in this book and the chapter by Morris and de Koker (2025) in this book.

[65] Financial exclusion remains a significant challenge in Africa. See Kawadza (2017), pp. 43–50.

rural dwellers—including poachers—do not have access to basic financial services and products such as bank accounts. Telecommunications infrastructure tends also to be limited in remote or rural areas. Unsurprisingly, therefore, cash has emerged as the dominant method of payment in respect of transactions occurring in source countries. The SAMLIT states:

> Cash remains one of the most prominent methods of transferring value amongst IWT actors, which remains difficult to track as, in many ways, the transfer of ownership circumvents the formal financial system altogether. Law enforcement agencies often find large amounts of cash when raiding homes or offices linked to suspected IWT cases. […] Poachers are mostly paid in cash or 'send-cash' options that create vouchers, redeemable at selected retail till-points or ATMs. Cash is the preferred and most frequently used method of payment as it minimises the risk of detection and allows for easier flows between legal and illegal economies. Cash transactions make it difficult to trace the linked role-players because this greatly limits the financial footprint.[66]

Funds entering the source country normally take the form of 'large or round amounts' and are typically made by way of electronic transfer.[67] These funds are used to facilitate the poaching and trafficking operations, including compensating low-level role players such as poachers. Generally, funds leave the source country through systems beyond the formal financial system.[68] In this regard, informal payment systems such as Hawala are suspected of being used in IWT transactions for the transfer of large amounts. The Hawala system entails the transferring of funds from one person to another without the physical movement of funds. Under this system, the sender provides cash to an intermediary, known as a 'hawaladar', in its physical location. The hawaladar then contacts another (second) hawaladar in the recipient's location and provides the details of the transaction, which invariably includes a password. The second hawaladar receives the password and provides the recipient with the funds upon collection. The hawaladars settle their accounts on a later date, either through transferring the funds or by balancing their accounts with other transactions. The system is built on the principle of trust.[69] The use of Hawala is well-documented in IWT studies[70] and, more broadly, AML/CTF reports by influential organisations.[71]

The use of Hawala in IWT poses a significant risk for terrorism financing due to its informal, trust-based nature and lack of regulatory oversight. This unregulated financial system enables IWT role players to discreetly transfer funds across borders, circumventing formal banking channels. In regions where terrorist groups operate alongside wildlife trafficking networks, Hawala can serve as a shared conduit for illicit financial flows. Consequently, terrorism groups may benefit directly

---

[66] SAMLIT (2021), p. 39. See also Lupton (2023), p. 184.

[67] SAMLIT (2021), p. 30.

[68] SAMLIT (2021), p. 37.

[69] Kagan (2023). For a detailed study on Hawala as an informal payment system, see World Bank Group (2003).

[70] See e.g. SAMLIT (2021); UNODC (2020), p. 128.

[71] See e.g. GIABA (2020); FATF (2020).

through involvement in IWT or indirectly through extortion, taxation or control of trafficking routes, thereby linking the proceeds of IWT to the financing of terrorism. As Hawala transactions do not lend themselves to the formal financial system, the risk of detection is low. This exacerbates the simplicity and ease with which IWT can be engaged as a terrorism financing method.

3.6 AML/CTF Considerations

In the process of financing terrorism, the funds generated from IWT may or may not penetrate the formal financial system, depending on various considerations such as the nature and intended purpose of the funds. In cases where funds move through the formal financial system, the AML/CTF obligations of regulated entities become relevant. This section focuses on AML/CTF regulatory frameworks in Africa and related developments. At a continental level, great strides have been made to address money laundering and terrorism financing in Africa. This can be evidenced through the work of the FATF-style Regional Bodies in Africa, namely GIABA, ESAAMLG, the Action Group Against Money Laundering in Central Africa (GABAC) and the Middle East and North Africa Financial Action Task Force (MENAFATF). At a country level, however, the situation is rather different. National AML/CTF regulatory frameworks tend to suffer from gaps and enforcement challenges, necessitating the exploitation of certain sectors or activities by criminals and terrorist groups.[72] This is especially pronounced in relation to IWT.

The starting point in this regard is the issue of fragmentation of AML/CTF frameworks. Throughout Africa, there is a tendency to establish AML/CTF laws across multiple regulatory instruments, which sometimes leads to regulatory inconsistency, overlap, and arbitrage.[73] Circumstances necessitating a flurry of legislative enactments, such as greylisting, may unintentionally further complicate these issues.[74] On a practical level, fragmentation contributes to the existing challenges on coordination between regulatory bodies and compliance by financial institutions and designated non-financial businesses and professions.[75] It also creates problems for supervision and enforcement as far as efficiency and effectiveness are

[72] This much is clear from the FATF mutual evaluation reports of various African countries, including Angola, Cameroon, Kenya, Mozambique, Nigeria and South Africa. These reports can be accessed at FATF (2025).

[73] South Africa represents a good case study in this regard. See generally FATF (2021). Many of the legal deficiencies identified in the mutual evaluation report of South Africa were subsequently cured by way of legislative amendment.

[74] A major possibility in this regard is the emergence of conflicting legal provisions, which may in turn lead to over- and under-compliance by regulated entities.

[75] The consequences of this kind of fragmentation is explored in the case study presented in the chapter by Ferrill and Southworth (2025) in this book.

concerned.[76] The relationship between IWT and AML/CTF ecosystems in Africa must be contemplated against this background.

IWT crimes are generally not prosecuted with reference to AML/CTF frameworks. Until recently, the focus was very much still on prosecuting only under wildlife conservation frameworks. The SAMLIT explains:

> [T]here has been limited attention given to investigating and understanding financial flows associated with IWT. Instead, offenders have been prosecuted for predicate offences such as poaching, possession, or trafficking of wildlife products. As a result of this limited focus on the financial side of IWT, authorities have not been effective in identifying and disrupting illegal networks, or in prosecuting higher-level offenders who operate in criminal organisations involved in IWT.[77]

There are many reasons for this development, but a limited awareness of the intersection of the regulatory frameworks and misalignment of the regulatory frameworks are especially noteworthy. Further research must be conducted to determine the extent to which a lack of resources and skills may have contributed to this development.

In 2020 the FATF emphasised the importance of regular or proactive collection, development and dissemination of financial intelligence to initiate or support financial investigations into wildlife crimes.[78] It, then, specifically recommends that parallel financial investigations in IWT cases be pursued. The FATF explains:

> Parallel investigations represent a powerful tool that jurisdictions can utilise to reduce the profitability of the illegal wildlife trade. In line with FATF Recommendation 30, it is important that jurisdictions launch parallel financial investigations where appropriate to identify broader criminal networks and to prevent criminal proceeds and instrumentalities from dissipating. Failure to utilise financial information and conduct a financial investigation sufficiently early may lead to relocation or concealment of the associated networks and assets that a financial inquiry after the predicate investigation is unable to detect.[79]

In 2021 Reid and Williams published, under the auspices of RUSI, research on IWT and parallel financial investigations in West Africa. Using a methodology comprising a targeted literature review, surveys, and interviews conducted at West African financial intelligence units (FIUs), the research found that 'Only three (25%) responding countries had conducted a financial investigation in an IWT case at the time of the survey in October 2020, meaning 75% of the responding countries had never conducted a financial investigation in an IWT case'.[80] The survey results similarly showed that very few parallel financial investigations had been conducted in wildlife cases in West Africa. Recent developments suggesting a gradual inclination towards financial investigations in wildlife cases are not convincing.[81]

---

[76] See GIABA (2020), pp. 56–58.

[77] SAMLIT (2021), p. 2.

[78] FATF (2020), p. 32.

[79] FATF (2020), p. 34.

[80] Reid and Williams (2021), p. 29.

[81] Reid and Williams (2021), p. 29.

Unfortunately, there are several impediments to financial investigations in wildlife cases. Reid and Williams provide a list of impediments of which the following were ranked by the participating FIUs as most problematic:[82]

1. Lack of awareness of IWT as a predicate offence to money laundering.
2. Lack of necessary training and skills.
3. Lack of financial resources.

The second and third impediments are underpinned by social and political considerations.[83] The first impediment, by contrast, falls within the scope of legal and operational structures. The UN calls upon member states to take seriously wildlife crime by strengthening legislation and regulations necessary for the prevention, investigation, prosecution, and appropriate punishment of IWT activities, as well as by strengthening enforcement and criminal justice responses, and to increase the exchange of information and knowledge among national and international crime authorities.[84] This call is especially important in the context of terrorism financing where prosecution is low and the dynamic and evolving nature of financing strategies yield limited information for the CTF community.

While domestic legal frameworks increasingly regard IWT as a predicate offence for money laundering (either expressly or implicitly),[85] rarely do they make a direct legal connection to terrorism financing. Defining IWT as a high-risk activity for terrorism financing under national CTF laws would serve to formally recognise the strategic use of wildlife trafficking by terrorist groups as a security threat. This legal designation would compel regulated entities, law enforcement agencies, and FIUs to treat transactions linked to IWT with heightened scrutiny, similar to how drug trafficking and arms smuggling are currently approached. It would also justify the application of enhanced due diligence, reporting obligations, and asset-freezing measures on individuals and entities suspected of engaging in wildlife crime to fund terrorist operations. Such a legislative enactment would be particularly appropriate in source countries, where the economic, environmental and social impact of IWT is most felt.

By codifying the link between IWT and terrorism financing, African countries can more effectively integrate environmental crime into national security agendas and align domestic CTF regulatory frameworks with evolving continental CTF shifts. As is clear from the experience of West Africa, however, there is a need to establish operational environments that support the implementation of the CTF legal framework.[86] Awareness campaigns and capacity-building exercises are likely to be instructive, but they should be complemented with ongoing skills development

[82] Reid and Williams (2021), p. 36.

[83] See the discussions in Reid and Williams (2021), pp. 36–41.

[84] UN (2021), p. 6.

[85] On this development, see Lupton (2023), pp. 192–194.

[86] Reid and Williams (2021), p. 21.

initiatives such as regular training exercises.[87] Ultimately, an appreciation for the link between IWT and terrorism financing may lead to a greater use of CTF regulatory frameworks in the prosecution of wildlife-related crimes, thereby widening sentencing options in relation to terrorists.

In the context of this study, two further impediments are noteworthy. The first is the use of cash and informal payment systems by criminals and terrorist groups which, as discussed above, presents serious challenges in identifying the financial flows of wildlife cases. The second is insufficient information sharing and cooperation capabilities between FIUs and other relevant national and regional agencies.[88]

Impediments to financial investigations in wildlife cases hinder the quantity and quality of data relating to the financial flows associated with IWT operations. More broadly, they illustrate the stark realities of the social and political landscape in Africa. Therefore, when assessing the effectiveness of African countries in tackling money laundering, terrorism financing, and proliferation financing, this background must be competently understood.

Of relevance to the present discussion, at the time of writing, is the proposed amendment of FATF Recommendation 16. Recommendation 16 was originally developed with the objective of 'preventing terrorists and other criminals from having unfettered access to wire transfers for moving their funds, and for detecting such misuse when it occurs'.[89] This construction necessitates an expectation to classify high terrorism financing risks. The language of the revised recommendation, read in conjunction with the revised interpretative note, however, implies an expectation to classify low or lower terrorism financing risks. The revised interpretative note provides:

> Due to the potential terrorist financing threat posed by small payments or value transfers, countries should minimise thresholds, while taking into account the risk of driving transactions underground and the importance of financial inclusion.[90]

On a practical level, a low- or lower-risk classification model may have significant compliance and reporting implications for financial institutions.[91] The essential question is, under what circumstances may a terrorism financing risk be classified as low or lower risk? The answer to this question is elusive. Moreover, anecdotal evidence suggests that such a model may not be compatible with the design of conventional AML/CTF systems.

Whether this revision will have a meaningful impact on the detection and prevention of IWT is unclear. Although a lower threshold would expand the scope of regulated entities' compliance and assessment functions, the cash-intensive nature of

---

[87] This statement finds support in the West Africa Strategy on Combating Wildlife Crime (WASCWC), which was recently adopted by the heads of state of the Economic Community of the West African States. See Reid and Williams (2021), p. 2.

[88] Further discussions regarding the centrality of information sharing can be found in the chapter by Chadderton (2025) in this book and the chapter by Goldbarsht and Goodrick (2025) in this book.

[89] FATF (2012–2023), p. 80.

[90] FATF (2024), p. 13.

[91] Southworth and Levi (2024), p. 101–121.

IWT activities, particularly at the poaching and transportation stages, means that IWT-related financial flows may be difficult to detect. This outcome would be even more acute where Hawala is the preferred payment system. In cases where IWT-generated funds are transferred using wire transfers in the formal financial system, even small payments may in principle be flagged for terrorist financing purposes—but this will likely only happen where multiple red flags (or a suspicion) for terrorist financing are present.

From the above analysis it is apparent that overlap exists between terrorist activities and IWT activities. The use of cash and informal payment systems and the exploitation of porous borders are especially noteworthy in this regard. It is also apparent, however, that the financial aspects associated with wildlife cases are not well-understood by the AML/CTF community, leading to ineffectiveness and unintended negative consequences. This is elevated due to pressing social and political considerations. It would therefore be fair to conclude that IWT could very well be perceived by terrorist groups as a 'low risk, high reward' financing method, potentially setting the stage for an increase in wildlife crimes.

4 Conclusion

Studies on terrorism in Africa typically include discourse on the historical underpinnings, the philosophies of specific terrorist groups and, to a large extent, the reasons for, and impact of, terrorism. Seldom is the focus on terrorism financing opportunities. This chapter focuses on a specific terrorism financing method: IWT.

While the link between IWT and terrorism financing has been acknowledged in the literature, a detailed study of this intersection was missing. The chapter therefore bridged the knowledge gap by integrating insights from the spheres of terrorism and wildlife crime, positioning IWT as a high-risk vulnerability for terrorist financing that requires proactive intervention. The identified factors (1) profitability, (2) proximity to poachers and wildlife, (3) porous borders, (4) reliance on cash and informal payment systems, and (5) AML/CTF considerations, probably do not take into account all applicable aspects, but they do represent the main features of the terrorism financing-IWT nexus.

From a risk management perspective, these factors may be approached by different disciplines. Factors (2) and (3) fall within the realm of wildlife protection and anti-poaching, while factors (1), (4), and (5) are relevant to the AML/CTF community and regulators. Factors (3) and (4) would also be relevant to customs and border control, and factors (1), (2), and (3) could effectively be considered the priorities of wildlife management agencies. Research suggests that the emerging risks, generally, are addressed in isolation, with little empirical data moving between the role players of the various disciplines.[92] In other words, there appears to be limited inter-

[92] See generally GIABA (2020); van Uhm and Wong (2021); van Uhm and Nijman (2022).

action and collaboration between the different spheres. This is regrettable. Therefore, the ability of the AML/CTF community to combat multi-dimensional threats should not be overemphasised in cases where the threat is not well-understood. This includes the terrorism financing-IWT threat.

To effectively address the terrorism financing-IWT nexus and terrorism in general, an integrated approach is essential. This approach would entail a focus on cross-discipline collaboration and cooperation to gain insights into the entire IWT spectrum as well as the multifaceted nature of terrorism. This is to say that it should go beyond current AML/CTF requirements, expectations and perspectives.[93] The approach would be particularly valuable in the facilitation of information sharing initiatives and the coordination of enforcement, regulatory, and other responses to imminent threats. The SAMLIT, which was established in South Africa as a public-private partnership, serves as an important case study in this regard.[94] Moreover, this approach could be implemented at both the regional and domestic levels with a view to promoting synergy across the relevant structures.[95] Importantly, these structures must be sufficiently supported by law to avoid being stifled unnecessarily by privacy and data protection concerns.

Substantive recommendations regarding the financial aspects of IWT have been proposed in the literature.[96] The recommendations by Reid and Williams are complementary and contextually appropriate—they are aimed at supporting West African countries to mainstream financial investigations in IWT cases.[97] These recommendations are not repeated here. It suffices to say that they can be applied, *mutatis mutandis*, in support of other regions where there is exposure to the terrorism financing-IWT threat. This includes Eastern and Southern Africa.

References

Abioye F (2019) Terrorist groups in Africa: *quo vadis*? Counc Dev Soc Sci Res Africa 44(3):5–30

ACLED (2023) Somalia: Al-Shabaab infighting — threat or opportunity for the counter-insurgency effort? https://acleddata.com/2023/11/17/somalia-situation-update-november-2023-al-shabaab-infighting-threat-or-opportunity-for-the-counter-insurgency-efforts/

Ali AM (2008) The Al-Shabaab Al-Mujahidiin – a profile of the first Somali terrorist organization. Institut für Strategie- Politik- Sicherheits- und Wirtschaftsberatung, Berlin. https://www.files.ethz.ch/isn/55851/AlShabaab.pdf

ATMIS (2025) New year message from the African Union special representative for Somalia. Somalia. https://atmis-au.org/new-year-message-from-the-african-union-special-representative-for-somalia/

[93] This resonates well with de Koker's 'collaborative approach' in de Koker (2024), pp. 156–157.

[94] For background on the SAMLIT, see SAMLIT (2023), pp. 6–8.

[95] This opens the door to greater consideration for public-private partnership models.

[96] ECOFEL (2021), pp. 36–65; FATF (2020), pp. 27–59. See also Lupton (2023), pp. 192–194.

[97] Reid and Williams (2021), pp. 47–49.

AU (2024) Press release: Boko Haram and other terrorist groups activities in Lake Chad Basin region suppressed in a joint forces operation. N'Djamena, Chad. https://au.int/sites/default/files/pressreleases/44012-pr-PR_Multinational_Joint_Task_Force_against_Boko_Haram.pdf

Azumah J (2015) Boko Haram in retrospect. Islam Christian–Muslim Relat 26(1):33–52

Bekele HK (2021) Problem of defining terrorism under international law: definition by the Appeal Chamber of Special Tribunal for Lebanon as a solution to the problem. Beijing Law Rev 12:619–630

Byrne JE, Marxen K, Kozakowski M, Byrne M (2022) Trade based financial crime compliance. Institute of International Banking Law and Practice, United States

Cannon BJ (2016) Terrorists, geopolitics and Kenya's proposed border wall with Somalia. J Terror Res 7(2):22–37

Chadderton P (2025) FATF and the conundrum of public-private sector intelligence and information sharing. In: Goldbarsht D, de Koker L, Ferrill J (eds) The financial war on crime and terrorism: opportunities and challenges. Springer, Cham

Duffy R (2022) Crime, security, and illegal wildlife trade: political ecologies of international conservation. Glob Environ Politics 22(2):23–44

ECOFEL (2021) Financial investigations into wildlife crime. ECFEL, Canada. https://egmont-group.org/wp-content/uploads/2021/09/2021_ECOFEL_-_Financial_Investigations_into_Wildlife_Crime.pdf

ESAAMLG (2016) A special typologies project report on poaching, illegal trade in wildlife and wildlife products and associated money laundering in the ESAAMLG region. ESAAMLG. https://www.esaamlg.org/reports/TYPOLOGIES-REPORT-ON-THE-WILDLIFE-CRIMES-AND-RELATED-ML.pdf

FATF (2012–2023) International standards on combating money laundering and the financing of terrorism & proliferation – the FATF recommendations. FATF, Paris

FATF (2016) FATF guidance: terrorist financing in west and central Africa. FATF, Paris. https://www.fatf-gafi.org/content/dam/fatf-gafi/reports/Terrorist-Financing-West-Central-Africa.pdf.coredownload.pdf

FATF (2020) FATF report: money laundering and the illegal wildlife trade. FATF, Paris. https://www.fatf-gafi.org/content/dam/fatf-gafi/reports/Money-laundering-and-illegal-wildlife-trade.pdf

FATF (2021) Anti-money laundering and counter-terrorist financing measures: South Africa mutual evaluation report. FATF, Paris. https://www.fatf-gafi.org/content/dam/fatf-gafi/mer/Mutual-Evaluation-Report-South-Africa.pdf.coredownload.inline.pdf

FATF (2024) Explanatory memorandum and draft revisions to recommendation 16. FATF, Paris. https://www.fatf-gafi.org/en/publications/Fatfrecommendations/R16-public-consultation-Feb24.html

FATF (2025) Mutual evaluations. FATF, Paris. https://www.fatf-gafi.org/en/publications/Mutualevaluations.html

Ferrill J, Southworth R (2025) Leadership in the evolving landscape of financial crime: navigating AML/CTF risks and controls. In: Goldbarsht D, de Koker L, Ferrill J (eds) The financial war on crime and terrorism: opportunities and challenges. Springer, Cham

Financial Intelligence Centre (2024) South African national terrorism financing risk assessment. FIC, South Africa. https://www.fic.gov.za/wp-content/uploads/2024/06/National-risk-assessment-%E2%80%93-Terrorist-financing-national-risk-assessment-2024.pdf

GIABA (2020) Assessment of counter terrorist financing capacities in West Africa. GIABA, Dakar. https://www.giaba.org/Frame/pdfviewer%7C%7C617f12f22b5b3d98bdf8719492be2960010811cdacf9259f238e2d5e0c0aaf3a%7C%7C1132_ENG-Assessment%20of%20the%20CFT%20Capacities%20in%20GIABA%20MS.pdf

Gilroy G (2024) The online frontline: decoding al-Shabaab's social media strategy. CTC SENTINEL 17(1):25–30

Goldbarsht D, Goodrick T (2025) Private to private: the next frontier of financial intelligence sharing. In: Goldbarsht D, de Koker L, Ferrill J (eds) The financial war on crime and terrorism: opportunities and challenges. Springer

Gow J, Olonishakin F, Dijxhorn E (2013) Militancy and violence in West Africa: religion, politics and radicalization. Routledge, London

Institute for Economics and Peace (2025) Global terrorism index. IEP, Sydney. file:///C:/Users/clupton/Downloads/Global-Terrorism-Index-2025.pdf

Kagan J (2023) What is Hawala? Money transfer without money movement. Investopedia. https://www.investopedia.com/terms/h/hawala.asp

Kawadza H (2017) A snapshot of financial exclusion in South Africa. In: Hugo C, du Toit S (eds) Annual Banking Law Update. Juta and Co, Cape Town, pp 43–50

de Koker L (2024) The FATF's combating of financing of proliferation standards: private sector implementation challenges. In: Goldbarsht D, de Koker L (eds) Financial crime and the law identifying and mitigating risks. Springer, pp 123–166

Lawson K, Vines A (2014) Global impacts of the illegal wildlife trade: the costs of crime, insecurity and institutional erosion. Chatam House, London

Lupton C (2023) Illegal wildlife trade: the critical role of the banking sector in combating money laundering. J Money Laund Control 26(7):181–196

MacFarlane D, Hurlstone MJ, Ecker UKH, Ferraro PJ, van der Linden S, Wan AKY, Veríssimo D, Burgess G, Chen F, Hall W, Hollands GJ, Sutherland WJ (2022) Reducing demand for overexploited wildlife products: lessons from systematic reviews from outside conservation science. Conserv Sci Pract 4(3):1–20

Maguire T, Haenlein C (2015) Occasional paper: an illusion of complicity terrorism and the illegal ivory trade in East Africa. RUSI, United Kingdom. https://static.rusi.org/201509_an_illusion_of_complicity.pdf

Mentan T (2017) Dilemmas of weak states: Africa and transnational terrorism in the twenty-first century. Routledge, London

Morris N, de Koker L (2025) The impact of the financial action task Force (FATF) standards and focus: from effectiveness to effect. In: Goldbarsht D, de Koker L, Ferrill J (eds) The financial war on crime and terrorism: opportunities and challenges. Springer, Cham

Mozer A, Prost S (2023) An introduction to illegal wildlife trade and its effects on biodiversity and society. Forensic Sci Int Anim Environ 3:100064

Nanima RD (2016) Prosecution of rhino poachers: the need to focus on the prosecution of the higher echelons of organized crime networks. Afr J Legal Stud 9(4):221–234

Nanima RD (2019) The Prevention of Organised Crime Act 1998: the need for extraterritorial jurisdiction to prosecute the higher echelons of those involved in rhino poaching. Potchefstroom Electron Law J 22(1):1–46

Obah-Akpowoghaha NG, Ojakorotu V, Tarro ML (2020) Porous borders and the challenge of national integration in Africa. J Afr Foreign Aff 7(3):89–111

OECD (2019) The illegal wildlife trade in Southeast Asia – institutional capacities in Indonesia, Singapore, Thailand and Viet Nam. OECD, Paris. https://www.oecd.org/content/dam/oecd/en/publications/reports/2019/09/the-illegal-wildlife-trade-in-southeast-asia_d91002c8/14fe3297-en.pdf4e2a7604120f3818d65&itemIGO=oecd&itemContentType=book

Reeve R, Pelter Z (2014) From new frontier to new normal: counter-terrorism operations in the Sahel-Sahara. Oxford Research Group, United Kingdom. https://www.files.ethz.ch/isn/182963/From%20New%20Frontier%20to%20New%20Normal%20-%20Counter-terrorism%20operations%20in%20the%20Sahel-Sahara.pdf

Reid A, Williams M (2021) Occasional paper: illegal wildlife trade and financial investigations in West Africa. RUSI, United Kingdom. https://static.rusi.org/273_op_iwt_west_africa_final_web_version_0.pdf

SAMLIT (2021) Financial flows associated with illegal wildlife trade in South Africa. Financial Intelligence Centre, South Africa. https://www.fic.gov.za/wp-content/uploads/2023/09/2021.11-SL-SAMLIT-IWT-Report-2021.pdf

SAMLIT (2023) Financial flows associated with illegal wildlife trade in South Africa: an updated perspective. Financial Intelligence Centre, South Africa. https://www.fic.gov.za/wp-content/uploads/2023/12/Financial-flows-associated-with-illegal-wildlife-trade-in-South-Africa.pdf

Solomon H (2013) Exploring the nexus between ethnicity and terrorism. Confl Trends 3:31–37

South African Government (2023) National integrated strategy to combat wildlife trafficking (NISCWT) securing South Africa's wildlife heritage: breaking the illicit value chain of wildlife trafficking. South Africa. https://www.saps.gov.za/dpci/site/RegulatoryFramework/documents/niscwt.pdf

Southworth R, Levi M (2024) Application of the risk-based approach (RBA) for financial crime risk management by banks. In: Financial crime and the law: identifying and mitigating risks. Springer, pp 101–121

Statista (2024) Number of violent deaths caused by political instability and citizen alienation in Nigeria between 2011 and 2023, by perpetrator. Hamburg. https://www.statista.com/statistics/1197776/deaths-caused-by-political-instability-in-nigeria/

Sullivan R, Weerd H (2021) The illegal wildlife trade and the banking sector in China: the need for a zero tolerance approach. TRAFFIC, United Kingdom. https://www.traffic.org/site/assets/files/17384/the_illegal_wildlife_trade_and_the_banking_sector_in_china_the_need_for_a_zero-tolerance_approach.pdf

Uhm DP, Nijman RCC (2022) The convergence of environmental crime with other serious crimes: subtypes within the environmental crime continuum. Eur J Criminol 19(4):542–561

Uhm DP, Wong RWY (2021) Chinese organized crime and the illegal wildlife trade: diversification and outsourcing in the Golden Triangle. Trends Organ Crime 24:486–505

UN (2021) Tackling illicit trafficking in wildlife. UNSC, New York. file:///C:/Users/clupton/Downloads/A_RES_75_311-EN.pdf

UNODC (2020) World wildlife crime report: trafficking in protected species. UNODC, Vienna. https://www.unodc.org/documents/data-and-analysis/wildlife/2020/World_Wildlife_Report_2020_9July.pdf

UNSC CTED (2022) Concerns over the use of proceeds from the exploitation, trade, and trafficking of natural resources for the purposes of terrorism financing. UNSC, New York. https://www.un.org/securitycouncil/ctc/sites/www.un.org.securitycouncil.ctc/files/files/documents/2022/Jun/cted_cft_trends_alert_june_2022.pdf

UNSC Resolution 2462 (2019). UNSC, New York. https://docs.un.org/en/S/RES/2462(2019)

US Department of Treasury (2023) Treasury designates terror operatives and illicit charcoal smugglers in Somalia. https://home.treasury.gov/news/press-releases/jy1499

Wildlife Justice Commission (2022). Value of rhino horn. Netherlands. https://wildlifejustice.org/wp-content/uploads/2022/10/Rhino-Horn-Trafficking-Report-2022-CAP.5.pdf

World Bank Group (2003) Informal funds transfer systems: an analysis of the informal hawala system. World Bank Group, Washington. https://documents1.worldbank.org/curated/en/410351468765856277/pdf/multi0page.pdf

World Bank Group (2019) Illegal logging, fishing, and wildlife trade: the costs and how to combat it. World Bank Group, Washington. https://thedocs.worldbank.org/en/doc/482771571323560234-0120022019/original/WBGReport1017Digital.pdf

Zabala ML (2023) Assessing the effectiveness of the Multinational Joint Task Force. Accord, Durban. https://www.accord.org.za/analysis/assessing-the-effectiveness-of-the-multinational-joint-task-force/

Cayle Lupton is an associate professor of banking law and director of the Centre for Banking Law at the University of Johannesburg. He is also an attorney of the High Court of South Africa, a member of the Global South Dialogue on Economic Crime and was recently appointed as chairperson of the Banking Commission of the International Chamber of Commerce South Africa. His research interests fall within the domain of international banking law, with a particular focus on trade finance, financial crime and targeted financial sanctions. His expertise in these areas has been recognised at the international level, most recently by the Court of Appeal of Singapore and the United Nations Office on Drugs and Crime. Prior to joining academia, Cayle practiced as a commercial lawyer with a particular focus on litigation and regulatory compliance. Cayle holds the degrees LLB, LLM and LLD from the University of Johannesburg as well as a Certificate in Trade Finance Compliance from the London Institute of Banking and Finance.

Practice to Deceive: A Taxonomy of Money Laundering Deception Based on US and Australian Case Studies

Ben Scott

Abstract The practice of deception is integral to financial crime in many of its forms. The criminal offence of money laundering involves knowingly conducting transactions, movements of funds or dealings in property that are derived from criminal activity. Concealing or disguising the criminal origins of crime-derived wealth is one of the acts which distinguishes money laundering from simply spending the proceeds of crime. Despite the centrality of deception to money laundering, there has been limited research into how money laundering deception operates and the forms it takes. The established three-stage conceptual model of the money laundering cycle provides a useful framework for understanding certain kinds of laundering activity. However, it does not support the granular analysis of deception practice which this chapter argues is fundamental to developing effective anti-money laundering control environments within advanced economies.

The chapter aims to develop deception as a lens through which to facilitate applied research into the detection and prevention of money laundering by combining legal analysis with financial intelligence case studies. It draws on frameworks developed within cybersecurity and intelligence to support a deeper analysis of deception practice in money laundering. The chapter begins with a review of the element of deception in the criminal law of money laundering, focusing on the common law jurisdictions of Australia and the United States. The chapter then applies a taxonomy of deception developed by cybersecurity researchers Rothstein and Rowe to two case studies of complex money laundering: the Toronto Dominion Bank and Changjiang Financial cases. The chapter posits a distinction between primary deception, which focuses on concealing the criminal origin of transactions, funds and assets through various means, and secondary deception, which involves plausible denial of criminal knowledge, usually by third-party facilitators.

B. Scott (✉)
Macquarie University and Financial Integrity Hub (FIH), Sydney, NSW, Australia
e-mail: ben.scott@afcx.com.au

D. Goldbarsht et al. (eds.), *The Financial War on Crime and Terrorism*, European Yearbook of International Economic Law,
https://doi.org/10.1007/978-3-032-06360-1_7

1 Introduction

Long before money laundering was defined in popular culture and legislation in the twentieth century, Sir Walter Scott's Marmion referred to the 'tangled web we weave/when first we practice to deceive.' Indeed, many money laundering schemes involve a bewildering sprawl of mule accounts, shelf companies, wire transfers, and cash deposits. However, money laundering is fundamentally a simple crime, and deception is at the heart of it. This is apparent in the framing of the Vienna and Palermo Conventions, which use the language of 'concealment' and 'disguise' to define money laundering offences,[1] and in the jurisdictions that have based their money laundering statutes substantially on the definitions in those conventions. Proving that a defendant's actions constituted a deliberate attempt to conceal or disguise the nature of illicit proceeds goes to distinguishing money laundering from the mere spending of criminal proceeds, and therefore to the success of a money laundering prosecution.[2]

Despite the centrality of deception in money laundering offences, there has been little research into the practice of deception in money laundering. This chapter argues that understanding deception is essential to going beyond mere pattern description, and more effectively detecting, preventing, and disrupting money laundering and other types of financial crime. There are other lenses through which money laundering methods can be analysed. The three-stage model of placement, layering, and integration is used extensively in law enforcement and the financial sector as a conceptual model to aid detection and train staff. This model has been criticised as prescriptive and static. Developed for cash-based scenarios in the 1980s, it is less suited to cashless methods such as trade-based money laundering. It suggests a uniformly sequential money laundering process and assumes that integration is invariably the end goal whereas proceeds of crime sometimes remain within a parallel criminal economy.[3]

However, the purpose of this chapter is not to supplant the three-stage model, which continues to have general explanatory value, particularly for complex, syndicated money laundering. The intention of this chapter is to draw on a scholarship of deception that exists in the fields of cybersecurity and intelligence studies. In these fields, deception analysis is paramount because practitioners generally deal with unknown adversaries seeking to infiltrate a system or network. The practices of red-teaming and kill chain analysis, which use structured techniques to anticipate the deceptive moves of adversaries, developed in these settings.[4] This chapter advocates

---

[1] See *United Nations Convention against Illicit Traffic in Narcotic Drugs and Psychotropic Substances* 1988 ('Vienna Convention'), art 1(b)(ii) and *United Nations Convention Against Transnational Organised Crime and the Protocols Hereto* 2000 ('Palermo Convention'), art 6(1)(a)(i) and (ii).

[2] *United States v Campbell*, 977 F.2d 854 (4th Cir. 1992), 858.

[3] Levi (2020), pp. 4–7.

[4] Scott (2021).

for the value of adapting frameworks for deception analysis from these fields, and suggests some directions for the application of deception research to the problem of money laundering.

The chapter starts with an overview of how the laws pertaining to money laundering have developed to deal with the concept of deception, focusing on the concepts of disguise and concealment, in two common law jurisdictions with relatively similar legal frameworks: the United States and Australia. It also reviews the ways these jurisdictions address the matter of an offenders' knowledge of money laundering. Knowledge of the criminal origins of funds or assets may be all that separates laundering activity from a legitimate business transaction, and so plausible denial of knowledge is an important aspect of secondary money laundering deception.

The chapter seeks to integrate these legal concepts with analysis of how money laundering deception works in practice. It does so by applying a taxonomy of deception developed by cybersecurity researchers Rothstein and Rowe[5] to two real-life case studies of complex money laundering: the Australian Changjiang Financial case (2023) and the US Toronto Dominion Bank case (2024). The Rothstein/Rowe taxonomy is used to analyse deception by breaking down any action into a series of building blocks called 'semantic cases.' Deception can be applied in relation to any of these semantic cases.

A distinction is made between two types of money laundering deception. Primary deception is practiced by criminal organisations attempting to launder the proceeds of crime. The goal of primary deception is to conceal and disguise the criminal origins of the funds or assets and provide a false 'legend' to legitimise them. Secondary deception is practiced by financial service providers and other intermediaries that knowingly facilitate money laundering transactions. Here the object of the deception is plausible denial of knowledge of their criminal origin. As we will see, this 'wilful blindness' was a key concern of legislators drafting money laundering laws in the 1980s and continues to be an important element of contemporary laundering.

The chapter concludes with a summary of the insights about money laundering deception which emerge from the application of the taxonomy to the case studies, and the implications of these insights for how governments and the private sector can more effectively detect, disrupt, and prevent financial crime.

---

[5] Rowe and Rothstein (2004).

2 Deception and the Law of Money Laundering

In military intelligence research, deception has been defined as consisting of two elements: dissimulation, which is hiding the real; and simulation, which is showing the false.[6] In the deception cycle defined by Bell[7], a deception planner first identifies a target. They then construct a ruse to achieve the desired outcome. The ruse is delivered by a channel in the 'decision arena'. This is the area in which a ruse is made visible to the target's perceptions. The target's response provides feedback to the deception planner, who then analyses that feedback. The planner can then respond to the feedback by adjusting the ruse, developing new ruses or abandoning the deception.[8]

In the law of financial crime, there is no universally accepted definition of deception. However, the language of the Vienna Convention, closely mirrored in the legislation of the US and other countries, is a useful starting point. It refers to concealment or disguise of the "true nature, source, location, disposition, movement, rights with respect to, or ownership of property."[9] US money laundering legislation refers to activity intended "to conceal or disguise the nature, the location, the source, the ownership, or the control" of criminal proceeds.[10] 'Conceal' and 'disguise' are not defined further in these provisions. There are various dictionary definitions of 'disguise,' including, relevantly, "to conceal or cloak the real state or character of something by a counterfeit show or appearance".[11] 'Conceal' can be defined as "to hide a person (or thing); to put or keep out of sight or notice".[12]

The United States was the first jurisdiction to establish a framework for prosecuting money laundering as a serious criminal offence in the 1980s. While the *Bank Secrecy Act* 1970 (BSA) contained criminal penalties for money laundering offences and civil penalties for reporting violations, these were seen as insufficient to address the systemic financial crime risks created by organised crime exploitation of the banking system. A 1984 report by the President's Commission on Organised Crime identified the low financial penalties imposed under the BSA as insufficient to deter money laundering, and its felony provisions difficult to apply. The report recommended that Congress make the use of financial institutions by money launderers a criminal offence.[13]

---

[6] Whaley (1982), pp. 182–3.

[7] Bell (2003), pp. 244–279.

[8] Ibid, pp. 252–3.

[9] Vienna Convention, art 1(b)(ii).

[10] Title 18 USC § 1956(a)(1)(B)(i).

[11] Oxford English Dictionary. Disguise. In Oxford English Dictionary. Retrieved 9 March 2025 from https://www.oed.com/dictionary/disguise_v?tab=meaning_and_use#6557718

[12] Oxford English Dictionary. Conceal. In Oxford English Dictionary. Retrieved 9 March 2025 from https://www.oed.com/dictionary/conceal_v?tab=meaning_and_use#8627813

[13] Ibid, p. 62.

The 1985 *Bank of Boston* case reinforced the Commission's case for change. In that case, the US Treasury fined the Bank of Boston $500,000 for failing to report transactions totaling over $1.6 billion as required under the BSA.[14] This was one of several investigations exposing systemic non-compliance with BSA requirements by US banks. Media coverage of the case focused not only on the formal reporting breaches, but on the actions of collusive bank employees who turned a blind eye to suspicious cash transactions by mafia-affiliated clients.[15]

The *Money Laundering Control Act* 1986 (MLCA) created money laundering offences under § 1956 and 1957 of the U.S. Code. § 1956, titled 'Laundering of monetary instruments,' prohibits a comprehensive range of criminal transactional activities and dealings with property and criminal proceeds.

At the time of drafting, legislators clearly understood and intended that the breadth of the offences would capture reckless misconduct by financial institutions in handling proceeds of crime. As Representative Clay Shaw put it in the discussions preceding the Bill which became the MLCA:

> I am sick and tired of watching people sit back and say "I am not part of the problem, I am not committing the crime, and therefore, my hands are clean even though I know the money is dirty I am handling." The only way we will get at this problem is to let the whole community, the whole population, know that they are part of the problem and could very well be convicted if they take these funds.[16]

§ 1956(a)(1) prohibits knowingly conducting transactions involving the proceeds of specified unlawful activity. Specified unlawful activity encompasses a range of serious criminal offences under U.S. law including racketeering offences, fraud, bribery, and extortion.[17] § 1956(a)(2) deals with offenses involving the transportation of funds or monetary instruments from, to or through the United States for the purpose of criminal activity or knowing that they are the proceeds of crime. § 1957 prohibits knowingly engaging in a transaction involving criminally derived property. It is a requirement of this section that the property is derived from specified unlawful activity, but not that the defendant knew that the offence from which the property was derived was specified unlawful activity.[18]

The internationalisation of money laundering as an offence followed soon after its criminalisation in the United States, motivated by the desire to act against narcotics trafficking. Signatories to the 1988 Vienna Convention agreed to criminalise a wide range of dealings with property for the purpose of concealing or disguising its connection with narcotics offences.[19]

[14] Morgan (1996), p. 11.

[15] Economist Intelligence Unit (1986).

[16] Comments of Representative Clay Shaw during markup of House Bill 5077, republished in Wolfteich (1988), footnote 136.

[17] Title 18 USC § 1956(c)(7).

[18] Title 18 USC § 1957(a) and (c).

[19] Vienna Convention, art 3.

The two money laundering offences described in the Vienna Convention use the language of concealment and disguise to place deception in the foreground. The first consists of the "conversion or transfer of property" knowing that is derived from narcotics offences, with the intention of concealing or disguising the illicit origin of the property or assisting a person involved in the offences to evade legal consequences.[20] The second consists of the concealment or disguise of the "true nature, source, location, disposition, movement, rights with respect to, or ownership of property," knowing that the property is derived from narcotics offences.[21] The language of both offences reflects the critical importance of actions taken to conceal or disguise the origins of crime-derived property in money laundering offences.

In 1990 the Financial Action Task Force (FATF) was established and published its 40 Recommendations. These included a recommendation that countries should criminalise "drug money laundering" as set out in the Vienna Convention,[22] and that where possible, corporations themselves should be subject to criminal liability as well as their employees.[23] The United Nations Convention against Transnational Organised Crime (the Palermo Convention'), signed in December 2000, broadened the concept of money laundering further. To combat transnational crime, signatories agreed to extend the range of predicate offences that could ground a money laundering charge.[24] Under Article 6 of the Palermo Convention, signatories undertake to establish as criminal offences:

The conversion or transfer of property with knowledge that it is the proceeds of crime for the purpose of concealing or disguising its illicit origin or helping any person involved in the predicate offence to evade legal consequences;

The concealment or disguise of the true nature, source, location, disposition, movement or ownership of rights with respect to property, knowing that it is proceeds of crime;

The acquisition, possession or use of property knowing that it is proceeds of crime; and

Providing assistance to the commission of any of the above offences.[25]

The knowledge or intent required for these offences can be inferred from factual circumstances.[26]

Australia was one of many jurisdictions to establish its own extensive framework for prosecuting money laundering based on the model provisions in the Vienna and Palermo Conventions. That framework is complex, comprising 19 different offences

[20] Ibid, art 3(1)(b)(i).

[21] Ibid, art 3(1)(b)(ii).

[22] Ibid, recommendation 4.

[23] Ibid, recommendation 7.

[24] See Palermo Convention, art 6(2)(a) and (b) and the definition of 'serious crime' at art 2(b).

[25] Ibid, arts 6(1)(a) and (b).

[26] Ibid, art 6(2)(f).

set out in Division 400 of the Commonwealth Criminal Code.[27] Australia is distinctive in differentiating money laundering offences by the value of the property or funds involved, and the offender's level of knowledge of its criminal origins. This results in a tiered offence structure. While the offence provisions originally focused on using indictable offences as predicate crimes, this created evidentiary challenges for proving specific knowledge of the crimes from which the proceeds were derived. This was addressed through the introduction of a definition of 'general crime,' and related laundering offences.[28]

Sections 400.2B to 400.8 criminalise dealing with the proceeds or an instrument of general crime or indictable crime. There are three tiers of offences in each of these sections based on the level of knowledge alleged; belief, recklessness, or negligence.[29] Each subsection pertains to dealing with proceeds or instruments of crime above a defined threshold of value, from 'any value' (section 400.8) to $10 million and above (section 400.2B). At the higher value thresholds (ss. 400.2B–400.4), each section includes an offence of dealing with the proceeds of general crime.

Section 400.9 criminalises dealing with property reasonably suspected of being proceeds or instruments of crime. To prove someone guilty under this section, the prosecution must establish that they dealt with money or property that could reasonably be suspected of being proceeds of indictable crime. The section defines eight scenarios in which such a suspicion is reasonable. These include where the conduct constituting the offence breached anti-money laundering regulations, and where the value of the money or property is grossly out of proportion to the defendant's income and expenditure.[30]

3 Knowledge, Concealment and Disguise in Money Laundering Law

Earlier in this chapter, reference was made to primary money laundering deception, where a criminal individual or group seeks to conceal the origin of criminal proceeds, and secondary deception, where a facilitator of money laundering seeks to conceal or deny their knowledge of its criminal origin by turning a blind eye. As the case studies will show, these behaviours can present separately or together. It has been a challenge for US and Australian legislators to criminalise the wide range of deliberately deceptive and negligent behaviours that can constitute money laundering while maintaining the definitional rigour the criminal law requires for serious criminal offences.

[27] *Criminal Code Act* 1995 ('CCA') (Cth).

[28] See discussion at 'Key issues and provisions,' Bills Digest No. 44, 2020–21, *Crimes Legislation Amendment (Economic Disruption) Bill* 2020 (Cth).

[29] CCA ss. 400.2B-400.8.

[30] CCA s.400.9(2)(a)-(e).

Knowledge is a particularly important element of the offence of money laundering in both the US and Australia. The US approach to the knowledge element is relatively simple. The three money laundering offences under § 1956 all require either knowledge that property is the proceeds of crime, or an intent to use it to promote unlawful activity. To prove violation of § 1956(a)(1), the prosecution must show that the defendant either:

Intended to promote specified unlawful activity;
Intended to engage in tax evasion or tax fraud;
Knew that the transaction was designed to conceal nature, location, source, ownership or control of proceeds of the specified unlawful activity; or
Knew that the transaction was designed to avoid transaction reporting requirements under state or federal law.

§ 1956(2) (the 'transportation' offence) has a similar knowledge requirement: that is either the defendant intended to promote a specific unlawful activity; or they knew the funds involved were proceeds of unlawful activity and that their activity was intended to conceal or disguise the specified aspects of those funds, or to avoid a transaction reporting requirement. The requirement for 1956(3) is belief rather than knowledge because this offence relates to money laundering activity carried out as a result of a 'sting' operation by law enforcement, where the funds involved are represented to be proceeds of crime but are in fact government funds.[31] § 1957 prohibits knowingly engaging or attempting to engage in a monetary transaction involving property derived from specified unlawful activity and worth more than $10,000.

Under § 1956, it is not necessary that the defendant knew which form of specified unlawful activity generated the proceeds, only that it was the proceeds of some form of felony.[32] US courts have resisted attempts to broaden the definition of knowledge to include what a defendant should have known; a conviction must be based on actual, subjective knowledge. Knowledge can be established through both direct and circumstantial evidence.[33]

US courts have developed a doctrine of wilful blindness to deal with circumstances where a person involved in money laundering deliberately avoided direct knowledge of facts pointing to criminal conduct. A jury may infer that a defendant deliberately ignored 'red flags' indicating criminal activity when they would have been obvious to a reasonable person, and this deliberate avoidance is equivalent to knowledge.[34]

The primary money laundering offences in Australian law address the knowledge elements of money laundering in a more detailed and comprehensive way. The

[31] Title 18 USC § 1956(3)(B).

[32] Title 18 USC § 1956(c)(1).

[33] *US v Heaps* 39 F.3d 479 (4th Cir. 1994), 485.

[34] See *US v Frigerio-Milano* 254 F.3d 30 (1st Cir. 2001),35 and *US v Rivera-Rodriguez* 318 F.3d 268 (first1st Cir. 2003), 272.

accused's level of knowledge forms the basis of the seriousness of the offence. Sections 400.2B to 400.8 use a similar structure for the knowledge element. There are three tiers of offence for each provision. The highest tier involves knowledge or belief that the money or property is proceeds of crime, or intent that it will become an instrument of crime. The second tier involves recklessness, and the third-tier, negligence.[35] Intention, knowledge, recklessness, and negligence are defined in Division 5 of the Commonwealth Criminal Code.[36]

Section 400.9 does not use the three-tier approach. It requires that a person deals with money or other property where it is reasonable to suspect that it is the proceeds of indictable crime.[37] The section lists conduct which, if proven, provides grounds for reasonable suspicion. This conduct includes structuring transactions to avoid transaction reporting obligations under anti-money laundering laws,[38] using bank accounts held in false names[39] and giving false or misleading information in relation to a reportable transaction.[40]

Both US and Australian legislation incorporate the concepts of disguise and concealment. In US law, concealment and disguise are part of the intention elements of offences under § 1956. A person can be convicted under this section if they carry out the required transactional or transportation elements knowing that the activity is designed in whole or in part "to conceal or disguise the nature, the location, the source, the ownership, or the control" of the specified criminal proceeds,[41] or to avoid a transaction reporting requirement under State or Federal law.[42] It is not necessary to this element that the person convicted themselves carried out the activity of concealment or disguise, but that they knew this was the activity's purpose.

In the Australian statutes, some of the tiered money laundering offences contain a conduct element. This requires that the offending conduct in relation to the money or property concealed or disguised its nature, value, source, location, any disposition, movement or rights in respect of it, or the identity of any person with rights or effective control in respect of it.[43] In addition, the offence of dealing with property reasonably suspected of being proceeds of crime (s.400.9) lists factors that can support a reasonable suspicion. These include various deceptive acts such as giving

[35] See, e.g. CCA s.400.3, which lists Tier 1 offences in ss. 400.3(1)-1(B), Tier 2 offences in ss.400.3(2)–(2)B and Tier 3 offences in ss. 400.3(3)–(3)B.

[36] CCA, Divisions 5.1–5.5.

[37] CCA, s. 400.9.

[38] Ibid, s. 400.9(2).

[39] Ibid, s. 400.9(2)(b).

[40] Ibid, ss. 400.9(da)(i) and (ii).

[41] Title 18 USC § 1956(a)(1)(B)(i).

[42] Title 18 USC § 1956(a)(1)(B)(ii).

[43] For an example of this structure see CCA ss. 400.2B(2)(c) and 400.2B(3)(c).

false and misleading information in relation to a reportable threshold transaction,[44] and structuring transactions in order to avoid reporting requirements.[45]

4 The Practice of Deception in Money Laundering

Money is laundered in a variety of ways, but the activity is underpinned by a common set of objectives that are relatively straightforward to understand. To systematically analyse how deception is used in money laundering, it is useful to develop a taxonomy. Taxonomies are used to organise, classify, and analyse information into categories to support detailed analysis. Several taxonomies of deception have been developed in the disciplines of military and intelligence studies.[46] For our purposes, the most detailed and granular of these is the case-based taxonomy developed by Rothstein and Rowe.[47] The Rothstein/Rowe taxonomy is based on the theory of semantic cases used in computer science, which says that every action is associated with a set of objects and methods used to accomplish it. Rothstein and Rowe identify seven semantic case types: participant, space, time, quality, causality, speech-act theory, and essence. Each case type contains multiple semantic cases, for a total of 32 cases in all. In theory, taken together, these semantic cases describe all the types of action a subject can take. To use the language of Bell, they represent the range of options available to a deception planner planning a ruse; deception can be applied in relation to any one of them. The taxonomy is set out at Table 1.[48]

We can see how this works in practice if we take the example of the 'Russian Laundromat' scheme which moved an estimated $20.8 billion out of Russia between 2010 and 2014.[49] The objective of the scheme was to move funds out of Russia through Europe and to various jurisdictions where they could be used to purchase assets. Funds were moved from Russia to Moldova using fictitious loans and debts as a cover, reinforced by court judgments facilitated by corrupt Moldovan judges. The laundering process can be summarised as follows:

1. A Russian business controlled by oligarchs held proceeds of crime in a Russian bank
2. The business controlling the proceeds created two shell corporations

[44] Ibid, s. 400(9)(2)(da).

[45] Ibid, s. 400(9)(2)(aa).

[46] See Bell (2003) and Whaley (1982).

[47] Rowe and Rothstein (2004) (n. 10).

[48] The examples of case types provided in Table 1 have been adapted to relate more closely to financial scenarios, as Rothstein and Rowes' original examples were more relevant to cybersecurity.

[49] Organised Crime and Corruption Reporting Organised Crime and Corruption Reporting Project (2017).

Table 1 Rothstein/Rowe taxonomy of deception based on semantic cases

Participant	**Quality**
Agent (the person who initiates the action), e.g. 'Joe' in 'Joe sent the funds' Beneficiary (the person who benefits), e.g. 'Tom' in 'Joe bought a house for Tom' Experiences (a psychological feature associated with the action), e.g. 'angry' in 'Joe became angry' Instrument (something that helps accomplish the action), e.g. 'credit card' in 'Joe bought the watch with a credit card' Object (what the action is done to), e.g. 'watch' in 'Joe bought a watch' Recipient (the person who receives the action), e.g. 'Tom' in 'Joe sent Tom the funds'	Accompaniment (additional object associated with the action) e.g. 'message' in 'Joe's payment included a message' Content (type of the action object), e.g. 'fraud notification' in 'Joe's fraud notification SMS' Manner (the way in which the action is done), e.g. 'compliant' in 'Joe's compliant AML program' Material (the atomic units out of which the action is composed), e.g. 'tranches' in 'The loan consisted of two tranches' Measure (the measurement associated with the action), e.g. '100K' in 'Joes's 100K loan repayment' Order (of events), e.g. 'last' in 'Joe's last transaction' Value (the data transmitted by the action), e.g. '37' in 'Joe emailed the password 37'
Space	**Causality**
Direction (of the action), e.g. 'forward' in 'The funds moved from Joe's account to Tom's account' Location-at, e.g. 'computer' in 'Joe's transaction on his home computer' Location-from, e.g. 'Joe sent the funds from Australia' Location-to, e.g. 'Joe sent the funds to Costa Rica' Location-through, e.g. 'Chinese account' in 'The funds passed through a Chinese account' Orientation (in some metric space), e.g. 'reply' in 'Joe's email reply'	Cause, e.g. 'court case' in 'The debt was created because of a court case' Contradiction (what this action contradicts if anything), e.g. 'outage' in 'The repayment was processed in spite of the outage') Effect, e.g. 'trading halt' as in 'The fraud event caused a trading halt' Purpose, e.g. 'to stop fraud losses' in 'Joe's email was sent to stop fraud losses'
Time	**Speech-act theory**
Frequency (of occurrence), e.g. 'daily' in 'Joe's daily cash deposit' Time-at, e.g. 'noon' in 'Joe's funds transfer at noon' Time-from, e.g. 'Joe's funds transfers sent from noon onwards' Time-to, e.g. 'Joe's online activity ending at noon' Time-through, e.g. 'Joe's funds transfer made at lunchtime'	Precondition (on the action), e.g. 'outage' in 'The outage prevented Tom from refunding Joe's payment' Ability (of the agent to perform the action), e.g. 'recognise' in 'Joe didn't recognise the activity as fraud'
Essence	
Supertype (generalization of the action type), e.g. 'Gift' in 'Joe sent the gift payment' Whole (of which the action is a part), e.g. 'document' in 'Joe sent the offer document'	

3. One of the shell companies ('the borrower') issued a promissory note to the other shell company ('the lender'), creating a fictitious debt
4. Moldovan citizens endorsed the promissory notes on behalf of Russian companies
5. The 'creditor' shell company took legal action in Moldova and obtained a judgment authorised by a corrupt judge directing the Russian business to pay the debt to an account held by the shell company with a Moldovan bank
6. From the shell company account, funds were disbursed to locations around the world[50]

Looking at the phases of money laundering in this case, we can see deception in multiple phases. Phase 2) (creation of the shell companies) involves deception concerning the first category of semantic cases—the Participant. The use of the shell companies conceals the identities of the oligarchs who are the agents and beneficiaries of the transactions, hiding their involvement and interests. Similarly Phase 3) (issuing the promissory notes) disguises the true agents and beneficiaries. Phases 2) and 3) also effect deception about Causality. They disguise the true cause and purpose of the transactions, which is to transfer illicit funds out of Russia and into other jurisdictions. Phases 4) (endorsement of the promissory notes) and 5) (legal action and judgment) also obscure the cause, purpose, agents, and beneficiaries of the transactions. The process cleverly inverts the agent and object of the activity, so that the Russian businesses appear to be the passive object of legal action initiated by the agent, which is the 'creditor' shell company. In fact, the shell company is a passive vehicle for the laundering scheme and the real beneficiaries are not visible.

Because the Rothstein/Rowe taxonomy is designed to analyse deception in a way that is descriptive and not prescriptive, it can be used to identify particular deception methodologies in much more detail than the three-stage model. While in theory, deception can be applied in relation to any one of the 32 cases, the case studies used in this chapter apply primary deception in only a small number of semantic cases: primarily those of Participant, Space, and Causality. Money laundering is a practical rather than an intellectual exercise. Arguably, if a criminal group can disguise or conceal the participants, direction, or location, and purpose of money laundering activity, they have achieved the purpose of that activity. However, the role of deception in money laundering is only fully described when we include the role of secondary deception. In both case studies analysed here, corrupt facilitators played a role in prolonging the deception by concealing their level of knowledge and ability to detect the activity.

The next section identifies money laundering deception across two recent money laundering case studies: the Australian case of Changjiang Financial, and the US Toronto Dominion case. What these two-case studies show is that, for criminal groups attempting to launder the proceeds of their own crime, or for Professional Money Laundering Organisations (PMLOs) undertaking laundering on behalf of another criminal organisation, the objectives of their deception plans are simple. They are generally seeking to disguise the cause, purpose, agent, and beneficiary of

[50] Cassella (2019), pp. 389–90.

the activity. The goal of this primary deception is that the criminal activity from which the wealth originated, and the criminal group that benefits from it, are hidden from sight, and a legitimate cover story put forward.

The reasons for doing this are also straightforward. The state has financial institutions collecting financial intelligence on its behalf, and powers to confiscate crime-derived assets. The processes for seizing and confiscating assets vary, but all of them require some level of evidence that links the assets to criminal activity, or to show that it is not explained by the legitimate income of the subject.[51] Therefore to enjoy the benefits of those assets, it is necessary for criminal groups not only to conceal links to the predicate offending, but construct a legitimate cover story to explain the origin of the funds or wealth. This is also necessary to enjoy ongoing access to the financial system. The Know Your Customer (KYC) and due diligence obligations of financial institutions are designed to help them determine the money laundering and terrorism financing risk presented by a prospective customer.[52] Even without facing criminal charges or confiscation, a criminal entity could find itself shut out of the mainstream financial system and unable to transact if its links to predicate crime are apparent.

Where financial service providers are implicated in the money laundering, the objectives of the deception are somewhat different. In this secondary deception, corporate knowledge of the scale and nature of money laundering happening within the enterprise is what must be disguised and concealed for as long as possible. The dividing line between primary and secondary deception is not always clear, and as the first case study show, one entity can practice both. However, the distinction is useful to maintain because secondary deception (about knowledge of the activity) can be practiced separately from primary deception (about the parameters of the activity itself).

5 Case Studies

5.1 Changjiang Financial

In the 2024 Australian money laundering case of Changjiang Financial, the principals of the Long River Money Laundering Organisation (MLO) were charged with money laundering offences. The MLO allegedly operated a currency exchange and money remittance business in Australia, and used it to launder the proceeds of crime, including the proceeds of 'pig butchering' romance scam activity. The

[51] For an Australian example, see *Criminal Assets Recovery Act* 1990 (NSW), s. 22 ('Making of assets forfeiture order') and s. 28A ('Making of unexplained wealth order').

[52] This is reflected in Recommendations 10 ('Customer due diligence') and 11 ('Record keeping') of the *FATF Recommendations* 2025, accessed at https://www.fatf-gafi.org/content/dam/fatf-gafi/recommendations/FATF%20Recommendations%202012.pdf.coredownload.inline.pdf

laundering methodology is set out in a judgment in a related asset confiscation case, and consists of a three-stage process:[53]

Placement of funds in accounts opened in the name of 'feeder companies' that are not registered remitters to avoid reporting obligations;
Movement of funds from feeder company accounts through other accounts to disguise the source of funds;
Integration of funds through the purchase of assets in a way that appears legitimate.

Media reports[54] further identify these deceptive elements:

- Registration of companies with trusted associates and family members as 'straw directors'
- False reporting of personal income to the Australian Taxation Office to disguise criminal wealth
- Use of false invoices to disguise the movement of tainted funds to and from China
- Posing as a legitimate remittance provider that was operating within the law
- Commingling of legitimate transactions (estimated at 98% of volume) with illicit funds (2% of volume) within the remittance provider's accounts
- Failure to report to Australia's Financial Intelligence Unit transactions and activity that was reportable under anti-money laundering laws
- Use of proxies to receive criminal cash and make funds transfers to companies and accounts secretly controlled by the Long River MLO, from which funds would be transferred to criminal groups
- Falsification of information in applications of loans to purchase property

Applying the Rothstein/Rowe taxonomy to this case, we can see that the focus of the primary deception activity by the Long River MLO is on concealing the agent and beneficiary. The purpose of deception elements 1) (placement of funds in feeder company accounts), 4) (registration of companies with straw directors) and 10) (use of proxies to receive cash) is to disguise the fact that the agent, and in some cases the beneficiary of transactions is an organised crime group. We can also see in deception elements 2), 3), 5), 6), 8) and 11) an attempt to disguise the 'cause,' or put another way, the origin of the funds as proceeds of money laundering, and the purpose of the transaction activity, which is to launder the proceeds of various crimes. The layering of funds through feeder and remittance accounts and the movement of funds on and offshore can also be seen as deception relating to space and time; funds are split into multiple transactions, sent on round trips, delayed, and substituted for other transactions in order to deceive bank staff and forensic investigators who are concerned with tracing funds from their origin to their destination.

Secondary deception is also at play here. The Long River MLO was a regulated reporting entity, with reporting obligations to the Australia's financial crime

[53] *45 Bonview Circuit Pty Ltd & Ors v Commissioner of the Australian Federal Police (No 2)* [2024] VSC 481, 56.

[54] Pearson (2023).

regulator, the Australian Transaction Reports and Analysis Centre (AUSTRAC). To continue to process transactions on behalf of criminal groups, the Long River MLO needed to maintain the appearance of a compliant remittance provider. Therefore, in addition to practicing deception and concealment of the agent, beneficiary, and cause of illicit funds flows, the Long River MLO concealed its complicity in and facilitation of money laundering from investigators and regulators. Rothstein and Rowe would describe this as deception about ability. We could also think of it as deception about knowledge. The Long River MLO had full visibility of the criminal activity it was facilitating but failed to report it to the regulator while maintaining the appearance of compliance. The Long River MLO may have also concealed the extent of illicit flows from AUSTRAC by not reporting, or only partially reporting cash deposits and international funds transfers.

5.2 Toronto Dominion

In October 2024 Toronto Dominion Bank ('TD Bank'), the tenth largest bank in the United States, pled guilty to money laundering and violations of the BSA, becoming the first US bank in history to plead guilty to conspiracy to commit money laundering.[55] In order to link TD Bank's compliance failures with the more serious matter of criminal money laundering, prosecutors focused on three main areas. The first of these was TD Bank's systemic under-resourcing of financial crime compliance and transaction monitoring, driven by prioritisation of a 'flat cost paradigm' and the 'customer experience.' The second was the knowledge of senior management within TD Bank, detailed in emails and messages, that this lack of resourcing was making TD Bank an attractive option for criminals to launder funds. The third was the exploitation of TD Bank by money laundering networks, two of which groomed and recruited bank insiders to assist in their schemes.[56]

Under the plea agreement with the US Department of Justice, TD Bank pled guilty to conspiracy to launder monetary instruments contrary to Title 18, USC 1956(a)(2)(B)(i). Over the period between 2013 and 2024, TD Bank failed to maintain an adequate AML program, instead prioritising 'flat costs,' meaning that business units, including the financial crime compliance function, were expected not to increase their costs year-on-year. This meant, among other things, that TD Bank's transaction monitoring program was not up-to-date and comprehensive, and failed to provide adequate coverage of the bank's products and services. For example, in 2017 TD Bank began to offer its customers access to the Zelle person-to-person payment platform, which allowed transfers between accounts at participating banks.

---

[55] US Department of Justice (2024).

[56] Ibid.

Between 2017 and 2024, TD Bank customers made approximately $75 billion in transfers, which were almost entirely unmonitored.[57]

The plea agreement links these failures to the exploitation of TD Bank's products and services by three MLOs. Between 2019 and 2021, one MLO, known as 'David's network,' laundered approximately $671 million through TD Bank. The network's principal, David, opened TD Bank accounts in the names of shell companies and acquired existing accounts, which were used to deposit cash. As part of his money laundering scheme, David distributed approximately $57,000 worth of retail gift cards to TD Bank employees to ensure they would continue processing his transactions.[58] The suspicious activity of David's network was readily apparent to TD Bank. It was detected in outlier reports and escalated by branch and back-office staff through Unusual Transaction Reports (UTRs).

However, the way TD Bank's AML function dealt with concerns about David's network created a false impression of the activity and impeded law enforcement's ability to detect it. For example, the UTR team, which was under-resourced, introduced a process whereby additional UTRs were not required on 'repeat subjects' who had previously been reported unless their behaviour changed.[59] Staff also filed materially inaccurate cash transaction reports which listed nominee account holders and shell companies as the persons conducting transactions, but failed to identify David himself when he was clearly conducting the transactions.[60]

Another MLO, referred to as 'MLO-2' in the statement of facts, used a method known as the Colombian ATM Typology to launder approximately $39 billion in illicit funds through TD Bank. Using this simple methodology, MLO-2 aggregated funds into accounts across various banks, wired those funds to a network of approximately thirty TD Bank checking accounts and used debit cards to withdraw the funds in Colombia. A group of TD Bank staff ('the TDBNA Insiders') assisted MLO-2 to launder these funds in exchange for bribes, which were paid in some cases using the unmonitored Zelle transaction channel and accessed via illicitly issued debit cards. [61] The TDBNA Insiders helped MLO-2 maintain accounts by overriding freezes on account activity, issuing new debit cards and bypassing internal controls. According to the plea agreement, the criminal misconduct of the TDBNA Insiders was enabled by TD Bank's failure to manage its employee risk. It stemmed in part from and was thus a reasonably foreseeable consequence of TD Bank's "pervasive AML failures."[62]

In the case of TD Bank, there were obvious failures to maintain an up-to-date transaction monitoring program, monitor entire transaction channels, apply account-opening controls, and report suspicious matters. There is evidence that, at the same

[57] Statement of facts, *United States v. TD Bank, N.A.*, 569 B.R. 12 (S.D.N.Y. 2017), 17–35.

[58] Ibid, pp. 48–58.

[59] Ibid, p. 55.

[60] Ibid, p. 56.

[61] Ibid, pp. 62–66.

[62] Ibid, p. 66.

time, individual staff had knowledge of, and in some cases, facilitated customer money laundering. While this was going on, Toronto Dominion held itself out to be a compliant financial institution with adequate money laundering controls, concealing its ability to detect money laundering, the way it was conducting its business and, through failure to report, the measure of the money laundering problem it had.

Applying the Rothstein/Rowe taxonomy to these case studies identifies some common themes. In both case studies, there is primary deception which focuses on disguising and concealing the agent, beneficiary, cause, and purpose of the activity. The use of proxies, straw directors, and false invoices and the commingling of legitimate and illicit funds in the Changjiang Financial case study concealed the agents, beneficiaries, cause, and purpose of the activity as well as obscuring the value of the funds involved. Similar patterns are observed in the activities of David's network and MLO-2 in the TD Bank case, where relatively unsophisticated but effective methods were used to conceal the agent and beneficiary of transactions: the use of shell companies and proxies, transfers via the unmonitored Zeller channel, and the use of debit cards to withdraw funds in Colombia. In both the TD Bank and Changjiang Financial case studies, the primary deception of the money laundering activity was amplified by secondary deception. The TD Bank insiders concealed their knowledge of the scale and nature of the laundering activity in exchange for bribes. In the Changjiang Financial case, primary and secondary money laundering were combined because the Long River MLO actually operated a remittance business which was a registered reporting entity. This allowed the deception planners of the Long River MLO to maintain a closed loop, minimising independent scrutiny of their activity by controlling access to information about it.

6 Conclusion

It is worth repeating the point that was made in introducing this chapter: money laundering is a simple crime which manifests itself in complex ways. In both jurisdictions studied in this chapter, money laundering offences are drafted broadly enough to capture the full range of primary and secondary deception activity outlined in these case studies. Both incorporate offence provisions that criminalise concealment and disguise of a broad range of attributes of criminal proceeds. The U.S. doctrine of wilful blindness and the case law around deliberate ignorance of red flags provides a basis for prosecuting enabling activity by facilitators based on secondary deception. The tiered money laundering offences in Australian law can be used effectively against secondary deception if it can be proven that a defendant was reckless or negligent in their handling of proceeds of crime.

However, the ability to prosecute is not the same as the capacity to detect. In both case studies, the primary deception practiced by the criminal groups was able to continue for an extended period, with hundreds of millions of dollars laundered, despite the relative lack of sophistication of the methods used. The key enabler for this primary deception was the secondary deception in relation to knowledge by facilitators who were obliged to detect and report money laundering activity. The case studies show that the problem of wilful blindness that occupied the minds of US legislators in the 1980s has not diminished since the Bank of Boston case.

Detection methods and controls designed to identify primary deception are vulnerable to secondary deception. In order to counter this, it is necessary to control for the presence of secondary deception rather than assume that it is not present. It is beyond the scope of this chapter to explore in detail how anti-money laundering controls can be developed with deception in mind. However, it is important to note that case studies and taxonomies are more than academic exercises. This chapter has shown that primary and secondary deception are enduring realities in the practice of money laundering, and that a taxonomy can be applied as a tool to money laundering case studies as a tool to identify how that deception works. Those learnings can then be applied in developing detective and preventative controls for future scenarios. Intelligence, enforcement, and risk professionals combating money laundering in the public and private sectors are constantly faced with new urgent cases, and there is pressure to stay in the present rather than applying the lessons of the recent past. However, where criminals have used primary and secondary deception to exploit gaps in existing controls and launder huge sums of money, it is important to bring the right specialists and information together to retrospectively analyse how this was done. The starting point is a common language and method for the analysis of this deception, a goal to which this chapter has contributed. Beyond that is an opportunity to develop counter-deception practices that work against primary and secondary money laundering deception as its 'tangled web' continues to evolve.

References

Bell JB (2003) Toward a theory of deception. Int J intell Counterintell 16(2):244–279. https://doi.org/10.1080/08850600390198742

Cassella S (2019) Illicit finance and money laundering trends in Eurasia. J Money Laund Control 22(2):388–399. https://doi.org/10.1108/JMLC-01-2018-0003

Economist Intelligence Unit (1986) Bank of Boston; Cash cropper. The Economist, p 87

Levi M (2020) Understanding the laundering of organised crime money. Crime Justice 49(1):579–631

Morgan MS (1996) Money laundering: the United States law and its global influence. University of London, London

Organised Crime and Corruption Reporting Project (2017) The Russian laundromat exposed. https://www.occrp.org/en/laundromat/the-russian-laundromat-exposed/

Pearson E (2023) 'Pig butchering' romance scam linked to $228m money laundering case. https://www.smh.com.au/national/victoria/pig-butchering-romance-scam-linked-to-228m-money-laundering-case-20231102-p5eh41.html Accessed 15 March 2025

Rowe NC, Rothstein HS (2004) Two taxonomies of deception for attacks on information systems. J Inf Warf 3(2):27–39

Scott BF (2021) Red teaming financial crime risks in the banking sector. J Financ Crime 28(1):98–111. https://doi.org/10.1108/JFC-06-2020-0118

United States Department of Justice (2024) TD bank pleads guilty to bank secrecy act and money laundering conspiracy violations in $1.8B resolution. https://www.justice.gov/archives/opa/pr/td-bank-pleads-guilty-bank-secrecy-act-and-money-laundering-conspiracy-violations-18b

Whaley B (1982) Toward a general theory of deception. J Strateg Stud 5(1):178–192. https://doi.org/10.1080/01402398208437106

Wolfteich PG (1988) Making criminal defense a crime under 18 USC section 1957. Vanderbilt Law Rev 41(4):843–877

Ben Scott is the Head of Industry, Government and Relationship Management at the Australian Financial Crimes Exchange and a PhD candidate at the Macquarie University Law School. Ben's career experience includes 8 years as a financial intelligence analyst in law enforcement, a range of intelligence and compliance roles in banking and engagement as a specialist advisor to AUSTRAC's Deputy CEO, Intelligence. He has degrees in history and law. His academic research has been published in peer-reviewed journals and edited collections. Ben's interests include intelligence methods, financial crime law and the history of organised crime. He also has a particular interest in the use of data analytics and intelligence technology in detecting financial crime.

Geopolitics of State Capture: Systemic Corruption as a Professional Service

Nicholas Donaldson and Christian Leuprecht

Abstract This chapter explores the geopolitical implications of systemic corruption by way of state capture. No longer a mere byproduct of weak governance, illicit gains from state capture have become an instrument of geopolitical leverage that large authoritarian states such as Russia and China use to project power and influence. State capture characterises a system where private interests collude to shape laws, policies, and regulations for their personal benefit by subverting public institutions. State capture endures due to systemic failures in domestic and international legal regimes and is exacerbated by economic globalisation, which enables transnational illicit financial flows associated with state capture. Case studies of South Africa under Jacob Zuma and the Eastern European Laundromat illustrate how financial institutions, corporate service providers, and public relations firms broker illicit influence. These professional enablers exploit legal asymmetries and regulatory gaps to launder wealth, obscure ownership, and legitimise corrupt regimes. The chapter reframes state capture as a political modality: a dynamic, transnational instrument of geopolitical competition that capitalises on an architecture of global finance and governance whose inadequate and inconsistent regulatory frameworks, notably FATF's gatekeeper model, foster rampant non-compliance.

The original version of the chapter has been revised. A correction to this chapter can be found at https://doi.org/10.1007/978-3-032-06360-1_14

N. Donaldson
Leiden University, Leiden, The Netherlands
e-mail: n.g.i.c.donaldson@fgga.leidenuniv.nl

C. Leuprecht (✉)
Royal Military College of Canada, Kingston, ON, Canada

Queen's University, Kingston, ON, Canada
e-mail: christian.leuprecht@queensu.ca

D. Goldbarsht et al. (eds.), *The Financial War on Crime and Terrorism*,
European Yearbook of International Economic Law,
https://doi.org/10.1007/978-3-032-06360-1_8

1 Introduction

The term *State Capture* was popularised by a series of working papers from the World Bank and European Bank for Reconstruction and Development. The papers described patterns of systemic corruption intent on weakening post-Soviet states' legal and regulatory frameworks. Private interests captured and colluded with public officials, extracting rents by manipulating state power. Rather than an epiphenomenon, systemic corruption has now become a design feature embedded in global capital markets. Elites instrumentalise the institutions of the state to capture large swaths of a country's economy—a phenomenon known as political capitalism—the proceeds of which they then launder by way of transnational professional enablers, notably financial institutions. However, the manifestation of state capture transcends self-serving transnational corruption. Countries such as China and Russia launder a significant portion of corrupt proceeds transnationally to fund insidious forms of conflict against which the West has proven unable to defend itself: hybrid warfare and grey-zone tactics such as dis- and misinformation, foreign interference, subversion, subterfuge and sabotage, etc. This chapter draws attention to the professional enablers and architects of transnational corruption that are embedded in global capital markets, and deficiencies in regulation and governance. Transparency regimes that are supposedly a vector to minimise the reach of autocrats and kleptocrats into democratic society are not having their intended effect. Instead, they are actually being leveraged by democracy's geopolitical adversaries as intermediaries of subversion.

Economic globalisation, especially embedded global capital markets, and the resulting growth and interdependence of transnational financial flows has had a multiplier effect on systemic corruption and state capture.[1] Globalisation intensifies and enables the process of state capture by making large sums more mobile to move across jurisdictions. As a result, state capture and associated laundering has scaled up. The shift from regional to transnational illicit flows is made possible by the emergence of a class of transnational professional enablers within the illicit transnational political economy. Professional enablers obfuscate illicit flows by way of information operations that leverage financial intermediaries and global markets to facilitating systemic corruption under the guise of legitimate business dealings.

This chapter analyses how globalisation has transformed state capture into a transnational phenomenon, with professional intermediaries operating as systemic brokers of illicit influence. Transnational refers to geographic spillovers of domestic corruption that are complemented by global networks of professionals outside the captured jurisdiction who are responsible for its construction, brokerage, and reproduction—primarily within finance. Economic globalisation, especially the embeddedness of global capital markets to which Saskia Sassen alerted us two decades ago, has radically altered the processes and mechanisms of corruption. This renders certain states, their institutions, and underlying structures, particularly susceptible to capture. Transnational professional enablers largely eschew legal and regulatory

[1] Belton (2021).

frameworks, which undermines the efficacy of efforts to contain state capture. Legal fragmentation and jurisdictional differences give rise to criminogenic asymmetry in the form of weak, under-resourced, and spotty regulation and enforcement whose vulnerabilities are subject to systematic exploitation at scale.

2 Background, Methods, and Data

Both economics/public administration (EPA) and scholarship on the Illicit International Political economy (IIPE) contribute to a better understanding of state capture.[2] EPA has largely focused on issues of bureaucratic efficiency, regulatory quality, and administrative constraints that allow or inhibit corruption. However, this scholarship tends to overlook the structural components of state capture in favour of routine corruption practices (i.e., bribery, embezzlement). Conversely, IIPE has little specific research on state capture beyond policy-oriented research.[3] Scholarship on IIPE and state capture tends not to account for mobility. It restricts analyses to territorial boundaries of the state. Such analyses interpret transnational phenomena through a state-centric lens.[4] This is manifest in the prevalence of single-country case studies of state capture informed by EPA, whereas comparative studies remain rare.[5] Nonetheless, IIPE provides a framework to understanding how capture is enabled, sustained, and amplified through globalisation. State captors do not act in isolation; they are embedded in a broader ecosystem of financial crime and exploit the pathways of this ecosystem.

This chapter makes three contributions to the state of knowledge. First, it identifies and discusses the various overlapping roles of the class of professional intermediaries who provide the necessary infrastructure for state captors to operate across jurisdictions. This chapter offers a proof-of-concept for a theoretically-driven comparative approach to state capture that draws on two case studies: the Eastern European Laundromat and the Zuma administration in South Africa. These cases are supplemented with intergovernmental reports—primarily from the Financial Action Task Force (FATF). In doing so, the chapter's secondary contribution is to conceptualise the failures of legal and regulatory regimes through a global state capture. It aims to reconcile the literature's conventional ontology of territory with a transnational epistemology of mobility. Its third contribution—while limited in scope—expands upon nascent research on state capture as a political modality. Capture is therefore not simply a static condition or legal aberration, but a dynamic and strategic mode of governance with significant geopolitical implications.

[2] Legrand and Leuprecht (2021).

[3] For this area of research, please see the World Bank publications on state capture, most prominently Hellman et al. (2000a, b); de Willebois et al. (2011) as well as recent research by Kaufmann (2024) and Dávid-Barrett (2023).

[4] Cooley and Sharman (2017), p. 733–34. Also see Cooley et al. (2018).

[5] Grzymala-Busse (2008).

3 State Capture: An Overview

3.1 Conceptualising State Capture

State capture describes the illicit influence and control of core functions of society and the state—its legislation, administration, and oversight—by private actors. Captors are diverse, internal and external to the state. They include political parties, individuals, local or foreign elites, organised criminal groups, as well as multinational corporations or even entire economic sectors. These associates double as gatekeepers and deal makers operating outside the rules and oversight that constrain formal government roles: the justice system is captured by the leader's loyalists; checks and balances are weakened or ignored; moral and ethical frameworks erode; oligarchs become richer and more powerful than institutions of the state. Such *systematisation* and *intent* set state capture apart from incompetent legislation or regulation. Other forms of grand corruption can be randomised and opportunistic. By contrast, state capture is directed towards core state institutions and functions to reorganise the nature of interactions in favour of its captors.[6] Moreover, it is an intentional and collusive project of elite factions against the public sphere with the aim of conflating political or economic actors.[7] This enmeshing of public and private interests creates power to control and distribute both political and economic resources within and outside captors' factions.

3.2 Mechanisms of Capturing the State

State capture is not a monolithic process, but an amalgam of interlocking subprocesses that target different pillars of governance. Three different logics inform state capture.[8] *Statutory capture* influences the texts and structure of legal regimes and regulatory requirements, most often via the exertion of influence over policymakers. Examples include captors' undue influence over independent regulatory assessments or consultations, the modification or amendment of bills and parliamentary procedures, and the abuse of emergency procedures or filibusters. *Administrative capture* restructures the implementation of policy. The public service and its bureaucracy are subverted to misallocate state resources in budgeting and procurement, alongside practices of nepotism, cronyism, bribery, intimidation, and coercion.[9] Lastly, capture of *accountability ecosystems* interferes in the function and independence of the judiciary, prosecutor offices, and other oversight mechanisms. These include arbitrary judicial proceedings, the delay of due process,

---

[6] Fazekas and Tóth (2016), p. 321–323.

[7] Dávid-Barrett (2023), p. 228.

[8] For a detailed theoretical discussion on this subject, see Dávid-Barrett (2023), pp. 229–230.

[9] Canen and Wantchekon (2022).

and packing courts and oversight bodies to create a culture of impunity for captors, with the aim of legitimising their power and frustrating efforts to impede them.

Capture is not guaranteed. The experience of South Africa teaches us that failure to subvert and capture administrative institutions—not just the bureaucracy but also the judiciary—can precipitate the subsequent prosecution of captors. With sufficient autonomy, public legitimacy, and resources, legal institutions, and civil society can pursue successful, transparent inquiries into misconduct.[10] Additionally, these three overarching categories subsume several distinct processes. The capture of accountability ecosystems includes forms of media capture, in which actors co-opt or control independent media and information capture, which involves monopolising and distorting alternative information channels. The purpose of such capture is to silence civil society and manipulate or undermine information channels such as bureaus of statistics or digital platforms.[11] Similarly, these distinct subprocesses often span overarching categories. For example, capture of electoral systems operates at the administrative and legislative level. Captors may target and manipulate electoral reform along with administrative institutions and staffers to entrench incumbents and patronage politics.[12]

State capture, then, is a differentiated process driven by diverse mechanisms. Captors subvert pillars of governance to suppress the state, its core functions, and the provision of public goods for private and corrupt ends by way of a host of disaggregated mechanisms. Actual mechanisms of state capture are a function of the composition of elite coalitions, their interests, and their ambitions.

3.3 Containing State Capture

At both the domestic and international level, enforcement actions against state capture are a function of two strands of legislation: anti-money laundering and counter-terrorist financing (AML/CTF), and anti-corruption. These are supplemented by both multilateral and unilateral sanction regimes. Transnational legal regimes focus on norm diffusion via policy expertise and authority by way of intergovernmental institutions such as the Organisation for Economic Co-operation and Development (OECD), FATF or United Nations (UN). Domestic regimes internalise these global standards and norms, adapt them to their own circumstances, and develop domestic tools to buttress regimes. In an ideal world, domestic translations and the development of novel tools in turn inform and push forward international standards in a mutually-reinforcing regulatory system.

On the one hand, international bodies such as the FATF institutionalise normative regimes to constrain state capture through AML/CTF legislation and regula-

[10] Khambule (2021).

[11] Dávid-Barrett (2023).

[12] Fazekas and Tóth (2016).

tions. By way of the 40 Recommendations and the process of black- and grey-listing non-compliant jurisdictions, the FATF leverages transaction costs and access to the global banking system.[13] By design, the FATF regime affords states ambit to implement and manage domestic AML/CTF frameworks. However, that ambit is limited to the FATF's risk-based approach. By design, it leaves little leeway to implement the framework, or elements thereof. FATF's framework for compliant AML/CTF legislation applies a "gatekeeper model" of privatised financial supervision by firms on their own clients.[14] As a result, domestic legislation demonstrably convergences around key principles of AML/CFT and anti-corruption. Actual implementation and compliance, however, varies greatly, in both intent and effect.[15]

On the other hand, anti-corruption legislation is fragmented across international jurisdiction. The United States' Foreign Corrupt Practices Act (FCPA) provided the original model for anti-corruption legislation that was subsequently emulated across jurisdictions including Canada, the UK, and Mexico.[16] Implementation and application, however, are subject to political whims. Faced with superpower competition from geopolitical rivals, for instance, the Trump administration appears to believe that constraints imposed by the FCPA disadvantages the US in geopolitical competition. Passed in 1977 in the wake of the Watergate scandal, the FCPA criminalises corrupt offers, payments, or promises of to foreign officials by firms of US origin, or whose funds flow through US institutions. The legislation's reach is extraterritorial insofar as it allows the US to levy broad sanctions, including on non-US entities. These laws are coupled with a host of individual pieces of legislation on civil forfeiture and asset recovery related to the proceeds of corruption or crime, such as the US global *Magnitsky Act* (2012) or the UK's *Proceeds of Crime Act* (2002).[17]

In parallel, states supplement existing legislation with novel forms of domestic enforcement. These often manifest as subdepartments of existing government agencies, or sanctions packages. The strongest examples are the US's inter-agency Anti-Kleptocracy initiatives which are embedded in authorities such as the Security and Exchange Commission (SEC) or Department of Justice (DoJ).[18] More recently, the EU has sought to establish the EU anti-corruption network of experts and civil society, with the backing of its new Anti-Money Laundering Authority (EU AMLA).[19] This decentralised supranational approach to monitor compliance and investigate corruption is largely untested as the legislation only entered into force in 2025.

In addition, states have pursued several regional and international conventions—most importantly the *OECD Anti-Bribery Convention* (1999) and *United Nations*

[13] de Koker et al. (2023); Morse (2019).

[14] FATF (2024). Also see Kellerman (2025).

[15] FATF (2025).

[16] Folsom (2019).

[17] Russia and Moldova Jackson-Vanik Repeal and Sergei Magnitsky Rule of Law Accountability Act (2012).

[18] Holder (2010); Garland (2022). In 2025 these initiatives were disbanded by the Trump administration.

[19] EU Regulation 2024/1620 Establishing the Authority for Anti-Money Laundering (2024).

Convention Against Corruption (2003)—to establish and promote common legal standards and mutual legal assistance across jurisdictions. Importantly, legislative reform of both AML/CTF and anti-corruption regulation tends to follow significant disruption to the existing equilibrium such as corruption scandals (e.g. 1MDB in Malaysia) and violent mass-casualty events (e.g. 9/11). That is, states tend to be reactive, rather than proactive, in managing both state capture and institutional corruption.

3.4 The Economic Globalisation of State Capture

Prior to the most recent wave of economic globalisation, state capture was largely confined within national borders with regional spillover effects on investment, migration, and political cooperation.[20] Owing to economic globalisation, state capture now operates across jurisdictions and capitalises on criminogenic asymmetries of integrated financial markets. As a result, state captors and their impact have gone transnational.

Tailored professional services are modular, marketed and sold as part of broader services utilised by everyday corporations. The technical expertise that underpins modern finance, banking, and real estate facilitates access to the global economy. Mid-twentieth century authoritarian regimes—such as Franco or Stalin—relied primarily on domestic banking systems and state patronage networks, constrained by capital controls and centralised economies. Conversely, modern counterparts exploit transnational financial infrastructures and regulatory arbitrage to externalise influence and obscure accountability. In a study of 150 cases of grand corruption, 128 involved offshore corporate vehicles, with over half using anonymous shell companies to obscure ownership and launder illicit wealth.[21] Ergo, Western entities are complicit in modern state capture. Hubs in Manhattan and London serve as critical financial chokepoints that allow captors to weaponise the same systems of interdependence that fuel the global economy.[22]

Economic globalisation of state capture in globally embedded capital markets has precipitated a qualitative shift: no longer solely an instrument of domestic regime consolidation, state capture is increasingly repurposed as an instrument of geostrategic transnational elite coordination and leverage. Capture is not merely an outcome but a political modality: a flexible mode of governance that encompasses a spectrum of behaviours from more subtle patron-clientelism to realigning institutions for corrupt ends. This modality is adaptive and scalar: often oriented inward to preserve power, outward it functions as a mechanism of geopolitical power projection. Authoritarian and hybrid regimes, particularly China and Russia, deploy

[20] Grzymala-Busse (2008).

[21] de Willebois et al. (2011), p. 34.

[22] Drezner et al. (2021); Also, Morgan and Kinossian (2024); Fishman (2025).

capture to monitor and control diasporas, neutralise regime critics, malign influence, foreign interference, and entrench spheres of influence.

The PRC's crackdown on capital outflows under the guise of "anti-corruption" precipitated a massive underground banking network: wealthy mainland Chinese citizens needed a vector to move wealth to the West—to fund their children's education, to purchase real estate assets, etc. At the same time, drug cartels needed to pay for precursor chemicals manufactured in China (and, increasingly, now across South-East Asia). The result was a low-cost and real-time reconciliation of transactions by way of an Informal Value Transfer System (IVTS). Networks use a variety of tools to move value over borders: cash collector networks, grey market gaming, South-East Asia scam centres and so on. They are enabled by professional intermediaries, Financial Institutions (FIs), Corporate and Legal Service Providers (CLSPs), and Public Relations (PR) firms serve as corporate avatars for the world's largest IVTS. To the extent that the PRC has weaponised laundering for state purposes, organisations such as the United Front Work Department (UFWD) can hide their transfers in the larger noise of that IVTS system. These professional intermediaries that launder funds by embedding them in global capital markets to render them legible as legitimate market or governance activity are the subject of the next section.

4 Professional Intermediaries

Professional intermediaries are network enablers of state capture, functioning as core nodes that connect financial edges. Previous research from IIPE has largely viewed such intermediaries as passive enablers or unwitting participants in state capture. This is echoed in the FATFs approach to enforcement, which privatises enforcement through a risk-based gatekeeping model. The FATF model presumes that professional actors are a positive force for change. Instead, this chapter posits the professions as active architects within a transnational ecosystem of corruption.

Professional actors are the brokers of global capital markets: they link edges of disparate domestic nodes into a network of transnational flows.[23] Their positionality within the transnational legal-financial infrastructure, and within the FATF's privatised approach to enforcement, endows them with networked power as brokers of information, market access, and regulatory evasion.[24] Expertise and professional connections make them brokers within networks of corruption; they provide captors with the financial services and reputational resources.[25] As transnational brokers, professional intermediaries provide legitimacy and global access, and make it possible to reproduce and scale state capture at the global level. The FATF identifies

[23] Drezner et al. (2021).

[24] Ibid.

[25] Cooley and Sharman (2017).

four sectors as gatekeepers of corruption: law, accounting, real estate, and trust and company service providers.[26]

This chapter's functionalist approach conceptualises three professional groups that are responsible for the brokerage and intermediation of state capture: FIs, CLSPs, and PR firms. Research seldom addresses internal variation of these actors beyond their sectoral or professional boundaries. However, as our Venn Diagram illustrates (Fig. 1), there are no clearly discrete capabilities or roles. Rather, professional intermediaries share several core functions, whilst maintaining exclusive competency over key strategic areas owing to their professional communities and expertise. The result is a competitive market for the provision of corrupt financial services for state captors, which bear a striking resemblance to their existing corporate services, such as aggressive tax avoidance or corporate structuring.

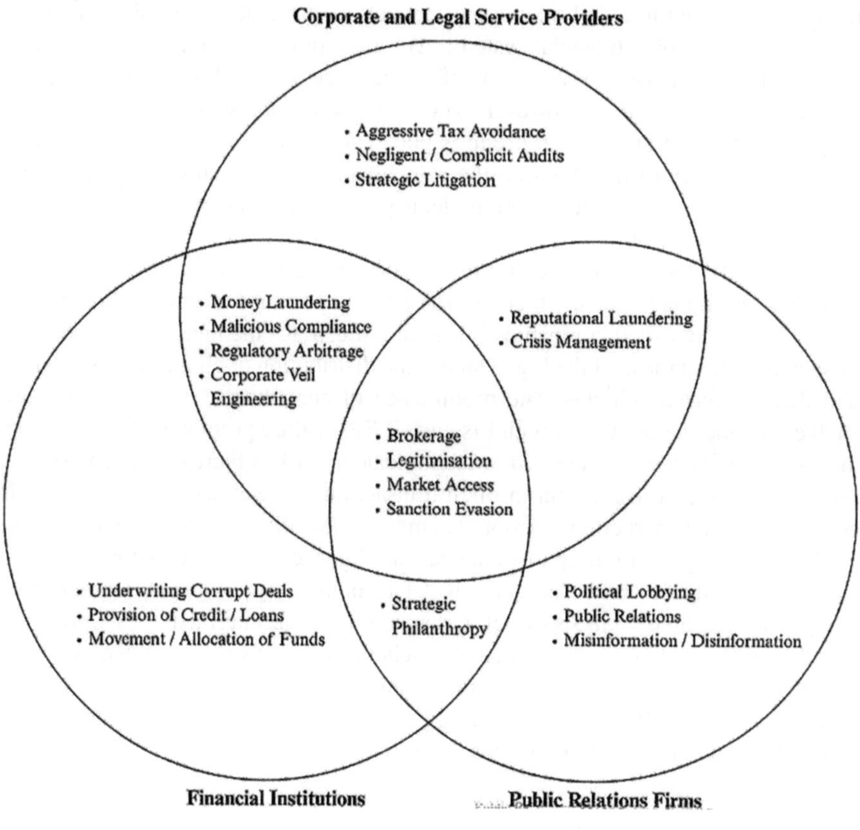

Fig. 1 Venn diagram of overlapping services provided by professional intermediaries

[26] FATF (2024), pp. 11–16. FATFs definition is wide ranging, including casinos, lawyers, notaries and other independent legal practitioners and accountants, trust and company service providers, real estate agents, dealers in precious metals and dealers in precious stones.

CLSPs and FIs jointly afford access to the global market. They act as primary conduits and architects for money laundering, malicious compliance with due diligence and Know Your Customer (KYC) rules, and regulatory arbitrage. Their fee-for-service model (usually a percentage of the total amount involved, driven by a risk premium) structures transactions and firm ownership to minimise exposure to taxation and financial surveillance. That allows captors to subvert the institutions designed to monitor and prosecute corruption. CLSPs and PR firms also launder reputation and perform crisis management. Clean audits of mismanaged or highly irregular firms legitimise illicit transactions and offshore vehicles, while external assessments of SOEs insulate against independent government agencies. Strategic litigation and public relations campaigns offer additional layers of defence: they provide legal cover and launder the reputation of Politically Exposed Persons (PEPs).[27]

Collectively, each professional group shares four overlapping functions that facilitate state capture: (1) brokerage of networks, information, and deals between captors and the global financial system; (2) transnational legitimation of state captors and their behaviour; (3) provision of market access; and (4) evasion of financial surveillance and sanctions. However, how their discrete and shared actions generate a shared coherent transnational group is poorly understood. The sociology of professions could afford insights into the roles of professional cultures, institutional autonomy, and embeddedness to help identify variation and continuity in enablers' behaviour and motivations.

Empirically, the growing centrality of professional intermediaries is evidenced by FCPA enforcement data, which reinforce the importance of financial intermediaries, brokers, and shell companies.[28] Figure 2 illustrates the increased prosecution of such intermediaries, whilst Fig. 3 shows the distribution of chosen intermediaries and their preferred vehicles. The prominence of consultants/brokers and opaque shell companies suggests that both FIs and CLSPs feature prominently in state capture. FATF enforcement trends likewise indicate a marked increase in professional service providers' involvement in illicit transactions, as well as their active role in constructing and marketing corrupt schemes to potential clients. A report by the FATF and the Egmont Group of Financial Intelligence Units (FIU) situates professional intermediaries on a "continuum" of responsibility: innocent, negligent, or complicit."[29] In their analysis of 150 cases, a third of all intermediaries were complicitly involved, having "designed the scheme themselves and promoted it to potential clients."[30] The complexity and sophistication of schemes disclosed in the LuxLeaks, Panama Papers, and Pandora Papers bolsters the shift of intermediaries from peripheral enablers to indispensable brokers.[31]

---

[27] Cooley and Sharman (2017).

[28] Stanford Law School & Sullivan & Cromwell, LLP (2025).

[29] FATF–Egmont (2018), p. 48.

[30] Ibid, p. 49.

[31] Cooley and Sharman (2017).

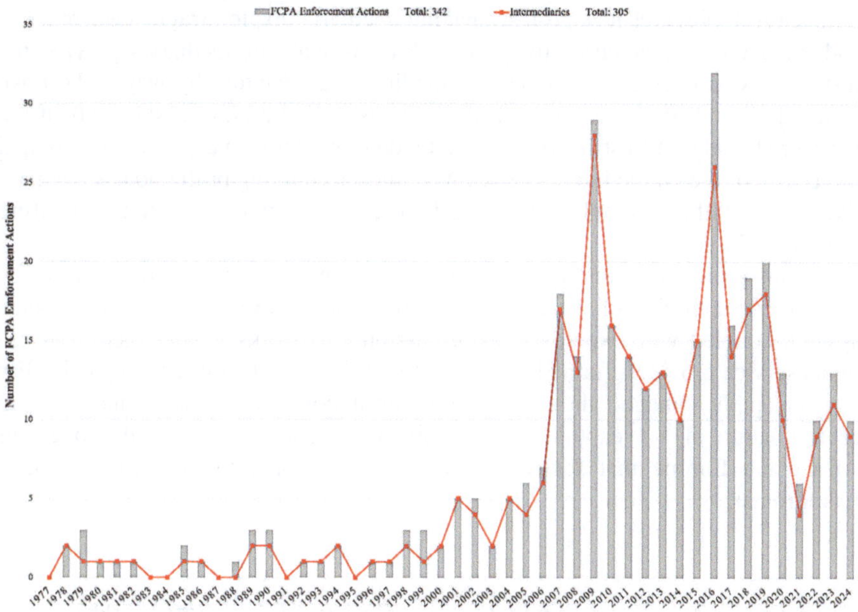

Fig. 2 FCPA enforcement data (1977–2025) by third-party intermediaries

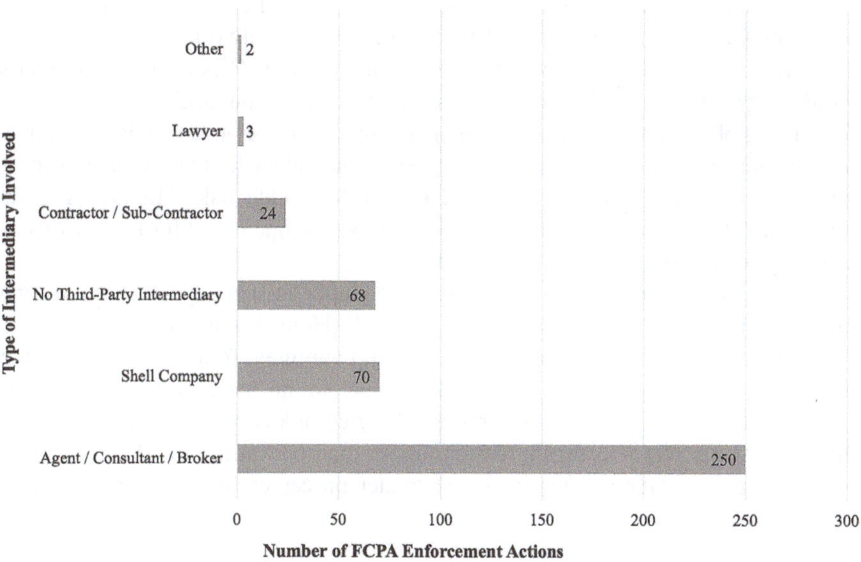

Fig. 3 FCPA enforcement data (1977–2025) by type of intermediary

The FATF observes how professional intermediaries exploit fragile legal regimes and regulatory asymmetries for profit.[32] Professional intermediaries provide the instruments and services necessary to facilitate state capture by way of bespoke "packages" with few questions asked of clients.[33] That raises questions about the appropriate balance to strike between individual freedoms in capitalist society and protection of the public interest. The FATF finds accounting professionals the most likely to be wilfully complicit, with legal professionals more likely to be unwitting or wilfully blind.

In sum, professional intermediaries and their industries support globalised "institutional corruption" within the state system.[34] Their centrality within the finance system, coupled with expertise and professional networks, render them transnational service providers for a globally oriented cadre of autocrats and oligarchs. Far from an epiphenomenon, the ecosystem of transnational brokers is an emergent and central feature of state capture. Case in point are two detailed case studies of South Africa and Europe that follow: the Zuma regime and the Eastern European Laundromat.

4.1 Jacob Zuma's Administration, South Africa, 2008–2018

Between 2008 and 2018, former South African President Jacob Zuma's administration facilitated the capture of the South African state in collusion with private actors, multinational corporations, FIs, CLSPs, and PR firms.[35] Networks embedded within the African National Congress, state-owned enterprises (SOEs), and private sector entities orchestrated the diversion of an estimated 3.7 billion USD from public coffers. The global financial crisis of 2008 galvanised corruption across BRICS countries insofar as financial intermediaries were nonetheless looking to capitalise on institutional failure. Large banks had taken on too much risk. Although governments bailed them out, institutions and individuals compensated for their losses by enabling corruption to bolster flagging profits.

Zuma and his associates—most notably the Gupta business dynasty—used complex beneficial ownership structures in the UAE, Hong Kong, the UK, and South Africa to launder and obscure the proceeds of procurement fraud. In 2014 transport firm Transnet procured 1064 locomotives where initial budgets were inflated by 1.116 billion USD, with 295 million USD diverted in kickbacks to Gupta intermediaries.[36] At the power company Eskom, more than 650 million USD in contracts were awarded to Gupta firms in rigged tender processes over 3 years.[37] Parallel

[32] FATF (2018), p. 12, 36.

[33] Ibid, p. 19.

[34] Brock and Russell (2015), p. 7–8.

[35] Perlo-Freeman (2017).

[36] Zondo Commission, Vol. 1, Pt. II. (2022).

[37] Zondo Commission, Vol. 3, Pt. I–IV (2022).

schemes at South African Airways and the Passenger Rail Agency of South Africa (PRASA) saw billions lost to inflated leases, consultancy fees, and phantom projects.[38] Simultaneously, Zuma manipulated appointments to critical patronage positions. His administration weakened oversight mechanisms, replacing at least 28 senior executives and board members across SOEs—including within the prosecution service, federal police, and tax authorities.[39]

The Gupta enterprise relied on FIs and their international networks to launder proceeds from corrupt contracts. Some schemes were simple: stolen funds were transferred directly into offshore accounts in the UAE or laundered through singular shell companies such as JJ Trading FZE and Century General Trading FZE to the UAE.[40] More sophisticated international networks routed money through complex transaction networks using global banks such as HSBC's Hong Kong branch. An internal HSBC investigation uncovered 92 companies that received payments from accounts held by Tequesta, Regiments Asia, and Morningstar.[41] Accounts still active in late 2016 had received 50,339 payments worth 234 million USD. These 60 accounts made onward payments to 5576 further beneficiaries, of which 55 were also paid by Regiments Asia, Tequesta, and Morningstar. The total value of 211 million USD across 32,653 transactions is likely a fraction of the picture at HSBC alone.[42]

An additional 251 million USD was laundered between 2007 and 2017 across 20 Gupta-linked front companies that held accounts at the Indian Bank of Baroda.[43] Baroda leveraged correspondence networks at South African Nedbank. Both shirked responsibility for reporting suspicious transaction by skirting KYC obligations.[44] Baroda's closure in 2017 precipitated the unravelling of the money laundering network. Notably, prominent South African Standard Bank and ABSA debanked Gupta-linked accounts through which they had processed over 95 million USD in suspicious transactions linked to Gupta-owned Sahara Computers between 2012 and 2016.[45] FIs thus find themselves at the centre of state capture: providing market access, laundering proceeds, and engaging in broad corporate negligence.

KPMG earned 1.3 million USD from the Gupta-linked Sahara Group. They had served as the auditors for Gupta-linked companies from 2003 to 2018. KPMG issued clean external audits of Gupta firms and provided standard services, including corporate structuring and aggressive tax avoidance.[46] In 2015 KPMG falsely accused SARS officials of operating an illegal investigative unit pursuing Zuma and his partners.[47] Likewise, Bain & Co. SA partnered with the Zuma administration to

[38] Zondo Commission, Vol. 1, Pt. I (2022); also Vol. 5, Pt. II (2022).

[39] Chipkin et al. (2018).

[40] Zondo Commission, Vol. 6, Pt. III (2022), pp. 798–801.

[41] Ibid.

[42] Ibid, p. 802.

[43] Sharife and Joseph (2018).

[44] Marchant et al. (2020).

[45] Zondo Commission, Vol. 6, Pt. III (2022).

[46] KPMG South Africa (2018).

[47] Ibid.

advise on the restructuring of the South African economy and "Profound Strategy Refresh" at the SARS.[48] Bain received 9.15 million USD in irregular contracts over 27 months. In short, consulting, law, and accounting firms legitimised corrupt procurement relationships and phantom transactions while weakening judicial enforcement mechanisms.

CLSPs such as the Gupta-affiliated Regiments Capital provided "financial advisory services" to state-owned entities, earning 62 million USD in excess profits from Transnet.[49] PwC, Bain & Co., and Deloitte were found to have circumvented procurement rules and inflated prices to obtain contracts.[50] Additionally, firms engaged in outright bribery and conspired to both uphold and bury corruption. Whilst consulting for both Eskom and Transnet, McKinsey & Company received 85 million USD for bribes paid as fees to Zuma-linked entities, acting on privileged information and violating procurement laws.[51] Gupta-linked firms—including Trillian Management Consulting, Islandsite Investments, and Oakbay Investments—acted as shell companies that structured illicit transactions as typical commercial interactions.[52] Whereas FIs move the money and ensure that flagged transactions are overlooked and AML/CTF protocols are not implemented, CLSPs are the architects of financial secrecy. Together, they provide modular financial services to launder billions in corrupt proceeds as active agents of state capture.

Firms also acted as public relations and lobbying agents, coordinating reputation laundering campaigns, strategic philanthropy, and crisis management efforts to deflect scrutiny and co-opt Western policymakers. Bain & Co. coordinated a media campaign to support their restructuring of the SARS, emphasising modernisation and improved efficiency, aiming to garner public support and mitigate criticism.[53] UK-based Bell Pottinger orchestrated a propaganda campaign to deflect scrutiny from Zuma and the Guptas. The firm coordinated a national influence operation through social media bots, fake news sites, and manipulated hashtags to discredit state capture allegations as a racially-biased conspiracy.[54] Moreover, transnational law firms such as Dentons and Hogan Lovells were hired to perform strategic litigation in an effort to discredit or silence critics and defend captors from credible allegations of corruption.[55] Together PR firms and CLSPs provide legal cover for captors through attacks on legal institutions and disinformation campaigns. Akin to FIs, they actively uphold state capture, provide spin for dictators and legitimise corruption before the eyes of the law.

---

[48] Bain & Company (2018).

[49] National Director of Public Prosecutions v. Wood and Others (2022).

[50] Deloitte & Eskom Holdings, SOC Limited (2020); Bain & Company (2018).

[51] US v. Mckinsey & Company, Inc. US (2024); Eskom Holdings, SOC Limited v. McKinsey & Company Africa Limited and Others (2019).

[52] Zondo Commission, Vol. 6, Pt. III (2022).

[53] Bain & Company (2018).

[54] Public Relations and Communications Association (2017).

[55] Zondo Commission, Vol. 3, Pt. I–IV (2022); Hogan Lovells (2023).

4.2 *Post-Soviet Capture and the Eastern European Laundromat*

Unlike South Africa, where state capture has been extensively documented through public inquiries and legal proceedings, post-Soviet capture is more opaque.[56] The 'Eastern European Laundromat' was a sprawling network of interconnected money laundering schemes that enabled the systematic extraction of illicit wealth from post-Soviet states. At the heart of this operation was the Danske Bank scandal, which exposed the scale and sophistication of financial intermediaries in laundering proceeds of state capture.

Between 2007 and 2015, Danske Bank's Estonian branch was at the centre of one of the largest money-laundering scandals in history[57]. An estimated 228 billion USD in suspicious transactions flowed through its non-resident accounts.[58] They ignored clear signs in favour of profits—in 2011, Danske Bank Estonia branch generated 11% of its parent company's total profits, and only held 0.5% of Danske Bank's assets.[59] Importantly, the Estonian branches' IT division, including its AML compliance regulations, lay outside Danske Banks Group-level infrastructure.[60] Non-resident clients—many of whom were linked to illicit financial networks in Russia, Azerbaijan, Moldova, and other post-Soviet states—represented a significant amount of the branches' profit.[61]

Key figures tied to accounts include members of the Aliyev ruling family of Azerbaijan, Russian secret service, and associates of Vladimir Putin (through companies linked to his cousin and friends).[62] In December 2022, Danske Bank pleaded guilty to fraud in the United States and agreed to a 2 billion USD fine.[63] In early 2024, Danish courts jailed two culprits who had helped launder billions through the bank. Their main branch ignored internal warning signs and concerns of external auditors as early as 2011. Multiple executives resigned in the wake of the scandal, including CEO Thomas Borgen.[64] Danske was not alone. Other Nordic and Baltic banks were caught in similar scandals or tied to Danske Banks and faced heavy fines. Deutsche Bank and SwedBank were found to have handled large volumes of suspicious payments, misrepresented customer relations, and falsified documents to regulators.[65]

---

[56] Belton (2021).

[57] Further details of the Danske case and the organisational complexities are outlined in the chapter by Ferrill and Southworth (2025) in this book.

[58] US DoJ v. Danske Bank, A/S (2022).

[59] NY Department of Financial Services v. Deutsche Bank, AG (2020), p. 27.

[60] Bruun & Hjejle (2018), p. 3.

[61] Ibid, pp. 31–35.

[62] Ibid; also Van de Ven (2019).

[63] US DoJ v. Deutsche Bank, AG (2022).

[64] Küngas (2023). Also see Bruun & Hjejle (2018).

[65] NY Department of Financial Services v. Deutsche Bank, AG (2020), p. 29; Finansinspektionen v. Swedbank, AB (2020).

Danske Bank's demise is one instance of a wider array of laundering schemes that feed into the Western financial system. The 'Russian Laundromat' systematically siphoned between 20 and 80 billion USD through falsified debt in UK shell companies certified by bribed Moldovan judges.[66] Deutsche Bank similarly faced sanctions for its role in the 'mirror-trading' scandal which funnelled 10 billion USD in similar methods to Danske Bank.[67] Weak AML controls, wilful blindness, along with outright complicity allowed billions to flows through accounts in Estonia, Latvia, and other entry points into the EU. Regulators levied record fines against Nordea and Skandinaviska Enskilda Banken and forced Latvia's ABLV Bank and Trasta Komercbanka to close.[68] As in South Africa, FIs in these cases are conduits for corrupt proceeds and turned a blind eye to the source of their profitable financial services. While at times negligent, FIs can be active enablers: they deliberately overlook internal warnings and stifle intervention by regulators.

While banks moved the money, an ecosystem of CLSPs obscured the network of suspicious transactions and undermined regulatory authorities. The methods described above allow funds to be routed into offshore shell companies' accounts at Danske as debt to be transferred out as ostensibly legitimate (re)payments. Corporate formation agencies such as ComForm established hundreds of these shell companies, often with the same false declarations of nominee directors and locations, with a preference for opaque vehicles such as English limited partnerships.[69] In many cases, employees at Danske Bank either brokered relationships between CLSPs and criminals, or established shell companies themselves in exchange for "consulting fees."[70] These were often controlled by anonymous offshore companies incorporated in the UK, Cyprus, the British Virgin Islands (BVI), and Seychelles. In one example, approximately 2.85 billion USD was funnelled through Danske Bank's Estonian branch for the 'Azerbaijani Laundromat' between 2012 and 2014.[71] This operation involved four UK-registered shell companies—Metastar Invest, Hilux Services, Polux Management, and LCM Alliance—whose accounts were held at Danske Bank Estonia.

Accounting firms and auditors from Ernst & Young and KPMG in Denmark reportedly knew of red flags and compliance failures at the Estonian branch but did not report them to authorities, whilst deliberately watering down internal reports at the behest of executives. Denmark's Business Authority later alleged that Ernst & Young had violated AML provisions and failed to report to FIUs when it discovered suspicious information in Danske's books, though state prosecutors have since dropped charges.[72] By setting up opaque corporate vehicles, issuing clean audit

---

[66] Van de Ven (2019).

[67] NY Department of Financial Services v. Deutsche Bank (2017).

[68] Finansinspektionen v. Nordea Bank, AB (2015); FinCEN (2018); ECB and FKTK (2016).

[69] Haddou and Bowers (2022).

[70] US DoJ v. Danske Bank, A/S (2022), p. A-2.

[71] Van de Ven (2019).

[72] Erhvervsstyrelsen v. KPMG Baltic & Ernst & Young (2020); Also, Reuters (2020).

opinions, or simply looking turning a blind eye, CLSPs provided the necessary infrastructure for offshore secrecy.

Putin's People laundered billions out of Russia, with the aim of subverting security, prosperity, and democracy.[73] Similarly, Azerbaijan's laundromat not only concealed illicit wealth but financed a vast lobbying apparatus in Washington and Europe. Funds wired through the Azerbaijani Laundromat, including payments from shell firms Metastar and Hilux, were funnelled into Renaissance Associates, which hired Bob Lawrence & Associates (BL&A) to conduct influence operations in Azeri interests, whitewash its human rights record for investment, and cultivate political allies.[74] U.S. lobby disclosures show BL&A received nearly 4.5 million USD in fees from 2006 to 2016, with 1.5 million USD flowing from 2012 to 2015, which matches funds siphoned off by the Azeri Laundromat.[75] Over a decade, the firm arranged visits for Azeri officials, testified in Congress, and enlisted former U.S. officials to lobby for Baku, including on strategic energy projects. Simultaneously, Azerbaijan engaged in *caviar diplomacy* in Europe, using laundromat funds to sway members of the Parliamentary Assembly of the Council of Europe (PACE), some of whom later faced corruption probes for accepting bribes in exchange for blocking human rights resolutions.[76] This campaign influence, orchestrated through PR firms and lobbying intermediaries, demonstrates how laundered capital was converted into political capital to suppress criticism and advance state interests abroad.

5 Transnational Professional Intermediaries as Network Brokers

As shown in our case studies, professional intermediaries are a crucial component of contemporary state capture. Without them, mechanisms of corruption in Eastern Europe and South Africa would be impossible to maintain. However, they were also crucial in undermining regulatory and legal frameworks meant to detect such forms of corruption. They act as brokers within international financial networks in circumventing financial surveillance, rather than just as gatekeepers or enablers. In this way, FIs, CLSPs, and PR agencies are the architects and salespeople of institutional corruption, brokering, and legitimation of transnational networks. In the following section, we explore the consequences of these activities across three interrelated areas: compliance, accountability, and enforcement.

---

[73] Belton (2021).

[74] Wrate (2018).

[75] US Senate (2025).

[76] Van de Ven (2019).

5.1 Professional Intermediaries and (Non)Compliance

Professional intermediaries show a brazen disregard for compliance and corporate good governance in the cases. With an obligation to act in the public good, they have an incentive to maximise utility. HSBCs Johannesburg branch had internally flagged transactions and accounts which were forwarded to executives. At Baroda, managers voided SARs on transactions including inter-company loans and government contracts with "no apparent legal or commercial purpose" to firms with "few employees."[77] After closing Gupta-linked accounts in 2016, Nedbank maintained its correspondent banking relationship with Baroda, allowing the laundering network to persist.[78] Deutsche Bank held meetings as early as 2011 on the volume of suspicious transactions from Danske Bank. Evidently, the FATF's privatised risk-based approach of compliance monitoring failed due to a powerful admixture of incentives in the global corporate industry.

Profits incentivised executives to overlook serious breaches in AML regulations. HSBCs London headquarters dismissed its Johannesburg branches internal warnings. By 2014, Danske Bank had received warnings from a European bank but declined to investigate on the grounds that "there were legitimate reasons for former Soviet businesses and individuals to use non-resident banks."[79] Ergoinvest had been flagged by Deutsche Bank's automated AML protocols but similarly never investigated, which precipitated the '2023 Mirror-Trading Scandal'.[80]

Utility-maximising behaviour is magnified by quarterly pressures for positive financial outlooks. Firms know the sheer scale of the corporate industry makes them replaceable. In both Eskom and Danske Bank, accounting and consulting firms identified clear breaches of internal corporate governance and abuse of procurement systems but watered down criticisms and recommendations due to political and financial pressure.

Even following disastrous scandals, firms continuously fail to enforce corporate governance standards. HSBC Johannesburg received 530,000 USD fine in 2024 for failure to perform KYC and due diligence.[81] Standard Bank similarly received 725,000 USD in fines in 2025.[82] SwedBank received another 89 million USD fine for failures in internal controls and AML protocols in 2023.[83] Ergo, institutional corruption is a product marketed and sold by a transnational industry of financial professionals that provides the modular architecture for state capture on a global level. While individual firms—such as Bell Pottinger, Danske Bank Estonia, or KPMG South Africa—may face closure or reduced investments, these industries

[77] Sharife and Joseph (2018).

[78] Ibid.

[79] NY Department of Financial Services v. Deutsche Bank (2020), p. 29.

[80] Bowers et al. (2020).

[81] South African Reserve Bank v. HSBC Bank, PLC – Johannesburg (2024).

[82] South African Reserve Bank v. Standard Bank of South Africa, Limited (2025).

[83] Finansinspektionen v. Swedbank, AB (2023).

offer illicit corporate services *à la carte* to autocrats while failing to enforce corporate governance standards.

Evidence of this thriving industry can be found in the continued prosperity of corporate formation agencies. A 2022 investigation found that just five UK-based formation agencies specialising in ex-Soviet clientele created thousands of shell companies registered to a mere handful of addresses in England and Wales. Some 28% of all English LPs formed in 2017 were set up by these five shops. Aforementioned ComForm has created at least 211 anonymous shells since 2014, almost 70% of which after the 2017 Scottish limited partnership reforms.[84]

5.2 Professional Accountability

States do not hold professional intermediaries to account. On the one hand, regulators use a soft touch, fearing damage to their financial sectors. On the other hand, state capture is characterised by uneven regulation and prosecution.

First, embedded capital markets are a source of economic vitality. They incentivise lax enforcement and soft intervention over harsh public punishment. Danish regulators approached Danske Bank quietly about ring-fenced IT systems and failures in their AML/CTF protocols. Repeated warnings and the threat of fines led to Danske winding down non-resident accounts, but only after it became clear that reputational risk and international pressure outweighed the benefits of regulatory forbearance.[85] In the case of South Africa, captive regulatory systems stifled actual enforcement.

Second, the global gap between states' compliance declarations and actual practices is substantial. Across 112 assessed jurisdictions, the FATF's Recommendations 24 and 25 on beneficial ownership transparency average just 47% on technical compliance and 22% on effectiveness, with nearly half (44%) scoring zero on effectiveness under Immediate Outcome 5.[86] Inherent conflicts-of-interest ensure that the FATFs existing privatised "gatekeeper model" fails due to perverse incentives at the firm and state-level. The World Bank observes that compliance officers know "any due diligence system can be beaten."[87] More stringent legislation is likely to be frustrated by "pressure groups or other lobbies" content to "prevent the passage of such legislation."[88] Additionally, there are 73 countries outside the FATF's network who are at least somewhat non-compliant. Due diligence is thus easily circumvented, and enforcement gaps are the rule, rather than the exception.

84 Haddou and Bowers (2022); also Bowers et al., (2022).

85 Bruun & Hjejle (2018).

86 Basel Institute of Governance (2021).

87 de Willebois et al. (2011), p. 8.

88 Ibid, p. 7.

Professional intermediaries are monitored as both FIs and designated non-financial business and professions (DNFBPs). While the average rate of compliance for so-called gatekeeper regulations is 74%, four countries (US, South Korea, China, Australia) are 5% or less.[89] FIs generally have a clear understanding of the risks they face and have implemented more effective risk mitigation measures.[90] In contrast, the non-financial sector, including DNFBs, generally have a poor understanding of risk, which they struggle to mitigate.

Legislation tends to be highly general and lacking in specificity regarding crimes of grand corruption. Laws focus primarily on AML/CTF compliance protocols. There are professional intermediaries not covered by these areas of legislation owing to legal fragmentation as well as gaps in compliance and effectiveness.[91] For example, consultancies may be partially covered by regulation, but their diverse services and global reach allows them to operate in areas not fully addressed by DNFBP legislation. Another legal grey zone persists between public political lobbying and private diplomacy, which enables largely unregulated foreign influence as exemplified by BL&A's ability to circumvent the United States' Foreign Agents Registration Act (FARA) while advancing Azerbaijan's interests. This is a challenge for regulators, as intermediaries form a coherent class of professionals who share roles and functions in capturing the state.

To an outsider, this lack of specificity might seem reasonable. State capture commonly involves bribery, kickbacks, and the laundering of illicit proceeds, which falls to prosecution services. New legislation and legal regimes are expensive to develop while externalising them globally poses a challenge. Ambiguity likewise allows for a degree of norm localisation in the implementation of AML/CTF legislation. The current approach reflects a classic problem in financial crime: regulators graft new or emergent threats onto existing legislation, rather than developing distinct purpose-built tools.

5.3 *Enforcement: Weak and Politicised*

Finally, enforcement is characterised by a high degree of unilateralism, especially on the part of the US. In recent years, executives have been held to account through criminal charges, such as McKinsey's Vikas Sagar.[92] However, the broad trend of enforcement data shows a preference for Deferred Prosecutions Agreements (DPAs) and plea bargains, as well as civil actions. DPAs (30.43%) and plea agreements (65.03%) make up a majority of actions from the US DoJ.[93] Half of the enforcement

[89] FATF (2024); also see FATF (2022).

[90] FATF (2024).

[91] FATF (2018); also see FATF (2024).

[92] United States v. Vikas Sagar (2024); also Küngas (2023).

[93] Stanford Law School & Sullivan and Cromwell, LLP (2025).

actions of the SEC are consent agreements (48.17%) and DPAs (1.83%).[94] These favour transnational firms: they can field legal armies with considerable financial resources; they can credibly threaten capital flight; and they generally enjoy special relationships with regulators.

With the advent of the second Trump Administration, the era of the FCPA and anti-kleptocracy initiatives may be coming to an end. As of February 2025, agency-based Anti-Kleptocracy initiatives have been dismantled, while the FCPA and FARA are being rescinded.[95] This reflects a long-held Republican opinion that anti-corruption legislation "impedes foreign policy objectives" and harms the "economic competitiveness" of US firms, as corruption is a "routine business practice in other nations."[96] It likewise highlights the continued and deeply politicised role of anti-corruption enforcement: Western states seem to prosecute and sanction state capture when it is in their self-interest.

5.4 Implications

Reforms that address transparency, the uneven regulatory terrain, the 'gatekeeper model', and enforcement challenges can curtail state capture.

First, states and firms must commit to transparency. As an example, foreign lobbying must be both documented and highly regulated. Adherence to FATF guidelines—particularly beneficial ownership transparency—is essential. However, transparency is limited in its effectiveness if not paired with robust monitoring and enforcement. In the case of beneficial ownership, verification of registries and public access are crucial and often lacking.[97]

Second, legislators need to even the uneven terrain of regulation by expanding existing regulatory frameworks, such as reporting requirements, to include actors currently on the periphery, such as DNFBPs. Harmonisation needs to reduce gaps across FATF member states. Operations of professional intermediaries should be regulated and not subject to differential treatment. Additionally, AML/CTF legislation needs to be strengthened through targeted legal provisions that specifically address the *'duty of care'* that professional intermediaries have, to the public good.

Third, states and the FATF secretariat should explore alternatives to the 'gatekeeper model.' The experiment of self-regulation in AML/CTF has seen transnational criminal activity proliferate, while placing extraordinary financial burdens on both states and minor or moderate corporate actors. One option is to establish a reward program for financial crime bounty hunters similar to that of hacking bounty

[94] Ibid.

[95] Bondi (2025); also, Executive Order, No. 14209 (2025).

[96] Executive Order No. 14209 (2025).

[97] de Willebois et al. (2011); Leuprecht et al. (2025).

programs.[98] The aim is to eliminate perverse incentives that drive the logic of firms in a competitive market.

Finally, states must deter firms and their agents with criminal and financial sanctions. Principal executives and their agents should face criminal sanctions for breaches, including of the aforenoted professional duties of care. Tepid financial penalties and restrictions on professional misconduct are insufficient. Absent credible deterrence, firms will internalise corruption and financial penalties as a cost of doing business. The current shifting political climate makes enforcement all the more important. As the case of South Africa shows, developing states lack the resources and political clout necessary to investigate, prosecute, and sanction state capture on their own.[99] The vacuum created by the Trump Administration can only be buffeted through international cooperation. By way of the newly fashioned AMLA and an eventual capital-markets union, both the UK and the EU can play a vital role in shaping anti-corruption enforcement to address regulatory arbitrage and enforcement gaps.

6 State Capture as Political Modality

A recent report by the Office of the Director of National Intelligence underscores a pivotal transformation in China's governance under Xi Jinping: corruption is no longer merely a vehicle for private enrichment but has become a strategic tool of centralised statecraft.[100] Prior to the Xi regime, kleptocracy largely centred on elite self-enrichment, facilitated through offshore networks and opaque jurisdictions designed to protect families and assets from political risk.[101] Under Xi Jinping, corruption has been repurposed as a mechanism of centralised control and a vehicle for geopolitical ambition. Xi's sweeping anti-corruption campaigns, despite targeting ideological impurity and high-level corruption, have left forms of systemic graft intact within upper party and military ranks. This signals a shift: from diffuse personal gain to centralised, regime-serving capture. China's model may now mirror the post-Soviet configuration yet distinguishes itself through its global orientation and strategic deployment—corruption as a modality of international power projection.

China's case reflects a shift in how corruption manifests: as a geostrategic instrumental rather than purely for private gain. In South Africa, under Jacob Zuma, the machinery of capture was driven by domestic rent extraction and political survival, enabled by global intermediaries who laundered wealth and reputations across jurisdictions. In contrast, post-Soviet elites institutionalised capture into the core of the state itself. They leverage transnational laundromats to channel billions into Western

[98] Kellerman (2025).

[99] This concept is explored further in the chapter "Corrupt Elites and Godfathers in Nigeria: Structural Impunity and the Undermining of Accountability" by Harvey and van Duyne (2025) in this book.

[100] ODNI (2025).

[101] Cooley and Sharman (2017).

financial systems in service of elite patronage, lobbying, and geopolitical leverage. China may reflect an emergent synthesis of these trajectories: that is, an evolution from the South African to the post-Soviet model.

Together, these cases demonstrate that transnational state capture is no longer—or never was—an aberration or symptom of weak governance. It is an adaptive and intentional strategy; a form of strategic corruption that thrives in an increasingly interdependent, multipolar world. As liberal norms recede, and institutional corruption is reconfigured as a tool of foreign policy, states and elites are increasingly weaponising corruption to navigate and exploit geopolitical ambition.

At the heart of this evolution lies an ecosystem of professional enablers: financial institutions, legal and corporate service providers, public relations firms, and lobbyists. They design the infrastructure of capture, sustaining elite influence while maintaining a façade of compliance and legality. This ecosystem of enablers is not merely an epiphenomenon of state capture, but its very crux.

However, the global legal response remains ill-equipped. Globally, AML/CTF regimes have promoted compliance-based enforcement models, which outsource oversight to financial institutions without confronting the professional intermediaries at the centre of these networks. These systems tolerate illicit flows, provided they are substantiated by 'compliant' paperwork. Meanwhile, multilateral frameworks focus on individual actors rather than the networks that sustain and operationalise capture.

The selective and politicised nature of enforcement exacerbates this problem. Western states often deploy anti-corruption measures as instruments of foreign policy. They ignore illicit wealth in their own financial centres while selectively targeting inconvenient foreign actors.[102] This uneven system of accountability allows professional enablers to operate with impunity. Nowhere is this clearer than in the United States' recent retreat from its historical role as a global anti-corruption watchdog. The dismantling of agency-based Anti-Kleptocracy initiatives and the weakening of FCPA and FARA enforcement under the current administration reflects a strategic de-prioritisation of corruption as a normative concern. Consistent enforcement is giving way to geopolitical expediency, where corruption is punished not for what it is, but for who wields it. Whether recent shifts in US posture are a function of a sense by the Trump administration that these rules are hamstringing the US in an era of geopolitical rivalry, or whether Trump's entourage intends to capture US institutions for private financial gain, or both, remains to be seen. Ambiguity on this matter illustrates the extent to which is this not just a technical or legal topic, but a political and architectural challenge. The shift to transnational state capture means having to confront not just illicit transactions or corrupt individuals, but global systems that enable and legitimise them. Without addressing this embedded infrastructure of complicity, anti-corruption efforts will remain performative and embolden state capture as a potent tool of geopolitical subversion.

[102] Morgan and Kinossian (2024).

References

Bain & Company (Dec 2018) Bain's initial response to the Nugent Commission's findings. https://www.bain.com/offices/johannesburg/sars-statement-dec17/

Basel Institute on Governance (2021) Basel AML index 2021. https://baselgovernance.org/sites/default/files/2021-09/Basel_AML_Index_2021_10th%20Edition.pdf

Belton C (2021) Putin's people: how the KGB took back Russia and then took on the West. William Collins

Bondi P (5 Feb 2025) Memorandum for all department employees for the total elimination of cartels and transnational criminal organizations. Office of the US Attorney General. https://www.justice.gov/ag/media/1388546/dl?inline

Bowers S, Kehoe K, Roonemaa H (2020) Inside scandal-rocked Danske Estonia and the shell-company "factories" that served it. https://www.icij.org/investigations/fincen-files/inside-scandal-rocked-danske-estonia-and-the-shell-company-factories-that-served-it/

Bowers S, Mukami P, Haddou L (3 Aug 2022) Exposed: how Russia-facing company formation agents took over the darkest corners of corporate Britain. Finance Uncovered. https://financeuncovered.org/stories/english-limited-partnerships-secrecy-formation-agencies-ios-las-lotus-comform-corruption

Brock G, Russell H (2015) Abusive tax avoidance and institutional corruption: the responsibilities of tax professionals. Edmond J. Safra working paper no. 56. https://doi.org/10.2139/ssrn.2566281

Bruun & Hjejle (2018) Report on the non-resident portfolio at Danske Bank's Estonian branch (internal report no. doc. 3151674). Bruun & Hjejle, Advokatpartnerselskab. https://danskebank.com/-/media/danske-bank-com/file-cloud/2018/9/report-on-the-non-resident-portfolio-at-danske-banks-estonian-branch.pdf

Canen N, Wantchekon L (2022) Political distortions, state capture, and economic development in Africa. J Econ Perspect 36(1):101–124. https://doi.org/10.1257/jep.36.1.101

Chipkin I, Swilling M, Bhorat H, Buthelezi M, Duma S, Friedenstein H, Mondi L, Peter C, Prins N, Qobo M (2018) Shadow state: the politics of state capture. Wits University Press. https://doi.org/10.18772/22018062125

Cooley A, Heathershaw J, Sharman JC (2018) Laundering cash, white washing reputations. J Democr 29(1):39–53. https://doi.org/10.1353/jod.2018.0003

Cooley A, Sharman JC (2017) Transnational corruption and the globalized individual. Perspect Polit 15(3):732–753. https://doi.org/10.1017/S1537592717000937

Dávid-Barrett E (2023) State capture and development: a conceptual framework. J Int Relat Dev 26(2):224–244. https://doi.org/10.1057/s41268-023-00290-6

Deloitte & Eskom Holdings, SOC Limited (20 Mar 2020) Joint statement between Eskom and Deloitte Consulting. https://www.deloitte.com/za/en/about/press-room/settlement-statement-as-agreed-with-eskom.html

Drezner DW, Farrell H, Newman A (eds) (2021) The uses and abuses of weaponized interdependence. Brookings Institute Press

EO No. 14209 (2025) Pausing foreign corrupt practices act enforcement to further American economic and national security, 14209 executive order. https://www.whitehouse.gov/presidential-actions/2025/02/pausing-foreign-corrupt-practices-act-enforcement-to-further-american-economic-and-national-security/

Erhvervsstyrelsen v. KPMG Baltic & Ernst & Young. Danish Ministry of Industry (28 Jan 2020) Business, and financial affairs. https://erhvervsstyrelsen.dk/sites/default/files/2020-01/Offentliggoerelse-Danske-Bank-english-version.pdf

Eskom Holdings, SOC Limited v. McKinsey & Company Africa Limited and Others (Jun 2019) High Court of South Africa, Gauteng Division, Pretoria. https://www.saflii.org/cgi-bin/disp.pl?file=za/cases/ZAGPPHC/2019/185.html&query=mckinsey

EU Regulation 2024/1620 Establishing the authority for anti-money laundering and countering the financing of terrorism and amending regulations (EU) No 1093/2010, (EU) No 1094/2010 and (EU) No 1095/2010, 2024/1620 Regulations (2024). https://eur-lex.europa.eu/eli/reg/2024/1620/oj/eng

European Central Bank, Finanšu un Kapitāla Tirgus Komisija (3 March 2016) Withdrawal of authorisation of JSC "TRASTA KOMERCBANK". https://www.centralbank.cy/images/media/pdf/Trasta_.pdf

Fazekas M, Tóth IJ (2016) From corruption to state capture: a new analytical framework with empirical applications from Hungary. Polit Res Q 69(2):320–334

Ferrill J, Southworth R (2025) Leadership in the evolving landscape of financial crime: navigating AML/CTF risks and controls. In: Goldbarsht D, de Koker L, Ferrill J (eds) The financial war on crime and terrorism: opportunities and challenges. Springer, Cham

Fishman E (2025) Chokepoints: American Power in the Age of Economic Warfare. Penguin RandomHouse

Financial Action Task Force (2018) Professional money laundering. Financial Action Task Force. https://www.fatf-gafi.org/content/dam/fatf-gafi/reports/Professional-Money-Laundering.pdf

Financial Action Task Force (2022) Report on the state of effectiveness and compliance with the FATF standards. https://www.fatf-gafi.org/content/dam/fatf-gafi/reports/Report-on-the-State-of-Effectiveness-Compliance-with-FATF-Standards.pdf.coredownload.pdf

Financial Action Task Force (2024) Horizontal review of gatekeepers' technical compliance related to corruption. https://www.fatf-gafi.org/content/dam/fatf-gafi/reports/HRGTC.pdf.coredownload.inline.pdf

Financial Action Task Force (2025) FATF annual report 2023–2024. https://www.fatf-gafi.org/en/publications/Fatfgeneral/FATF-Annual-report-2023-2024.html

Financial Action Task Force – Egmont Group (2018) Concealment of beneficial ownership. https://www.fatf-gafi.org/content/dam/fatf-gafi/reports/FATF-Egmont-Concealment-beneficial-ownership.pdf

Financial Crime Enforcement Network (2018) Proposal of Special Measure Against ABLV Bank, AS as a Financial Institution of Primary Money Laundering Concern: Notice of proposed rulemaking. https://www.fincen.gov/system/files/federal_register_notices/2018-02-16/2018-03214.pdf

Finansinspektionen (19 May 2015) Finansinspektionen v. Nordea Bank, AB: Decision. Government of Sweden. https://www.fi.se/contentassets/97ef5372bd4a4397bb5c4247ef206757/nordea-13-1784-eng2.pdf

Finansinspektionen (19 March 2020) Finansinspektionen v. Swedbank, AB: Decision. Government of Sweden. https://www.fi.se/contentassets/fd722f1e092b42c98910914969812a26/swedbank-beslut-2020-03-19-eng.pdf

Finansinspektionen (15 March 2023) Finansinspektionen v. Swedbank, AB: Decision. Government of Sweden. https://www.fi.se/contentassets/ee66531f570f4e738f897d4c15a4b257/beslut-swedbank-2023-03-14-eng.pdf

Folsom R (2019) A commentary on the globalization of foreign corrupt practices law. San Diego Legal Studies Paper No. 19-373. https://doi.org/10.2139/ssrn.3314302

Garland M (2 Mar 2022) Attorney General Merrick B. Garland announces launch of task force KleptoCapture. US Department of Justice. https://www.justice.gov/archives/opa/pr/attorney-general-merrick-b-garland-announces-launch-task-force-kleptocapture

Grzymala-Busse A (2008) Beyond Clientelism: incumbent state capture and state formation. Comp Pol Stud 41(4–5):638–673. https://doi.org/10.1177/0010414007313118

Haddou L, Bowers S (3 Aug 2022) Meet the old school friends running a UK formation agency linked to the Russian laundromat scandal. Finance Uncovered. https://financeuncovered.org/stories/english-limited-partnerships-comform-company-formation-agencies

Hellman J, Jones G, Kaufmann D (2000a) "Seize the state, seize the day": state capture, corruption, and influence in transition. Policy Research Working Paper no. WPS2444 World Bank Group. http://documents.worldbank.org/curated/en/537461468766474836

Hellman J, Jones G, Kaufmann D (2000b) Measuring governance, corruption, and state capture - how firms and bureaucrats shape the business environment in transition economies. Policy Research Working Paper no. WPS2312. World Bank Group. http://documents.worldbank.org/curated/en/241911468765617541

Hogan Lovells (25 Jan 2023) We regret our work was associated with State Capture. Hogan Lovells. https://www.politicsweb.co.za/documents/we-regret-our-work-was-associated-with-state-captu

Holder E (25 July 2010) Speech: Attorney General Holder at the African Union Summit. US Department of Justice. https://www.justice.gov/archives/opa/speech/attorney-general-holder-african-union-summit

Kaufmann D (2024) State capture matters: considerations and empirics toward a worldwide measure. In: Rose-Ackerman S (ed) Public sector performance, corruption and state capture in a globalized world. Routledge

Kellerman M (2025) Licensed detection agents: the case for financial crime bounty hunters. https://papers.ssrn.com/abstract=5106992

Khambule I (2021) Capturing South Africa's developmental state: state-society relations and responses to state capture. Public Adm Dev 41(4):169–179. https://doi.org/10.1002/pad.1912

de Koker L, Howell J, Morris N (2023) Economic consequences of Greylisting by the financial action task Force. Risks 11(5):Article 5. https://doi.org/10.3390/risks11050081

KPMG South Africa (2018) KPMG South Africa baseline report 2018: embracing change and rebuilding trust. https://assets.kpmg.com/content/dam/kpmg/za/pdf/2018/July/KPMG%20South%20Africa%20Baseline%20Report%202018.pdf

Küngas K (17 Apr 2023) Prokuratuur esitas rahapesu süüdistuse. Eesti Prokuratuur. https://www.prokuratuur.ee/uudised/prokuratuur-esitas-rahapesu-suudistuse

Legrand T, Leuprecht C (2021) Securing cross-border collaboration: transgovernmental enforcement networks organized crime and illicit international political economy. Policy and Society 40(4):565–586. https://doi.org/10.1080/14494035.2021.1975216

Leuprecht C, Ferrill J, Ozga M, Milind T, Karunakaran J (2025) Containing sex trafficking: the enabling role of beneficial ownership registries. Curr Issues Crim Just 37(2):264–286. https://doi.org/10.1080/10345329.2025.2466869

Low CK, Low TY (2020) Corporate criminal liability and Section 17A of the Malaysian Anti-Corruption Commission Act. Singap Acad Law J 32:563–610. https://doi.org/10.3316/informit.838683001273497

Marchant M, Mosiana M, Holden P, van Vuuren H (2020) The enablers: the bankers, accountants, and lawyers that cashed in on state capture. Open Secrets. https://www.opensecrets.org.za/the-enablers/

Morgan K, Kinossian N (2024) Dismantling Londongrad: the dark geography of dirty money. Eur Plan Stud 32(1):169–185. https://doi.org/10.1080/09654313.2023.2221283

Morse JC (2019) Blacklists, market enforcement, and the global regime to combat terrorist financing. Int Organ 73(3):511–545

National Director of Public Prosecutions v. Wood and Others (2022) High Court of South Africa, Gauteng Division, Pretoria. https://www.saflii.org/za/cases/ZAGPJHC/2022/272.html

NY Dept. of Financial Services (January 2017) New York State Department of Financial Services v. Deutsche Bank, AG: Consent Order. https://www.dfs.ny.gov/system/files/documents/2020/03/ea170130_deustche_bank.pdf

NY Dept. of Financial Services (July 2020) New York State Department of Financial Services v. Deutsche Bank, AG: Consent Order. https://www.dfs.ny.gov/system/files/documents/2020/07/ea20200706_deutsche_bank_consent_order.pdf

Office of the Director of National Intelligence (2025) Wealth and corrupt activities of the leadership of the Chinese Communist Party. Office of the Director of National Intelligence. https://www.dni.gov/files/ODNI/documents/assessments/ODNI-Unclassified-CDA-CCP-Leadership-202503.pdf

Perlo-Freeman S (2017) The south African arms deal. World Peace Foundation. https://sites.tufts.edu/corruptarmsdeals/the-south-african-arms-deal/

Public Relations and Communications Association (5 Sep 2017) PRCA announces expulsion of Bell Pottinger. https://prca.mena.global/prca-announces-expulsion-bell-pottinger/

Reuters (29 May 2020) Danish state prosecutor drops investigation of Danske Bank auditor EY. Reuters. https://www.reuters.com/article/markets/danish-state-prosecutor-drops-investigation-of-danske-bank-auditor-ey-idUSL8N2DB35W/

Sharife K, Joseph J (2018) India's Bank of Baroda played a key role in South Africa's Gupta scandal. Organized Crime and Corruption Reporting Project. https://www.occrp.org/en/investigation/indias-bank-of-baroda-played-a-key-role-in-south-africas-gupta-scandal

South African Reserve Bank v. HSBC Bank, PLC – Johannesburg (4 Oct 2024) South African Reserve Bank. https://www.resbank.co.za/content/dam/sarb/publications/media-releases/2024/pa-sanctions/hsbc-joburg/South%20African%20Reserve%20Bank%20imposes%20administrative%20sanctions%20on%20HSBC%20Bank%20Plc%20Johannesburg%20Branch.pdf

South African Reserve Bank v. Standard Bank of South Africa, Limited (24 Jan 2025) South African Reserve Bank. https://www.resbank.co.za/content/dam/sarb/publications/media-releases/2025/pa-sanctions/standard-bank/SBSA-sanction-2025-1.pdf

Stanford Law School & Sullivan & Cromwell, LLP (2025) Stanford Foreign Corrupt Practices Act Clearinghouse [Dataset]. https://fcpa.stanford.edu/index.html

United States v. Danske Bank A/S (12 Dec 2022) Plea agreement. US District Court, Southern District of New York, US Department of Justice. https://www.justice.gov/d9/press-releases/attachments/2022/12/13/danske_plea_508_compliant_0.pdf

United States v. Mckinsey & Company, Inc. US (13 Dec 2024) Deferred prosecution agreement. US District Court, Western District of Virginia Abingdon, US Department of Justice. https://www.justice.gov/usao-ma/media/1380231/dl

United States v. Vikas Sagar (Dec 2024) US District Court, Southern District of New York, US Department of Justice. https://www.justice.gov/d9/2024-12/sagar_information_0.pdf

US Senate (2025) US Senate lobbying disclosure report database. https://lda.senate.gov/filings/public/filing/search/?registrant=&registrant_country=&registrant_ppb_country=&client=Renaissance+Associates+S.A+&client_state=&client_country=&client_ppb_country=&lobbyist=&lobbyist_covered_position=&lobbyist_conviction_disclosure=&lobbyist_conviction_date_range_from=&lobbyist_conviction_date_range_to=&report_period=&report_year=&report_dt_posted_from=&report_dt_posted_to=&report_amount_reported_min=&report_amount_reported_max=&report_filing_uuid=&report_house_doc_id=&report_issue_area_description=&affiliated_organization=&affiliated_organization_country=&foreign_entity=&foreign_entity_country=&foreign_entity_ppb_country=&foreign_entity_ownership_percentage_min=&foreign_entity_ownership_percentage_max=&search=search

Van de Ven M (2019) Laundromats: responding to new challenges in the international fight against organised crime, corruption and money laundering (Report for the Committee on Legal Affairs and Human Rights no. doc. 14847). Parliamentary Assembly Council of Europe. https://assembly.coe.int/nw/xml/XRef/Xref-XML2HTML-EN.asp?fileid=27474&lang=en

de Willebois VD, Halter EM, Harrison RA, Park JW, Sharman JC (2011) The puppet masters how the corrupt use legal structures to Hide stolen assets and what to do about it (No. 65125). World Bank. https://documents.worldbank.org/en/publication/documents-reports/documentdetail/784961468152973030/the-puppet-masters-how-the-corrupt-use-legal-structures-to-hide-stolen-assets-and-what-to-do-about-it

Wrate J (2018) US lobbying firm launders Azerbaijan's reputation—and gets "laundromat" cash. Organized Crime and Corruption Reporting Project. https://www.occrp.org/en/project/the-azerbaijani-laundromat/us-lobbying-firm-launders-azerbaijans-reputation-and-gets-laundromat-cash

Zondo CJRMM (2022) Judicial commission of inquiry into allegations of state capture, corruption and fraud in the public sector including organs of state, vol 1–6. Zondo Commission, Constitutional Court of South Africa. https://www.statecapture.org.za/site/information/reports

Nicholas Donaldson is a Junior Lecturer at Leiden University's Institute for Security and Global Affairs and a graduate researcher with Queen's University's Institute of Intergovernmental Relations, where he leads a project on transnational state capture. He is also a Junior Research Fellow at *The Hague Journal of Diplomacy* and previously worked at ISGA on ERC-funded projects related to counter-terrorism , global economic governance, and quantitative foreign policy analysis.

Christian Leuprecht is an award-winning professor at the Royal Military College of Canada, director of the Institute of Intergovernmental Relations at Queen's University, Editor-in-Chief of the *Canadian Military Journal* and Adjunct Research Professor at the Australian Graduate School of Policing and Security. He is the recipient of RMC's Cowan Prize for Excellent in Research and an elected member of the College of New Scholars of the Royal Society of Canada.

Corrupt Elites and Godfathers in Nigeria: Structural Impunity and the Undermining of Accountability

Jackie H. Harvey and Petrus C. van Duyne

Abstract Corruption would appear to be almost 'hardwired' into the fragile democracy of Nigeria. Well-endowed with natural resources, Nigeria should have been one of the wealthiest countries in West Africa. Instead, it has one of the highest levels of inequality with a large part of the population living below the poverty line in contrast to a small elite that has reserved access to the national wealth. Based on a review of literature on the subject that is supported by documentary analysis of media sources and of known cases, our chapter seeks to understand the social historical context of corruption of the ruling elite.

Within many countries there is an inevitable tension between the ideals of equality across the wider population and the favourable position of a far smaller group of political elitist entrepreneurs. A small part of it manifest itself as 'godfathers', wealthy political patrons, who form the political elite class. Of interest is the position of this godfatherism in Nigerian society, whether that be within the political or economic sectors, and how they are able to influence decisions of social and economic importance by influencing the instalment into high positions of their nominees (godsons). But the godson remains dependent as he must pay back the investment. This can lead to rigged election outcomes and processes. When elitism becomes corrupted in this manner, we find that established norms and traditional hierarchical deference to authority actually protect those politically powerful elitist entrepreneurs, which would place them 'above the law'. This position will only

This chapter was submitted for review the day before the sad and untimely death of my co-author em Prof. Petrus C. van Duyne on 20th March 2025. I hope that the post-review modifications I have made do justice to his memory.

J. H. Harvey (✉)
Newcastle Business School, Northumbria University, Newcastle upon Tyne, UK
e-mail: jackie.harvey@northumbria.ac.uk

P. C. van Duyne (Deceased)
Tilburg University, Tilburg, The Netherlands

D. Goldbarsht et al. (eds.), *The Financial War on Crime and Terrorism*, European Yearbook of International Economic Law,
https://doi.org/10.1007/978-3-032-06360-1_9

change when there is far greater transparency within the decision-making process as currently the case.

1 Introduction

In the history of most societies, two contrasting concepts recur: the first concerns the equality of mankind; the second is the obvious differences that exist, *e.g.* in skills, social position or esteem. Of concern to politicians and policy makers is the unequal distribution of wealth and income. This wealth gap may be experienced as an injustice if it mainly benefits a limited number of people, together denoted as the 'elite', encompassing persons in the higher levels of society. This wealth gap can and has led to social and political tensions between the 'haves' and 'have nots': the latter striving for equality, and the former (favouring the *status quo)* resisting (too much) change in society. Such tensions have, in the past, contributed to violent upheavals, such as the French Revolution when attempts were made to create an egalitarian society and included the abolition of the hated nobility with all its titles and privileges. These extreme manifestations of striving for equality were ultimately undone by Napoleon who created his own titled elite in which his family were positioned at the pinnacle.

Equality of mankind remains a lofty aim. However, history teaches us that in daily life, elites will always surface, whether in politics, business, or culture. Elitism may have a positive or a negative association, ranging from striving to get 'on top' in the cultural sectors to involvement in politics. Elitism is not a static concept: elites have the inherent problem of having outlived themselves, which poses the question of replacement and whether that occurs gradually or violently. Though the top may have fallen, elite status still matters.

The fact that 'elite status matters' does not imply that the concept is clearly delineated. The most common notion is 'belonging to' a highly esteemed social group. The reasons for belonging can be diverse. For example, because of excellent skills, knowledge, employment, or some other specialism. However, high esteem may also be attributed for reasons other than personal excellence; it may be a consequence of heritage, as is the case with nobility, inherited wealth, or just having the right connections.

Clearly, the concept of 'elite' covers a wide variety of groups, some of which have little in common. For example, there is likely no connection between an excellent artist and the indulged son of an aristocrat who is manoeuvred into a high position by 'friends of friends'. Conflating different types of elites cannot provide insight into the social sectors where elitism is important; for example, in political decision making where it is all about Who get what, when and how.[1] For this reason, we limit our study to the arena of political decision making. In a democratic state,

[1] Yawa (2020), p. 11.

to comply with the demand of transparency, it is also about the question 'why?' In elite policy making 'why' is often absent, making elitism a problematic phenomenon: how opaque is elitist decision making?

Our study is focused on Nigeria, where political elitism has grown into a very specific manifestation: that of 'godfatherism'[2] enabled by a surrounding field of political grand corruption. Nigeria should be one of the wealthiest countries in West Africa.[3] Instead, it has one of the highest levels of inequality with a large part of the population living below the poverty line. This is in contrast to a small elite group of wealthy political patrons that has reserved access to the national wealth. As will be elaborated, godfatherism consists of the support (usually financial but it can also be by way of endorsement) of the election campaigns of candidates for one of the representative bodies or other high office in return for a political favour at some later date.[4] The problematic nature of political elitism has not escaped the attention of critical scholars.[5] These critical authors are of the opinion that this phenomenon, undermines the fragile democracy in Nigeria.[6] There is a broad consensus about the negative effects of godfatherism, sometimes referred to through synonymous terms such as patron-client relationship or neopatrimonialism.[7]

The sources of wealth belonging to the godfather may have been legitimately earned but are often acquired through the benefits obtained from prior political favours. This can involve acts of corruption and plundering of state resources for personal gain.[8] Undertaken at scale, such acts rob the country of the funds that could otherwise be deployed for economic growth and development.[9] As will be discussed, going back to colonial times, such activity is interwoven with public administration and remains a continuing characteristic of Nigerian governance.[10] The traditional deference to authority and the elite status afforded to politicians (including godfathers) holding senior roles in the legislature has enabled those who would wish to do so, to acquire the resources of the state with apparent impunity. The godfather's illicitly acquired wealth is deployed both locally to influence the

---

[2] Within Nigeria the terms 'Godfather' and 'Godfatherism' tend to be used interchangeably but refer to wealthy individuals who use their status to influence political activity. They may operate openly or behind the scenes.

[3] Harvey et al. (2025).

[4] Human Rights Watch (2007); Albert (2005).

[5] See for example Ameh et al. (2025); Human Rights Watch (2007); Igbini and Okolie (2020).

[6] Also see Sule, Sani & Mat (2018).

[7] Animasawun (2013); Hoffman (2010); Erdmann and Engel (2006).

[8] Also see Donaldson and Leuprecht (2025).

[9] Refer to the cases of grand corruption by government officials involving the embezzlement of billions of naira that are detailed in the various reports produced by the Human Environmental Development Agenda (HEDA), the Nigerian human rights non-governmental organisation (NGO) available at https://hedang.org/ accessed 27/05/2025.

[10] Van Duyne and Harvey (2022).

election of a 'godson'[11] (to secure a future income stream) as well as to finance their own asset accumulation within Nigeria and overseas.

Though concerns about such negative effects are justified, given its opaque nature, obtaining hard facts on the extent of political elitism and godfatherism in Nigeria remains difficult. The few qualitative studies cannot be considered as commensurate to the apparent seriousness of its threat.

2 Approach

Based on a review of literature, supported by descriptive analysis of media sources and of known cases, our chapter seeks to understand the social historical context of corruption of the political elite. In doing so, it aims to provide a more systematic explorative analysis of elitism and of godfatherism in Nigeria together with their link to corruption. The research for this chapter has been carried out through an extensive desk review of English language publications (academic articles and NGO publications) on elitism and godfatherism in Nigeria. The starting point is 1999, this being the end of military rule and the start of the fourth republic. The articles were available open access and sourced through University library resources. Cross-reference was also made to on-line newspaper articles mainly published by the Nigerian press. This enabled us to enhance our assessment of content through media discourse.[12] We used 'elite' and 'godfather'[13] as key words alone and combined, and in combination with 'corruption'. The last search was important as a way of uncovering articles on corruption that might also mention elitism or godfatherism. Our search was inevitably subjective, selecting from publications only those that had these phenomena as a main subject of discussion. We also utilised the series of compendia reports produced by the Human and Environmental Development Agenda (HEDA) NGO.[14] HEDA produced its first report in 2017 and is currently in its eighth edition. The aim of the HEDA reports is to raise public awareness of ongoing high-level cases of corruption and to highlight those that 'get delayed in courts'.[15]

The remainder of the chapter presents our analysis and synthesis of these various sources of information. We focus first on elites and their operation in Nigeria, and consider the challenges associated with delineating the concept before unpicking the characteristics and functions of this group. We use our exploration of the data from HEDA to illustrate how these socio-political structures facilitate high-level

[11] The term 'Godson' refers to an individual who is groomed for high office with the support of a godfather.

[12] Wincup (2017).

[13] We included plurals and derivatives and conducted a separate search on 'godfather' and 'godson' together.

[14] Refer to note 10.

[15] HEDA (2024), p. i.

corruption. We then turn our attention to godfathers and the challenges faced in identifying the individuals who occupy this position within Nigeria and how corruption is manifested within this specific group.

3 Elites

3.1 Limitations of Delineating 'Elite'

As already mentioned, depending on its context the term 'elite' (and its derivatives: 'elitism' and 'elitist') is defined in various ways. The term 'elite' originally indicated something very concrete: the recognition of a 'master' craftsman in a craft guild. With time, its coverage was broadened to 'excellence' by esteemed professionals across the arts and science, and amongst the military and clergy. Each group has its own characteristics determined by its role in society and by public appreciation. However, that role may be one that is given or acquired by association rather than by intrinsic effort. In short, 'elite' matters, but its core meaning remains evasive. This does not prevent exploration of its social or political function.

Political elites have been identified as a power elite, a status group among citizens comprising <1% of the population.[16] This suggestion is not supported by other data and is rather an indication of the size of the relevant social groups within a surrounding 'mass'. More accurately, elites may comprise only a 'ruling minority, a group that controls and disputes the most important power sources'.[17] This corresponds to the more precise delineation: 'Elites represent a small group of influential people that control a disproportionate amount of wealth, privilege or power in society'.[18] We think this a useful working definition, while recognising open components such as 'influential' or 'proportional'.

In this approach there is less attention paid to social sectors with different elite cultures. Cultural elites may respond to different incentives, though power politics may just as well step over the thresholds of science, literature, and fine arts, where rich collectors want to show-off their elite status by dominating markets and fairs and play the role of wealthy patrons. In the field of power politics this would be called 'godfatherism'.[19] Closer investigation should determine the overlapping aspects of the various sectors.

One aspect is shared across all kinds of elitism: the social perception of *belonging* to an elite for which one is esteemed. Elite is in the eye of the beholder and is, therefore, a subjective and fragile attribute: elite-ness ends when the beholders shift their fashion or if populist agitation attacks elitism to strip it of its power and

[16] Bolarinwa and Osuji (2022).

[17] Yawa (2020), p. 1.

[18] Nakpodia and Adegbite (2018), p. 17.

[19] Obodo (2009).

privileges. This elite-ness concerns political power and top-down decision making along a hierarchical line of decision making.[20]

3.2 Nigerian Perception/Judgement of Elite

Though the analysis of the core concept fails to lead to an unambiguous outcome, the issue of elitism still matters if we are to understand the political economy of high-level financial crime within Nigeria. Therefore, it is of interest to have an overview of its meaning from a small selection of experts and academic authors located as outlined in the *Approach* section.

As misconduct is not a built-in feature of elitism, we leave it to the authors as summarised in Table 1 to identify any examples. Historically, elitism has not always been seen as beneficial. During the colonial era and the early years of the first republic elitism was compatible with the existing local social and political institutions.

Table 1 Summary of "the meaning of…"

Author(s)	Year	Elites are …	Examples given
Afolabi	2019	…those who predominate in corruption offences	Senior office holders, godfathers, political party bosses and community chiefs (and unspecified others)
Bolarinwa and Osuji	2022	…those who should rule. The political elite is the power elite	List of office holders (the President) downwards to traditional leaders (Christian and Muslim)
Fisayo et al.	2023	Elite capture basically means the capture of government decision-making or resources	Godfatherism (clientelism)
Ogele	2021	Political elite holding power	Success at the ballot box Organised electoral and criminal law breaking to remain in power by any means including violence
Prince	2023	…those individuals occupying influential positions within the political realm	None
Yawa	2020	the capability of imposing one's will, even if against the will of others	Institutional (e.g. the military, health care system) or personal. Access to public resources, political power in economic sectors and being able to determine "*who gets what, when and how*"

[20] Odubajo, and Alabi (2014).

The local institutions were ruled and represented by a local chief, mayor, or other authority under the flag of 'indirect rule' which was considered the most efficient way of administrating the exploitation of Nigeria's riches.[21] At the same time, with wider access to education a new, young elite class developed.[22] That was a positive development; after independence in 1960, a new political cohort could take over. Unfortunately, it failed, and from 1966, Nigeria experienced the first of a series of *coups d'état* (and attempts) that ended in 1999 with the transition to civilian rule, although there was an amnesty of the military staff involved who were allowed to keep any illicitly obtained wealth.

This short survey of 'the meaning of...' could be extended by including other publications that also contain the keyword 'elite' in the main text but not in the title. We doubt whether that will bring more clarity: there are no generally accepted criteria to determine what belongs to the 'true' elitism group which will keep its fluidity within boundaries. We think it more fruitful, therefore, to list recognised distinctive features noting they are not exclusive and may even overlap.

3.3 Characteristics of Elitism

The following characteristics are identified as belong to the 'semantic tree of elitism':

(a) Elite groups are always small and must be exclusive relative to the masses;
(b) Elite groups can determine '*who gets what, when and how*';[23]
(c) For this reason, the elites need access to resources, for self-enrichment and to reward or seduce newcomers (through corrupt acts generating illicit finance);
(d) Perception of being an elite is a social condition: what is the use of being 'elite' if nobody sees it?

Under the political elite groups there are the many sub-elites: the cultural elite and the performance or artistic elite. As far as can be assessed, these elites have no power outside their own expert circle of art, sport and other rare skills. Although this does not exclude an overlap of interests with those within political circles.[24] The Nigerian literature on the allegedly corrupt political elite contains such judgements but without differentiating between the different types of corruption.

---

[21] Oghovbu (2023).

[22] Ogele (2021).

[23] Yawa (2020), p. 11.

[24] For example: Oligarchs buying football clubs and interest groups lobbying for certain government policies.

3.4 The Function and Corruption of Elites

There is no necessary causal connection between elites and corruption: one can be bribed without belonging to the elite. Also, one can belong to the elite while staying away from corrupt opportunities: '*noblesse oblige*'. Historically, in many states in Europe, the ruling (conservative) elite disapproved the ostentatious display of wealth, considering it vulgar. This social attitude can function as a counterweight to the temptations, that may be within easy reach, to corruptly seek personal profit. Can the weight of '*noblesse oblige*' as a social counterweight have an impact in a society in which the materialistic display of personal success is generally accepted if not admired?[25] This makes the association of corruption with elitism more than a mere *cliché*. Unfortunately, wealth accumulation by the individual without productive added value is always at the expense of wealth available elsewhere. As has been observed in Nigeria: 'The fruits of economic growth, and the country's natural resources, have long been gobbled up by the nation's tiny but overbearing elite, while the vast majority remains ruinously poor.'[26]

Elitism has important personal and societal functions. Some of the functions reinforce the fluidity of the elite concepts. However, what is certain, is that members of the elite group may expect to receive privileged treatment. We identify four distinct functions of elitism which are evidenced in Nigerian society and that facilitate financial crimes:

(a) '*Belonging to*'

Despite the lack of an unambiguous definition of elitism, the idea of belonging to an 'elite' has maintained its attractiveness and not only for reasons of self-esteem but also for personal vanity. This is a basic condition for elite sustainability: *social recognition*. Hence the importance of mutually recognised elite markers such as manifestations of wealth and distinctive modes of behaviour.

Apart from this personal self-esteem, belonging to a particular elite may also have more practical advantages, such as providing personal leverage in deal making or to open doors to the 'right people' who in their position of power can decide over the distribution of positions or jobs to those who are perceived as 'belonging to'.[27]

(b) *The protection or 'cushion' function*

Belonging to an elite group also has a protective function. In the face of revelations of wrongdoing by one or more elite members, there can be a closing of ranks to fend-off possible reputation damage. This action provides a social or political shield or cushion against various forms of (criminal) misfortune. The effects of the cushioning should not be underestimated. If successful, it

---

[25] Adekoya (2023).

[26] Adekoya (2023).

[27] See UNODC (2017, 2019, 2024) for discussions about corruption and the workplace in Nigeria.

contributes to the perception of *impunity* in cases of criminal liability.[28] This undermines the rule of law if only because of a decreased willingness to report cases of elite wrongdoing to the authorities who are themselves seen as supporters of the elite. This protective cushioning can involve an initial policy of denial. If denial proves untenable, professional delaying techniques can be used, slowing the court process; ultimately, there can be leniency in the sentencing and in the execution of the sentence.[29]

(c) *Social and political control and 'role modelling'*

'Belonging to' can also extend social and political control by more senior or higher status members demonstrating acceptable boundaries of behaviour. This might involve avoidance of flaunting an extravagant lifestyle that might lead to unwanted media investigation into the assets and activity of one or more of the groups. This is a fuzzy function, particularly as it can also be very compelling: deviating too much from implicit standards may see other people in the elite turning against you. The deviant member may be offered as some type of scapegoat, protecting the others. Elitism may provide a protected latitude of behaviours, but the role model can also function as an internal control mechanism, screening the group.

(d) *Impunity*

The three functions of elitism mentioned above culminate in the most important function of impunity: wrongdoers can get away with their misbehaviour because formal or informal institutions fail to respond adequately. There may well be social disapproval, but it is the criminal law institutions that have responsibility for prevention of law breaking. Their failure to act opens the door to high level financial impropriety.

It appears that the higher the alleged perpetrators are on the political or social ladder, the less they have to fear from the law. This has been observed during elections when incumbent office holders and potential candidates fight for power at the ballot box, spilling into violence between opposing factions with no police intervention.[30]

When looking at misdeeds perpetrated by those at the high end of the social-economic ladder we see the process of law bogged down in a system of delays, postponements, and appeals that display a stable pattern over the years.[31] Impunity is more than a violation of a specific code of penal law; it is a reflection of power which can be exploited in a way that ultimately undermines democracy.[32]

---

[28] Examples of this are found in the various reports by HEDA and in the Human Rights Watch Report (2007).

[29] See van Duyne and Harvey (2022).

[30] Human Rights Watch (2007) and ACLED (2023).

[31] Ojo (2024).

[32] OyozeBaje (2023); also see US Department of State (2017).

3.5 Analysis of the HEDA Compendia

The HEDA reports provide an overview of what they identify as the 100 high profile on-going corruption cases brought to court from 2005 onwards, involving public office holders and 'substantial' sums of money.[33] This list can, and has, changed across the various editions and provides a short unstandardised description of each of the cases. While bringing attention to these cases, there is a lack of transparency: the sampling procedure is not disclosed with the result that the compendia are like a family picture album without structure. The narrative case descriptors do not report a consistent set of research variables[34] and where cases are removed and subsequently reappear, there is no cross referencing between the different reports, while their case numbering system appears somewhat random.[35] Nevertheless, in view of the scarcity of systematised empirical data in Nigeria, it is still useful to inspect and evaluate the HEDA studies.

Table 2 indicates the status of those offenders included in its reports. Because it is produced by others, we cannot say anything about the relationship between these 100 cases and the totality of all known cases. Furthermore, as cases can and do appear across multiple editions of the compendia it is not possible to produce a simple total for each category across all years. The 2020 edition removed some 50 cases (replaced by others) that had been included in earlier editions. This was because a large number had been concluded through defendants being sentenced or discharged. The removed cases included 21 Governors, 6 Senators, 3 ministers and advisers, and 20 categorised as 'others'. While this provides some explanation for

Table 2 Category of offender as recorded by HEDA

Category	2018	2019	2020	2021	2022	2023	2024
Former minister/advisor	12	12	11	13	8	12	9
Senators	3	5	5	2	5	7	2
Former Governor	44	41	17	15	14	12	15
Others	41	41	67	70	73	69	69
Total	100	99	100	100	100	100	95

Source information the analysis section of the various HEDA reports. The total for 2019 is incorrectly shown as 100 in the report. The report for 2024 contains 95 cases pertaining to Nigeria with a further 5 drawn from the region of West Africa, we have excluded these

Source: HEDA Reports 2018–2024 (HEDA 2018, 2019, 2020, 2021, 2022, 2023, 2024)

[33] The case selection is derived from the Economic and Financial Crimes Commission (EFCC), the Independent Corrupt Practices and other Related Offences Commission (ICPC) documents or other sources.

[34] For example, named defendants, criminal law offence, court case number and sums involved.

[35] By way of example: the ongoing case of the National Security Advisor under President Goodluck Jonathan. He and co-defendants were first arraigned in court in 2015 for two separate cases concerning criminal misappropriation of public funds. For the editions 2019–2021 the case was assigned the number 1; in 2022 it was case 81; case 100 in 2023 and case 56 in 2024.

the fall in the number of cases against former state governors it does not explain the increase in the number in the category 'others'.[36]

Though one may consider this the top of elite corruption, the offences with which they are charged cover a wide typology of criminal profit-making. Within Nigeria, corruption can take many different forms: embezzlement; tender and procurement fraud including facilitation payments and kickbacks; lobbying; campaign financing as well as patronage; regulatory capture; and rent-seeking.[37] Despite the powers vested in the authorities to bring anti-corruption charges, it has been found that few corruption cases are prosecuted successfully. Consequently, fraud and money laundering dominate as the main offences being prosecuted (Table 3).

The prosecuting agencies typically bring charges under three main pieces of primary legislation.[38] All of which contain AML provisions, that 'are complex in their drafting and, in practice, overlap in their reach. Their use is varied and at times, inconsistent'.[39] The overlapping mandates of the two main agencies (and their unwillingness to cooperate)[40] have negatively impacted their successful completion of cases.

Table 3 Main charge recorded by HEDA

Type of crime	2018	2019	2020	2021	2022	2023	2024
Fraud	40	40	40	43	63	45	49
Corruption	11	11	11	7	6	5	5
Embezzlement	3	3	3	3	4	0	2
Money laundering	28	28	18	26	20	31	23
Bribery	2	2	2	6	1	2	2
Forgery	1	1	1	7	1	6	4
Misappropriation	9	9	9	7	5	7	11
Conspiracy	2	2	2	1	0	0	0
Election scandal	1	1	1	0	0	0	0
False declaration of assets	3	3	3	0	0	2	2
Abuse of office	0	0	0	0	0	2	2
Total	100	100	90	100	100	100	100

The total in the 2020 edition of the compendia incorrectly sums to 100. The total of 100 for 2024 has included the five cases from West Africa. We cannot remove these as it is not possible to know how those cases were originally classified by HEDA as the cases mention multiple charges
Source: HEDA Reports 2018–2024 (HEDA 2018, 2019, 2020, 2021, 2022, 2023, 2024)

[36] From our inspection, 'others' includes prominent individuals who do not fall into the elected government positions. This includes judges, senior office holders of government agencies, police inspectors, bankers, and businessmen, particularly within the oil sector.

[37] Shehu (2015).

[38] An explanatory note is required here: the Anti-Money Laundering powers lie primarily with the ICPC and the EFCC as conferred through their establishing acts. These are respectively the Corrupt Practices and Related Offences Act, 2000 and the Economic and Financial Crimes Commission Act of 2004. A third piece of legislation, the Advance Fee Fraud and Other Fraud Related Offences Act 2006 also contains additional AML provisions.

[39] Sproat et al. (2024).

[40] Harvey et al. (2021).

We found that the HEDA reports do not give a proper analysis of these criminal law concepts. For example, money laundering can be an independent 'standalone' offence by way of financial criminal service providing. It can also point at a 'follow-up crime' of self-laundering to wash the revenues of bribery, embezzlement, misappropriation or mismanagement as far as this is a criminal offence.

Earlier work provided further detail on the HEDA cases; this analysis informed a composite spreadsheet compiled from the first three versions of the compendia (2018–2020).[41] We updated this data set by including information from the next four versions of the compendia (2021–2024).[42] Of interest for the purposes of this chapter are cases that involve individuals holding offices of state that consistently appear across multiple versions of the compendia. These cases may be so complex that they are difficult to prove, requiring vast amounts of evidence from many witnesses. Their inclusion may also indicate the ability of high-profile individuals with excessive wealth to hire the very best legal teams who are able to use professional delaying tactics, stalling the cases in courts. These cases can also, however, indicate the ability of the elite to control or influence the legal process (both prosecutorial and judicial) and fend off reputation damage in a way that provides 'a protective cushion'. For those cushioned by the elite system or having the funds that can be used to stretch the case processing, there is an advantage in belonging to the elite.

We identified 60 cases that appear across all editions of the compendia from 2018 to 2024. Table 4 shows that almost half of these 60 cases are either adjourned or remain ongoing. Eighteen cases were discharged, dismissed, or struck out with the defendants having no case to answer. Only nine were sentenced, and a further four had sentences overturned on appeal. So, for 60 cases covering a period of 6 years, only nine have resulted in a custodial sentence being passed. Of those nine, three were given the option of a fine in place of incarceration and one was pardoned by the government.[43] We are of course dealing with incomplete data: we can say nothing about those high-profile individuals who pleaded guilty and were sentenced accordingly or those against whom the evidence was compelling and who were found guilty within a court session. Given our discussion thus far we venture that these probably represent only a small number.

For the 29 cases that are 'adjourned/ongoing' we further analysed the subset to find out how long they had been in the court system (see Table 5). A note on interpretation is needed. Of the 12 cases lasting up to 2 years, ten of the cases were last included in HEDA (2021). We cannot say anything about why they no longer appear. It may be that the cases remain stuck in the court system with no further information

[41] This version of the spreadsheet is available at https://giace.org/projects/benowner/ accessed 04/12/2024

[42] Reports available on-line at https://Hedang.org/ Accessed 08/12/2024.

[43] Also see 'SPECIAL REPORT: 11 forgotten cases of alleged corruption by former Nigerian state governors' Kunle Sanni Premium Times, 20th August, 2022 *"The Economic and Financial Crimes Commission (EFCC) has investigated 31 state governors for corruption and taken 11 of them to court, but the agency has recorded only two convictions, both of whom were pardoned without completing their sentences"* https://www.premiumtimesng.com/politics/549627-special-report-11-forgotten-cases-of-alleged-corruption-by-former-nigerian-state-governors-2.html Accessed 05/03/2025.

Table 4 Outcome of cases

Category	Outcome					Total
	Sentenced	Sentence overturned on appeal	Discharged/ acquitted	Dismissed/ struck out/ closed/no case	Adjourned/ Ongoing	
Ministers/ Advisors	3	1	2	0	13	19
Senators	1	1	1	0	3	6
Governors	1	1	3	3	8	16
Other	4	1	4	5	5	19
Total	9	4	10	8	29	60

Source: HEDA Reports 2018–2024 (HEDA 2018, 2019, 2020, 2021, 2022, 2023, 2024)

Table 5 Period between date of case first filing and date of last process mention for those 29 cases that remain ongoing

Category	Case length		
	0–2 years	3–5 years	6–10 years
Ministers/Advisors	4	3	6
Senators	2	0	1
Governors	4	1	3
Other	2	1	2
Total	12	5	12

Source: HEDA Reports 2018–2024 (HEDA 2018, 2019, 2020, 2021, 2022, 2023, 2024)

released into the public domain or that HEDA considered other cases to be of more interest. The cases that remain ongoing for a period of 6–10 years commenced around the time of the election of President Buhari (who campaigned on an anti-corruption ticket) in 2015. As has been pointed out[44] Buhari was praised for pursuing some very high-profile individuals early on in his second term of office.

The evidence of widespread abuse of office or position is fragmentary and should therefore be used with reservation. However, the political and business elite, due to their position, have access to public funds that can be illegally diverted to personal accounts. Most often such acts are perpetrated by a small group of officials in and around a central office,[45] as illustrated in the case of the office of the Accountant General (AG) of the Federation.

The AG of the Federation embezzled ₦ 84.7 billion which was distributed by former aides. The AG was aided by his technical assistant and a former director. Additionally, five small groups helped handle his office's money through an Exchange Office; these groups either worked directly in his office or functioned as intermediaries with the banks, which were apparently not vigilant in their oversight. No Suspicious Activity Reports were submitted.[46]

[44] Adeleke (2023); Harvey et al. (2021).

[45] van Duyne and Harvey (2022).

[46] For a summary of the case refer to https://v1.corruptioncases.ng/export/frn-vs-ahmed-idris-former-accountant-ge accessed 02/02/2025.

This case does not differ much from cases of grand corruption described in the HEDA publications, suggesting that grand corruption is an elite matter.[47] Although, the converse does not hold: not all elites are involved in corrupt dealings, though some authors lean towards an almost full overlap.[48] Nevertheless, this assumed overlap follows from an historic-cultural interpretation, beginning with colonialism, where the roots of corruption were borrowed, such as rent seeking and clientelism. The colonial administration was seen as a greedy and clientelist (indirect) ruler, and when they left in the beginning 1960s their local elite successors simply stepped into their shoes. During President Obasanjo's rule from 1999–2007, they managed their position in the public administration as a "self-interested exploitation of the people and the country".[49] This clientelism and rent-seeking did not change under his successor President Goodluck Jonathan (2010–2015). It may also be said that President Muhammadu Buhari (2015–2023) who twice won presidential election (2015 and 2019) on his anti-corruption ticket failed in preventing the ongoing corrupt practices. However, despite this, corruption continues to be referred to as being intractable.[50]

It is interesting to observe how President Obasanjo implemented his anti-corruption policy. In 2000, Obasanjo established the Independent Corrupt Practices and other Related Offences Commission (ICPC) and in 2004, the Economic and Financial Crimes Commission (EFCC). These were amongst several institutional attempts that have been criticised for their lack of success against corruption,[51] as well as against criminal abuse of office, both partly due to the inefficiency of the judicial system and partly to criminal law complexities. The handling of many high-profile cases by the courts dragged on for years.[52] The anti-graft institutions were also accused of allowing themselves to be used in vendettas between opposing elite factions: '*if you were a friend no matter how corrupt you may be, nobody would touch you, and if you were an enemy, real or imaginary, the commission would go after you*'.[53] This reproach appears to be cross-government: it was a complaint under President Obasanjo as well as under the self-proclaimed corruption fighter President

[47] Also see Anaedozie (2017); van Duyne and Harvey (2022); Harvey et al. (2021).

[48] See for example, Ojukwu and Shopeju (2018).

[49] Ojukwu and Shopeju (2018), p. 2.

[50] See for example The Conversation 'Why Buhari's government is losing the anti-corruption was' Oludayo Tade, March 7th, 2021. Available at https://theconversation.com/whybuharis-government-is-losing-the-anti-corruption-war-155488; also see Premium Times 'Buhari's anti-corruption failure fuels insecurity, undermines democracy – Report', June 13th, 2021, available at https://www.premiumtimesng.com/news/headlines/467455-buharis-anti-corruption-failure-fuels-insecurity-undermines-democracyreport.html; and Centre for Democracy and Development, Buhari's Anti-Corruption Record at Six Years: An Assessment. Available at https://www.cddwestafrica.org/wp-content/uploads/2021/06/Buhari-Anticorruption-record-at-6years.pdf

[51] These include: the Code of Conduct Bureau, Ethical Revolution Commission, Mass Mobilization for Social Justice and Economic Recovery (MAMSER); and the Judicial Commission of Inquiry.

[52] Refer to the HEDA reports.

[53] Ojukwu & Shopeju (2018), p. 6; also see Adeleke (2023).

Buhari.[54] It is a description of law enforcement that does not instil much confidence in the rule of law, particularly if the administration silently flouts its own anti-corruption policy, maintaining weak institutions to suit their own purposes[55] or using their position to create unneeded or duplicate agencies or bodies who then are expected to 'provide contracts and appointments to their supporters'.[56]

Elites gain dominance in weak law enforcement environments, enabling them to exploit weak institutions characterized by organizational or 'institutional voids.[57] They can manipulate these institutions for their own ends and implement self-serving policies as public policy.[58] This allows the elite to maintain their positions at the expense of the wider, poorer population.

Of course, just as not all elites are corrupt, neither is there total immunity for those who break the law. There is always the risk of exposure and of being held accountable for wrongdoing. How is this risk managed? One way is to finance other people. As we discuss next, this is not only the hooligans on the streets, but others wishing to climb the ladder to assume the trapping of success and for whom the risk is one they are willing to take. This formulation is the essence of what is denoted as Godfatherism: a system of supporting or grooming someone else (the godson) to take on the political role. But this is rarely an act of pure altruism, as already noted; there is an expectation by the godfather of a return on their investment.

4 Godfathers

4.1 The Phenomenon of the Godfather

Absent a clear definition, there has been an attempt to provide a distinction between different types of godfathers. The demarcation provided is not sharp, but the characteristics are helpful in recognising the different ways in which godfathers can operate:

(a) 'Geopolitical or ethnic organisation that arrogate to themselves the right to decide who represent their jurisdiction in government;'
(b) 'Geo-political or ethnic father figures. These are some prominent individuals within some geo-political or ethnic organisation who are popularly respected;'
(c) There are 'Political godfathers consist[ing] of some rich Nigerians who see sponsorship of political candidates as a source of upward social and economic mobility;'

[54] Adeleke (2023).

[55] Afolabi (2019).

[56] Page (2018), p. 8.

[57] Nakpodia and Adegbite (2018), p. 18.

[58] Okeke and Idike (2016).

(d) Some godfathers are not themselves rich, but they know how to secure grass roots support and votes. The 'client provides the money and the godfather delivers the votes;'
(e) the final group 'consists of rich patrons who are willing to provide support for either rich or poor clients to win elections'.[59]

In addition to these categories, godfathers can also be serving public officials with access to public funds which they can deploy in support of 'lower-level officials'.[60] While this typology makes clear that there are diverse types of godfathers, it does not present a clear differentiation: the same godfather can behave differently depending on his aims and the political capacities of his godsons. Godfathers can also act with the best of intentions and for the benefit of their communities or corruptly for their own personal benefit and enrichment.[61]

It is not possible to estimate the godfather-son prevalence across 36 states and one Federal State Capital. Obviously, there is no 'godfather register' nor is there a clear definition for delineating the concept. In addition, in this field we have the problem of missing observations or 'dark numbers': cases of godfatherism which are not recognised or reported. A wise godfather avoids media attention and remains in the background, particularly when their actions are suspect. The presence of a godfather is only likely to draw media attention when the godfather-son relationship breaks down. Mostly this is caused by the godson's reticence when it comes to paying back the godfather's investment or fulfilling other demands. Investment payback can lead to the godson engaging in or facilitating financial crimes such as embezzlement or contract fraud in order to raise the necessary funds. Other demands may concern the staffing of the son's office with the godfather's nominees such as the role of commissioner or secretary of an important commission in the senate. These senior appointments could themselves facilitate financial crime, taking decisions that directly benefit the godfather. Resulting feuds between godfather and son, each having their own often violent retainers and that affect public order, are of obvious interest to the media.

4.2 *Corruption as Manifested Through Elections, Violence and Feuds*

Where studies on godfathers do share commonality is in their references to violence, which is allegedly linked to these figures' roles as 'strong men'. This requires a methodological warning as violence can take many forms as direct or as

[59] Albert (2005), pp. 90–91.

[60] Human Rights Watch (2007), p. 34.

[61] In an ideal world the HEDA compendia that we analysed in the previous section would have included a category of 'godfather' to help identify those perceived as performing this role but for their own illicit enrichment.

intimidation. It could well have been different at the start of the fourth Republic as from the most recent elections and certainly the prevalence of violence in general is exacerbated by the many fault lines in Nigeria.[62] While research is limited, structural conditions have been identified that make harmful godfatherism and its associated violence more likely. These include a landscape of poverty, unemployment, and the general neglect of public administration.[63] This neglect is more so given the dominance of state control of resources[64] and the perception that state office holders can accumulate personal wealth through diversion of these resources.[65] A further driver is the 'politicisation of security and law enforcement institutions and questions about their neutrality'.[66] As will be described, there is evidence of instigators of violence being able to act with apparent *impunity* with no one held accountable for the hundreds of people killed in and around the particularly violent elections of 2011 and 2015.

Some cases draw attention to the *greed* of the godfathers seeing themselves as major political investors claiming the right of a full return plus extra profits or the right to nominate several other followers to high positions, which increases his power. If the godson refuses leading to a fall out with the godfather, the latter can take drastic measures. Apart from impeachment, the godson may be physically assaulted, kidnapped, and be forced at gunpoint to sign his letter of resignation. Such refusal to cooperate can arise from a power struggle between godfather and godson resulting in drawn out feuds encompassing their respective supporters and followers.

4.3 Nigerian Perception of Godfathers

While the literature consulted[67] alluded to these corrupt activities by godfathers, we had no real information on the extent of their operation. We should point out the evidence is fragmentary. The academic literature alludes to the phenomenon as widespread—with local strong men exerting power over office holders. Yet specific examples are limited and the same ones repeated across multiple texts. We used the family names as they were mentioned in the articles.

We can draw only a broad picture from discussions in the literature (see Table 6). Over the timespan of 1999–2019, eight states were mentioned as affected by godfathers. The three oldest cases were from 1999; two of them lasted more than 5 years.

[62] Foundation for Partnership Initiatives in the Niger Delta (2023).

[63] Human Rights Watch (2007).

[64] Principally the redistribution of oil revenues.

[65] Kwarkye (2019).

[66] Kwarkye (2019).

[67] For this section we used the material generated from our separate search of godfathers and godsons.

Table 6 Godfather/sons mentioned in academic papers from 1999–2019

Source	State	Godfather	Position/Role	Godson	Position/Role	Year(s)	comments
Asogwa (2017)	Abia	Orji Uzor Kalu Theodore Orji	Former Governor Current Governor	None mentioned		2011	Battle between two 'strongmen' with Theodore (Ochendo) Orji the winner Note from HEDA: Orji Uzor Kalu was sentenced to 12 years on money laundering charges in 2019 but sentence was overturned by the supreme court in 2020 and a government request for a retrial was dismissed by Abuja Court of Appeal in 2024 due to process errors
Asogwa (2017) Oghovbu (2023) Offor and Eze (2018) Albert (2005) Hoffman (2010) Human Rights Watch (2007) Edigin (2010)	Anambra	Chris Uba (self-styled)	PDP Board of Trustees	Chris Ngige	Governor	2003–2005	Signed multiple legal documents in favour of Uba, pledging to stand down after one term and agreement to do his bidding. Ngige reneged on agreements once elected and was abducted by police. Uba allegedly organised riots and arson attacks 'to discredit the governor' Failed to payback N2.5bn—the sum expended in getting Ngige elected or to allow Uba to nominate appointments and siphon off state funds Godfather was also special advisor to the president. Uba claimed to be 'the greatest godfather in Nigeria' (HRW, 2007)

Offor and Eze (2018) Hoffman (2010) Asogwa (2017) Edigin (2010)	Anambra	Emika Offor	Financier and friend to the President	Chinwoke Mbadinuju	Governor	1999–2003	Fell out with Offor and served only a single term as lost financial support to run again. Replaced by Chris Ngige.
Offor and Eze (2018) Human Rights Watch (2007)	Anambra	Peter Obi	State Governor	Chief Willie Maduabuchukwu Obiano	State Governor	2013	Obi served two terms (including a period of impeachment for gross misconduct which was then overturned when he was reinstated). Replaced by Obiano who also served two terms. Sponsored by Obi with Obiano stating that Obi demanded payback of N7.5bn in addition to there being a complex financial disagreement.
Oghovbu (2023) Albert (2005) Edigin (2010)	Borno	Ali Modu Sherriff	State Governor and Senator	Malla Kachalla	Governor	2003	Albert (2005) indicates that Kachalla 'chose' Sherriff as godfather for the 1999 elections due to his wealth and influence. They were former friends and equal godfathers. Very public falling out. Godfather ensured 'disobedient' godsons not elected for second term.

(continued)

Table 6 (continued)

Source	State	Godfather	Position/Role	Godson	Position/Role	Year(s)	comments
Offor and Eze (2018) Albert (2005) Edigin (2010)	Enugu	Chief Jim Ifeanyichukwu Nwobodo	Chief and Benefactor	Dr. Chimaroke Nnamani.	State Governor	1999–2016	Godson installed as first governor of the state as a relative unknown. Godfather 'provides a lifeline and direction' to the 'subservient' godson whom he aims to subjugate. However, he stood up to demands of his benefactor and himself then moved to be a godfather.
Offor and Eze (2018) Edigin (2010)	Enugu	Dr. Chimaroke Nnamani.	State Governor	Sullivan Chime	State Governor	2007	Nnamani—selected Chime as his successor. Denounced godfather and completely reduced his influence.
Offor and Eze (2018)	Enugu	Sullivan Chime	State Governor	Ifeanyi Ugwuanyi	State Governor	2015	Chime supported Ugwuanyi as his replacement. Subsequent feuding and breakdown in relationship.
Oghovbu (2023)	Lagos	Bola Tinubu	State Governor	Akinwunmi Ambode	Governor	2015–2019	Godfather ensured 'disobedient' godsons not elected for second terms. No other evidence.
Asogwa (2017) Oghovbu (2023) Edigin (2010) Offor and Eze (2018)	Kwara	Olusola Saraki	Financier/ Benefactor (former senate president)	Mohammed Lawal Dr. Abubakar Bukola Saraki (son) replaced by sister	State Governor State Governor	1999–2003 and 2003–2011	Lawal died 2003. Fell out with godfather over sharing of 'political commissions and gains' (Oghovbu 2023) led to inter-group extreme violence with major casualties. Unusually Lawal was independently wealthy (Albert 2005). Son was Governor 2003–2011. Rift between father and son and movement across political parties. Saraki apparently installed some four state governors.

Asogwa (2017)	Ogun	Olusegun Osoba	Former Governor	Olumide Osoba	State Representative	2011–2015	None.
Asogwa (2017)	Ogun	Olusegun Obasanjo Gbenga Daniel	Former President Governor	Olurin (supported by Obasanjo) Isiaka (supported by Daniel)	No information	2003–2011	Fractional party clash and falling out between Obasanjo Daniel (who had been the godson) on who would be then next state godfather. Neither prevailed.
Human Rights Watch (2007)	Oyo	Lamidi Adedibu	Chief and power broker	Christopher Alao Akala	State Governor	2006	Interim governor during impeachment of Ladoja.

Asogwa (2017); Oghovbu, (2023); Offor and Eze (2018); Albert (2005); Hoffman (2010); Human Rights Watch (2007); Edigin (2010)

The most recent case stems from 2019. However, the essays contain insufficient accurate data about the duration of the godfathers' operations. We have no data to determine 'at this time godfather X began grooming godson Y'. Three states were affected by two or more godfathers. In two cases the godfathers developed something of a family dynasty. One godfather in Anambra operated over an extended number of years and self-claimed to have sponsored all appointments made within the state.

Compared with the 'serious concern' about godfatherism expressed throughout scholarship, the number of identified godfather cases looks to be small. This may be due to our restrictive approach of using published literature. To broaden the scope of our work, we also scanned the digital print media and searched for newspaper articles that mentioned godfathers. This was not intended as a replacement for a proper quantitative database but rather as an illustrative indication of the current presence of godfatherism (see Table 7). While we identified numerous mentions of godfathers in the press, there was little in the way of concrete discussion. The references that we found covered ten states and indicated that godfatherism might be a limited issue and more a statement of fact rather than a 'serious concern'. Of the cases located none indicated, apart from an oblique reference to financial controversy, anything criminal in the actions of the godfathers. In some of the publications respondents denied the existence or need of a godfather in their specific state.

Given the time scales, there is not much overlap between the states mentioned in Tables 6 and 7, nor with the criminal cases listed by HEDA. The most noticeable overlap is in connection with Abia State, where two former Governors are described as godfathers in both the academic papers and in the media. According to HEDA, one was sentenced to prison having been found guilty of money laundering, but the case was subsequently overturned by the Supreme Court. The EFCC brought charges of money laundering against the other but now appears to have abandoned the case. There is little to provide concrete proof that godfathers are automatically corrupt, engaging in financial crime and acting in their own interests.

5 The Challenge of Linking Elitism, Godfatherism and Corruption

In the previous sections we discussed the constructions of elitism and godfatherism but without properly connecting them to a specific facet of the public administration that goes through all the veins and fabric of society: corruption. As established, elitism and corruption are according to their definition different phenomena. The term 'elitism' is used as if it is a self-evident social phenomenon. When there is a reference to political elite, it is presented as something that should be eliminated, suppressed, or replaced by something that 'the people'can steer. In political practice elitism can be combined with corruption which does not clarify the discussion but does have an emotional resonance.

Table 7 The recent prevalence of godfatherism as mentioned in the digital print sources

State	Godfather	Godson	Years of office	Source	Comments
Abia	Theodore Orji (Governor)	Dr Okezie Ikpeazu (Governor)	2015–2023	'Breaking the grip of godfatherism in Abia' The Sun, 14th April, 2022 https://thesun.ng/breaking-the-grip-of-godfatherism-in-abia/	Orji was alleged to be the sole reason that Ikpeazu became Governor. Article suggests that the State lost over a decade to failed leadership. Note from HEDA: a case for money laundering and embezzlement from 2018 in connection with security votes but in their edition 2022 HEDA notes that EFCC appears to have abandoned the prosecution of the case.
Akwa Ibom	Godswill Akpabio (Governor)	Udom Emmanuel (Governor)	2015–2023	'How Akwa Ibom Governor Overshadowed His Former Godfather, Akpabio' This Day no date other than '3 years ago' https://www.thisdaylive.com/index.php/2022/08/14/how-akwa-ibom-governor-overshadowed-his-former-godfather-akpabio/	Article states Emmanuel overshadows his godfather in terms of performance but also as the former is alleged to be mired in financial controversy.
Anambra	Chief Chris Uba	Peter Obi (Governor)	2006 (impeached) 2007 (reinstated)–2010	'Obi ended godfatherism in Anambra—Bianca Ojukwu' Dennis Agbo Vanguard, December 31,2022 https://www.vanguardngr.com/2022/12/obi-ended-godfatherism-in-anambra-bianca-ojukwu/	Article states Obi brought godfatherism to an end in the state coinciding with a statement from Uba claiming that he made many governors in Anambra but Obi was not one of them. Note: Obi headed the Labour Party in the 2023 that saw success amongst the youth vote.
Bayelsa	Seriake Dickson (Governor)	Douye Diri (Governor)	2020–	'Dickson does not play godfather in Bayelsa—Diri' The Sun 28th December, 2023 https://sunnewsonline.com/dickson-does-not-play-godfather-in-bayelsa-diri/	Article notes that Diri stated his predecessor Seriake refused to act as Godfather.

(continued)

Table 7 (continued)

State	Godfather	Godson	Years of office	Source	Comments
Benue	George Akume (Party godfather)	Hyacinth Alia (Governor)	2023–	'Nigeria: In Benue State, a governor priest battles a godfather' Eniola Akinkuotu, The Africa Report 2nd January, 2024 https://www.theafricareport.com/331603/nigeria-in-benue-state-a-governor-priest-battles-a-godfather/	Article refers to a former priest backed by Akume for Governor but the latter defied the patronage and allegedly refused recommended appointees, ignoring establish processes. The report questions *'the viability of godfather-style politics in Nigeria's evolving political landscape'*.
Lagos	Bola Ahmed Tinubu (governor and now President)		1999–2007	'Godfather of Lagos' is the man to beat in pivotal Nigerian election' Jason Burke The Guardian 24th February, 2023 https://www.theguardian.com/world/2023/feb/24/godfather-of-lagos-is-the-man-to-beat-in-pivotal-nigerian-election	The article refers to Tinubu (now President) as 'godfather of Lagos' and draws attention to his significant improvements in Lagos and to his being the power behind the two-term outgoing President Buhari. It states that his power rests *on 'a complex web of patronage networks'*.
Kaduna	Malam Nasir Ahmad El-Rufai (Governor)	Uba Sani (Governor)	2023–	'Uba Sani: A governor under siege of 'godfatherism' in Kaduna politics' Samson Atekojo Usman Capital Post 27th June, 2023 https://www.capitalpost.ng/uba-sani-a-governor-under-siege-of-godfatherism-in-kaduna-politics/ 'I don't want to be a godfather, says El-Rufai' Olatunji Omirin, Daily Trust 15th April 2024 https://dailytrust.com/breaking-i-dont-want-to-be-a-godfather-says-el-rufai/	Article refers to the former and current governors as *'political godfather and godson'*. Article refers to El-Rufai declining to be a godfather in the state, this follows an apparent dispute over the allegedly huge debts and contractual liabilities of the administration inherited by Sani.

Kano	Rabiu Kwankwaso (Governor)	Abba K Yusuf	2023–	'Kano Governor Nominates Political Godfather's Son as Commissioner' Kano Times March 26th 2024 https://kanotimes.com.ng/2024/03/26/kano-governor-nominates-political-godfathers-son-as-commissioner/	Article states that Yusuf nominated the son of his 'godfather' to the post of commissioner.
Rivers	Peter Odili	None mentioned	1999–2007	'Peter Odili: A Citizen of Humanity at 76' Christopher Unuigbe This Day no date other than 7 months ago https://www.thisdaylive.com/index.php/2024/08/15/peter-odili-a-citizen-of-humanity-at-76/	Article states *'Odili is seen as the godfather of Rivers'* and *'a man of unimpeachable integrity'*. Note from HEDA: There is an ongoing case against Odili from 2020 in connection with Diversion of funds for personal use between 2004 and 2007. Odili filed counter suit also in 2020 to restrain EFCC from investigation saying it was bound by a 2007 judgement of Federal High Court on the perpetual injunction against his arrest and prosecution.
Jigawa	None mentioned	Sule Lamido	2007–2015	'Sule Lamido: I have no godfather….I was in PDP before Obasanjo' was president 29th August, 2018 The Cable https://www.thecable.ng/sule-lamido-no-godfather-pdp-obasanjo-president/	Interview article states *'he says he does not have any godfather in politics'* interview at the time he was presidential aspirant on the PDP platform. Note from HEDA: Embezzlement and money laundering case from 2015 was discharged by court of appeal in 2023 ruling no case to answer. In same year EFCC filed notice of appeal to supreme court for decision to be set aside but outcome still pending.

Corruption is a concept with many meanings and a correspondingly broad coverage. Most often it is used to denote the abuse of public resources for personal gain. In the context of the United Nations and other international bodies and NGOs against corruption, this description had been broadly accepted, even if it is imprecise and comprises a large variety of wrongdoing. However, an essential point is missing: the *power of decision making* according to a set of accepted standards, which serve to hold decision makers accountable for their decisions.

Cases of large financial gains involving public office holders have been referred to as 'grand corruption',[68] though the threshold of 'grand' remains imprecisely defined and might have been better subsumed under the broader concept of 'elitist corruption' as has been adopted elsewhere.

We already established that not all political elite engage in corrupt conduct, but opportunity exists for them to do so. This would involve abuse of decision-making powers in the public administration.

In the media and academic studies we found references to the phenomenon of a 'godfather' who is presented as a local strong man capable of exerting locally a lot of informal power over office holders in a hierarchical relationship.[69] The reason why this power appears to be easily assumed is that their interaction with ordinary Nigerians is shaped by the presentation of a godfather as a benign or paternal father figure "a protector and provider which masterfully disguises the exploitative nature of their role".[70]

To what extent are the godfather-godson arrangements corruptive? In principle one can imagine that they can be corruption free: the godfather invests money in a promising but poor politician who in return promises to promote the legal interests of his benefactor. That can be elaborated in the way the godfathers in the early years of independent Nigeria aimed to let the still young political elite gain office.

However, during the military rule and after the establishment of the fourth republic acting as a godfather became opaquer, ruling through the godsons who function as proxies. As set out in the examples in Table 6, in their capacity as governor or senator they appear to act independently, but it is the godfather who in the background pulls the hidden strings. This is particularly important with recruiting and nominating of the godson's new staff. Such cases are significant for the godfather because he can demand that his own people will be nominated. This means a personal extension of power in the cabinets of the godson-governor or the offices of the representative bodies. While this may imply a weakening of the affected public bodies taking care of 'crony staff' is not criminal *per se*. It would be criminal if there is an underlying hidden transaction such as facilitating or ignoring financial crime that impacts on a decision-making process, the latter being the essence of corruption.

---

68 Van Duyne and Harvey (2022).

69 Offor and Eze (2018).

70 Hoffman (2010), p. 292.

If the godson acts as a proxy, his law breaking is also committed as proxy. But is acting as a proxy for some principal a criminal offence? Unless there is evidence of abetting, provoking or furthering the commission of crime, the godfather remains hidden behind his anointed grandson and out of the reach of the law, hindering the successful prosecution of complex financial crimes. This implies that acting within the framework of godfatherism entails a high degree of impunity, one of the basic conditions for the prolongation of corruption. It does not, however, imply a direct positive correlation.

6 Conclusion

This chapter set out to understand the social historical context of corruption of the ruling elite in Nigeria and aimed to provide a theoretical delineation of corruption, elitism, and godfatherism—terms which are often used in conjunction. To understand our subject, we surveyed the academic literature and media coverage of elites and of godfathers and sought evidence of who might fall into which classification and what the implications were of such 'belonging'. We found an assumed overlap between elites and corruption and of godfathers and corruption in academic articles. As they point out, corruption would appear to be almost 'hardwired' into the fragile democracy of Nigeria. Well-endowed with natural resources, Nigeria should have been one of the wealthiest countries in West Africa. Instead, it has one of the highest levels of inequality with a large part of the population living below the poverty line. This contrasts sharply with a small elite that has reserved access to the national wealth. Despite this, uncovering evidence of malfeasance is difficult.

From the limited and incomplete survey that we have conducted, one important conclusion is the problematic opacity surrounding the decision making of political elites. This lack of transparency can mean that resource allocation decisions are not open to debate and challenge. Elites can take advantage of weak institutions, manipulating them for their own ends by implementing self-serving policies that maintain their position at the expense of the wider (poorer) population. The work of HEDA suggests the operation of the 'cushion' aspect of the functions of elite but does not identify the role of the local godfather in Nigeria. As discussed in the media, godfatherism is certainly a facet of the Nigerian political elite but not all godfathers are corrupt, and many fulfil their functions in the interests of the wider public. At this stage of knowledge, we have little else to conclude that corrupt godfatherism is a small phenomenon but with big consequences for the rule of law and social fabric of the country. It is evident that when godfathers are tempted to divert public resources for their own personal use, the sums involved can be spectacular.

Similarly, the operation of godfathers in manipulating election results in favour of their nominated godsons can lead to rigged election outcomes and processes.

When elitism becomes corrupted in this manner, we find that established norms and traditional hierarchical deference to authority actually protect those politically powerful elitist entrepreneurs, placing them 'above the law'. This type of nepotism presents a significant challenge. If the cycle is to be broken, the decision-making process has to be far more transparent than is currently the case.

We have observed that elite-ness ends when the beholders shift their fashion or if populist agitation attacks elitism to strip it of its power and privileges. It may be that the rise of the Labour vote at the last election in 2023,[71] mainly amongst the young, is beginning to challenge the established status quo. Though the top may have fallen, elite status still matters.

We fear that despite extensive digging we must conclude that there are fewer godfathers than has been suggested, although the paternal metaphor clearly shapes the interaction of politicians with ordinary Nigerians. We imagine they operate behind the scenes, projecting a protective image that hides their acquisition of power for personal enrichment. They can operate behind the curtain, in the shadows, because the facilitators (the lack of transparency and accountability together with competition rather than collaboration between government departments and agencies) are hardwired into the country.

References

Adekoya R (24 Feb 2023) The threat to Nigeria's political elite This election could produce a real-life Wakanda. Unheard. https://unherd.com/2023/02/the-threat-to-nigerias-political-elite/. Accessed 02 Feb 2025

Adeleke A (26 Dec 2023) Five worst corruption scandals under Buhari regime. Premium Politics. https://premiumpolitics.com/five-worst-corruption-scandals-under-buhari-regime/?utm_source=punch&utm_medium=punch_backlink. Accessed 04 Feb 2025

Afolabi O (2019) Political elites and anticorruption campaigns as "deep" politics of democracy. A comparative study of Nigeria and South Africa. Taiwan J Democr 15(1):159–181

Albert I (2005) Explaining 'godfatherism' in Nigerian politics. Afr Sociol Rev/Revue Africaine de Sociologie 9(2):79–105

Ameh S, Anande T, Nnam E (2025) Political godfatherism as a catalyst for corruption and impunity in Nigeria. Int J Multidiscip Curr Educ Res 7(2):48–58

Anaedozie F (2017) A critical analysis of grand corruption with reference to international human rights and international criminal law: the case of Nigeria. Doctoral thesis. https://doi.org/10.21427/D7V983

Animasawun G (2013) Godfatherism in Nigeria's fourth republic: the pyramid of violence and political insecurity in Ibadan, Oyo-State, Nigeria. [Research Report] IFRA-Nigeria. Working Papers Series 27 (hal-03750517), pp 1–24

[71]The two traditional parties, the APC and the PDP lost heavily: ruling party of Buhari (APC) dropped from 46 to 36%; the opposition party PDP went from 42 to 29%, while, buoyed by the largely youth vote, the new Labour Party jumped to 25% of the popular vote.

Armed Conflict Location and Event Data (ACLED) (22 Feb 2023) Political violence and the 2023 Nigerian election. https://acleddata.com/2023/02/22/political-violence-and-the-2023-nigerian-election/. Accessed 18 Mar 2023

Asogwa JO (2017) The politics of godfatherism in Nigeria. Online J Arts Manag Soc Sci 2(1):261–272

Bolarinwa O, Osuji U (2022) Political elitism in Nigeria: challenges, threats and the future of citizenship. Open J Philos 12:105–122

Donaldson N, Leuprecht C (2025) Geopolitical implications of embedded corruption in global capital markets: the professional brokers who enable the transnational illicit political economy of systematic state capture. In: Goldbarsht D, de Koker L, Ferrill J (eds) The financial war on crime and terrorism: opportunities and challenges. Springer, Cham

Edigin LU (2010) Political Conflict in Nigeria: A Focus on the Fourth Republic. Africa 4(4):174–186

Erdmann G, Engel U (Feb 2006) Neopatrimonialism revisited – beyond a catch-all concept. GIGA research program: legitimacy and efficiency of political systems. Working paper no. 16

Fisayo D, Nte N, Adejok A, Ayoola O (2023) Elite capture syndrome and anti-corruption control in Nigeria: the Economic and Financial Crimes Commission and The Independent Corrupt Practices Commission in perspective. Int J Bus Educ Humanit Soc Sci 5(2):144–152

Foundation for Partnership Initiatives in the Niger Delta (2023) Why was violence lower in Nigeria's 2023 election: implications for peacebuilding? https://fundforpeace.org/wp-content/uploads/2023/08/Post-Election-Early-Warning-Brief-Nigeria_2023.pdf. Accessed 18 Mar 2023

Harvey J, Bello A, Doig A, van Duyne PC, Gonul S, van Koningsveld J, Shehu A, Sittlington S, Sproat P, Turner S, Ward T (Oct 2021) Tracking beneficial ownership and the proceeds of corruption: evidence from Nigeria. Final project report, Northumbria University, Newcastle. https://ace.globalintegrity.org/wp-content/uploads/2022/02/FINAL-REPORT-TRACKING-BENEFICIAL-OWNERSHIP-AND-THE-PROCEEDS-OF-CORRUPTION-EVIDENCE-FROM-NIGERIA.pdf. Accessed 13 Feb 2024

Harvey J, Sproat P, Turner S, Ward T (2025) CansATF'S focus on beneficial ownership aid anti-corruption efforts in a 'low-capacity' country? Challenges from the front line in Nigeria. In: Azinge-Egbuiri N, Esoimeme E, Ryder N (eds) Global anti-money laundering regulations: developing countries' compliance challenges. Routledge, London

HEDA (2018) A compendium of 100 high profile corruption cases in Nigeria. Human and Environmental Development Agency

HEDA (2019) A compendium of 100 high profile corruption cases in Nigeria, 3rd edn. Human and Environmental Development Agency

HEDA (2020) A compendium of 100 high profile corruption cases in Nigeria, 3rd edn. Human and Environmental Development Agency

HEDA (2021) A compendium of 100 high profile corruption cases in Nigeria, 5th edn (Revised). Human and Environmental Development Agency

HEDA (2022) A compendium of 100 high profile corruption cases in Nigeria, 6th edn. Human and Environmental Development Agency

HEDA (2023) A compendium of 100 high profile corruption cases in Nigeria, 7th edn. Human and Environmental Development Agency

HEDA (2024) A compendium of 100 high profile corruption cases in Nigeria (Special edition with some West African corruption cases), 8th edn. Human and Environmental Development Agency

Hoffman L (2010) Fairy godfathers and magical elections: understanding the 2003 electoral crisis in Anambra State, Nigeria. J Modern Afr Stud 48(2):285–310

Human Rights Watch (Oct 2007) Criminal politics violence, "godfathers" and corruption in Nigeria. https://www.hrw.org/report/2007/10/11/criminal-politics/violence-godfathers-and-corruption-nigeria. Accessed 31 Jan 2025

Igbini D, Okolie U (2020) Godfatherism and its threat to the Nigeria's nascent democracy. J Public Adm Finance Law 17:93–105
Kwarkye S (2019) Roots of Nigeria's election violence. Institute for Security Studies. https://issafrica.org/iss-today/roots-of-nigerias-election-violence. Accessed 19 Mar 2025
Nakpodia F, Adegbite E (2018) Corporate governance and elites. Account Forum 42(1):17–31
Obodo E (2009) The Nigerian art scene: patrons and patronage. Int J Res Arts Soc Sci 1:388–401
Odubajo T, Alabi B (2014) The elite factor in Nigeria's political-power dynamics. J Stud Soc Sci 8(1):121–139
Offor MA, Eze CO (2018) Godfatherism and Nigerian politics: a study of the fourth republic 1999–2018. IMTIJOTAS 3(1):78–90
Ogele E (2021) Elitism, election, and governance in Nigeria's fourth republic. A study of Rivers State, 2003–2019. J Polit Sci Leadersh Res 7(1):24–38
Oghovbu E (2023) Godfatherism and its effects on Nigeria's democracy. Global J Polit Sci Adm 11(2):58–71
Ojo J (23 Oct 2024) How impunity fuels Nigeria's underdevelopment. Punch. https://punchng.com/how-impunity-fuels-nigerias-underdevelopment/. Accessed 18 Mar 2025
Ojukwu C, Shopeju J (2018) Elite corruption and the culture of primitive accumulation in the 21st century Nigeria. Int J Law Legal Stud 6(2):001–010
Okeke R, Idike A (2016) The dialectics of political economy and elite corruption in a postcolonial state: a Nigerian case study. Kuwait Chapter Arab J Bus Manag Rev 5(7):55–60
OyozeBaje A (12 April 2023) Goodbye to the culture of impunity. The Guardian. https://guardian.ng/opinion/goodbye-to-the-culture-of-impunity/. Accessed 18 Mar 2025
Page M (2018) A new taxonomy for corruption in Nigeria. Carnegie Endowment for International Peace, Washington
Prince A (2023) Analyzing the effects of political power on criminal behavior among political elites in Nigeria. Int J Soc Sci Manag Res 9(6):1–28
Shehu A (2015) Nigeria the way through corruption to the well-being of a people. National Open University of Nigeria, Lagos
Sproat P, Ward T, Harvey J, Turner S, Shehu A, Bello A (2024) A non-conviction based asset recovery in Nigeria—an additional tool for law enforcement agencies? In: de Koker L, Golsbarsht D (eds) Financial crime, law and governance. Ius Gentium: comparative perspectives on law and justice, vol 116. Springer, Cham, pp 21–44
Suel B, Sani M, Mat B (2018) Godfatherism and political party financing in Nigeria: Analysing the 2015 general election. Malays J Soc Space 14(1):1–14
UNODC (July 2017) Corruption in Nigeria bribery: public experience and response. Vienna
UNODC (Dec 2019) Corruption in Nigeria: patterns and trends. Second survey on corruption as experienced by the population. Vienna
UNODC (July 2024) Corruption in Nigeria: patterns and trends. Third survey on corruption as experienced by the population. Vienna
US Department of State, Bureau of Democracy, Human Rights and Labor (2017) Country reports on human rights practices: Nigeria. https://2021-2025.state.gov/reports/2017-country-reports-on-human-rights-practices/nigeria/. Accessed 18 Mar 2025
van Duyne P, Harvey J (2022) Grand corruption in Nigeria: Nigeria's grabbing political elite. In: van Duyne PC, Larsson P, Harvey J, Antonopoulos G, von Lampe K (eds) Narrating organised crime stories and Aristotelian principles of drama. Eleven International Publishing, The Hague, pp 133–170
Wincup E (2017) Criminological research: understanding qualitative methods. SAGE Publications
Yawa G (2020) The elite theory and democracy in Nigeria, 2011–2018. Bingham J Econ Allied Stud 4(2):1–12

Jackie H. Harvey is Emeritus Professor in the Newcastle Business School, Northumbria University. She previously had worked as a fiscal and macro policy economist and in commercial banking. She is a leading authority on the phenomenon of money laundering and has also published in the field of anti-corruption, fraud and asset recovery. She was most recently the principal investigator on a Foreign, Commonwealth & Development Office (FCDO) funded Global Integrity Anti-Corruption Evidence multi-disciplinary project investigating beneficial ownership as a mechanism for recovering the proceeds of corruption in Nigeria.

Petrus C. van Duyne is an internationally known researcher on organised (economic) crime, money-laundering and corruption. As psychologist and jurist, he has done research in this field since the 1980. He is known for his strict analytic and critical approach and independent view.

Dangerous Play: AML/CTF/CPF Risks in the Gaming Sector

Jeffrey Simser

Abstract Money laundering is a foundational function for transnational organized crime, back office activity moving illicit profits to the right place without interdiction by law enforcement or criminal rivals. Gaming is popular around the world, functioning in regulated, under-regulated and unregulated markets. The chapter explores the exploitation of gaming systems by money launderers, hiding illicit financial flows in the larger stream of gaming revenue.

The chapter begins with a discussion of money laundering, gaming and the regulatory systems used to manage risk. The Canadian system is offered as an example. The chapter then explores money laundering typologies that have pierced the regulatory systems governing land-based casinos in Canada, the United States and Australia. Typologies that can penetrate the regulated online gaming system in Europe are then considered.

The chapter then moves to the massive gaming grey market, where gaming is either unregulated or under-regulated. Junkets and an intense demand to evade Chinese restrictions on gaming and capital flight have created a perfect storm, opening up a massive informal value transfer system that has spread from Southeast Asia into all corners of the world. The resultant underground banking network has matched professional money launderers with transnational organized crime worldwide, including Central American drug cartels and European organized crime.

The chapter briefly notes the challenges posed by match-fixing and corruption in sport. The links between gaming, cryptocurrency and terrorism/proliferation financing are considered. Finally, the chapter concludes with three examples that show the linkages between gaming, transnational organized crime and money laundering. The chapter concludes by observing that while there is ample literature discussing money laundering and research into gaming, more work needs to be done on the linkages between the two activities.

J. Simser (✉)
Barrister and Solicitor, Toronto, Canada

D. Goldbarsht et al. (eds.), *The Financial War on Crime and Terrorism*, European Yearbook of International Economic Law,
https://doi.org/10.1007/978-3-032-06360-1_10

1 Introduction

Money laundering observed is property legerdemain, an art of trickery that paints criminal gains with the patina of legitimacy.[1]

Money laundering capability is a foundational function for organised crime. This chapter examines the interplay between gaming and money laundering. A UNODC report recently concluded that transnational organised crime groups (TOC) have grown at an unprecedented pace, starting, for example, with gaming and fraud enterprises in Southeast Asia and expanding into Pacific Island Territories and Countries, Africa and South Asia.[2] Those TOC groups developed sophisticated professional money laundering networks and underground banking structures that are now used by South American drug trafficking organisations, the Italian mafia, and the Irish mob, amongst others[3] This chapter asks a number of questions. What is money laundering? Which aspects of the gaming sector, licit and illicit, are vulnerable to money laundering and why?

Using Canada as an example, this chapter looks at how regulatory systems oversee gaming and mitigate money laundering risks. Then the chapter examines money laundering typologies within the regulated market, considering examples in Canada, the United States and Australia. The chapter briefly reviews some of the related risks posed by match fixing and proliferation financing. Finally, the chapter examines gaming in regulated, under-regulated and unregulated marketplaces (the latter are collectively "grey markets"). The nexus between gaming and money laundering is underexamined in the literature. More study is needed: as we shall see, gaming is at the heart of an ever-expanding organised crime eco-system that includes cyber-enabled crime, scam centres, and even kidnapping. Regulated gambling is at risk of exploitation by professional money launderers and cheats. Grey market gaming is at the foot of an underground banking network capable of "integrating billions in criminal proceeds into the formal financial system with impunity."[4] The chapter concludes with a look at the gaps in research and knowledge as well as an assessment as to what might be needed to face this challenge.

2 What Is Money Laundering

Money laundering disguises the source of ill-gotten gains. Criminals launder money for many reasons: to place profit beyond the reach of predatory criminal rivals, to present to the casual observer as a legitimate and upstanding citizen, and to conceal their control of significant assets. Not all laundering is carefully planned: at times,

---

[1] Simser (2023), p. 387.

[2] UNODC (2025), p. 9.

[3] UNODC (2025), p. 58.

[4] UNODC (2025), p. 36.

it is adventitious and just good enough.[5] Simple arrangements will pass muster as long as no one examines them in detail. Sophisticated arrangements, in contrast, will challenge the most competent financial investigator. The goal: paint dirty money the appearance of clean and legitimate wealth.

In Canada, as in most countries, money laundering is a criminal offence.[6] Canada's financial intelligence unit (FIU), the Financial Transactions and Reports Analysis Centre of Canada (FINTRAC) regulates entities at risk of enabling, often unwittingly, money launderers (e.g., banks and casinos).[7] FINTRAC tells those reporting entities that money laundering has "three recognised stages" namely placement, layering and integration (PLI). Placement occurs when illegally generated wealth is initially lodged into the legitimate economy. In a simple case, drug cash might be deposited into a bank account. Layering involves moving that wealth through transactions, perhaps transferring the deposited drug money into other accounts with a different ownership structure. The goals of layering: obscure the audit trail, making it challenging to follow the money and then moving the "cleansed" funds to a secure location. Money laundering investigations are a race against time and across borders, challenges that professional money launderers take full advantage of. Integration, the final stage, involves bringing those "cleansed" assets into an apparently legitimate ownership structure.

This chapter will discuss a number of typologies whereby gaming provides a modality for money laundering. Using cash to buy-in at a casino cage creates a placement risk, which can be mitigated by requiring the casino to know their customer's source of funds. Placement isn't a helpful concept when considering illicit wealth generated by grey market online gaming, computer hackers or fraudsters.[8] For example, a ransomware victim may pay the ransom in bitcoin, or a fraud victim may e-transfer funds. Those funds can be moved quickly online and placement through a gaming site can disguise its provenance. Integration assumes that the criminal wants to openly control apparently cleansed assets, but this is not always so. For example, some criminals will want to disguise all relationships with their wealth. Wealth makes them a target for predatory rivals. Tax authorities use a net worth approach to compare holdings with known legitimate income (levying tax on the difference). As this chapter will discuss, organised crime groups use integrated funds to pose as legitimate foreign investors for capital intensive ventures (like hotel/casino complexes) in jurisdictions with a weak ability to scrutinize investors and who often offer "citizen-by-investment" schemes.[9]

---

[5] Levi (2013), p. 3.

[6] *Criminal Code*, RSC 1985, s. 462.31(1).

[7] Established by the *Proceeds of Crime (Money Laundering) Terrorist Financing Act*, SC 2000, c.17, referred to as the PCMLTFA.

[8] Many drug dealers now operate using e-transfers, FINTRAC (2025), p. 1.

[9] UNODC (2025), p. 47.

3 Gambling

Gambling revenue, worldwide, in the regulated sector, is expected to be USD $449.67 billion in 2025.[10] A significant portion of that revenue comes from land-based casinos, but consumers are increasingly moving to online gambling platforms. There are social harms associated with gambling: 449 million adults worldwide experience some risk with gambling and 80 million adults have a gambling disorder or engage in problematic gaming.[11] The UK Gambling Commission observed some emerging AML/CTF risks in the regulated sector, including remote and land-based casinos offering money service business functions (foreign exchange and money transfers), artificial intelligence used to bypass due diligence and customer identification (particularly a problem with remote operators), and puppet accounts (gamblers are offered money to open an account that is then used by a launderer). Open loop payment systems allow value transfer from one payment method to another, which can disguise the origin of funds. The UK Gambling Commission also identified risks in the grey market. Crash games, typically involving crypto, begin with a bet and then a multiplier. Customers can cash out at any time, but if the game "crashes" before withdrawal, the gamer loses their stake, which can happen from within a few seconds to a few minutes and can result in significant losses. The Commission also identified white label partnerships and unregistered providers as a risk.[12] As will be addressed later in the chapter, organised crime groups have built the infrastructure for white label gaming platforms that can be deployed quickly and with little technical expertise; those platforms are part of the broader criminal ecosystem, including underground banking, and can be the vector of serious malware.[13] The UNODC estimates the illegal betting market is worth between USD$340 million and $1.7 trillion a year, which includes $140 billion in laundering.[14] The wide margin of error is consistent with estimates of money laundering, which UNODC estimates ranges between 2 and 5% of GDP (a margin of error of USD$1.2 trillion dollars annually).[15] Illegal gaming and money laundering are furtive activities. Criminals don't want researchers to know how much money they are earning or moving.

[10] Statista (2025), p. 1.

[11] Tran et al. (2024), p. 602.

[12] Gambling Commission (April 2025), pp. 1–5.

[13] The Vigorous Viper system, for example: Infoblox (2024); see also UNODC (2025).

[14] UNODC (2023), p. 1.

[15] UNODC *Money Laundering* (2025).

4 An Example of a Regulatory System: Canada

Most countries regulate gaming, although in weaker states, there is little to no actual regulation (an environment that organised crime seeks out). Robust regulatory regimes support tax collection, social harm mitigation, and anti-money laundering (AML). In Canada's federal political system, constitutional responsibilities are distributed among a national government, ten provincial governments, three northern territorial governments, and municipal governments. Criminal law is a federal responsibility. Part VII of Canada's *Criminal Code* broadly criminalises all gaming activities, but carves out an exception where a province or territory conducts and manages the gaming.[16] Two levels of government regulate portions of gaming activity. FINTRAC operates both as the national FIU and as a regulator, creating barriers to money laundering. Provinces and territories regulate gaming activity. In this chapter, the focus is on Canada's largest province, Ontario, which happens to have an interesting regulatory gaming model. There are provincial regulators, like the Alcohol and Gaming Commission of Ontario (the AGCO).[17] To conduct and manage gaming within the *Criminal Code* exemption, Ontario has two operating entities, the Ontario Lottery and Gaming Corporation and iGaming Ontario (which, bizarrely, was created as a subsidiary of AGCO, the regulator). The system is slightly confusing. Technically, the province conducts and manages all gaming activities, but in practice, private operators actually run many of the enterprises in terms of day-to-day operations. This applies to land-based casinos as well as internet gaming, where private companies are licensed to operate. As discussed below, collectively, these private "operators" have AML obligations to the provincial regulator, the AGCO and the provincial entities have ultimate responsibility to the AML regulator, FINTRAC.[18]

An operator has obligations under their license with the province to assess money laundering risk as it applies to their line of business and then develop a compliance plan to mitigate and manage that risk.[19] An operator has mandatory record-keeping obligations, client identification requirements, and reporting obligations. While some elements of the AML system are purely prescriptive (for example, there must be reporting on all cash transactions and disbursements over $10,000), overall, the architecture of the AML system is risk-based. Understanding risk requires an operator to know their client, which requires client disclosure and operator verification through customer due diligence, which must be updated periodically in a way that is commensurate with risk. An operator must verify a patron's identity (typically through government issued identification like a passport or driver's license) and assesses patron risk (are they in a high-risk occupation, e.g., one that handles cash,

---

[16] *Criminal Code*, RSC 1985, s. 207.

[17] Established under the *Gaming Control Act*, SO 1992, C. 24.

[18] Simser and Kroeker (2017), p. 15.

[19] *Gaming Control Act,* 1992 which has detailed regulations and registrar's standards for entities wishing to enter and operate in the gaming sector.

or a low-income occupation, e.g., like a student). This assists an operator to assess on-going risk: where the client acts in a manner inconsistent with the operator's understanding, then extra due diligence is needed to reassess AML risk.[20]

An operator must ensure that their AML system can properly identify and effectively report on suspicious transactions. Under the *Proceeds of Crime (Money Laundering) and Terrorist Financing Act*, a financial transaction is suspicious if it occurs (or is attempted) and gives rise to reasonable grounds to suspect that the transaction is related to the commission or attempted commission of a money laundering, sanctions evasion, or terrorist financing offence.[21] For the provincial regulator, an operator must also report on criminal offences beyond money laundering (e.g., like cheat at play). There is no monetary threshold attached to this reporting requirement. Prior to filing, the operator must carefully establish that in fact reasonable grounds to suspect money laundering exists. The operator is required to identify and report on any cash deposit of $10,000 or more in a single transaction or two or more transactions that a customer makes within a consecutive 24-h window.[22]

There are reasons to be concerned about the state of AML oversight for online gaming in Ontario. By 2026, the worldwide online gaming market is expected to be $100 billion.[23] In Canada, the Ontario government has brought a reference to the Court of Appeal which is opposed by other Canadian jurisdictions. Ontario wants to allow for pooled liquidity on peer-to-peer (P2P) games like poker, and has asked the Court whether this step would fall within the "conduct and manage" exception of the *Criminal Code*.[24] Other provinces have not opened their gaming systems up to international private operators (although Alberta may soon change course on this point)[25] and they complain that Ontario's approach is diverting Canadian customers away from regulated sites to international subsidiaries in under-regulated jurisdictions. To sign into an Ontario site, a customer has to satisfy the geo-fencing requirements to show they are Ontario gamers (something that likely could be defeated by a reasonably competent teenager with a VPN network). Customers who are outside of Ontario, say located in Montreal or Vancouver, are directed to the dot com addresses of the operator. This poses a problem on a number of levels. Gaming enterprises relentlessly advertise. One cannot watch a live sporting event in Canada without pervasive and persistent ads. Montreal and Vancouver gamblers that might normally go to a government site with AML controls can find themselves on a site

[20] Simser (2024) pp. 207–208.

[21] PCMLTFA s. 7.

[22] AGCO (2022), p. 1; see also Simser and Kroeker (2017), Chapter 3.

[23] FINTRAC (2024a), p. 1.

[24] *Criminal Code*, RSC 1985, s. 207.

[25] *Red Tape Reduction Statutes Amendment Act*, 2024, Bill 16 not in force at the time of writing.

regulated in Malta or Samoa.[26] As discussed later, those jurisdictions also host problematic "white label" casino sites.[27]

5 Money Laundering Typologies in Canada's Regulated Gaming Sector

In Canada, two significant reports have been issued documenting money laundering risk in casinos. Dr. Peter German issued a report commissioned by the Attorney General of British Columbia in 2018 entitled *Dirty Money,* which noted that the Canadian casino business was cash intensive and therefore at risk of misuse by money launderers.[28] The Commission of Inquiry into Money Laundering in British Columbia led by Mr. Justice Cullen (the Cullen Commission) investigated land-based casinos and other businesses susceptible to laundering activity in the lower mainland of British Columbia. The Commission report, issued on June 3, 2022, found that over a 10-year period, hundreds of millions of dollars in proceeds of crime had been laundered in B.C. casinos. Over 133 hearing days, the Commission heard from 199 witnesses and received over 1000 exhibits considering money laundering, particularly in the gaming sector. Wealthy gamblers with legitimately acquired wealth worked with cash facilitators who were affiliated with criminal networks. Casino operators wanted the trade from high end patrons who would acquire the cash from a local facilitator. The facilitators received offsetting payment for the cash abroad. The currency presented at the cage frequently consisted of $20 bills, oriented in a non-uniform fashion, bundled in bricks of specific values (as opposed to the number of notes), bound by elastic bands, and transported in various conveyances (suitcases, backpacks, shopping bags and so on). For the launderers, the bulky and suspicious cash was converted into a safe, fungible and easily moved source of wealth abroad. The Cullen report noted that the implementation of Dr. German's recommendations significantly reduced the amount of laundering in casinos.[29] Those recommendations, like mandatory logs for transactions of $3000 or more, have since effectively been implemented in Ontario.[30]

Canada's FIU, FINTRAC, publishes and regularly updates indicators and typologies for money laundering, including sector specific "red flags" for casinos. A red flag is something that is suspicious or unusual in the absence of a reasonable explanation. A red flag can arise from "facts, behaviours, patterns or other contextual

[26] Atlantic Lottery Corporation, Factum (2024), p. 10. The Court of Appeal reference is under reserve at the time of writing.

[27] UNODC (2024), p. 20.

[28] German (2018), Chapter 3.

[29] Cullen (2022), Chapter 13.

[30] AGCO (2022), p. 4.

factors that identify irregularities related to a client's transactions."[31] The behaviour itself may be unusual, or it may be inconsistent with what you know about your patron. Operators faced with a red flag are expected to determine whether other facts or context requires further investigation. There are roughly 60 red flags presented by FINTRAC and they focus on onboarding (client identification), know your client (is their behaviour consistent with their profile?), changes in account activity, atypical transactions, transactions that appear to be structured (e.g., multiple transactions below the $10,000 threshold to evade reporting scrutiny), wire transfers, transactions outside of Canada, and the use of third parties. For example, red flag cash indicators include the bundling of currency (e.g., different denominations, with elastics) and unusual markings (e.g., dyed cash as banks and security delivery services often use dye packs when transporting cash and in the event of theft, the dye pack explodes). Staff in the casino cage are expected to be trained on these types of risks. FINTRAC provides reporting entities with advisories to deepen their understanding of indicators.[32]

Cullen noted that money launderers take advantage of a casino with poor controls. For example, collusion in games between players occurs when a group of seemingly unrelated players at a high stakes' poker table coordinate the loss of their tainted money at the table to a pre-determined winner.[33] That winner's source of funds? Professional gambling. Another technique, refining, involves the conversion of smaller denomination bills into larger denomination bills. Five $20 bills are obviously bulkier than a single $100 bill. If an illegal enterprise is managing millions of dollars, this scale matters. Cocaine is sold to users on the street for cash; that cash, particularly if the denominations are small, is heavy and bulky (44 pounds of cocaine can translate into 220 pounds of $10 bills).[34] Chip walking occurs when a patron buys in, engages in limited (or no) play and then leaves with the chips. Those chips might be passed to another player: players are screened at buy-in, and this is a technique to evade AML scrutiny. The German report also notes that chips can be fungible for underworld for transactions.[35]

The term the "Vancouver Method" was coined by Professor John Langdale to unpack a typology whereby vast amounts of money have been laundered through an informal value transfer system (IVTS), an underground banking network that matches supply and demand.[36] An IVTS enables Chinese nationals to work around Communist government currency controls: regardless of their wealth, without prior government approval, a citizen is limited to transmitting $50,000 a year outside China which they must transact through a state-sanctioned bank.

---

[31] FINTRAC *STR Guidance* (2024b), s. 3.

[32] FINTRAC, *STR Guidance* (2024b), Annex B.

[33] Sometimes called "chip dumping"—Cullen (2022), p. 621.

[34] Simser (2008), p. 15.

[35] German (2018), p. 182.

[36] Langdale (2023), p. 100.

To avoid state oversight, a mainland Chinese citizen can legally transfer money within China to a local underground banker. The money may be legitimately earned (or not). The Chinese underground banker notifies their Vancouver counterparty. When that Chinese citizen visits Canada, the Vancouver counterparty provides them with Canadian cash (less a fee). That cash did not physically move over the border; the cash was collected from street drug dealing (frequently in the form of $20 bills). The Chinese national could then take the Canadian cash to a casino to buy in (ironically transported at times in an ice hockey equipment bag). Many of the gamblers put their money at risk and lost all or most of it. Some gamblers, after a bit of gambling, might seek from the casino higher denomination bills (refining) or a cashier's cheque. As noted, some casinos use chips that are fungible in other locations (Macau, Las Vegas and so on).[37]

Underground bankers offer lower fees, insurance (in case law enforcement interdicts cash), and rapid pay-out options. They operate real-time mirror transactions, typically through encrypted communications. The underground bankers are "insular and often decentralized, making them difficult to penetrate."[38] The gambler pays fees to skirt currency controls; in some instances, the underground bankers make North American bank accounts available to the Chinese national. The cash broker pays fees to convert street drug money. There might be a mirror transaction made in Mexican pesos that can reconcile transactions between the drug wholesaler (typically a Mexican cartel) and other entities in China that typically supply precursor chemicals to the cartel to manufacture drugs like fentanyl (although some of that trade is now being displaced into Southeast Asia).[39] FINTRAC has also identified a money laundering typology associated with the proceeds of illicit synthetic opioids. Traffickers frequently exchange drugs for e-transfers of funds, which are then forwarded on to online gaming sites. In turn, they receive remittances from online payment processors in Canada, the United Kingdom and Malta. The FIU suspects that the traffickers are disguising their drug sale proceeds as online casino winnings.[40]

6 Regulated Markets: The Crown and Wynn Casino Cases

Over a decade ago, the Chinese government cracked down on gambling, treating enforcement as an anti-corruption measure. These crackdowns didn't reduce demand, but they did displace three classes of gamblers: mass market (small gamblers), premium mass market (medium), and VIP or high roller patrons (very, very important patrons are referred to as whales in China). Virtually every gaming market around the world rushed to grab as much of this lucrative VIP market as they

[37] German (2018), p. 182.

[38] U.S. Treasury (2024), p. 29.

[39] Langdale (2024). p. 228.

[40] FINTRAC (2025), p. 1.

could. Crown Casino (Crown) in Australia partnered with junket operators. Those junket operators eluded legal prohibitions on promoting gambling in China, provided credit to VIPs (as mini-banks) and collected debts (legally unenforceable in China).[41] Two casinos in particular, Crown Melbourne and Crown Perth, aggressively courted junket operators with names like Suncity, Neptune (later renamed Guangdong), Meg-Star, Song, Chinatown, Tak Chun, Jimei, and the Oriental Group. The returns were spectacular, but those profits came at a cost. The Australian Transaction Reports and Analysis Centre (AUSTRAC), the Australian FIU, determined that there were 546 AML breaches and levied penalties of $281 million.[42] Following investigative reporting that exposed both laundering in casinos as well as a "free-wheeling approach to regulation," a commission of inquiry, the Bergin Inquiry, was struck to conduct a comprehensive investigation into Crown.[43]

Junket operators provide visiting VIPs with dead chips: non-negotiable chips that can be played at the tables but cannot be cashed in at the casino cage. VIP winnings are collected in live chips, that in fact can be cashed in at the cage. Through play, dead chips became rolling chips, allowing the junket operator to track how much they are bringing into the casino for remuneration purposes. Junket providers were granted front money accounts for buy-ins and then paid through commissions for rolling chip turnover as well as discounts and rebates for losses. Junkets operators took on the risk (and the profit). Crown essentially rented rooms for the junkets: private salons where VIPs could gamble without mass market gamblers looking over their shoulder. They allowed the junket operators to flow money, often from dubious sources, into two shelf companies, unimaginatively named Southbank and Riverbank. HSBC, who banked the casinos, became concerned with the AML risk and de-risked[44] Crown in 2013. They moved to banking relations with ANZ and CBA, but those financial institutions also became concerned about 100s of millions of dollars flowing through the accounts, and de-risked as well.

The AML controls were so poor at Crown that the de-risking (a red flag if there ever was one) was not reported up to the board. Companies would make remittances into the casino shelf companies: for example, in 2016, Pai Pai Supply Chain Ltd. lodged 53 deposits in a 4-month period for 20 different gamblers (USD $31.8 mil); those funds would flow from the shelf company to the casino, where the gambler could present their patron identification at the cage to buy in from their front money account. Patrons were allowed to charge their credit cards for "hotel services" when in fact they were using the money for gaming. Between 2012 and 2016, USD $100 million was transferred using China's UnionPay process, ostensibly for hotel services, but "in reality for gambling"[45] a technique that evaded Chinese currency con-

[41] Langdale (2023), p. 103.

[42] UNODC (2024), p. 6.

[43] Bergin Inquiry (2022). The Bergin Inquiry was followed the Finkelstein Inquiry in Victoria (2021), the Perth Royal Commission (2022), the Bell Inquiry in New South Wales and the Gotterson Inquiry in Victoria (2022). Langdale (2023), p. 101.

[44] See Goldbarsht and Goodrick (2025) in this book for more on de-risking.

[45] Langdale (2023), p. 107.

trols as well as Australian AML laws. The Bergin Inquiry determined that Crown had partnered with at least seven junket operators connected to organized crime. Crown isn't the only Australian operator accused of poor AML controls. At the time of writing, casinos run by the Star Entertainment Group in Sydney, Brisbane, and the Gold Coast have been the subject of fines and scrutiny by the Australian Securities and Investments Commission, as have Star's directors.[46]

The American state of Nevada prohibits junket operators but does allow for the registration of agents who operate under strict limitations: they receive only flat fees, cannot extend credit, and function essentially as executive travel agents. The Wynn casino in Las Vegas agreed as part of a non-prosecution agreement on September 6, 2024, to a criminal forfeiture of USD $130 million (the largest such forfeiture in the US). Like Crown, the Wynn casino was chasing the VIP gaming market. To do so, they partnered with offshore third-party agents who guaranteed markers for patrons, deposited patron front-money and paid off patron loans. Money would move with little AML oversight, frequently through shell companies and structured remittances, into Wynn's California bank accounts. From there the amounts would be consolidated and then sent, as needed, to the casino's cage account in Nevada where it would be credited to individual patrons. There was no AML oversight.[47] The casino also permitted proxy gambling by the "human head" or "human hat" method. A person, the human head, would buy in at the casino and then head to a private salon. Another patron, likely an individual who would not pass AML screening (e.g., someone who might be associated with a Mexican drug cartel and show up on open-source screening), would sit beside the human head at the gaming table and direct play. Every centimetre in a casino gaming room is carefully monitored and controlled: cheat-at-play diminishes the operator's bottom line. There is no question that Wynn staff were colluding with the human head.[48]

Two other typologies showed up in the Wynn case. One third party affiliate of several VIPs approached a Wynn employee and his boss, handing them winnings of USD $3 million in cash. The employee was asked to place that money in his office safe (outside of AML monitoring) and then would be directed from time-to-time by his boss to disburse the cash to other patrons in the casino.[49] Finally, the casino enabled the "flying money" or "qian chen" process (part of the IVTS system this chapter has been discussing). A casino employee would introduce a patron to a money processor who collects proceeds of crime within the United States. The patron would be sold cash in exchange for a commission and a transfer within China an equivalent amount of yuan or renimbi. The broker was part of a larger IVTS, moving value around to pay for precursor chemicals in China to offset the

[46] Guardian (2025), p. 1.

[47] U.S. Wynn Agreement (2024), attachment A, para 9.

[48] U.S. Wynn Agreement (2024), attachment A, para 11.

[49] U.S. Wynn Agreement (2024), attachment A, para 14.

obligations of cartels in Mexico (where the precursors are used to manufacture fentanyl) using cash proceeds of drug sales in America.[50]

7 Online Gaming Typologies in the Regulated Marketplace

Fourteen percent of the national income on the Isla of Man comes from online gaming. The FIU has issued a typology report, noting that there is serious risk of criminal misuse of online gaming. The simplest typology listed is "cash in, cash out" where tainted funds are entered into the system, the criminal engages in some low risk gameplay and then cashes out. Organised criminal groups can split proceeds across a broad range of seemingly unrelated accounts and payment platforms in small volumes (below the reporting threshold), using technology to speed up processing and eliminate the need to recruit individual mules for accounts. Crypto assets, mixers, bridges, and peer-to-peer exchanges are layering techniques that can further obfuscate the trail.[51] So-called "even money" betting can be used to launder. In roulette, a bet on red doubles the wager; if two gamblers collude and place simultaneous bets on red and black, one will win and one will lose, but collectively they will end up with the same amount of money they started with.[52] As with land based casinos, players in peer-to-peer games can engage in chip dumping: some players repeatedly lose and one player wins, giving the winner funds—either to settle a criminal debt or to move value offshore.[53]

8 Grey Market Typologies

The UNODC estimates the illegal betting market is worth between USD $340 million and $1.7 trillion a year, which includes $140 billion in laundering.[54] There are unregulated and under-regulated land-based casinos in Southeast Asia, particularly in the Mekong region.[55] iGaming systems (including white label franchised systems) operate through servers in places like Samoa (which in theory is regulated by the Samoan Gambling Control Authority, but not so much in practice). Money laundering occurs through a range of typologies. As with regulated markets, proceeds of crime might be lodged into a betting account and then later withdrawn (cash-in, cash-out). Grey market operators are largely indifferent to source of funds, meaning

[50] U.S. Wynn Agreement (2024), attachment A, para 15.
[51] Isle of Man (2025), pp. 4–5.
[52] Isle of Man (2025), p. 6.
[53] Isle of Man (2025), p. 7.
[54] UNODC (2023), p. 1.
[55] Langdale (2024), p. 230.

that shell companies can move funds through their gaming system. Some professional gamblers will take a commission to bet on behalf of nominees. Collusive peer-to-peer play can be used to launder funds.[56]

The Chinese government crackdown on gambling, noted earlier, had far-reaching impacts. Gaming is still popular with Chinese consumers, and currency controls created a massive appetite within China to get money out of the country. Wealthy Chinese nationals seek out nest eggs in the stable west and want to send their children to schools in Australia or Canada. To meet those aspirations, a massive underground banking network has been developed. To move value over borders, underground bankers partner with organised crime. Typologies include the technique of "offsetting" to transfer value between countries using various credit and debit relationships. In the context of gaming, a junket operator might receive funds in one country (e.g., China) and then make those funds available for the customer to game in another jurisdiction (e.g., Vietnam). The junket operator will establish a front-money account in the casino. They frequently avail themselves of money brokers and cash collectors, who need to launder proceeds of crime and cryptocurrencies (e.g., from fraud or theft). The customer in our example might be directed to deposit funds in China or they might be told to purchase shares in an offshore company. Either way, the customer is agnostic: they evade currency controls and get their day at the gaming table. The junket operator profits from a lucrative and relatively safe business, getting to "clip their ticket at both ends," earning money from the gambler as well as the launderers. Operating at scale across multiple jurisdictions, the fees for such professional money launderers are low, making them an attractive venture for organised crime groups. Finally, junket operators take advantage of weak anti-money laundering systems in grey markets.[57]

Gaming junket operators in Macau responded to the crackdown by aligning with organised crime networks. Gaming debts are not enforceable in China. This means that a junket operator needs their own enforcement mechanism, something that violent and connected organised crime groups can execute on.[58] This is big business. By 2030, these gaming enterprises are expected to grab a majority of the $205 billion a year market share.[59] Volume and scale have led to some creative money laundering typologies. For example, online casinos hosted elsewhere were promoted in Hong Kong and China. Gamblers would register and buy-in with crypto and debit transfers which the operators received through a series of stooge accounts in Hong Kong. The betting volumes in one enterprise were USD $3.3 million a month, and over a 9-month period, 32 people were arrested after laundering $38.5 million dollars.[60] The stooge account technique is used in a variety of different ways. For example, the "moving ants" method of laundering starts with the recruitment of

[56] UNODC (2025) p. 58.

[57] UNODC (2024), p. 46.

[58] UNODC (2024), p. 2.

[59] UNODC (2024), p. 30.

[60] Asia Pacific Group (2024), case study #28, p. 44.

unemployed (and underemployed) individuals who agree to allow the money laundering enterprise to use their accounts and credit cards as a pass-through for funds for a marginal fee. This disperses transactions broadly and optimizes the layering process. The motorcade method is a variation on this technique. Again, transactions are dispersed across a range of actors and the front car participant, who bears the highest risk of incarceration, takes commissions of between 20 and 40%. Both methods use casinos in Laos, Myanmar, and so on to "whitewash" the money.[61]

9 Match Fixing and Corruption in Sport

The topic of match-fixing is beyond the scope of this chapter, but it is part of the criminal ecosystem surrounding gaming.[62] Sports betting is a big business. In North America alone, the market was expected to be $16.52 billion in 2024.[63] That amount of money comes with risk. In 2024, The European Union extended their AML measures to apply to football agents and professional clubs (Anti-Money Laundering Regulation EU).[64] The EU regulations recognise that match-fixing, corrupting players or officials to generate a result that a bet can be placed on, is a perennial concern. Match-fixing includes the deliberate loss of a game (or a portion of a game), deliberate underperformance (tanking), micro manipulation, (spot-fixing), and the deliberate misapplication of the rules by an official.[65] Gambling operators encourage prop bets: gambling on a proposition that something will or won't occur. In spot-fixing, a sporting participant, a player or official, will agree to influence a specific part of the match: kicking a ball to touch in football or throwing a no-ball in cricket. Toronto Raptor basketball player Jontay Porter was banned for life by the league in April 2024 for this. Porter disclosed his health status to someone he knew would be betting on a match in March. That gambler placed an $80,000 prop bet which would have paid out at $1.1 million. Porter then limited his play in the match, withdrawing after 3 min claiming ill health. The gambling operator froze the account based on the unusual betting activity and the resulting investigation revealed the spot-fixing. Porter had also used the account of an associate to place $54,094 in bets over the previous 3 months.[66] The net winnings from betting were $21,965 and Porter's earnings as an athlete, in the previous 4 years, were just over $2.7 million.[67]

---

[61] UNODC (2024), p. 6.

[62] See, for example, Europol (2021) and UNODC (2021).

[63] Statista (2024), p. 1.

[64] *Anti-Money Laundering Regulation* (EU), 2024/1624.

[65] UNODC (2016), p. 4.

[66] NBA (2024), p. 1.

[67] Ostly (2024), p. 1.

10 Crypto, Terrorism, and Proliferation Financing

Cryptocurrency offers users pseudo-anonymity, which can be enhanced by the use of tools like mixers, and obviously poses a money laundering risk.[68] Blockchain analytics firm Chainalysis estimates that $2.2 billion in crypto assets were stolen from platforms and wallets, with state sponsored North Korean hackers stealing $1.34 billion.[69] North Korea poses a persistent state level cybersecurity threat having focused immense resources with military precision on evading international sanctions. North Korean criminals exploited security lapses to steal $80.8 million from the central Bank of Bangladesh in 2016. The New York Federal Reserve spotted problems with beneficiary details and refused to authorize 35 SWIFT transactions which would have stolen a further $951 million. Unlike a smash-and-grab criminal, the hackers lurked and trolled through the central bank's security system with military efficiency, stealing credentials, finding gaps and exploiting vulnerabilities. Following the theft, a portion of the funds were sent to the Philippines to be laundered. Nominees opened accounts in Manila with the Rizal Commercial Banking Corporation (who were later fined) and then moved the money through junket operators at two casinos.[70] Casinos in the Philippines, at the time of the heist, were exempt from AML oversight. Even where casinos are regulated, they are at risk of exploitation: while AML and CTF risks are understood, proliferation financing risks are less understood.[71] A 2024 report concluded that the casino and gaming sector was being abused by North Korea to launder and earn income for their weapons of mass destruction program.[72]

11 Three Examples of Gaming in the Criminal Ecosystem

Three cases discussed in this section highlight that fact that for TOC, gaming is, invariably, only one part of a much larger criminal ecosystem. In 2023, Filipino Chinese businessman Anson Que. was kidnapped; in 2025, police determined that the multi-million-peso ransom payment paid by his family found its way into the hands of private casino junket operators linked to Philippine offshore gaming operators. The government initially licensed these operations, but recurrent problems with laundering, fraud, and human trafficking led to de-licensing and expulsion by Philippine authorities.[73] The ransom collecting junket operators exploited both "fiat

[68] UNODC (2023), p. 7.

[69] Chainalysis (2025) Annual Report, p. 2.

[70] BBC (2016); White (2022); note also the litigation in *Republic of the Philippines* (2020).

[71] Asia Pacific Group (2024).

[72] Owen and Seshadri (2024), p. 17.

[73] Porteus (2024), pp. 5–6.

and digital rails" to move the money, and at the time of writing, the case is still under investigation.[74]

In the second example, a Turkish Cypriot "businessman" was ambushed in 2022 and killed by automatic weapon fire. Halil Falyali ran hotels and licensed casinos in Cyprus but following his murder, a sprawling illegal online betting empire was exposed. Dozens of gaming websites, claiming Curacao licenses, operated illegally in Europe. To hedge risk, the websites operated on sequential domains; if authorities took down a website, it could be replaced in 16 s. Earnings were allegedly funnelled into bribes in Cyprus and Turkey to keep the "licensed" operations running without interference. Complex networks of mules and crypto accounts were used, along with a land-based casino in Belarus, to launder. Following the murder, most of the operation appears to have decamped to the United Arab Emirates.[75]

The third example demonstrates TOC's ability to find optimal conditions to protect their illicit business interests. As with the Falyali case, discussed above, having a licensed casino gives cover to grey market operations. In Southeast Asia, casinos operate in jurisdictions with low regulatory friction, often in special economic zones. They are important to the local economy, providing employment and financial services in an under-serviced market.[76] The Vault Viper network started in Taiwan over 20 years ago but evolved into a global structure consisting of thousands of shell companies and subsidiaries formed in jurisdictions adverse to beneficial ownership disclosure. Their business started with gaming in environments with weak to non-existent regulatory frameworks, poor investor screening, weak threat awareness, and minimal enforcement capacity. Corruption suborned local officials. The Vault Viper network developed the "white label" gaming platforms noted earlier, a turnkey product allowing nearly anyone to launch an online casino or betting forum with minimal technical expertise. The software was highly customisable, adopting to languages and cultures in various markets. Domain Name System (DNS) infrastructure was resilient and dispersed, making website origins hard to track, and as with Falvali's Cypriot enterprise, difficult to take down.[77] Vault Viper also provided backend management tools, including payment gateways with unlicensed fiat and crypto options to evade AML regulation. This "trusted" payment platform then became the bridgehead for malware deployment.[78] The payment systems evolved as a result of the COVID pandemic, which interrupted traditional cash smuggling networks as borders were shut down. Groups like Vault Viper took advantage of several conditions. As noted earlier, currency controls in countries like China created a massive demand for offshore currency. Technology and encryption were used to create a fast, efficient and anonymous way of moving value over borders, with some professional money laundering networks lowering the cost to

---

[74] TRM (2025), p. 1.

[75] OCCRP (2025).

[76] UNODC (2024), p. 20.

[77] UNODC (2025), p. 37.

[78] UNODC (2025), pp. 38–39.

between 0 and 6% of funds laundered (which completely undercut less efficient operations).[79] Joint ventures with drug cartels led to the creation of new cash courier networks, making weekly pick-ups of between USD $150,000 and $1 million based on coded communications. Those funds were then placed and layered into pools, which in turn were laundered into crypto, real estate, and other assets.[80]

12 Conclusions: Money Laundering Risks and the Future of Gaming

Money laundering is a critical back-office function for organised crime. Criminals need to move their lucre, undetected by law enforcement. This not only allows them to enjoy the fruits of their crime, but it also provides working capital for ongoing criminal enterprises. All of that activity forms an underworld eco-system. This chapter has examined a number of aspects of that eco-system. A 2025 UNODC report recommended that the threat posed by money launderers exploitation of gaming be met by increased political awareness of the challenges, improvement of regulatory systems, and operational capacity with a view to creating whole of government solutions. Practical operational cooperation on a regional basis is necessary.[81] The dyad of gaming and laundering is under-examined in the literature. What needs to be examined? Within the regulated market, we need to stay abreast of changing threat vectors. As online gaming grows, the ability of operators to effectively identify their customers can be undermined by artificial intelligence which is capable of producing realistic counterfeit identification.[82] We struggle to create effective ultimate beneficial ownership registers, leaving operators susceptible to abuse by shelf companies and false identities.[83] Video gamers are proliferating and their potential for money laundering is emerging.[84] Money laundering is about moving value: where an in-game object has value, a professional launderer can take advantage of weak controls. TOC groups are using regulated and grey market to support underground banking networks that pollute our legitimate financial system with dirty money and sustain all manners of crime around the world. That threat cannot be ignored. We need further study and deeper awareness of the challenges in order to properly confront them.

[79] UNODC (2025), p. 58.

[80] UNODC (2025) p. 59.

[81] UNODC (2025) p. 12.

[82] Gambling Commission (2025); for further discussion on the use of AI, see Tiwari (2025).

[83] MONEYVAL (2013), p. 10.

[84] Higgs and Flowerday (2024).

References

Alcohol and Gaming Commission of Ontario (2022) Registrar's standards for gaming. Toronto
Asia Pacific Group (2024) 2024 APG typologies report. Sydney
BBC (10 March 2016) Bangladesh Bank Hackers Fail in Bid to Net $1 billion
Bergin Inquiry (2022) Report - Inquiry under section 143 of the Casino Control Act 1992 (NSW). New South Wales
Chainalysis (2025) Annual report, 2025, New York
Cullen (2022) Commission of inquiry into money laundering in British Columbia. Attorney General, Victoria
Europol (2021) The involvement of organized crime groups in sports corruption. Brussels
FINTRAC (Jan 2024a) Special bulletin on laundering the proceeds of crime through online gambling sites. FINTRAC-2024-SB001, Ottawa
FINTRAC (2024b) FINTRAC'S compliance guidance: reporting suspicious transactions to FINTRAC. Ottawa
FINTRAC (Jan 2025) Operational alert: laundering the proceeds of illicit synthetic opioids. Cat. No. FD4-39/2024E-PDF, Ottawa
Gambling Commission (April 2025) Emerging money laundering and terrorist financing risks. London
German P (2018) Dirty money, an independent review of money laundering in lower mainland casinos conducted for the Attorney General of British Columbia, Victoria
Goldbarsht D, Goodrick T (2025) Private to private: the next frontier of financial intelligence sharing. In: Goldbarsht D, de Koker L, Ferrill J (eds) The financial war on crime and terrorism: opportunities and challenges. Springer, Cham
Guardian Australia (10 Feb 2025) Star heads accused in court. Sydney
Higgs J, Flowerday S (2024) Towards definitive categories for online video game money laundering. J Money Laund Control 27(6):1051–1062
Infoblox (24 July 2024) Infoblox threat intell: Vigorish Viper
Isle of Man Online Gaming Typology (2025) https://www.fiu.im/media/1245/online-gambling-typology-2025.pdf
Langdale J (2024) Combatting money laundering in South Asian and Australian Casinos. In: Goldbarsht D, de Koker L (eds) Financial crime and the law: identifying and mitigating risks. Springer, pp 225–245
Langdale J (2023) Money laundering in Australian Casinos. J Money Laund Control 26(7):99–109
Levi M (2013) Money-laundering typologies: a review of their fitness for purpose. Government of Canada, Ottawa
MONEYVAL (2013) Council of Europe. The use of online gambling for money laundering and terrorism financing purposes. Paris
National Basketball Association (17 April 2024) Jontay Porter banned from NBA for violating league's gaming rules. New York
OCCRP (Organized Crime and Corruption Reporting Project) (13 Feb 2025) Inside the global online betting empire of a Slain Turkish Cypriot businessman
Ostly A, (17 April 2024) Jontay Porter's contract details. USA Today, New York
Owen A, Seshadri C (2024) North Korean activity in the casino and gaming sector: how do jurisdictions respond? Royal United Services Institute, London
Porteus J (2024) The ban on Philippines POGOs and the consequent global expansion of illegal gaming hubs. The International Federation of Horse Racing Authorities Council on Anti-Illegal Betting and Related Crime, pp 5–12
Statista (2024) Online sports betting North America 2024. Hamburg
Simser J (2008) Money laundering and asset cloaking techniques. J Money Laund Control 11(1):15–24
Simser J, Kroeker R (2017) Canadian anti-money laundering law: gaming sector. Thomson Reuters, Toronto

Simser J (2023) In: Leuprecht, Ferrill (eds) Responses to money laundering in dirty money. McGill, Montreal, pp 387–410
Simser J (2024) Money laundering and structuring: a Canadian perspective. Company Lawyer 45(6):207–212
Statista (2025) Gambling – worldwide. https://www.statista.com/outlook/amo/gambling/worldwide
Tiwari M (2025) Network analytics and generative artificial intelligence: a hybrid approach to money laundering detection. In: Goldbarsht D, de Koker L, Ferrill J (eds) The financial war on crime and terrorism: opportunities and challenges. Springer, Cham
Tran L, Wardle H et al (2024) The prevalence of gambling and problematic gaming: a systemic review and meta-analysis. The Lancet 9(8):594–613
TRM Solutions (24 May 2025) Philippines Police trace kidnapping ransom to casino junket operators in laundering probe
UNODC (2016) Resource guide on good practices in the investigation of match-fixing. Vienna
UNODC (2021) Illegal betting and sport. Section 9. In: Global report on corruption in sport. Vienna
UNODC (2023) Safeguarding sport from corruption. Vienna
UNODC (2024) Casinos, money laundering, underground banking, and transnational organized crime in East and Southeast Asia: a hidden and accelerating threat. Bangkok
UNODC (2025) Inflection point: global implications of scam centres, underground banking and illicit online marketplaces in Southeast Asia. Bangkok
UNODC Money laundering (2025) https://www.unodc.org/unodc/en/money-laundering/overview.html
U.S. Department of Justice (6 Sep 2024) Deferred prosecution agreement with Wynn Las Vegas, LLC, San Diego
U.S. Department of Treasury (2024) National money laundering risk assessment, 2024. Washington
White G (2022) The Lazarus Heist: from Hollywood to high finance – inside North Korea's global cyber war. Penguin, London

Cases and Statutes

Anti-Money Laundering Regulation (EU), 2024/1624
Atlantic Lottery Corporation Factum filed October 25, 2024, IN THE MATTER OF A REFERENCE to the Court of Appeal pursuant to section 8 of the Courts of Justice Act, RSO 1990, c. C.34, by Order in Council 210/2024 respecting permitting international play in an online provincial lottery scheme (COA-24-CV-0185), Toronto (currently under reserve by the court)
Criminal Code, RSC 1985, c. C-46
Gaming Control Act, SO 1992
Proceeds of Crime (Money Laundering) Terrorist Financing Act, SC 2000, c.17
Red Tape Reduction Statutes Amendment Act, 2024, Bill 16 (Alberta)
Republic of the Philippines represented by the Anti-Money Laundering Council (AMLC), Petitioner v. Bloomberry Resorts and Hotels, Inc. (Solaire) and Banco de Oro, Respondents, 2020 G.R. No. 224112

Jeffrey Simser, a Canadian lawyer, was Canada's first director of civil forfeiture and served with the Ministry of the Attorney General in Toronto, Canada for over 30 years. He is a senior associate fellow at RUSI (the Royal United Services Institute) and one of Canada's leading experts on money laundering and asset forfeiture law. He holds law degrees from Queens University at Kingston and Osgoode Hall Law School. Mr. Simser is the author of two published books, *Canadian Anti-Money Laundering Law: The Gaming Sector* and *Civil Asset Forfeiture in Canada* (loose-leaf). He has published dozens of peer reviewed articles. Mr. Simser was twice qualified as an expert witness at the Commission of Inquiry into Money Laundering in British Columbia (the Cullen Commission) and recently testified before Canada's Standing Committee on Finance to address money laundering issues. Mr. Simser provides advice, training, and support to law enforcement in jurisdictions across Canada and around the world (including South Africa, the Democratic Republic of Congo, the Philippines, Guatemala, and Kenya).

International Arbitration and Money Laundering: Is There an Actual Issue?

Robert Walters

Abstract International commercial arbitration (ICA) has long been considered an effective tool to resolve cross border trade and investment disputes. However, with technology and the potential for arbitrators to be exposed to, and placed in complex situations where, for instance, resolving financial transactions disputes that for part of an arbitral procedure could directly or indirectly be associated with Money Laundering (ML).

ICA is a non-judicial mechanism for public and private disputes, where the parties agree (Redfern and Hunter, Law and practice of international commercial arbitration. Oxford University Press, 1986, p 23), through either a contract and/or arbitration agreement to resolve disputes. While arbitration is voluntary, the process itself provides a high level of confidentiality to the parties. It keeps the dispute out of the courts. One of the fundamental features of international arbitration is confidentiality. This well understood principle could be in conflict with ML activities that arise from arbitral proceedings. This chapter will compare the arbitral laws of the United National Commission on International Trade Law, and the national laws of Australia, India, United Kingdom, United States, European Union, and selected Arbitration Institutions from these economies, to confirm or otherwise whether they adequately address ML activities. The chapter will confirm or otherwise as to whether there is a need for the laws, standards and rules used by arbitrators in arbitral proceedings are in need of updating.

Notwithstanding this, the above is based on the fact that from time to time, there could be contracts that parties have agreed upon, prior to a dispute, raise complex issues related to burden of proof, evidentiary requirements, applicable criminal laws, enforcement, and judicial review (Born, International commercial arbitration, vol I–III, 2nd edn. Kluwer Law International, 2014). The question arises, what are the obligations of an arbitrator under the rules of confidentiality and impartiality to the arbitral process, when having to deal with issues of ML? This chapter will look

R. Walters (✉)
Victoria University, Melbourne, VIC, Australia
e-mail: robert.walters2@live.vu.edu.au

D. Goldbarsht et al. (eds.), *The Financial War on Crime and Terrorism*, European Yearbook of International Economic Law,
https://doi.org/10.1007/978-3-032-06360-1_11

at whether there have been technology breakthroughs such as blockchain that could assist in managing these issues. It will look at the international and national definition of ML and contracts the definition/s with the arbitral rules and standards.

Significantly, this chapter will address the rules of evidence as they pertain to the well founded and generally applied rules of the balance of probabilities for arbitration proceeding, versus the principle of beyond reasonable doubt for criminal offences such as ML. This alone will be complex to reconcile as arbitrators begin to use and apply technology to an arbitral proceeding. The technology itself may be able to mask or hide such activities; therefore an arbitrator will require new skills so as to ensure they are not compromised. That said, it will be argued how overcoming confidentiality in arbitration will be problematic, when compared to the current day laws and selected arbitration institutional rules. In concluding this chapter, the arbitrator will need to reconcile how they deal with a detection of ML, and how they manage the issue and/or whether there is an obligation to report the alleged criminal activity. This will need to be finely balanced between an arbitrator's obligation to confidentiality, and the implementation of relevant rules and arbitration laws.

1 Introduction

To the lay person, international commercial arbitration is not widely understood. Yet across the commercial world, contracts routinely provide for dispute resolution clause, in the form of allowing parties to agree go to arbitration. Therefore, when a dispute between parties arises, there is generally the option for both parties to agree to arbitration rather than litigate. ICA has become a preferred option for parties to resolve disputes, because they do not need to go to the courts. By keeping a dispute out of the courts, there is a higher level of confidentiality as opposed to the courts, whereby, it is open for all the public to view. One of the key components to ICA is the arbitration agreement and the arbitration panel that can comprise of a sole arbitrator or a panel of three. International arbitration comes in two different forms. First, is ICA has been established to resolve international commercial disputes generally involving parties from different countries. Second, is transnational investment disputes. Otherwise referred to as investment treaty arbitration, it is used for disputed between nation states, or, a nation state and a commercial entity.

ICA has a broad reach in and across international commercial activities. It can be utilised across a number of different sectors including finance, cybersecurity, artificial intelligence, data flows and data storage, amongst others. Generally, arbitration has been widely accepted to resolve disputes related to intellectual property, contracts, investments, and construction.

Gary Born summarises ICA as a creature that owes its existence to the will of the parties alone.[1] For ICA to be initial, the parties' 'consent is essential for an

[1] See Born (2022), p. 1.

agreement to arbitrate; the ultimate efficacy of an international arbitration agreement depends in large part upon its validity and enforceability in national courts, applying rules of national and international law'.[2] Born notes that for the 'essential to the enforcement of international arbitration agreements are contemporary international arbitration conventions. Particularly significant in this regard are the New York Convention, the European Convention and the Inter-American Convention'.[3] In a period of heightened changes in commercial and financial transactions being undertaken over the internet, the opportunity and risk of money laundering is real. This is evidenced by the many different scams[4] that have been well documented by international organisations.

Andrew McDougall made 20 years ago that money laundering is not a new phenomenon. [5] McDougall briefly described the concept of money laundering as originating from criminal activity in the 1920, where coin-laundries were used as a means of concealing the criminal origin of the revenues.[6] McDougall notes that the definition of money laundering is a 'process by which criminals attempt to hide and disguise the true origin and ownership of the proceeds of their criminal activities, thereby, avoiding prosecution, conviction, and confiscation of criminal funds'.[7] Money laundering for McDougall occurs in three stages:

- Soaking, smurfing, or placing, which is aimed at putting proceeds from criminal activity not the banking system by way of cash deposit in local currency,
- Washing or layering which is aimed at separating the proceeds from their original source (achieved through a series of transactions, including co-mingling of clean and dirty money), and
- Drying or integrating, which is aimed at converting the washed money into legitimate investments.[8]

In adopting and applying what McDougall has defined as money laundering to ICA, the author believed that up to 2005, criminal organisations have recourse to international arbitration as the very means of laundering money, such as, where a commercial dispute is simulated between two related corporate entities that appear on their face to be unrelated. For McDougall:

> Company A commences a fake claim for damages based on forged evidence against company B. Company A obtains an arbitral award for damages against Company B, and Company B pays damages to Company A out of proceeds obtained from criminal activity.[9]

---

[2] See Born (2022), p. 1.

[3] See Born (2022), p. 1. The Convention on the Recognition and Enforcement of Foreign Arbitral Awards, 1958.

[4] Interpol, Financial Fraud Assessment: A Global Threat boosted by Technology, 2024.

[5] See McDougall (2005), pp. 1021–1054.

[6] See McDougall (2005), p. 1022.

[7] See McDougall (2005), p. 1022.

[8] See McDougall (2005), p. 1023.

[9] See McDougall (2005).

However, even under this scenario, McDougall noted in 2005 that it would be rare. Although, in a more recent study, arbitration itself can be used to in a way to assist in the money laundering process.[10] Thus, the question arises, is how or to what level if an arbitrator liable for money laundering in arbitration? This question alone is complex, as it will relate and change, at the stage of arbitration that the arbitrator is made aware of money laundering. Yet, when applied to technology, for instance, arbitration that involves blockchain, artificial intelligence, cybersecurity, and soon to possibly commercialised quantum.

Notwithstanding the above, these technological areas have all emerged across the new areas of digital finance such as online banking, online payment and transfer services, tokens, crypto currencies, peer-to-peer lending, personal investment advice, and services. These products and services are utilising e-money, digital wallets, digital payment platforms, for loans, savings, insurance and investment.[11] These products and services are being applied on technology that supports 'mobile network operators, payment service providers (PSPs), merchant aggregators, retailers, FinTech companies, neo-banks, and super platforms, are leveraging these technologies and altering the competitive landscape for financial services'.[12] The resulting effect, is new innovations that provide greater access for consumers. These technologies have enabled greater collaboration and engagement between citizens located in different countries.

Centrally though, the international community has been slowly tackling the impact of financial gain from the trafficking of illicit substances, which in turn, involves a level of money laundering for many decades. For instance, *The Convention against Transnational Organized Crime* and the United Nations Convention Against Illicit Traffic *in Narcotic Drugs and Psychotropic Substances* (1988)[13] while not specifically mentioning money laundering, draws the connection between illicit substances and financial gain. The Preamble states that 'illicit traffic generates large financial profits and wealth enabling transnational criminal organizations to penetrate, contaminate and corrupt the structures of government, legitimate commercial and financial business, and society at all its levels'.[14]

Against the backdrop of the above, the 1999 United Nations *The Convention for the Suppression of the Financing of Terrorism,*[15] *does not mention money laundering, although Article 18 states that* 'measures for the supervision, including, for example, the licensing, of all money-transmission agencies'.[16] Additionally, the Financial Action Task Force (FATF) has been established and today, leads global

[10] Teichmann et al. (2023).

[11] See World Bank, Inclusive Digital Financial Services.

[12] See International Finance Corporation, Digital Finance.

[13] See UN (1988).

[14] Preamble, p. 1, UN (1988).

[15] United Nations, *The Convention for the Suppression of the Financing of Terrorism, 1999.*

[16] See Article 18. UN 1999.

action to tackle money laundering, terrorist financing, and proliferation financing.[17] The general principles for member countries to consider is to leverage their Anti-Money Laundering (AML) controls in carrying out their obligations relating to proliferation financing.[18] In Australia, AML falls under the *Anti-Money Laundering and Counter-Terrorism Financing Act 2006*[19] and for the United Kingdom, *Proceeds of Crime Act 2002*,[20] the United States *The Anti-Money Laundering Act 2020*, modified subchapter II of Chapter 53 of title 31 United States Code,[21] and the European Union established the 2024 Regulation (EU) 2024/1620 on AML.[22] While it is beyond the scope of this chapter to compare each of these jurisdictional laws on AML, it is argued that there has been considerable attention been given by governments and regulators post the terrorist attacks of September 11, 2001 in the United States. What exactly do these laws mean for ICA, is not clear, however, under the legal framework of arbitration, a long-standing feature has been the concept of confidentiality. This could provide the opportunity for parties to conceal where and how they have received money. To put this into context, and not suggesting or making any assumptions, arbitration can involve small to large amounts of money—and it is not uncommon to have millions, if not, billions of dollars involved. On the other hand, and more generally, the above jurisdictional laws provide a framework for specific sectors such as the financial sector to monitor transactions for AML activity.

This chapter will explore the evolving area of the potential for money laundering in international arbitration. The chapter will first examine a selected number of arbitration rules to confirm or otherwise their response and management of money laundering at the commencement, during, or conclusion of an arbitral proceeding. Second, this chapter will highlight the ensuing developments in technology such as blockchain, artificial intelligence-machine learning, cybersecurity and quantum, and how they apply to arbitration and money laundering. Third, the chapter will analyse a selected number of arbitration institutional rules from Australia, the

[17] See The Financial Action Task Force (FATF), https://www.fatf-gafi.org/en/the-fatf/what-we-do.html The FATF Recommendations contain specific measures that complement the United Nations Security Council Resolutions with respect to proliferation financing: The global approach aimed at preventing non-state actors from taking part in proliferation-related activities (United Nations Security Council Resolution 1540 (2004) and its successor resolutions).

[18] See FATF (2018), p. 12.

[19] See The *Anti-Money Laundering and Counter-Terrorism Financing Act 2006.*

[20] See Institute of Financial Accountants, Proceeds of Crime Act 2002 (POCA) (as amended by the Serious Organised Crime and Police Act 2005 (SOCPA)), the Money Laundering, Terrorist Financing and Transfer of Funds (Information on the Payer) Regulations 2017 (MLR 2017) and the Terrorism Act 2000 (TA 2000) (as amended by the Anti-Terrorism, Crime and Security Act 2001 (ATCSA 2001) and the Terrorism Act 2006 (TA 2006)).

[21] See Federal Deposit Insurance Corporation, Anti Money Laundering (2024).

[22] See Regulation (EU) 2024/1620 of the European Parliament and of the Council of 31 May 2024 establishing the Authority for Anti-Money Laundering and Countering the Financing of Terrorism and amending Regulations (EU) No 1093/2010, (EU) No 1094/2010 and (EU) No 1095/2010 (Text with EEA relevance) PE/35/2024/INIT, *Official Journal of the European Union, 2024/1620, 19.6.2024.*

United Kingdom, the United States, and the European Union, to confirm or otherwise the management of money laundering during an arbitration proceeding. It will also discuss the challenges of confidentiality in ICA as a fundamental and core feature that has been well entrenched in arbitral proceedings. To overcome this core principle will not only be challenging, but also, problematic. Fourth, the chapter concludes by determining whether any issue of money laundering in an arbitration, once detected, is the fault of the arbitrator, and what is any liability rests with the arbitrator to report the activity. It will argue for further research to be undertaken, and that there is a diverged approach to the application of confidentiality in arbitration, which will need to be finely balanced upon the detection of money laundering during an arbitral proceeding.

2 Technology: Blockchain

Blockchain technology and distributed ledgers have emerged as the technology of choice for the developing and fast evolving area of tokens and crypto currency. To understand the technology behind blockchain, is a decentralised framework that can allow anyone access, and no single person or entity has control. However, for governments and regulators this poses challenges, whereby, they have for more than a century been highly centralised for of control of the population and business. The challenge has been described 'due to the decentralized nature of public, permissionless blockchain-based networks'.[23] Primavera De Filippi and others go onto say how the 'operations of these networks are determined by a computer protocol enforced by a decentralized network of nodes responsible for processing transactions and recording them into the blockchain'.[24] The resulting effect is that all 'network nodes follow the same protocol, no single party can unilaterally dictate or influence the operations of the network'.[25] Today, there are three blockchain categories: the public blockchain that enables anyone to join and operate the network; the consortium blockchain that is restricted to only those that are provided access; and, a private blockchain that is significantly restricted to only those individuals that have access.[26] A 2020 study undertaken by Fabian Teichmann and others have argued that:

> Money laundering is one of the most pressing concerns when it comes to cryptocurrencies. Time and time again, data published by blockchain experts, researchers and firms illustrate that large proportions of cryptocurrencies such as Bitcoin are misappropriated for financial crime. Cryptocurrencies are a highly feasible vehicle for a variety of financial crimes because they provide high degrees of anonymity paired with a lack of regulation. Difficulties in cryptocurrency regulation can be attributed to the fact that cryptocurrencies are powered

[23] See De Filippi et al. (2022), pp. 358–37.

[24] See De Filippi et al. (2022), p. 358.

[25] See De Filippi et al. (2022), p. 358.

[26] See De Filippi et al. (2022), p. 358.

> by blockchain. Because of its decentralization, this public ledger is out of the reach of governments, which also makes it suitable for the circumvention of sanctions or other financial crimes. Because the blockchain is a decentralized network, there is no person responsible for the network that could be sanctioned for illicit activity taking place on it. Prior efforts to regulate blockchain technology have had limited success.[27]

The response by regulators, to date, recognised the need develop and/or strengthen the AML laws. This is largely in part due to the lack of regulation of blockchain technology. The extent of the use of this technology by the banking and financial sector is not fully understood. As digital payments become more accessible, banks and financial institutions are constantly competing to be ahead of the market. This includes the adoption of blockchain technology. That said, Thommandru and Chakka (2023) note that when investigating AML compliance within the context of the costs associated and evaluating the use of blockchain, it is significant: in 2020 was estimated to be in the vicinity of USD $213 billion.[28] Importantly, the costs are associated with assessing the use of a blockchain by individuals and/or entities. More specifically, because blockchain may be private (restricted access), to would involve a highly specialised and skilled person to access the technology. The authors further note that by 2021, FATF stated that high-risk nations have also raised concerns about the impact AML requirements may have on their economy.[29] Therefore, as the world becomes more contested and countries and regions compete across the economy, the potential of this technology to be used to assist in AML will be problematic.

Having said that, artificial intelligence (AI)[30] and machine learning can be used within and by a blockchain or distributed ledger. They can be integrated together, and generally the commentary has been what and how AI is benefiting blockchain by providing a higher level of security to its users. The next section explores the use of AI and machine learning technology.

2.1 *Artificial Intelligence [AI]: Machine Learning [ML]*

The application and use of AI across money laundering activity is being viewed as not so much as an enabler, but rather, a response to improved reporting processes. For instance, AI is being developed and used to assess 'transaction monitoring, customer due diligence, and the generation of intelligence and suspicious activity reports—that traditionally require significant human intervention and are prone to errors'.[31] However, there are concerns regarding the potential for bias, management

---

[27] See Teichmann et al. (2023), p. 99.

[28] Thommandru and Chakka (2023).

[29] Thommandru and Chakka (2023).

[30] Polas et al. (2022).

[31] See Menz (2024).

of data, and generating inaccurate and misleading information.[32] At the same time, ML is being used to develop methods to 'identify organisations prone to money laundering activity'.[33] Noteworthy too, is how the algorithms used in machine learning are increasingly being used to detect and predict criminal behaviour.[34] It is the algorithms used by ML technology that can be used to detect and monitor transactions, and ensure there is a level of compliance with local money laundering laws. They require the application and use of complex coded rule based on algorithms.

Nevertheless, Georgios Pavlidis, in referring to Jonathan McCarthy and others, makes the point of how these new technologies 'promise to improve AML compliance and enhance the delivery of regulatory requirements through the use of artificial intelligence (AI) and its various subsets, such as machine learning and natural language processing'.[35] Moreover, Pavlidis reaffirms how the use of AI in AML/CFT can help detect and prevent money laundering by analysing vast amounts of financial data and identifying suspicious activity promptly and accurately. At the same time, however, it poses new regulatory challenges, including privacy, fairness, explainability, and oversight.[36] Arguably, the development, application and use of these technologies are far from being settled, to fully manage the cycle of money laundering.

Significant also, is how these technologies are being use in arbitration. For instance, AI 'technologies are being integrated into the dispute resolution mechanism and fundamentally altering how disputes are managed and resolved. AI technologies have the potential to revolutionie international arbitration in several key areas'.[37] Layan Al Fatyri believes that, AI used in arbitration is able to 'analyse vast amounts of data to identify past rulings, potential biases—to the drafting of awards and briefs'.[38] By utilising AI, Fatyri states that the technology can enhance data analysis and researching document, whereby the cost of time of the arbitrator is reduced.

Over time as the technology continues to advance, the efficiencies will further improve for the arbitrator, and in turn for the parties. Significant too, for complex cross border international arbitration, these AI tools can analyse and compare 'legal precedents, case laws, and arbitration awards from various jurisdictions to identify relevant patterns and provide predictive analytics'.[39] For Fatyri, 'one of the most significant impacts of AI in international arbitration is its potential to bridge the gap between different legal traditions'.[40] This will be the case where the parties are from

[32] See Menz (2024); see the chapter by Tiwari (2025) in this book for further reading.

[33] See Domashova and Mikhailina (2021), pp. 184–185.

[34] See Bertrand et al. (2021), pp. 276–293.

[35] See Pavlidis (2023), p. 155. See also, McCarthy (2023), Brynjolfsson and McAfee (2017).

[36] See Pavlidis (2023), p. 162.

[37] See Al Fatyri (2024).

[38] See Al Fatyri (2024).

[39] See Al Fatyri (2024).

[40] See Al Fatyri (2024).

different legal systems, and the choice of law has not been either specified by the arbitration agreement or agreed upon by the parties via the arbitrator.

Under these circumstances, AI can be used by the tribunal to assess and evaluate the gaps or differences in the laws. However, and while AI may be able to assist in this area, it is another unsettled area of technology, because there is insufficient evidence confirming its accuracy. Simply put, the accuracy of today's technology lacks the sophistication to identify the nuances and contextual meaning of terms between the country's different laws. This is whether it is civil law or common law or both parties are from the same legal family, yet the laws are different. The next section briefly examines the developments in quantum technology.

2.2 *Quantum*

Quantum technology is closely aligned with AI and machine learning technologies. Simply put, 'Quantum Artificial Intelligence (QAI) is the intersection of quantum computing and AI, a technological synergy with expected significant benefits for both.'[41] Klusch et al. note how:

> QAI algorithms could indeed make a positive difference in solving certain computationally hard problems such as for combinatorial optimization in AI applications compared to classical solutions. So far, the potential quantum utility of direct quantum or hybrid quantum-classical methods of QAI is under investigation for applications in diverse domains such as manufacturing, automated driving, transport and logistics, energy management, healthcare, finance, aerospace, climate and earth sciences, and pharmaceutical and chemical industries. In this regard, quantum AI use cases are concerned with, for example, portfolio optimization in finance, traffic management, capacitive vehicle routing, safe navigation of self-driving vehicles, satellite network constellation and mission planning, energy network management, job-shop scheduling in manufacturing, weather simulation and forecasting and simulation of materials and chemicals for drug discovery and material design.[42]

Of importance is the current day industry sector where this technology can be applied. Most notably, all these sectors can and do rely of levels of commercial relations that involve contracts, and in turn, can rely on arbitration as the dispute resolution mechanism. Furthermore, the propensity for money laundering across these sectors is real. It is beyond the scope of this chapter to provide statics on this activity.

Quantum technology, while been in existence for some time is only recently being considered as to its impact[43] or otherwise to ICA. The issue for Peter O'Neill is how the developments in deception detection, the use of AI, ML, and quantum computing have the potential to disrupt arbitral systems. This is because the technology is invariably aligned, and any disruption/s are far from being fully understood. It can be used for 'detecting patterns of illegal activity, and even though it is

[41] See Klusch et al. (2024).

[42] See Klusch et al. (2024).

[43] See O'Neill (2022).

not conclusive, the technology may be able to unravel concealed transaction chains, simultaneously exploring multiple paths through transaction networks. This would enable the discovery of hidden connections between seemingly independent accounts that cannot be identified by conventional computers'.[44] When fully realised, the technology has the potential to provide as many benefits as it does challenges to money laundering activities and international arbitration.

Nonetheless, James Dargan wrote in 2020[45] that quantum arbitration tools are being developed, which essentially incorporate algorithms and AI, to make the arbitral process more efficient. This can be done by improving efficiencies in assessing financial outcomes pertaining to an award, discovery of documents, and managing evidence more generally. It is an area of vigilance and of high note, as it could be used very effectively to differentiate between laundered money and legitimate money. This technology has the potential however to pose challenges to cybersecurity. The technology, when commercialised is highly advanced whereby it can detect and break[46] current day encryptions. Arguably, it is the current day encryptions that have provided the world with a high level of security of commercial, personal, and state data and information. Should that ever be diluted, it poses a significant economic challenge to the world in the area of reporting criminal activity, and international arbitrations. Moreover, cybersecurity is an issue in arbitration and helps facilitate money laundering activities. The next section discussed some of the issues related to cybersecurity in these areas.

2.3 Cybersecurity

Cybersecurity in international arbitration has been generally viewed through the lens of what and how to protect sensitive and confidential information. With the growing trend of arbitral proceedings being undertaken online, the threat of cybersecurity intrusions and loss of commercial information and data is increasingly vulnerable. To date, the response by arbitration tribunals has been to develop protocols and/or rules such as the 2022 *Protocol by the international Council for International Arbitration* that provides a 'framework to determine reasonable information security measures for individual arbitration matters'. [47] That framework includes 'procedural and practical guidance to assess security risks and identify available measures that may be implemented'.[48] Specifically, the Protocol has established 14 Principles that address information security issues in an individual arbitration. Of note is that

[44] Anti Money Laundering, Quantum Computing (2024).

[45] Dargan (2020).

[46] See Can quantum computing break tradition encryption: What the experts say? (2024).

[47] See International Council for Commercial Arbitration, ICCA – NYC BAR – CPR Protocol on Cybersecurity, The ICCA Reports No. 6, in International Arbitration (2022).

[48] See International Council for Commercial Arbitration, ICCA – NYC BAR – CPR Protocol on Cybersecurity, The ICCA Reports No. 6, in International Arbitration (2022).

according to Principle 14, it does not 'establish liability or a liability standard for any purpose whatsoever'.[49] Mauricio Duarte notes, some of the main impacts of cybersecurity breaches include: (a) economic loss to parties, arbitrators, and arbitral institutions; (b) reputational damage to arbitral institutions, arbitrators and counsel, as well as to the system of international arbitration overall; and (c) potential liability under applicable laws and other regulatory frameworks.[50] In a recent report that outlined the intensity and trends of cybersecurity in 2024, it has been noted how AI has been weaponised 'enabling attackers to enhance every stage of an attack and to do so better and faster than before.

Cybercriminals increasingly use AI to support a multitude of malicious activities, ranging from thwarting the algorithms that detect social engineering to mimicking human behaviour through activities such as AI audio spoofing and creating other deepfakes.[51] To what extent these activities are being used to undermine the arbitral process is not fully understood. What is well understood is that where there is a lack of cybersecurity in place, there is a heightened risk of an arbitral proceeding being compromised.

On the backdrop of the above, the similarities in the detection of cyber intrusions, cybersecurity breaches that have resulted in a loss of commercial and other confidential information in arbitration is and would be considered a criminal offence. This is the same as when an arbitrator detects a level of money laundering: the extent of obligation to report these offences become complex. The impact and consequences of confidentiality in arbitration from the reporting of a detected criminal offence is contrary to the long-standing rules of ICA. In reaffirming this point, Edna Sussman in referring to Geisinger and Ducret conclude that reporting duty is in complete contradiction with the confidential nature of international commercial arbitration and suggest that most legal systems would not impose any such duty. They allow for possible exceptions for extremely serious violations of fundamental legal principles, such as human trafficking, where the confidentiality of the arbitration becomes a 'minor consideration.'[52]

The use and application of the above technologies in arbitration is evolving. It is well understood that there is 'broad discretionary powers to manage the procedure in arbitral proceedings. This discretion arises both in national laws applicable to arbitration and in the rules adopted in the proceedings'.[53] As noted by Tamlyn Mills and Mrithula Shanker, Article 17(1) of the United Nations Commission on International Trade Law (UNCITRAL) Arbitration Rules provides:

> …the arbitral tribunal may conduct the arbitration in such manner as it considers appropriate, provided that the parties are treated with equality and that at an appropriate stage of the

[49] See International Council for Commercial Arbitration, ICCA – NYC BAR – CPR Protocol on Cybersecurity, The ICCA Reports No. 6, in International Arbitration (2022).

[50] See Duarte (2019).

[51] Fortinet (2024).

[52] Geisinger and Ducret (2018), p. 12.

[53] Mills and Shanker (2024).

> proceedings each party is given a reasonable opportunity of presenting its case. The arbitral tribunal, in exercising its discretion, shall conduct the proceedings so as to avoid unnecessary delay and expense and to provide a fair and efficient process for resolving the parties' dispute.[54]

In taking this view, the level of discretion afforded by Article 17 (1) would prima facie allow for the use of technology such as blockchain, AI, cybersecurity, and quantum. However, reliance on broad tribunal discretion over the management of procedure does not necessarily: deal with disclosure of what, when and how these technologies are used; help those involved in arbitral proceedings to understand the acceptable use cases for these technologies; or provide parties, counsel or tribunal members with clarity about how they can expect these technologies to be managed throughout the arbitral process.[55] However, and as highlighted in the next section, confidentiality in arbitration is a well-grounded concept that will be problematic to overcome, for the disclosure of evidence or otherwise that constitutes money laundering.

3 Confidentiality

Arguably, most commentators of ICA regard confidentiality as an important and essential advantage of the arbitral process.[56] A significant advantage of arbitration[57] is confidentiality. Confidentiality is an important component of arbitration and has enabled the process to be a 'popular choice for parties, in both state-to-state and commercial dispute resolution, since the beginning of recorded history'.[58] Most notably, information, if confidential, will most likely constitute evidence in an arbitral proceeding. It is this evidence that can be in the form of documents or provided orally that may disclose the laundering of money. The ability for the arbitrator and tribunal to manage such confidential information is problematic and challenging. This section will discuss the well-grounded principle of confidentiality in arbitration and how it would impact on the tribunals ability to disclose a criminal offence related to the laundering or money.

Gary Born (2020) makes the point that a core objective international arbitration:

> is to provide the possibility of confidentiality, or at least private dispute resolution mechanism. Most national court proceedings are not confidential. Hearings and court dockets are

---

[54] Mills and Shanker (2024). United Nations: United Nations Commission on International Trade Law, UNCITRAL Arbitration Rules (2021), UNCITRAL Expedited Arbitration Rules, UNCITRAL, Rules on Transparency in Treaty-based Investor-State Arbitration, 2021.

[55] Mills and Shanker (2024).

[56] Born (2020), pp. 2248–2255. In Mandhan, https://cc.bingj.com/cache.aspx? Accessed 2 Jan 2022. Note this section in relation to confidentiality draws upon the early work undertaken by the author in Walters and Rajwanshi (2023).

[57] Redfern and Hunter (2004), p. 23. In Walters and Rajwanshi (2023).

[58] Born and Miles (2015).

> open to the public, competitors, press and regulators in many countries, and parties are often to disclose submissions and evidence to the public. Public disclosure can encourage trial by press release and may impede compromises.[59]

For Born, international arbitration is substantially private and more confidential than court proceedings. He goes on to say arbitration are virtually always closed to the press and public, and in practice the parties' submissions and tribunals' awards often remain confidential.[60]

Notably, as stated by Born, in some jurisdictions, 'confidentiality obligations are implied in international arbitration agreements as a matter of law, while some arbitration agreements or institutional arbitration rules impose such duties expressly'.[61] Further, most 'international business prefer, and actively seek, the privacy and confidentiality that the arbitral process offers. Viewed thus way, confidentiality, reduces the risks of aggravating the parties' dispute, limits the collateral damage of a damage and focuses the parties on an amicable, business-like resolution of their disagreements'.[62] Confidentiality is 'used to refer to the 'parties' asserted obligations not to disclose information concerning the arbitration to third parties'.[63] By taking the view and approach by these leading international arbitration practitioners, confidentiality in arbitration poses significant challenges to the reporting of money laundering offences.

More centrally, the UNCITRAL Model Law on Arbitration does not specifically refer to confidentiality.[64] Likewise, the UNCRITAL Arbitration Rules does not specifically mention confidentiality. However, Article 34.5 of the UNCITRAL Arbitration Rules,[65] arguably provides for confidentiality by requiring the consent of both parties for the arbitration award to be made public.

Article 30 of the Rules of the London Court of International Arbitration (LCIA) regulates the duty of confidentiality in a well-defined manner. Article 30(1) stipulates that the parties undertake 'as a general principle to keep confidential all awards in the arbitration, together with all materials.'[66] Article 30(2) provides further that '[t]he deliberations of the Arbitral Tribunal shall remain confidential to its members.'[67] The *Australian International Arbitration Act* (1974) for instance defines confidential information to include all statements and evidence, notes, transcripts,

[59] See Born (2016), pp. 13–14.

[60] See Born (2016), pp. 13–14.

[61] See Born (2016), pp. 13–14.

[62] See Born (2016), pp. 13–14.

[63] See Born (2009), p. 2251.

[64] See The United Nations Commission on International Trade Law (UNCITRAL) Model Law 2006.

[65] See The United Nations Commission on International Trade Law (UNCITRAL) Arbitration Rules 2010.

[66] See Article 30.1.

[67] See Article 30.1.

rulings, or award.[68] Confidential information defined under the Australian Act includes a level of personal data, as defined in the different data protection laws of Australia's states and territories.

In contrast, neither the Arbitration Act (1996) of the United Kingdom (UK) nor the *Indian Arbitration Act 1940*,[69] provided for the scope of confidentiality. However, a recent addition to the legal framework in India, under section 42A of the 1996 Indian *Arbitration and Conciliation Act*, requires the arbitrator, the arbitral institution and the parties to the arbitration agreement shall maintain confidentially of all arbitral proceedings except award where its disclosure is necessary for the purpose of implementation and enforcement of award.[70] However, India has diverged from the UK approach and chosen to include confidentiality within the law. The question arises whether the words in section 42A where necessary extend the public interest test. That said, section 42A is a recent phenomenon in India and the duty of confidentiality as not applicable when the arbitral award is to be disclosed for the purpose of its implementation and enforcement. In effect, this balancing test of legitimate interest, or public interest, forms the foundation of the exception within the section, and is a testament to the intention of protecting the legitimate interest of a decree/award holder.[71]

Most notably, Jaideep Khanna (2021), is of the view that Indian courts must also consider observations laid down by common law jurisdictions in the *Ali Shipping*[72] case (see below) where the court stated that one of the exceptions to the implied duty of confidentiality is the protection of 'the legitimate interests of an arbitrating party'.[73] Khanna, argues that the insertion of section 42A reveals legislative intent to codify confidentiality obligations in arbitration proceedings. However, section 42A has cast a blanket duty of confidentiality without qualifying its exceptions and applicability. The author argues that it is anticipated that Indian courts would have to develop exceptions to confidentiality obligations under section 42A under the broad umbrella of Balance of Interests, Court Proceedings and Regulatory Obligations.[74] To date it would appear that this section does not, which was expressed by Lord Peter Goldsmith[75] in 2023. Therefore, and on this basis alone, the divergence in acceptance of the public interest test in confidentiality, limits those jurisdictions that do not apply the concept, to a stricter application of the concept. In practice this would mean that unless the parties' consent to dispensing of confidentiality for the disclosure of evidence that constitute money laundering, such a

[68] Section 15 International Arbitration Act 1974.

[69] Indian Arbitration Act 1940.

[70] India, The Arbitration and Conciliation Act 1996.

[71] Khanna (2021), pp. 90–97.

[72] See Khanna (2021), pp. 90–97. see also, *Ali Shipping Corporation v Shipyard Trogir* [1997] APP.L.R. 12/19, http://www.nadr.co.uk/articles/published/ZzzzarbitrationLawReports/Ali%20v%20Trogir%201997.pdf

[73] See Khanna (2021), pp. 90–97.

[74] See Khanna (2021), p. 97.

[75] Lord Peter Goldsmith (2023).

disclosure would be contrary to the principle of confidentiality as set out in section 42A of Indian law.

Article 26.2 of the Australian Centre for International Arbitration (ACICA) rules provide that an Arbitral Tribunal shall 'treat as confidential and shall not disclose to a third party without prior written consent from the parties all matters relating to the arbitration (including the existence of the arbitration), the award, materials created for the purpose of the arbitration and documents produced by another party in the arbitration proceedings and not in the public domain'.[76] Article 29 of the Indian Council of Arbitrator Rules on International Commercial Arbitration provides that unless the parties have otherwise agreed, the tribunal and the parties at all times shall follow a general principle to maintain the confidentiality of the arbitration and the award. The tribunal or a party, without prior written consent of all the other parties, shall not disclose any such matter to a third party unless: a) disclosure may be required of a party by legal duty; or b) it is to protect or pursue legal right; or c) to enforce or challenge an award in bona fide legal proceedings before a Court or other judicial authority.[77] A saltatory conclusion that can be taken from the Indian Rules is that while it protects confidentiality, there is the ability for the parties to consent (agree) on what evidence can be disclosed. Despite this, it is difficult to comprehend that a party would self-incriminate by consenting to the disclosure of money laundering. It is argued that the tribunal would continue to be bound by confidentiality.

The EU has no specific arbitration decision, directive or regulation governing commercial disputes. It does however have a dispute resolution directive that addresses confidentiality in arbitration.[78] The EU has left the regulation of ICA to its member states. Slovenia's Arbitration Law (2008) was modelled on the 2006 UNCITRAL Model Law and enacted shortly after Slovenia's accession to the EU.[79] Article 1 (1) of the Slovenian Arbitration law provides that an arbitration is considered as being domestic if the seat is in Slovenia, irrespective of the nationality of the parties to proceedings (or the country of incorporation of legal persons). Article 1(2) provides further than an arbitration is considered foreign (or as international) if its seat is abroad. Article 1(3) adds that, until the seat of arbitration has been determined, Slovenian courts have jurisdiction to decide matters referred to in Article 9

---

[76] Article 26.2 Australian Centre for International Arbitration (ACICA).

[77] Article 29, Indian Council of Arbitration, Rules of International Commercial Arbitration.

[78] Directive 2013/11/EU of the European Parliament and of the Council of 21 May 2013 on alternative dispute resolution for consumer disputes and amending Regulation (EC) No 2006/2004 and Directive 2009/22/EC (Directive on consumer ADR), OJ L 165. (29) Confidentiality and privacy should be respected at all times during the ADR procedure. Member States should be encouraged to protect the confidentiality of ADR procedures in any subsequent civil or commercial judicial proceedings or arbitration.

[79] Law on Employment and Social Courts (Official Gazette of the Republic of Slovenia no. 2/04 and 10/04), art 11; Law on Employment Relations (Official Gazette of the Republic of Slovenia, nos. 42/02, 79/06, 46/07 and 103/07), art 205(3); Law on Electronic Commerce (Official Gazette of the Republic of Slovenia no. 61/06), art 19(3); Law on Collective Bargaining (Official Gazette of the Republic of Slovenia no. 43/06), art 20(5); and Law on the Participation of Employees in Management (Official Gazette of the Republic of Slovenia no. 42/07), art 105.

provided that one of the parties has its permanent or temporary residence in the Republic of Slovenia.[80]

The divergence in national laws governing arbitration has eroded the general principles that traditionally regulated confidentiality, undermining its global attractiveness.[81] Yet, confidentiality in international arbitration has long been the subject of debate[82] including uncertainty over to its scope and enforceability.[83] As the number of applicable jurisdictions, including international arbitration institutions, have grown among the laws, rules, and standards by which confidentiality is applied to arbitration, the attraction for arbitration has abated. Such divergence over the nature and application of arbitration laws are accentuated by the different expectations of parties over the scope of their obligations to maintain confidentiality and how to comply with and enforce them.[84] In contrast, arbitrators, counsel, and parties have devised inventive ways in which to preserve confidentiality in arbitration proceedings, consistent with fairness and equality between the parties.[85] Confidentiality is also conceived as encouraging efficient and dispassionate dispute resolution; marginalising emotive 'trial by press release'; and reducing the risks of damaging disclosure of commercially sensitive information to competitors, customers and others.[86]

Centrally, it is noted how parties to transnational arbitration encourage threats to confidentiality at two stages of proceedings: first, in presenting evidence in support of their cases; and second, when being requested to produce evidence by their opponent.[87] On that basis, confidentiality can be categorised into four groups: (1) the redaction of confidential information; (2) restricted access to confidential information, including materials submitted by the parties; (3) prohibiting the use of confidential data by third parties; and (4) adopting specific measures to protect the confidentiality of testimony.[88] In adopting this approach, the extent of confidentiality in ICA will also be subject to the tribunal that includes, but is not limited to, evidence adduced before, during, and after proceedings; the preparation and communication of the award, and other information the parties agree to treat as confidential. There may be circumstances where the parties agreed not to treat information and evidence as confidential. Should this arise in a proceeding where money laundering is detected, there could be ability for the arbitrator to report such a matter. Even so, this would need to be treated with caution. Taking such an approach is likely to invoke the public interest test, and the courts are likely to address such a disclosure if challenged.

---

[80] Articles 1 and 9.

[81] Articles 1 and 9.

[82] See de Ly et al. (2012), p. 355.

[83] See Born (2009), p. 2499.

[84] See Born (2009), p. 2499.

[85] See Born (2009), p. 2499.

[86] See Born (2009), p. 2251.

[87] Baizeau and Richard (2016), p. 54.

[88] Baizeau and Richard (2016), p. 54.

In *Esso Australia Resources Ltd v The Honourable Sidney James Plowman and others*,[89] the High Court of Australia concluded that confidentiality was not an essential attribute of a private arbitration. Specifically, it held that the requirement to conduct proceedings in camera did not translate into an obligation prohibiting disclosure of documents and information provided in, and for the purpose of, the arbitration. Thus, the disclosure of documents is likely to be evidence that is important to evaluating the arbitral dispute. The Court then concluded that, although a certain degree of confidentiality might arise, it was not absolute. Ultimately and in turning to the public interest test, the Court concluded that, 'the public's legitimate interest in obtaining information about the affairs of public authorities' prevailed.'[90] On the other hand, in *Cockatoo Dockyard Pty Ltd*,[91] the Australian Court decided that an arbitrator had no power to make a procedural direction imposing an obligation of confidentiality that would have had the effect of preventing the government from disclosing to a state agency, or to the public, information and documents generated in the course of the arbitration that ought to be made known to that authority or to the public. The Court elaborated on the public health and environmental issues arising in its judgement:

> Whilst private arbitration will often have the advantage of securing for the parties a high level of confidentiality for their dealing, where one of those parties is a government, or an organ of government, neither the arbitral agreement nor the general procedural powers of the arbitrator will extend so far as to stamp on the governmental litigant a regime of confidentiality or secrecy which effectively destroys or limits the general governmental duty to pursue the public interest.[92]

Viewed this way, the Australian courts have adopted the approach that where it is in the public interest for confidentiality to no longer apply, it may be dispensed with[93] and certain information may be disclosed. While this is a brief illustration of how Australia would deal with the issue of confidentiality, most noteworthy is how the courts will invoke the 'legitimate interest' test in relation to the disclosure of evidence. Even though an arbitration in Australia applying the ACICA rules allow for the consent of the parties for the disclosure of information, the principles of confidentiality would continue to apply. Therefore, the parties are unlikely to consent to the release of evidence that confirms money laundering. The arbitrator continues to be bound by the principles and rules of confidentiality.

In the UK case of 1977 *Ali Shipping*,[94] the Court pointed how the English law has recognised the following exceptions to the broad rule of confidentiality:

> (i) Consent where disclosure is made with the express or implied consent of the party who originally produced the material; (ii) order of the Court, an obvious example of which is an

[89] [1995] 193 CLR 10.

[90] [1995] 193 CLR 10.

[91] *Commonwealth of Australia v Cockatoo Dockyard Pty Ltd* [1995] 36 NSWLR 662.

[92] *Commonwealth of Australia v Cockatoo Dockyard Pty Ltd* [1995] 36 NSWLR 662. para 682.

[93] Ibid.

[94] *Ali Shipping Corporation v Shipyard Trogir* [1997] APP.L.R. 12/19.

> order for disclosure of documents generated by an arbitration for the purposes of a later court action; (iii) leave of the court. It is the practical scope of this exception, the grounds on which such leave will be granted, which gives rise to difficulty. However, on the analogy of the implied obligation of secrecy between banker and customer, leave will be given in respect of (iv) disclosure when, and to the extent to which, it is reasonably necessary for the protection of the legitimate interests of an arbitrating party.[95]

While this historical case is nearly 50 years old, it arguably laid the foundations of where there is consent between the parties (the parties agree) to produce material (evidence), confidentiality can be dispensed with. Even though here is no specific mention of the public interest, it could be argued that it could be derived from the terms legitimate interest. Therefore, a legitimate interest could be in circumstances that involve money laundering that the information no longer has confidentiality attached. Problematically though, what is obvious is how that a level of consent is required by the parties to dispense with confidentiality and allow for the disclosure of information. This alone would pose a significant challenge to the parties and arbitrator/s, because upon disclosure to or by the parties or money laundering, the arbitrators would effectively require a level of consent to disclose the information to the relevant authorities. This is, and unless, as part of the procedural steps upon commencing arbitration, the arbitrator has clearly established agreement between the parties that any evidence presented that constitutes a criminal or other offence there is an obligation to report.

In the United States, confidentiality arises in disclosing materials introduced its arbitral proceedings' such as in discovery.[96] United States' law generally restricts the scope of confidentiality, and sometimes admit the production of submissions, evidence, and transcripts from arbitration proceedings, without addressing either express provisions for confidentiality in the agreement of the parties, nor implied obligations of confidentiality under the law of the arbitral seat.[97] In the case of *Lawrence*[98] the plaintiff subpoenaed all arbitration documents from a third party relating to an earlier, separate arbitration, against the Respondent, Household. This would amount to a substantial body of evidence. Yet, the arbitral proceeding itself included a blanket confidentiality agreement which was endorsed by the arbitrator.[99] The third party was willing to produce the subpoenaed documents while not wishing to violate the confidentiality order. Household moved to quash the subpoena. The Court refused to reach what it viewed as the novel issue of whether it had authority to countermand the arbitrator's order. It stayed the discovery against the third-party and required the parties to address the discovery issues in the underlying action. Given that the material sought through discovery had already been adduced,

---

[95] *Ali Shipping Corporation v Shipyard Trogir* [1997] APP.L.R. 12/19. para 36.

[96] Born (2014), ch 20, pp. 2790–2796.

[97] Born (2014), ch 20, pp. 2790–2796.

[98] *Lawrence E Jaffe Pension Plan v Household Int'l Inc* [2004] WL 1821968 (D Colo 2004).

[99] *Lawrence E Jaffe Pension Plan v Household Int'l Inc* [2004] WL 1821968 (D Colo 2004).

the Court made no further ruling.[100] This case demonstrates how when there is agreement on the level of confidentiality between the parties, the court allow for continued discovery of documents that amounted to important evidence. In the 2023 case of *Eletson*[101] noted that "confidential documents obtained in an arbitration are appropriately sealed when a petition to confirm an arbitral award has become moot and the purpose of counsel in placing the documents in a court file was not to obtain satisfaction of the award but to 'evade the confidentiality provision to which the plaintiff agreed in the arbitration agreement' and to use the documents in other proceedings".[102] Importantly, the Court, while not specifying a public policy test, went onto highlight that a level of caution will be undertaken when parties are attempting to 'force the disclosure of otherwise-confidential materials',[103] which is contrary to the rules of confidentiality. Rather, the court relied on the concept of 'improper purpose' of the use of documents-evidence, where that evidence is confidential.

The Singapore International Commercial Court in the case of *CZT*[104] in 2023, made the point that 'it is also common ground that the protection of the confidentiality of deliberations is not absolute but is subject to exceptions.' However, the Court applied the test of in the interest of justice, for the production of evidence—being documents. The Court stated that interests of justice in ordering production of the records of deliberations outweigh the policy reasons for the protection of the confidentiality of deliberations.[105] What has emerged is that each jurisdiction has applied a public policy test, which applies different terminology. The use of legitimate interests and the interest of justice are being used in similar manner by the courts to apply the public policy test for the production and disclosure of evidence. This could extend to any documents or evidence that confirms a level of money laundering activity. However, when weighed against the laws and rules of arbitration, the arbitral tribunal remains substantially bound by the obligation of confidentiality.

In reaffirming the above, and according to the FATF 40 recommendations, certain legal professionals are obliged to report reasonable suspicions of money laundering.[106] Moreover, under the 40 Recommendations it clearly states that:

> Lawyers, notaries, other independent legal professionals, and accountants acting as independent legal professionals, are not required to report their suspicions if the relevant information was obtained in circumstances where they are subject to professional secrecy or legal professional privilege.[107]

---

[100] *Lawrence E Jaffe Pension Plan v Household Int'l Inc* [2004] WL 1821968 (D Colo 2004).

[101] *Eletson Holdings, Inc v Levona Holdings Ltd*, No 23, cv, 7331, LJL.

[102] *Eletson Holdings, Inc v Levona Holdings Ltd*, No 23, cv, 7331, LJL.

[103] *Eletson Holdings, Inc v Levona Holdings Ltd*, No 23, cv, 7331, LJL.

[104] *CZT v CZU*, https://www.elitigation.sg/gd/sic/2023_SGHCI_11.

[105] *CZT v CZU*, para 80.

[106] Financial Action Task Force Recommendations 20 and 23(a) of the FATF 40 Recommendations.

[107] Ibid, p. 8.

In taking the literal and purposive approach to the interpretation of the above, it can be argued that an arbitrator and/or tribunal would not be required under the FATF standards, which are not rules, to report ML activity, if detected. Of note though is that these are only standards and are not rules or law. Applicable domestic law that responds to the standards may however create such obligations.

4 Conclusion

This chapter has examined and demonstrated the developments in technology and how it can be used in transnational arbitration. The chapter further highlighted how money laundering in arbitration is a highly complex issue, when evaluated against the long standing and well settled principle of confidentiality. To date, the jurisdictional arbitration laws compared in this chapter and selected arbitration institutional rules do not provide a clear pathway forward for how an arbitrator or tribunal is to deal with money laundering, should it be detected within and arbitral proceeding.

ICA has become an important feature of resolving commercial disputes, based on party autonomy. However, there are conflicts that do arise when criminal matters have been detected within an arbitral proceeding. It places the tribunal and arbitrator in a position that has to be finely balanced with the long-standing substantive law and procedural rules, such as, confidentiality. This is because an arbitration proceeding is not a court case and the rules within the courts do not necessarily apply to an arbitration.

The rules of evidence generally applied in arbitration will be the rule of the seat, choice of law, and/or determined by the tribunal. This has been reaffirmed by the courts, that 'parties' allow the tribunal to determine evidence's relevance according to evidentiary rules'.[108] In *BQP*, the Court stated that:

> the parties appeared to take the admissibility of the pre-contractual negotiations for granted during the proceedings before the Tribunal. The Defendant points out that: (i) the Plaintiff had never objected to the admissibility of evidence of the negotiating history of the agreements, and (ii) the Plaintiff had *itself* relied on such evidence to advance its case.[109]

While the rules of evidence are generally settled in arbitration, they will be impacted from the application and use of technology. This will vary from AI, blockchain, quantum, and cybersecurity. First, there will be the evidence that these technologies provide. Second is the evidence that the technology can collect, store, and secure. It has been highlighted, for example, that:

> …blockchain evidence provides proof of transactions carried out within the system itself. The transaction can be proved through a blockchain receipt, as it is tracked, validated, registered and time-stamped in the chain through a hash. If admissible, it would be a verified

[108] *BQP v BQQ* [2018] SGHC 55, para 127 https://www.elitigation.sg/gd/s/2018_SGHC_55

[109] *BQP v BQQ* [2018] SGHC 55, para 98.

proof of the time, place and nature of the transaction; and as an authentication system for information produced outside the blockchain.[110]

However, AI can be used to collate, review, analyse, and locate critical evidence within documents and documents. Moreover, cybersecurity can be used to protect evidence and also provide a level of evidence that there was an intrusion, and that the impact was to the party from that intrusion.

Notwithstanding the above, any evidence of money laundering activities will need to be weighed against the principles of confidentiality in arbitration. This principle has been a long standing and is well grounded in the substantive laws and procedural rules of arbitration. Even though there has been considerable discussion and writing on the topic, the courts continue to support the principle and ensure that only under specific circumstances such as in the public interest or legitimate interest that it should be dispensed with. It is also arguable whether parties would consent to an arbitrator or tribunal in disclosing money laundering evidence. This would be a form of self-incrimination. Therefore, it can be ruled out.

Despite the law and rules on confidentiality being restricted by an arbitration agreement, or the law and arbitration rules, it can be expressly or implied. What has emerged is how the courts will apply a general test of legitimate interest in determining how far, and if, any exceptions would or could be applied to the disclosure of evidence in arbitration. It is argued that there exists a level of protection to specific legal professionals such as arbitrators under the international finance rules that there is no actual requirement to report suspicious information, where the professional is subject to professional secrecy. By applying this to arbitration, it is argued that an arbitration through the rules on confidentiality meets the requirements of professional secrecy. This protects the arbitrators and/or tribunal from any obligation to report any criminal activity.

References

Álvarez O, Vidal O, and Vallespinós L (2022) 'Unlocking Blockchain Evidence in International Arbitration'. 2022 Spain Arbitration Review, Revista del Club Español del Arbitraje 19, Wolters Kluwer España.

Al Fatyri L (2024) AI in international arbitration: what is the big deal? https://aria.law.columbia.edu/ai-in-international-arbitration-what-is-the-big-deal/?cn-reloaded=1#:~:text=In%20international%20arbitration%2C%20AI%20tools,in%20making%20more%20informed%20decisions

Baizeau B, Richard J (2016) Addressing the issue of confidentiality in arbitration proceedings: how is this done in practice? In: Geisinger E (ed) Confidential and restricted access information in international arbitration (ASA special series no. 43). JurisNet, LLC, p 54

Bertrand A, Maxwell W, Vamparys X (2021) Do AI-based anti-money laundering (AML) systems violate European fundamental rights? Int Data Priv Law 11(3):276–293. https://doi.org/10.1093/idpl/ipab010

[110] Álvarez et al. (2022).

Born G (2014) International commercial arbitration, vol I–III, 2nd edn. Kluwer Law International. E-book, accessed through Kluwer Arbitration online database. http://www.kluwerarbitration.com/. in Christoffer Coello Hedberg. International Commercial Arbitration and Money Laundering. https://www.diva-portal.org/smash/get/diva2:948822/FULLTEXT01.pdf

Born G (2016) International arbitration law and practice. Kluwer Law, pp 13–14

Born G, Miles W (2015) Global trends in international arbitration. https://biblioteca.cejamericas.org/bitstream/handle/2015/812/Global-Trends-in-International-Arbitration.pdf?sequence=1&isAllowed=y

Born GB (2009) International Commercial Arbitration, Kluwer

Born GB (2020) International Commercial Arbitration (Kluwer Law International 2020)

Born GB (2022) International Commercial Arbitration, 3rd edition, Kluwer Law International; Kluwer Law International

Brynjolfsson E, McAfee A (2017) What's driving the machine learning explosion. Harvard Business Review

Dargan J (2020) How a quantum arbitration tool plans to change the practice of law. https://thequantuminsider.com/2020/07/21/how-a-quantum-arbitration-tool-plans-to-change-the-practice-of-law/

De Filippi P, Mannan M, Reijers W (2022) The alegality of blockchain technology. Polic Soc 41(3):358–372. https://doi.org/10.1093/polsoc/puac006

Domashova J, Mikhailina N (2021) Usage of machine learning methods for early detection of money laundering schemes. Procedia Comput Sci 190:184–185. https://doi.org/10.1016/j.procs.2021.06.033

Duarte M (2019) Essential tips on cybersecurity for arbitrators: identify, protect, detect, respond and recover. https://legalblogs.wolterskluwer.com/arbitration-blog/essential-tips-on-cybersecurity-for-arbitrators-identify-protect-detect-respond-and-recover/

FATF (2018) Guidance on Counter Proliferation Financing – The Implementation of Financial Provisions of United Nations Security Council Resolutions to Counter the Proliferation of Weapons of Mass Destruction, FATF, Paris, p 12, https://www.fatf-gafi.org/content/dam/fatf-gafi/guidance/Guidance-Countering-Proliferation-Financing.pdf.coredownload.pdf

Federal Deposit Insurance Corporation (2024). https://www.fdic.gov/banker-resource-center/anti-money-launderingcountering-financing-terrorismamlcft#:~:text=The%20Anti%2DMoney%20Laundering%20Act,laundering%20and%20the%20financing%20of Can quantum computing break tradition encryption: What the experts say? December 2024, https://sptel.com/quantum-computing-breaking-encryption/

Fortinet (2024) Cyberthreat predictions for 2024: an annual perspective from FortiGuard Labs

Geisinger E, Ducret P (2018) The uncomfortable truth: once discovered what to do with it. In: The search for "truth" in arbitration: is finding the truth what dispute resolution is about? JurisNet, LLC, pp 113–114

Goldsmith P (2023) Confidentiality in arbitral proceedings: an Indian perspective. https://www.mondaq.com/india/arbitration-dispute-resolution/1353704/confidentiality-in-arbitral-proceedings-an-indian-perspective

Khanna J (2021) Confidentiality under the Indian arbitration regime. In: Indian arbitration law review, vol 3, pp 80–93

Klusch M, Lässig J, Müssig D et al (2024) Quantum artificial intelligence: a brief survey. Künstl Intell. https://doi.org/10.1007/s13218-024-00871-8

de Ly F, Friedman M, Radicati di Brozolo L (2012) International Law Association International Commercial Arbitration Committee's report and recommendations on 'confidentiality in international commercial arbitration'. 28(3):355–396. https://academic.oup.com/arbitration/article-abstract/28/3/355/196598

McCarthy J (2023) The regulation of RegTech and SupTech in finance: ensuring consistency in principle and in practice. J Financ Regul Compliance 31(2):186–199

McDougall A (2005) International arbitration and money laundering. Am Univ Int Law Rev 20(5):1021–1054

Menz M (2024) The pros and cons of generative AI in AML compliance. https://www.int-comp.org/insight/the-pros-and-cons-of-generative-ai-in-aml-compliance/

Mills T, Shanker S (2024) New frontiers: regulating artificial intelligence in international arbitration. https://www.nortonrosefulbright.com/en/knowledge/publications/3cb82b55/new-frontiers-regulating-artificial-intelligence-in-international-arbitration

O'Neill P (2022) Transformative technology and arbitration's emerging future. Am Rev Int Arbitr 32(3) https://aria.law.columbia.edu/issues/32-3/transformative-technology-and-arbitrations-emerging-future-vol-32-no-3/

Pavlidis G (2023) Deploying artificial intelligence for anti-money laundering and asset recovery: the dawn of a new era. J Money Laund Control 26(7):155–166

Polas M, Jahanshahi A, Kabir A, Saleh Md A, Uz-Zaman S, Osman A, Karim R (2022) Artificial intelligence, blockchain technology, and risk-taking behavior in the 4.0IR metaverse era: evidence from bangladesh-based SMEs. J Open Innov Technol Market Complex 8(3):168. https://doi.org/10.3390/joitmc8030168

Redfern A, Hunter M (1986) Law and practice of international commercial arbitration. Oxford University Press

Redfern A and Hunter M (2004) Law and Practice of International Commercial Arbitration (Sweet & Maxwell 4th ed.)

Teichmann F, Boticiu S, Sergi B (2023) Compliance issues in arbitration proceedings–bribery, money laundering and other abuses. J Financ Crime 31(3):759–767

Thommandru A, Chakka B (2023) Recalibrating the banking sector with blockchain technology for effective anti-money laundering compliances by banks. Sustain Futures 5:100107. https://doi.org/10.1016/j.sftr.2023.100107

Tiwari M (2025) Network analytics and generative artificial intelligence: a hybrid approach to money laundering detection. In: Goldbarsht D, de Koker L, Ferrill J (eds) The financial war on crime and terrorism: opportunities and challenges. Springer, Cham

UN (1988) United Nations convention against illicit traffic in narcotic drugs and psychotropic substances

Walters R and Rajwanshi H (2023) Reconciling "Confidentiality" in Data Protection, Cyber Security, Artificial Intelligence in International Arbitration, Yearbook od Privat International Law, De Gruyter 2023.

Dr. Robert Walters is an Associate Professor Law and Director Technology Law and Legal Research, Victoria University-Australia, Adjunct Professor European Faculty of Law, Advisor Corporate Insolvency Centre Gujarat National Law University, India, Honorary Lecturer Liverpool Law School, United Kingdom, Adjunct Research Fellow University Western Australia. Dr. Walters is a practicing Solicitor and International Arbitrator, holding an LLB (Victoria), MPPM (Monash), PhD Law (Victoria), and been engaged by national governments to address commercial and private law matters across the digital economy.

The Impact of the Financial Action Task Force (FATF) Standards and Focus: From Effectiveness to Effect

Nicholas Morris and Louis de Koker

Abstract The Financial Action Task Force (FATF) is the global intergovernmental standard-setting body for anti-money laundering and the combating of terrorist and proliferation financing (AML/CFT/CPF). More than 200 jurisdictions globally are committed to complying with its standards. They are subject to peer-based evaluation of the quality of their compliance and to black- and grey-listing, with accompanying negative economic impact, when their systems are found wanting. This has placed considerable burden on smaller, less-developed, countries. The FATF reformed its greylisting processes in 2024 to provide some protection for smaller economies in the fifth round of mutual evaluations, with increased focus on larger economies.

This chapter considers the time and attention that the FATF has focused to date on smaller economies compared to larger economies and whether there is evidence of positive crime-combating and governance benefits resulting from the attention. Applying a FATF Activity Score, it finds that the FATF has focused extensively on lower-middle income countries while devoting the least time to the rich countries that generally hold and process the largest share of global illicit funds. The chapter also considers whether there are correlations between the FATF's activity and focus and higher governance and crime-combating levels in a country. The study finds little correlation between FATF-related activities aimed at raising country compliance levels, the country's FATF effectiveness scores, and positive governance and crime prevention outcomes of the country. The FATF activity and pressure to date has resulted mostly in higher levels of technical compliance with the FATF standards. This is out of proportion with other key indicators and development factors for smaller economies, resulting in a 'rhino horn' effect in spider diagrams of key

N. Morris
La Trobe University, Melbourne, VIC, Australia

L. de Koker (✉)
La Trobe University and Financial Integrity Hub (FIH), Melbourne, VIC, Australia

University of the Western Cape, Belville, South Africa
e-mail: l.dekoker@latrobe.edu.au

D. Goldbarsht et al. (eds.), *The Financial War on Crime and Terrorism*, European Yearbook of International Economic Law,
https://doi.org/10.1007/978-3-032-06360-1_12

indicators, with high technical compliance levels that are not proportionately reflected by achievements in the related indicators.

The lack of impact may be due to incorrect assumptions that compliance with the FATF standards would lead to such positive outcomes. Poor implementation of laws and structures could, however, explain in part the lack of clear correlation with positive governance and crime prevention outcomes. Unfortunately, effective implementation may not improve for low-income countries during the new round of mutual evaluations. Lack of resources and capacity is often a key constraint in these economies and this is unlikely to change. A greater focus on effective implementation of the FATF standards by richer economies in FATF's fifth round of mutual evaluations commencing in 2025 may in fact deliver better overall governance and crime prevention outcomes. Political will is, however, a key constraint in these economies, and this constraint may become more challenging in the current period of geopolitical fragmentation and repositioning.

1 Introduction: The Role of FATF

The Financial Action Task Force (FATF), the global intergovernmental standard-setting body for anti-money laundering and the combating of terrorist and proliferation financing (AML/CFT/CPF), plays a crucial standard-setting role in combating money laundering and terrorist and proliferation financing (ML/TF/PF). Over 200 jurisdictions worldwide have committed to adhering to the FATF Recommendations.[1]

The FATF itself is a relatively small body. It has a global network of 40 members (38 countries and two regional organizations, the European Commission and the Gulf Cooperation Council (GCC)) and a secretariat housed by the OECD in Paris.[2]

The FATF membership is limited to strategically-important countries. This has skewed its membership towards the Global North. Since 2000, however, the FATF engaged in a limited expansion of FATF membership to include a small number of strategically important countries that would enhance the FATF's geographic balance.[3] Malaysia (2016), Israel (2018) Saudi-Arabia (2019) and Indonesia (2023) are countries that have been allowed to join during the past few years. The FATF manages its lack of wider international representation through the global network of FATF-Style Regional Bodies (FSRBs). FSRBs enjoy associate membership of the FATF, providing their non-FATF members with an indirect voice into the global standard-setting process, and a role in the FSRB's compliance and effectiveness assessment processes.

The FATF sets AML/CFT/CPF standards and provides guidance on their interpretation and implementation. While the FATF standards themselves lack legal

[1] FATF (2024a).

[2] FATF (2024a).

[3] FATF (2000), par 18; FATF (2014), p. 4.

force, they have shaped national laws and institutional practices by leveraging economic pressure, mainly through FATF's mutual evaluation and grey- and black-listing processes.

All this effort has cost a significant amount, both for the organisations and for the countries involved. A 2023 LexisNexis Risk Solutions study estimated that annual financial crime compliance costs to financial institutions globally amounted to US$ 206 billion.[4] The additional cost impact of these measures on customers has not been calculated. The FATF also recognises that 'unintended consequences' are linked to the implementation of its standards including impacts on access to financial services for vulnerable populations, loss of correspondent banking, difficulties with inter-country remittances, and abuse of AML/CFT/CPF measures by governments to suppress civil society.[5] There is also evidence that FATF listings adversely impact GDP growth rates, bank non-performing loans, and official aid flows.[6] Concerns have also been expressed that these listings have historically been focused on smaller, non-white, poorer jurisdictions that are not FATF members.[7]

The FATF standards therefore impose costs and their implementation may hold unintended negative consequences. They are however advancing important crime combating objectives. Are these objectives being achieved or at least achieved at a rate that justifies the costs? This is the question considered in this chapter.

2 The FATF and the Effectiveness of Its Standards

The FATF was first established by the G7 in 1989. In the first two decades of its operation and standards, discussions around FATF mostly focused on their effectiveness as a standard-setter. This was measured by the number of countries that made political commitments to implement the standards.[8]

The FATF and its associated FRSBs evaluate country compliance with the FATF standards in terms of a mutual evaluation methodology, first adopted in 2004.[9] This methodology was amended in 2022 and updated in 2024 for the fifth round of mutual evaluations commencing in 2024.[10] Mutual evaluations, which can be conducted by the FATF, the FSRBs, the IMF or the World Bank, employ a standard assessment methodology.

Mutual assessment processes result in the publication of a 'Mutual Evaluation Report' (MER) and, where compliance levels are not satisfactory or where

---

[4] LexisNexis Risk Solutions (2023), p. 9; De Koker and Goldbarsht (2024).

[5] FATF (2021); D'Hulster et al. (2023); Van Broekhoven (2020).

[6] de Koker et al. (2023).

[7] Littrell (2024).

[8] de Koker and Turkington (2015).

[9] Kyriakos-Saad (2005).

[10] FATF (2024b).

compliance improvements are monitored or reported for re-rating of the MER outcomes, also in further 'Follow-up Reports' (FURs). Where countries fail to make sufficient progress to address strategic deficiencies in their compliance levels, they may be "greylisted" by the FATF and, where the political will to comply is absent, also "blacklisted". These listings may impact negatively on such countries. Greylisting normally results in fast-tracked country action to improve compliance levels in order to be "delisted".[11]

In the past, the mutual evaluation methodology focused on country compliance with the FATF standards. As the system became more mature, the FATF was prepared to address growing concerns that countries were merely ticking boxes by adopting laws but were not implementing them effectively. A new evaluation module was introduced in 2013 which focuses on the effectiveness of the country's AML/CFT/CPF system. The technical compliance component considers, for example, whether the required legal provisions were enacted, while the effectiveness component of the evaluation considers whether the legal provisions are operating effectively in practice.[12]

The effectiveness evaluation requires the assessors to exercise a judgement as to whether, and to what extent, specific outcomes are being achieved. The assessment is constructed around a hierarchy of defined outcomes. The High-Level Objective of implementing AML/CFT measures is defined as follows: 'Financial systems and the broader economy are protected from the threats of money laundering and the financing of terrorism and proliferation, thereby strengthening financial sector integrity and contributing to safety and security.'[13]

At the lowest level 11 Immediate Outcomes (IOs) are identified. These in turn are clustered into three Intermediate Outcomes that, collectively, should result in the High-Level Objective (FATF 2024b, par. 51):

1. Policy, coordination and cooperation mitigate the money laundering and financing of terrorism risks (IO 1 and 2).
2. Proceeds of crime and funds in support of terrorism are prevented from entering the financial and other sectors or are detected and reported by these sectors (IO 3, 4 and 5).
3. Money laundering threats are detected and disrupted, and criminals are sanctioned and deprived of illicit proceeds. Terrorist financing threats are detected and disrupted, terrorists are deprived of resources, and those who finance terrorism are sanctioned, thereby contributing to the prevention of terrorist acts (IO 6-11)

Neither the High-Level Objective nor the Intermediate Outcomes are directly assessed in the mutual evaluation processes but the extent to which they are met is assumed based on the outcomes of the assessments of the IOs. It is not clear how the

[11] de Koker et al. (2023).

[12] de Koker and Turkington (2015).

[13] FATF (2024b), par. 51.

outcomes for different IOs clustered in relation to a single Intermediate Outcome are weighted or how strongly the Intermediate Outcomes contribute to the High-Level Objectives.

The actual effectiveness assessment therefore focuses primarily on the extent to which a country meets 11 specified Immediate Outcomes, as listed below. In essence, countries that meet these Immediate Outcomes are assumed to meet the three Intermediate Outcomes and, in turn, the High-Level Outcome as well:[14]

1. Money laundering and terrorist financing risks are understood and, where appropriate, actions coordinated domestically to combat money laundering and the financing of terrorism and proliferation.
2. International cooperation delivers appropriate information, financial intelligence, and evidence, and facilitates action against criminals and their assets.
3. Supervisors appropriately supervise, monitor and regulate financial institutions, DNFBPs, and VASPs for compliance with AML/CFT requirements commensurate with their risks.
4. Financial institutions, DNFBPs, and VASPs adequately apply AML/CFT preventive measures commensurate with their risks, and report suspicious transactions.
5. Legal persons and arrangements are prevented from misuse for money laundering or terrorist financing, and information on their beneficial ownership is available to competent authorities without impediments.
6. Financial intelligence and all other relevant information are appropriately used by competent authorities for money laundering and terrorist financing investigations.
7. Money laundering offences and activities are investigated and offenders are prosecuted and subject to effective, proportionate and dissuasive sanctions.
8. Proceeds and instrumentalities of crime are confiscated.
9. Terrorist financing offences and activities are investigated and persons who finance terrorism are prosecuted and subject to effective, proportionate and dissuasive sanctions.
10. Terrorists, terrorist organisations, and terrorist financiers are prevented from raising, moving and using funds, and from abusing the NPO sector.
11. Persons and entities involved in the proliferation of weapons of mass destruction are prevented from raising, moving, and using funds, consistent with the relevant UNSCRs.

The methodology requires assessors to consider all 11 IOs and also to examine in greater detail those linked to the higher risk issues and factors identified by the assessment team.[15] For each IO, the methodology provides the characteristics of an effective system, as well as core issues to be considered by the assessors and examples of information or data to be considered to support the conclusions relating to

[14] FATF (2024b), par. 51.

[15] FATF (2024b), par. 52.

the core issues.[16] While the methodology provides a measure of consistency in the assessment approach, much depends on the country risk factors identified by the assessment team. The methodology also provides assessors a measure of flexibility, e.g. to vary the degree of detail with which they examine each core issue to reflect the degree of risk and materiality associated with that issue in the country and even, in exceptional circumstances, to consider additional issues which they identify as core to the effectiveness outcome.[17]

As pointed out above, it is uncertain how these IO-effectiveness building blocks support the Intermediate Outcomes and ensure that the High-Level Objective is achieved. The effectiveness outcomes were identified more than two decades after the key standards were adopted. The linkages between the IOs themselves and between the IOs, the Intermediate Outcomes, and the High-Level Objective are not clear. The weight of the contribution of each to the High-Level Objective is uncertain too. The attempt to retro-fit objectives and outcomes on the existing standards framework may furthermore have left some gaps and ignored other factors in the framework itself. The original standards themselves were not formulated after a robust and objective evidence-based analysis of the impact that they would have on crime, and this lends a further element of uncertainty regarding the crime combating impact of FATF compliance.

A 2015 analysis pointed out that the FATF standards have not been formulated to appropriately protect "the broader economy" and that the exclusionary effects of AML/CFT/CPF controls that may serve to strengthen financial sector integrity, may not contribute to safety and security when it displaces criminal activity into the informal economy.[18] A 2016 paper held that the design of the effectiveness assessment weakened the usefulness of the assessment outcomes when answering the question whether the strategy is effective in countering organised crime.[19] Pol, analysing criminal asset forfeiture and confiscation, has highlighted the limited effect of AML/CFT measures on money laundering and crime combating.[20]

It therefore seems possible that even if countries are held to be effective on all 11 Immediate Outcomes, the High-Level Objective of protection of its financial system and the broader economy against the threats of money laundering and the financing of terrorism and proliferation may still remain elusive.[21]

AML/CFT/CPF scholars are however not yet in a position to observe the effect when a country is rated as highly effective on all 11 IOs. The MERs produced during the so-called fourth round of mutual evaluations, that generally drew to a close in 2024, still do not point to particularly high levels of effectiveness as assessed in terms of the FATF's mutual evaluation methodology. In April 2022 the FATF

[16] FATF (2024b), par. 55–65.

[17] FATF (2024b), par 58.

[18] de Koker and Turkington (2015).

[19] de Koker and Turkington (2016), p. 216.

[20] Pol (2020).

[21] de Koker and Turkington (2016), p. 216.

published the *Report on the State of Effectiveness and Compliance with the FATF Standards*.[22] The report drew on data from 120 MERs that were completed by December 2021. While the report reflected high levels of technical compliance (85% and 73% respectively for FATF members and FSRB members), the average effectiveness ratings were much lower. FATF members scored 43%, and FSRB members only 14%.[23]

The averages mask individual country performance. Though there is much room for improvement, some countries perform significantly better than others on the effectiveness of their AML/CFT/CPF systems. Are these better performing countries safer and more secure as a result of their FATF performance, or, alternatively, are the lowest performing countries subject to higher levels of crime? Is there evidence that the high level of technical compliance and the current levels of effectiveness have resulted in improved governance and a lower crime threat in countries?

Littrell (2024) makes the point that while the FATF's technical compliance ratings are based upon detailed standards, the effectiveness ratings rely more on "the opinions of the international MER assessment team, and… adjustments… by the FATF secretariat and the FATF plenary."[24] Effectiveness scores are important in deciding which countries should be greylisted: "countries with poor effectiveness assessments will be grey listed even if they display perfect or near-perfect technical compliance".[25] So, the practical details of what is measured under effectiveness are important, especially for small and non-white countries.

The FATF's focus in the fifth round of mutual evaluations is more on larger economies. To ensure that the FATF gives assessment priority to countries with important financial sectors, it will now consider the relative size of a country's economy and financial sector as one of the key prioritisation criteria.[26] The greylisting processes of the FATF's International Co-operation Review Group (ICRG), the group overseeing the process of reviewing jurisdictions that may have deficiencies in AML/CFT, were also amended to ensure that it better targets the countries that pose the greatest risk to the international financial system.

A country will now be prioritised for active greylisting review if it meets one of the following indicators[27]:

(a) the country is an FATF member;
(b) the country is a high-income country based on data from the World Bank (excluding high-income countries with a financial sector of two or fewer banks); or.
(c) the country has broad money of more than 10 billion USD (or the equivalent in another currency).

[22] FATF (2022).

[23] FATF (2022), p. 11.

[24] Littrell (2024), p. 193.

[25] Littrell (2024), p. 201.

[26] FATF (2024c), par. 9.

[27] FATF (2024c), par. 154.

When a country has broad money more than 10 billion USD (or the equivalent in another currency) and is a Least Developed Country (LDC) based on data from the UN[28] the new procedures provide for two pathways:

(a) if the ICRG achieves consensus that the LDC does not present a significant ML/TF/PF risk, the LDC will be placed in the new ICRG pool where it will not be actively reviewed for greylisting but will be reviewed at least annually to consider whether it should be placed under active ICRG review;
(b) if the LDC is placed under active ICRG review, (1) it will have an observation period of 2 years to meet the FATF standards, unless, based on risk, the ICRG agrees that only 1 year should be allowed; and (2) appropriate progress reports should be provided.

This is an important policy shift. The FATF has, in the past, not differentiated this formally between non-compliant countries. In view of this change this chapter considers two broad questions: Firstly, has the focus of the FATF and FATF-related assessment and listing activities been on smaller or larger economies? Secondly, are there correlations between FATF-related activities, the size of a country's economy, the country's technical compliance levels with the FATF standards, its FATF effectiveness scores, and positive governance and crime prevention outcomes?

3 Methodology

To consider the impact of the FATF itself, this chapter takes the view that FATF impact includes the impact of the FATF and FSRB MERs and FURs on countries and institutions and the FATF black- and greylisting of countries but also goes beyond those. The standards inform a range of actions taken by a number of different stakeholders in relation to their countries and other countries, especially those that do not adequately comply with the standards. Such activities include the publication of higher risk third country lists, especially the EU and UK lists, and IMF and World Bank Reports on Observance of Standards and Codes (ROSC) which relate to FATF technical compliance and to effectiveness since 2013.

The authors therefore developed a 'FATF Activity Score' for all the countries covered by FATF and the FSRBs for the period 1998–2023.[29] In doing this, we have assembled and reviewed over 1600 MERs, FURs, ROSCs and other documents published by FATF, FRSBs, the IMF and other stakeholders. The FATF Activity Score therefore reflects the intensity of FATF compliance and effectiveness-related attention that a country received in a range of forms over across more than two

[28] FATF (2024c), par 154*bis*.

[29] Earlier reports were not always available but see for example reports reflected in the FATF (1998), part C.

decades, As we have noted in a previous article,[30] this attention will create signals, which may (or may not) affect market responses, including the behaviour of the banks.

We hypothesised that a high FATF Activity Score would be triggered by low levels of technical compliance and, since 2013, low effectiveness scores. Greylisted countries have strategic compliance deficiencies while blacklisted countries lack the political will to comply with the standards.[31] Good governance in these countries would therefore be under pressure and criminal activity would be high.

To consider whether there is evidence that higher FATF technical compliance ratings and/or higher FATF effectiveness levels result in improved governance outcomes and less criminality in a country, a range of data was considered, including measures of criminality, sustainability, informality and governance.

Criminality

If the FATF's intermediate outcomes and high-level objectives are achieved by a country, that success should reflect in enhanced resilience against criminality, especially organised crime, and in lower levels of such criminality. The *Global Organised Crime Index* of the Global Initiative Against Transnational Organized Crime (GI-TOC) reflects "criminality" scores for 193 jurisdictions (based on prevalence of criminal markets and the structure and influence of criminal actors) and "resilience" scores for each (reflecting the existence, capacity and effectiveness of country responses to organized crime based on 12 factors, including AML/CFT).[32] The Index was first published in 2021 (reflecting 2020 data) and the second edition was published in 2023 (reflecting 2022 data). This Index provided country scores for "criminality" (primarily organised crime) and "resilience" (against organised crime).

Sustainable Development Goals

If the FATF's intermediate outcomes and high-level objectives are achieved by a country, that success should be reflected in part in its achievement of the United Nation's Sustainable Development Goals. Effective measures against money laundering, and terrorist and proliferation financing, should result in improved flows of funds to the government and lower levels of corruption. This should enable a country to perform relatively better on the attainment of the SDGs compared to counterparts who are not performing as well on the FATF standards.

Many factors contribute to a country's SDG performance and the contribution of FATF-compliance in that regard may be too limited to be reflected in the general SDG data. The study therefore also considered specific performance on SDG 16—Peace, Justice and Strong Institutions. This SDG addresses the combating of crime and corruption, promotion of the rule of law, the reduction of illicit financial and arms flows, the strengthening of the recovery and return of stolen assets, the combating of all forms of organised crime, and the strengthening of relevant national

[30] See de Koker et al. (2023).

[31] de Koker et al. (2023).

[32] Global Initiative Against Transnational Organized Crime (2023).

institutions to prevent violence and combat terrorism and crime. If a country performs well on FATF technical compliance and effectiveness, it should also perform well on SDG 16 indicators. There should therefore be some correlation between the criminality and resilience scores of the *Global Organised Crime Index* and performance on SDG 16 indicators as they broadly consider the same subject matter. In assessing this, it is important to note that while both sets of indicators deal with justice and security, SDG 16 indicators are broader, covering human rights, governance, and institutional accountability, whereas the Global Organised Crime Index indicators are more crime-focused, analysing criminal networks and resilience strategies.

3.1 ILO Informal Employment

To explore the relationship between FATF activity and the extent of the informal economy, we used the International Labour Organization database on informal employment.[33] Where data on a particular country was not available, comparison was made to countries with similar GNI per capita and other characteristics. Small and mid-sized countries have the greatest informal employment share. In previous work, we have shown that informal employment share is detrimental for SDGs (those countries with highest informal share do least well relative to World average, especially mid-sized).[34]

3.2 World Bank Governance Indicators

The World Bank publishes governance indicators for most countries, reflecting: perceptions of the rule of law; control of corruption; stability and state of violence and terrorism; government effectiveness; and voice and accountability.[35] These are indicators that are closely associated with the FATF's IOs, Intermediate Objectives and High-Level Objective. Countries with higher levels of technical compliance and effectiveness should therefore score higher on these indicators than countries that do not perform as well on the standards.

The creation of these indicators is a complex process[36] and the indicators have been compiled since 1996. The aggregate indicators are based on several hundred individual underlying variables, and reflect the views of "survey respondents and

---

[33] International Labour Organization (2025).

[34] Morris et al. (2026).

[35] The data is available at https://www.worldbank.org/en/publication/worldwide-governance-indicators

[36] Described in Kaufman and Kraay (2024).

public, private, and NGO sector experts worldwide". Annex B provides a summary of their derivation.

3.3 Focus

Not all countries publish a full set of SDG and governance data. We have focused on 141 countries for which a reasonably complete set of data exists, the same set as used in a related chapter.[37]

3.4 Heatmap

Annex A provides a 'heatmap' which shows when various relevant activities occurred for each country, using colour-coding as shown in Fig. 1.

Based on the scores, the overall FATF Activity Score for a country is the sum of all identified FATF-related activities during the period 1998–2023. This is a simple, unweighted, measure—activities in any particular year score the same as in earlier or later years, and we have not had access to FATF and government expenditure data which would permit assessment of whether particular MERs and FURs were carried out more- or less- comprehensively for individual countries.

As the heatmap shows, less compliant countries have received a substantial amount of reported attention over the whole period for which some were fast-tracked, while more compliant countries may only have an MER and subsequent standard reporting to the FATF. It should be noted that these scores reflect activity which is reported in the public domain, but it is possible that other activities also occurred which were not reported publicly.

Figure 2 reflects the very large effort that has been put into seeking to get Iran, North Korea and Myanmar to comply with international norms over AML/CTF/CPF, as well as the considerable attention that has been given to countries like Pakistan, Trinidad and Tobago, the Philippines, Panama, Guyana, and Nigeria. In contrast, countries like Tonga, Solomon Islands, the Maldives, Timor-Leste, and Swaziland/Eswatini have received considerably less attention. Yemen and the Syrian Arab Republic also feature on the list of countries that received the most attention of the FATF. They have been languishing on the FATF greylist as they have been in the grips of conflict. In June 2014, the FATF determined that the countries had substantially addressed the concerns about their technical compliance levels. Due to the security situation in the country, the FATF has, however, been unable to conduct an on-site visit to confirm the improved compliance levels of these countries and hence it has not been able to implement processes to delist them.

[37] Morris et al. (2026).

Scoring for FATF actions			Score
Mutual Evaluation Report adopted	MER		15
Follow-up Report	FUR		5
MER+FUR same year	MER+FUR		17
Two (or more) FUR same year	FUR2		8
On 'watch list', greylisted, monitoring	L+		30
Listing+MER same year	L+MER		42
Listing+FUR(s) same year	L+FUR		34
Listing+MER+FUR(s) same year	L+MER+FUR		47
Black List	BL		65
IMF ROSC(s) completed	IMF		10
IMF + MER	IMF+MER		18
IMF + FUR(s)	IMF+FUR		12
IMF + FATF Listing	L+IMF		38
IMF + FATF Listing + MER	L+IMF+MER		51
EU Higher Risk Third Country Listing	EU		20
EU/UK + Black List	EU+BL		80
EU/UK + MER	EU+MER		32
EU/UK + FUR(s)	EU+FUR		23
EU/UK + FATF Listing	L+EU		45
EU/UK + FATF Listing + MER	L+EU+MER		52
EU/UK + FATF Listing + FUR(s)	L+EU+FUR		49
EU/UK + FATF Listing + IMF	L+EU+IMF		53
No FATF, EU or IMF Action	-		0

Fig. 1 Colour-coding and Scoring of FATF-related activities

4 Relating FATF Activity to Other Indicators

Figure 3 groups countries by GNI per capita, and by economic size, as measured by GDP. It also identifies the 21 "Least Developed Countries" in our sample.[38] The table shows that the most FATF and related activity in the period 1998–2023 has been applied to Lower-Middle-Income countries. In general, this has achieved >80% technical compliance (shown as "FATF Compliance"), although FATF effectiveness is still measured as low. Despite this attention, these countries have below-average achievement of SDGs, low resilience, and lower-than average prevention of criminality.

To create the "All SDGs" indicator in Fig. 3, we selected between one and six indicators for each of 13 SDGs which are relevant to the FATF analysis, and

[38] LDCs are defined by the United Nations Office of the High Representative for the Least Developed Countries, Landlocked Developing Countries, and Small Island Developing States (UN-OHRLLS) based on poverty, human resource weakness and economic vulnerability. See https://www.un.org/ohrlls/

Highest 20 by FATF Activity	Overall Score	Lowest 20 by FATF Activity	Overall Score
Iran, Islamic Republic of	1170	Central African Republic	40
Korea, Democratic People's Republic of	965	Chad	40
Myanmar	621	Cote d'Ivoire	40
Pakistan	544	Guinea	40
Uganda	490	Palau	40
Trinidad and Tobago	468	Swaziland/Eswatini	40
Philippines	455	Dominican Republic	38
Panama	416	Curacao	37
Guyana	387	Congo	35
Nigeria	384	Congo, the Democratic Republic of the	35
Indonesia	373	Tonga	35
Ethiopia	365	Virgin Islands, British	35
Syrian Arab Republic	361	Guernsey	30
Cambodia	357	Solomon Islands	30
Sri Lanka	355	Chinese Taipei	30
Zimbabwe	354	Maldives	25
Nicaragua	351	Timor-Leste	25
Türkiye	349	Jersey	20
Lao People's Democratic Republic	345	Comoros	18
Yemen	345	Equatorial Guinea	15

Fig. 2 Highest 20 and Lowest 20 of countries by FATF Activity Score 1998–2023

averaged to provide a single score for each SDG.[39] For example, SDG 16 is represented by indicators for violence, robbery and bribery. Our book chapter on the relationship between FATF regulations and SDGs goes into these patterns in more detail.[40]

We used the 'Organised Crime Index'[41] mentioned above to identify "criminality" scores for 193 jurisdictions (based on prevalence of criminal markets and the structure and influence of criminal actors) and "resilience" scores for each (reflecting the existence, capacity and effectiveness of country responses to organised crime based on 12 factors, including AML/CFT).[42] The latest version, used here, was published in 2023. An indicator for degree of informal employment has been developed by the International Labour Organization (ILO), published in ILOSTAT. These data have been enhanced for countries where data was not available by comparison to countries with similar GNI per capita and other characteristics.

Figure 3 highlights how poorer countries (with lower GNI per capita) and very small countries (with GDP less than US$3 billion) perform less well on both effectiveness and technical compliance with FATF requirements. They also have done less well with SDGs overall, and particularly with SDG 16. Low-income countries tend to have lower crime resilience, and correspondingly higher incidence of organised crime, and to have larger shares of employment in the informal sector.

---

[39] For details of this process, see the Annex to Morris et al. (2026).

[40] Morris et al. (2026).

[41] See https://ocindex.net/

[42] Where data is not available, the indicator was set to the average for those countries for which data is available.

Country Grouping	FATF Activity Score 1998-2022	FATF Effectiveness	FATF Compliance	All SDGs	SDG 16*	OCI Resilience	OCI Criminality	ILO Informal %	GNI per capita	GDP US$bn	No of countries covered
Low income - to US$1,036 GNI per capita	138.7	16%	78%	27%	36%	36%	54%	90%	726	24.5	14
Lower Middle Income - $1,037-$4,046	235.3	24%	83%	40%	40%	42%	54%	78%	2,430	104	32
Upper Middle Income - $4,046-$12,535	153.2	42%	87%	52%	49%	49%	52%	55%	7,305	816	31
Higher income - $12,536-$30,000	149.3	45%	90%	58%	58%	57%	44%	23%	20,333	174	28
Rich Countries - >$30,000	91.2	56%	92%	64%	68%	68%	43%	17%	63,754	1,506	36
Least Developed Countries	171.5	16%	78%	31%	36%	37%	54%	89%	1,083	25.7	21
Very small - <US$3bn GDP	107.8	27%	82%	50%	51%	48%	40%	42%	14,163	1.39	20
Small - $3-20bn	158.9	32%	89%	49%	53%	47%	48%	63%	24,608	12	33
Mid-sized - $20-100bn	197.7	35%	86%	48%	46%	49%	52%	52%	11,928	52	34
Large - $100-500bn	165.8	46%	90%	51%	54%	57%	51%	37%	25,242	305	30
Largest > $500bn	113.1	58%	90%	62%	61%	63%	53%	21%	38,545	3,196	24
All countries	**153.8**	**39%**	**87%**	**51%**	**52%**	**52%**	**49%**	**48%**	**22,545**	**624**	**141**

Fig. 3 FATF Activity Score and other indicators, for various country groupings. The indicator for SDG16 has been normalised to make it comparable to the ranges for other SDGs

4.1 World Bank Governance Indicators

The study also considered the correlations between the FATF Activity Score and the World Bank's governance indicators on perceptions of the rule of law; control of corruption; stability and state of violence and terrorism; government effectiveness; and voice and accountability.

Figure 4 reports the average of these governance indicators, normalised to a scale of 0–100%.[43]

4.2 Correlations Between FATF Activity Score and Selected Indicators

Figure 5 explores correlations (using Coefficients of Determination (CoD), which are also sometimes simply called 'R-squared') which measure what proportion of the variance in one series can be explained by the other) between the FATF Activity Score and outcomes for these various indicators in 2022. Such correlations do not prove causation, they are simply a measure of how far the final outcome in 2022 reflects, across the sample of countries, the country-specific activity of the FATF and related organisations.

Figure 5 explores the correlation between a variety of indicators of the outturn (2022) position of countries (with respect to a variety of development and governance indicators), and the FATF Activity Score for the period 1998-2022. The left hand column reports Coefficients of Determination (CoD): a low CoD indicates that there is little correlation between FATF activity during the 25-year period and the outcomes for

[43] The WB Governance indicators are provided by the World Bank on a scale of −2.5 to +2.5. We have normalized so that −2.5 becomes zero (worst) and +2.5 becomes 100% (best). An average score of below 50% means that that group of countries, on average, have below-average performance on the relevant indicator.

Country Grouping	FATF Activity Score 1998-2022	FATF Effectiveness	FATF Compliance	WB Rule of Law	WB Control Corruption	WB Regulatory Quality	WB Stability Violence Terrorism	WB Government Effectiveness	WB Voice and Accountability	GNI per capita	GDP US$bn	No of countries covered
Low income - to US$1,036 GNI per capita	138.7	16%	78%	37%	38%	36%	33%	34%	41%	726	24.5	14
Lower Middle Income - $1,037-$4,046	235.3	24%	83%	39%	38%	36%	41%	38%	39%	2,430	104	32
Upper Middle Income - $4,046-$12,535	153.2	42%	87%	48%	46%	50%	49%	50%	48%	7,305	816	31
Higher income - $12,536-$30,000	149.3	45%	90%	60%	60%	61%	60%	60%	63%	20,333	174	28
Rich Countries - >$30,000	91.2	56%	92%	76%	77%	77%	66%	78%	68%	63,754	1,506	36
Least Developed Countries	171.5	16%	78%	37%	38%	35%	36%	34%	39%	1,083	25.7	21
Very small - <US$3bn GDP	107.8	27%	82%	54%	55%	48%	62%	49%	59%	14,163	1.39	20
Small - $3-20bn	158.9	32%	89%	50%	50%	51%	53%	51%	52%	24,608	12	33
Mid-sized - $20-100bn	197.7	35%	86%	47%	46%	50%	48%	48%	48%	11,928	52	34
Large - $100-500bn	165.8	46%	90%	59%	58%	59%	48%	61%	52%	25,242	305	30
Largest > $500bn	113.1	58%	90%	66%	67%	68%	56%	69%	62%	38,545	3,196	24
All countries	**153.8**	**39%**	**87%**	**54%**	**54%**	**55%**	**52%**	**55%**	**53%**	**22,545**	**624**	**141**

Fig. 4 Relationship between FATF Activity and World Bank Governance Indicators in 2022

Correlation with FATF Activity Score 1998-2022	Coefficient of Determination (CoD)	Rank Correlation (RC)
All SDGs	5.5%	-14.1%
SDG 16 enhanced	6.7%	-26.2%
Resilience	9.0%	-24.4%
Prevention of Criminality	9.9%	21.3%
WB Rule of Law	17.1%	-36.9%
WB Control Corruption	17.5%	-37.0%
WB Regulatory Quality	14.0%	-32.1%
WB Stability Violence Terrorism	15.6%	-29.3%
WB Government Effectiveness	14.0%	-31.3%
WB Voice and Accountability	9.1%	-24.0%
ILO Informal %	12.6%	24.1%
GNI per capita	9.0%	-28.8%
GDP US$bn	1.2%	0.1%
LDCs	0.4%	4.4%

Fig. 5 Coefficients of determination between FATF Activity Score and various indicators, 2022

each indicator. The right hand column reports Rank Correlations (RC): a negative RC that as one variable increases in rank, the other tends to decrease in rank. In simpler terms, higher ranks of one variable are associated with lower ranks of the other.

CoDs are generally low, indicating that FATF and related organisations predominantly used other criteria, and in particular the outcomes of MERs, which are mostly focused on technical compliance, in deciding where to initiate most activity. The development and governance indicators in Fig. 5 are however, what the FATF activity is in the end trying to improve, so it is arguable that greater focus on these measures in deciding which countries to focus on might have led to greater effectiveness in outturn.

RCs are largely negative, indicating that countries that rank highly on, for example, rule of law, control of corruption and effectiveness of government have received the least attention over the period 1998 - 2022. The latter observation is not surprising, as it is clear that FATF's focus to date has been on less developed, and often

Dependent Variable: FATF Activity Score Rank	*Coefficients*	*t Stat*
Intercept	128.57	11.28
Low and low-middle income - to US$4,084 GNI per capita	76.00	3.81

Dependent Variable: FATF Activity Score Rank	*Coefficients*	*t Stat*
Intercept	122.82	10.50
Small countries - to US$20bn pa	81.26	4.26

Fig. 6 Focus on low and low-middle income and low GDP countries

smaller, countries, and also on countries such as Iran and North Korea where these indicators are particularly poor. As pointed out, the FATF activity has been triggered by the lack of sufficient compliance with its standards rather these indicators.

Various authors have highlighted the extent to which FATF has, so far, focused its attention on poorer and smaller countries.[44] To explore the extent of this, we carried out some simple econometrics (Fig. 6). This related the rank position of countries for the FATF Activity Score to a dummy variable as to whether the countries had GNI per capita of less than US$4084 (Low and Low-Middle Income); and whether they are small in terms of GDP (less than US$20bn pa). In both cases, the dummy variables are highly significant, with positive coefficients, reinforcing the concerns of other authors.

5 Has FATF Activity Coincided with Improvements in Governance?

We now turn to more detailed exploration of whether there is evidence that FATF activity has coincided with improvements in the governance indicators over the period 1998–2023. As noted above, even where there is movement in the same direction, this does not necessarily imply causation, as other, non-FATF influences may have caused the change.

Focusing on control of corruption as measured by the World Bank for the 30 countries that have received the greatest FATF and related activity during the period, Fig. 7 shows that Myanmar and Pakistan have improved slightly, while Iran has become worse. Among the other countries in the top 30 which have received the greatest FATF attention, a majority have experienced deteriorating perceptions, particularly Trinidad and Tobago, Syria, Zimbabwe, Yemen and Mongolia. Indonesia, Ukraine, and Albania stand out as having improved.

The situation with regard to the other governance indicators shows a similar pattern, although there are differences in detail and in the degree of change. Perceptions of regulatory quality in Pakistan, for example, have deteriorated, while those in Iraq have improved. Indonesia stands out as a country which has improved on all

[44] See, for example, Littrell (2024).

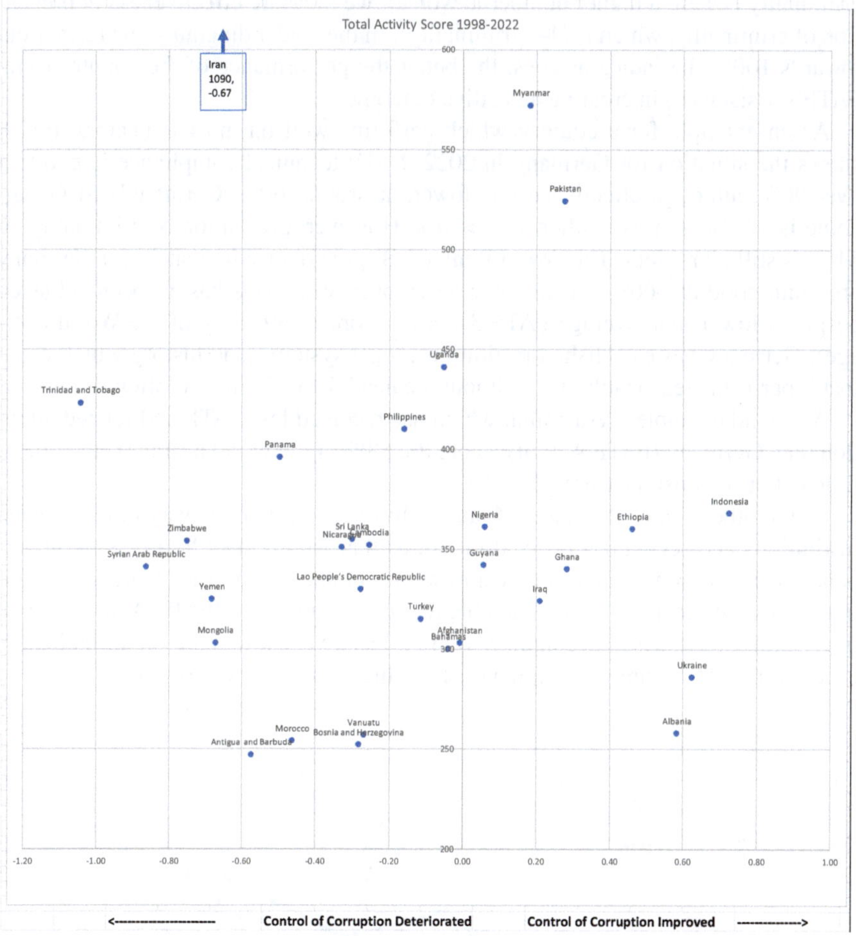

Fig. 7 Change in Control of Corruption 1998–2022, related to FATF Activity Score

indicators, while Syria has deteriorated. The detailed graphics for the other five World Bank Governance Indicators are provided in Annex B. The general observation of more countries (among the group which has received most FATF attention) facing deterioration in these indicators than improvement persists across all the indicators.

6 Focus on Specific Countries

In what follows, we present all the various indicators in what is often called a 'spider diagram'. Here the indicators have all been normalised to a scale of 0–100% and calculated so that a higher number is better. So, for example, instead of measuring criminality (where a higher number is worse), we measure effectiveness in prevention of criminality, which is (1—criminality). In the spider diagrams, the further out towards 100% the indicator goes, the better the performance of the country (with FATF's assistance) in creating a positive outcome.

As an example for a country which performs well on most indicators, Fig. 8 shows the situation for Germany in 2022. FATF technical compliance is good, at over 90%, although effectiveness is lower, at around 60%. Germany's SDG outcome is >60%, and its resilience is >70%. However, prevention of criminality, at 51%, is still a problem. The World Bank (WB) governance indicators for Germany are quite good at >60% and in some cases over 80%. This has all been achieved despite a lower-than-average FATF Activity Score of 99 (65% of the World average): Germany has established institutions, legal systems, and history which mean that it performs reasonably well without the need for FATF intervention.

A second example is Australia, which has received less FATF and related attention than Germany (FATF Activity Score 88, 58% of the world average), and does a little better on most measures (Fig. 9).

At the other end of the scale, Myanmar has very little in the way of established institutions and regulatory or legal measures that would meet World Bank governance or FATF compliance (i.e. technical compliance) and effectiveness expectations. Despite receiving a considerable amount of attention (FATF Activity Score 621, 406% of the world average), Myanmar has a very low score on all indicators except for FATF technical compliance, for which it scores over 80% (Fig. 10).

Fig. 8 Comparison of various FATF, criminality and governance indicators: Germany

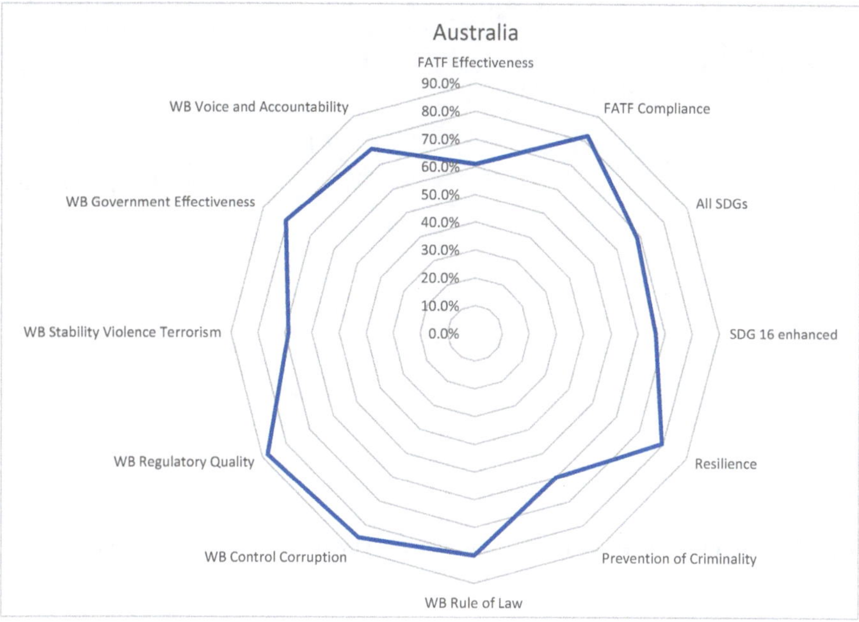

Fig. 9 Comparison of various FATF, criminality and governance indicators: Australia

Pakistan, which has a FATF Activity Score of 544 (356% of the world average) shows a similar pattern, though it performs slightly better than Myanmar on rule of law, criminality, corruption and government effectiveness (Fig. 11).

An example of a developing country with a more balanced score card is Indonesia. It has a FATF Activity Score of 373, 274% of the world average, and has achieved technical compliance of around 90%. Indonesia has also become the latest country to join the FATF. Indonesia invests heavily in the development of its regulatory system and has a substantial, if complex, governmental system. However, it still scores relatively poorly on control of corruption and criminality, and is intermediate on terrorism and accountability (Fig. 12).

7 Reflections and Conclusion

Applying the FATF Activity Score, it is clear that the FATF has focused extensively on lower middle-income countries while devoting the least time to the rich countries that generally hold and process the largest share of global illicit funds. The chapter has considered whether there are correlations between the FATF's activity and focus on a country, and higher governance and crime combating levels in a country. The study finds little correlation between FATF-related activities aimed at raising country technical AML/CFT compliance and effectiveness levels, the size of a country's

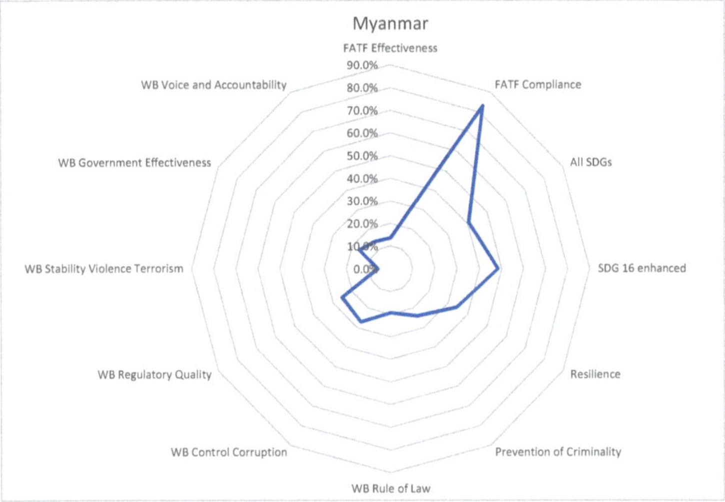

Fig. 10 Comparison of various FATF, criminality and governance indicators: Myanmar

economy, a country's actual technical compliance levels with the FATF standards, its FATF effectiveness scores, and positive governance and crime prevention outcomes.

The FATF activity and pressure to date has resulted in higher levels of technical compliance with the FATF standards. This level is out of proportion with other key indicators and development factors of smaller economies, resulting in a "rhino horn" effect in spider diagrams of key indicators with high technical compliance levels that are not supported proportionately by achievements in the related indicators.

Lower income countries are resource-constrained, and this limits their ability to implement the FATF standards effectively. That, in turn, would limit their broader impact on crime prevention and good governance. From that perspective the FATF's increased focus on larger economies in the fifth round of mutual evaluations makes sense. Larger economies, that also have higher levels of proceeds of crime, have more resources to implement the FATF standards effectively. Such a focus would increase the general level of global effectiveness of the implementation of the FATF standards as defined and assessed by the FATF.

While the shift in country focus is commendable, the actual change is limited. The new greylisting processes provide more protection to the smaller economies with less than $10 billion in broad money. This is helpful to small economies that were greylisted by the FATF in the past. However, it does not assist the lower-middle-income countries that have featured extensively in greylisting. It is unlikely that ongoing FATF attention to these resource-constrained countries will

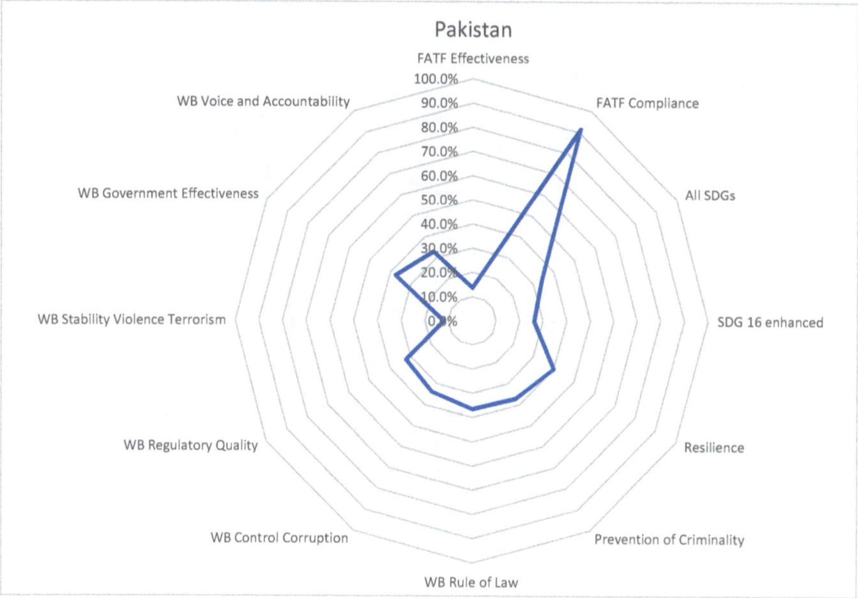

Fig. 11 Comparison of various FATF, criminality and governance indicators: Pakistan

be generating significant improvements in effectiveness levels as defined by the FATF.

However, the research raises a fundamental question: Will increasing the effectiveness of the FATF standards implementation significantly advance the objectives these standards are meant to achieve? After 30 years of considerable effort and coercion, most countries now technically comply with FATF standards, with the majority achieving compliance levels above 80%. However, there is little evidence that this has translated into a meaningful 'real-world' impact. In fact, we find little correlation between FATF-related activities, FATF technical compliance, and FATF effectiveness scores in relation to positive governance or crime prevention outcomes. It is possible and probably likely that countries scoring well on various sustainability and governance indicators do so because of pre-existing political, institutional, or societal conditions rather than because of FATF compliance.

To set against this, in other work,[45] we have established correlations between FATF activity and "unintended consequences". Clearly the effort that has been put in to developing the regulatory systems, listing and delisting, and mutual evaluation, has had a significant direct cost, both for FATF and related organisations, and for the countries themselves. We observe that the response of the market and institutions to

[45] Morris et al. (2026).

Fig. 12 Comparison of various FATF, criminality and governance indicators: Indonesia

FATF signals has contributed to financial exclusion, debanking, withdrawal of correspondent banking services, loss of aid flows, and higher remittance costs, and that it may have had an impact on trade flows. None of these effects are easy to quantify, and causal relationships are hard to establish, but the balance of available evidence does suggest that these unintended consequences may be significant.

There is a measure of subjectivity to the calculation of the FATF Activity Score. The date sources selected do not cover all countries comprehensively and the general analysis and correlations identified may not fully reflect the FATF impact, especially in an individual country. At a minimum, however, the analysis in this chapter suggests this a subject which is worth exploring further, with better data. We have assembled the data that is available in the public domain, but we expect that more and better data is available to FATF and to official bodies. Some of the propositions we have set out above could be tested by further enquiry in specific countries, to develop case studies of what has worked, and what hasn't. These studies could inform standardised impact assessments and be fed into policy management cycles. This can inform a more thoughtful and evidence-based approach by the FATF. The new round of mutual evaluations provides an excellent framework in which such studies can be conducted.

8 Annex A: Heat Map of FATF and Related Activities: Highest and Lowest 20 Countries

Highest: Most FATF Activity 1998–2022

Country	FATF Activity 1998-2022	1998/9	2000	2001	2002	2003	2004	2005	2006	2007	2008	2009	2010	2011	2012	2013	2014	2015	2016	2017	2018	2019	2020	2021	2022	2023
Iran, Islamic Republic of	1170	-	-	-	IMF	-	-	-	-	-	BL	BL	BL	BL	BL	BL	BL	BL	EU+BL	EU+BL	EU+BL	EU+BL	EU+BL	EU+BL	EU+BL	EU+BL
Korea, Democratic People's Republic	965	-	-	-	-	-	-	-	-	-	-	-	-	BL	BL	BL	BL	BL	EU+BL	EU+BL	EU+BL	EU+BL	EU+BL	EU+BL	EU+BL	EU+BL
Myanmar	621	-	-	L+	L+	L+	L+	L+	L+	-	MER	-	L+	L+	L+	L+	L+	L+	L+	-	MER	FUR	L+EU+FUR	L+EU+FUR	L+EU+FUR	L+EU+FUR
Pakistan	544	-	-	-	-	-	IMF	-	-	IMF	L+IMF	L+MER	L+	L+	L+	L+	L+	L+	-	-	L+EU	L+EU+MER	L+EU+FUR	L+EU+FUR	L+EU+FUR	EU
Uganda	490	-	-	-	-	IMF	-	-	IMF	MER	-	-	-	-	-	-	L+	L+	L+EU+MER	L+EU+FUR	L+EU+FUR	L+EU+FUR	L+EU+FUR	L+EU+FUR	L+EU+FUR	L+EU+FUR
Trinidad and Tobago	489	-	-	-	-	-	-	-	IMF	MER	-	FUR	L+FUR	L+FUR	L+FUR	FUR2	FUR2	FUR	MER	L+	L+EU	L+EU	L+EU	L+EU	L+EU	L+EU
Philippines	455	-	L+	L+	L+IMF	L+	L+IMF	IMF	-	-	-	MER	L+	L+	L+	L+	-	-	-	-	-	MER	FUR	L+FUR	L+EU	L+EU
Panama	416	-	L+	L+	-	-	-	-	IMF	-	-	-	-	-	-	-	L+IMF	L+	L+	L+	L+MER	L+FUR	L+EU+FUR	L+EU+IMF	EU	EU
Guyana	387	-	-	-	-	-	-	-	-	-	-	-	-	MER+FUR	FUR2	L+FUR	L+FUR	L+FUR	L+EU	EU	EU	EU	EU	L+EU	L+EU	L+EU
Nigeria	384	-	-	L+	L+	L+	L+	L+	L+	-	MER	FUR	L+FUR	L+FUR	L+FUR	L+FUR	FUR	FUR	-	-	-	-	-	MER	-	EU+FUR
Indonesia	373	-	-	L+	L+	L+	L+	L+IMF	-	-	MER	-	L+	L+	L+	L+	L+	L+	-	-	MER	-	-	-	-	FUR
Ethiopia	365	-	-	-	-	-	-	-	-	-	-	-	L+	L+	L+	L+	L+	MER	FUR	L+EU	L+EU	L+EU	L+EU	FUR	FUR	FUR
Syrian Arab Republic	361	-	-	-	-	-	-	-	MER	-	-	FUR2	L+FUR	L+FUR	L+FUR	L+FUR	L+FUR	FUR	EU	EU	EU+FUR	EU	EU	EU	EU	EU
Cambodia	357	-	-	-	-	-	-	-	-	MER	-	-	-	L+FUR	L+FUR	L+FUR	L+FUR	L+	-	MER	FUR	L+FUR	L+EU	L+EU+FUR	EU+FUR	FUR
Sri Lanka	355	-	-	-	IMF	-	-	IMF	MER	-	IMF	-	L+	L+	L+	L+	-	MER	FUR2	L+EU	L+EU+FUR	L+EU	EU+FUR	FUR	-	-
Zimbabwe	354	-	-	-	-	-	-	-	-	MER	-	-	-	L+	L+	L+	L+	L+	MER	FUR	-	L+FUR	L+EU	L+EU	L+EU	-
Nicaragua	351	-	-	-	IMF	-	-	-	-	-	-	MER	IMF	L+	L+	L+	L+	L+	-	MER	-	FUR2	L+EU+FUR	L+EU+FUR	L+EU	-
Turkey	349	-	-	-	IMF	IMF	-	-	IMF	MER	FUR	IMF+FUR	L+FUR	L+FUR	L+FUR	L+FUR	L+FUR	-	-	-	-	MER	-	L+FUR	L+FUR	L+FUR
Lao People's Democratic Republic	345	-	-	-	-	-	-	-	-	-	-	-	-	MER	-	L+	L+	L+	L+EU	L+EU	L+EU	L+EU	L+EU	-	-	MER
Yemen	345	-	-	-	-	-	-	-	-	-	MER	-	L+FUR	L+FUR	L+FUR	L+FUR	L+FUR	-	EU	EU	EU	EU	EU	EU	EU	EU

Lowest: Least FATF Activity 1998–2022

Country	FATF Activity 1998-2022	1998/9	2000	2001	2002	2003	2004	2005	2006	2007	2008	2009	2010	2011	2012	2013	2014	2015	2016	2017	2018	2019	2020	2021	2022	2023
Central African Republic	40	-	-	-	-	-	-	-	-	-	-	-	MER	-	-	-	-	-	-	-	-	-	-	IMF	-	MER
Chad	40	-	-	-	-	-	-	-	-	IMF	-	-	-	-	-	-	MER	-	-	-	-	-	-	-	-	MER
Cote d'Ivoire	40	-	-	-	-	-	-	-	-	-	-	-	-	-	-	MER+FUR	FUR	-	-	-	-	-	-	-	-	IMF+MER
Guinea	40	-	-	-	-	-	-	IMF	-	-	-	-	-	-	MER	-	-	-	MER	-	-	-	-	-	-	-
Palau	40	-	-	-	-	-	-	-	-	-	MER	IMF	-	-	-	-	-	-	-	-	MER	-	-	-	-	-
Swaziland/Eswatini	40	-	-	-	-	-	-	-	-	-	-	-	MER	-	-	-	-	-	-	FUR	FUR	-	-	-	MER	-
Dominican Republic	38	-	-	-	-	-	-	-	IMF+MER	-	-	-	-	-	-	-	-	-	-	-	MER	FUR	-	-	-	-
Curacao	37	-	-	-	-	-	-	-	-	-	-	-	-	-	MER+FUR	FUR	FUR	FUR	FUR	-	-	-	-	-	-	-
Congo	36	-	-	-	-	-	-	-	-	-	-	-	-	-	-	-	-	MER	-	-	-	-	-	-	MER	FUR
Congo, the Democratic Republic of the	35	-	-	-	-	-	-	-	-	-	-	-	-	-	-	-	-	-	-	-	-	-	-	MER	-	EU
Tonga	35	-	-	-	-	-	-	-	-	-	-	-	MER	-	-	-	-	-	-	-	-	-	-	MER	-	FUR
Virgin Islands, British	35	-	-	-	-	-	-	-	-	-	MER	FUR	FUR	FUR	FUR	-	-	-	-	-	-	-	-	-	-	-
Guernsey	30	-	-	-	-	-	-	-	-	-	-	-	-	IMF	-	MER	-	FUR	-	-	-	-	-	-	-	-
Solomon Islands	30	-	-	-	-	-	-	-	-	-	-	-	MER	-	-	-	-	-	-	-	-	MER	-	-	-	-
Taiwan, Province of China	30	-	-	-	-	-	-	-	-	MER	-	-	-	-	-	-	-	-	-	-	-	MER	-	-	-	-
Maldives	25	-	-	-	-	-	-	-	-	-	-	-	-	MER	IMF	-	-	-	-	-	-	-	-	-	-	-
Timor-Leste	25	-	-	-	-	-	-	-	-	-	-	-	IMF	-	MER	-	-	-	-	-	-	-	-	-	-	-
Jersey	20	-	-	-	-	-	-	-	-	-	-	-	-	-	-	MER	-	FUR	-	-	-	-	-	-	-	-
Comoros	15	-	-	-	-	-	-	-	-	-	-	-	IMF+MER	-	-	-	-	-	-	-	-	-	-	-	-	-
Equatorial Guinea	15	-	-	-	-	-	-	-	-	-	-	-	-	-	-	-	-	-	MER	-	-	-	-	-	-	-

9 Annex B: World Bank Governance Indicators

The World Bank Governance Indicators (WGI) are a set of metrics designed to measure the quality of governance in over 200 countries.[46] They cover six key dimensions of governance:

Voice and Accountability: This indicator captures the extent to which a country's citizens can engage in the political process, including through free and fair elections. It also reflects freedoms of expression, assembly, and the press.

Political Stability and Absence of Violence/Terrorism: This measures the likelihood of political unrest, violence, or instability, including terrorism. It also reflects how secure and predictable the political environment is.

Government Effectiveness: This assesses the quality and efficiency of public services and civil servants, the quality of policymaking and implementation, and the government's commitment to such policies.

Regulatory Quality: This indicator examines how well the government can design and implement policies and regulations that support private sector development while protecting public interests.

Rule of Law: This measures public confidence in legal systems and the enforcement of laws, including protection of property rights, fair judicial processes, and contract enforcement.

Control of Corruption: This evaluates how well corruption is prevented, including measures against bribery and misuse of public resources for personal gain. It reflects transparency and accountability in governance.

The World Bank Governance Indicators (WGI) are composite measures of governance derived from over 30 distinct data sources. These sources are adjusted and merged to produce the six aggregated indicators, utilizing a statistical technique called the Unobserved Components Model (UCM).

Control of corruption has already been highlighted above. The following diagrams show which countries have improved or deteriorated on the other five World Bank Governance indicators, and relate this to the FATF activity score for the period 1998–2022.

[46] Kaufman and Kraay (2024).

Changes to Governance Indicators for Top 30 countries on FATF Activity Score

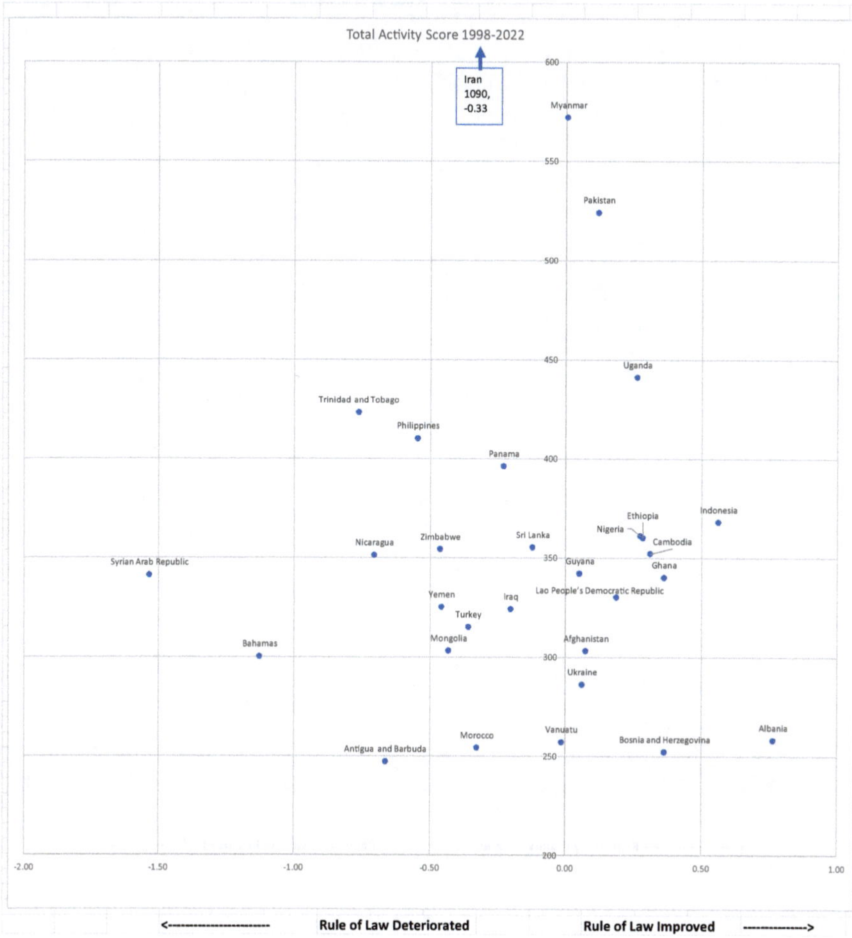

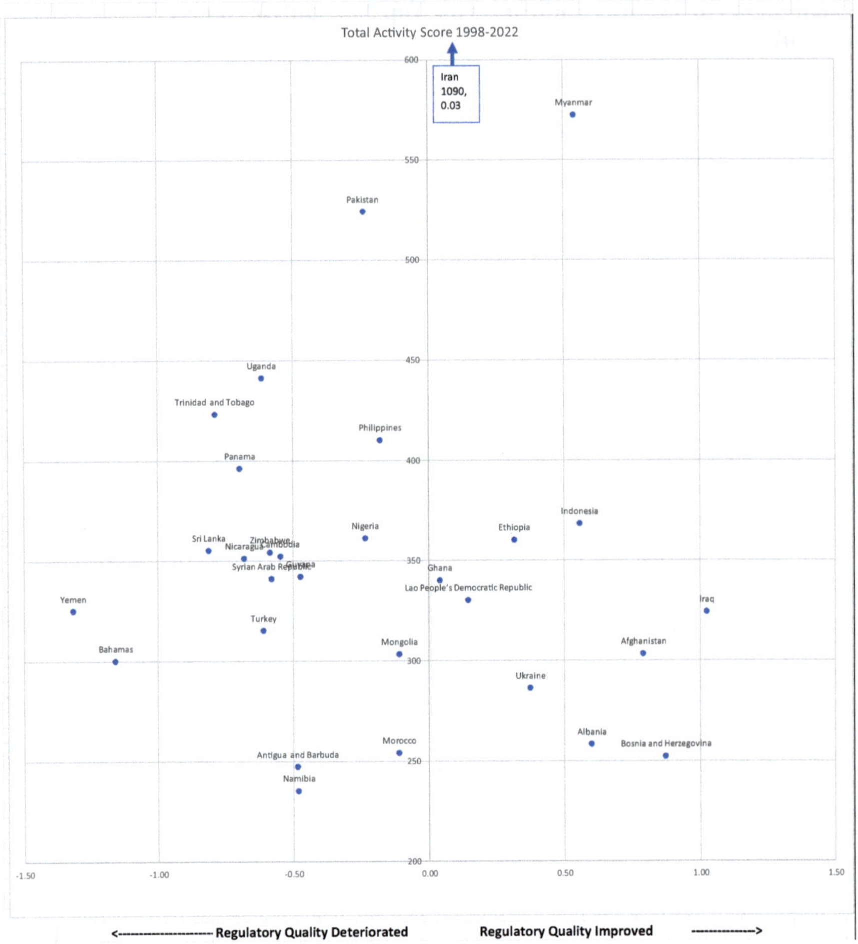
Total Activity Score 1998-2022
Iran 1090, 0.03
Myanmar
Pakistan
Uganda
Trinidad and Tobago
Philippines
Panama
Indonesia
Nigeria
Ethiopia
Sri Lanka
Zimbabwe
Nicaragua
Cambodia
Syrian Arab Republic
Guinea
Ghana
Lao People's Democratic Republic
Yemen
Iraq
Turkey
Mongolia
Afghanistan
Bahamas
Ukraine
Albania
Morocco
Bosnia and Herzegovina
Antigua and Barbuda
Namibia
600
550
500
450
400
350
300
250
200
-1.50
-1.00
-0.50
0.00
0.50
1.00
1.50
<---------------------- Regulatory Quality Deteriorated
Regulatory Quality Improved -------------->

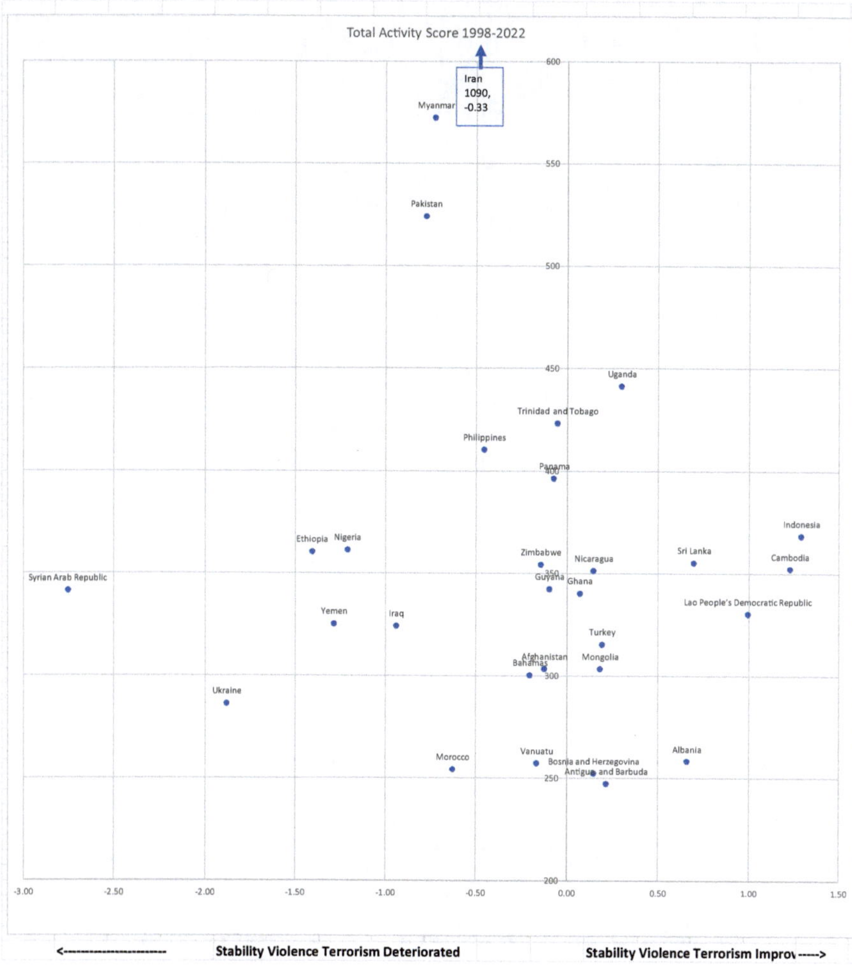
Total Activity Score 1998-2022
Iran
1090,
-0.33
Myanmar
Pakistan
Uganda
Trinidad and Tobago
Philippines
Panama
Indonesia
Ethiopia
Nigeria
Zimbabwe
Nicaragua
Sri Lanka
Cambodia
Syrian Arab Republic
Guyana
Ghana
Lao People's Democratic Republic
Yemen
Iraq
Turkey
Afghanistan
Bahamas
Mongolia
Ukraine
Morocco
Vanuatu
Bosnia and Herzegovina
Antigua and Barbuda
Albania
600
550
500
450
400
350
300
250
200
-3.00
-2.50
-2.00
-1.50
-1.00
-0.50
0.00
0.50
1.00
1.50
<------------------------ Stability Violence Terrorism Deteriorated
Stability Violence Terrorism Improv ---->

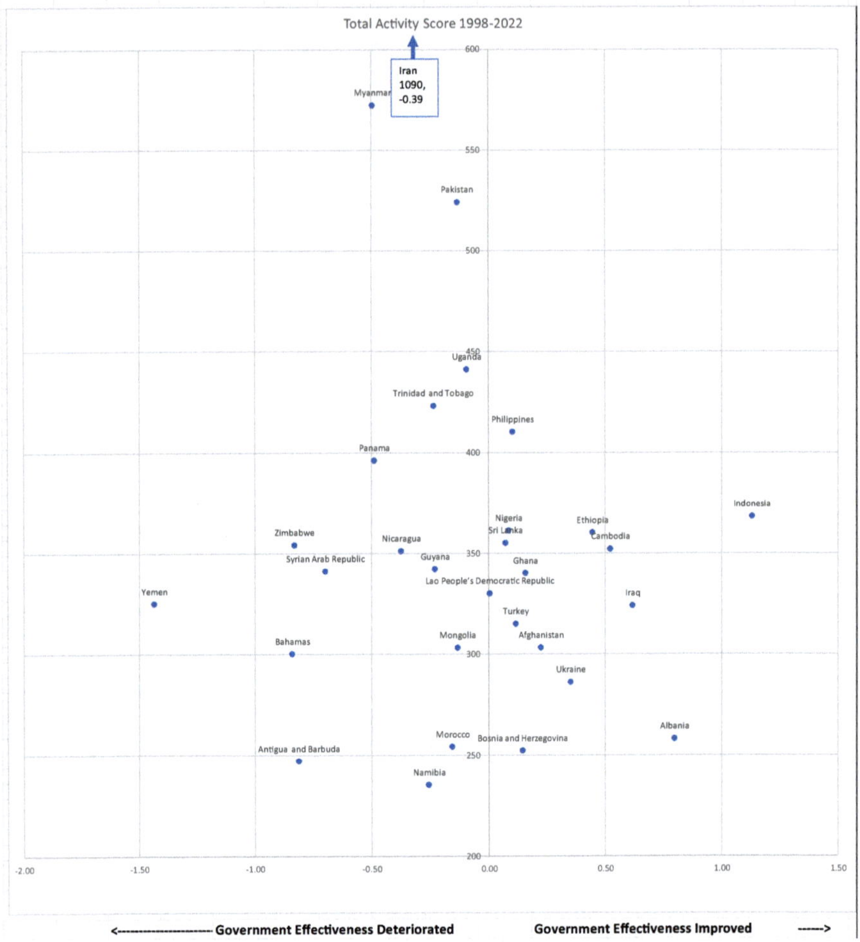
Total Activity Score 1998-2022
Iran 1090, -0.39
Myanmar
Pakistan
Uganda
Trinidad and Tobago
Philippines
Panama
Indonesia
Nigeria
Sri Lanka
Ethiopia
Cambodia
Zimbabwe
Nicaragua
Guyana
Ghana
Syrian Arab Republic
Lao People's Democratic Republic
Yemen
Iraq
Turkey
Mongolia
Afghanistan
Bahamas
Ukraine
Albania
Morocco
Bosnia and Herzegovina
Antigua and Barbuda
Namibia
600
550
500
450
400
350
300
250
200
-2.00
-1.50
-1.00
-0.50
0.00
0.50
1.00
1.50
<---------------------- Government Effectiveness Deteriorated
Government Effectiveness Improved ------>

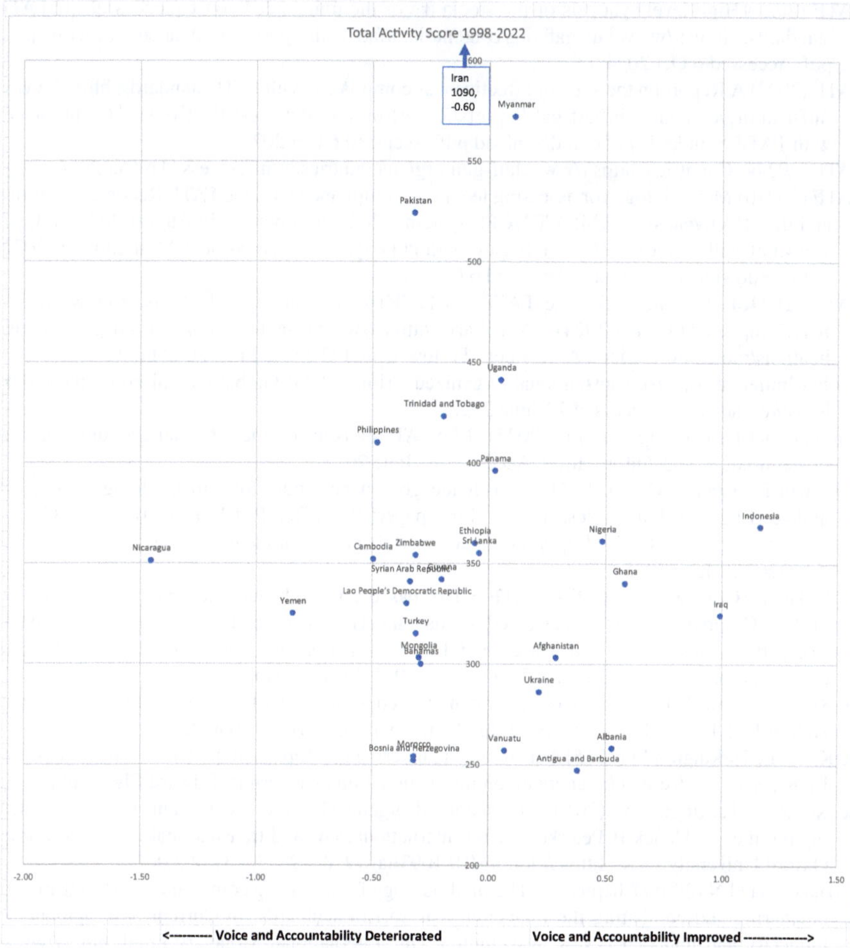

References

D'Hulster K, Morris N, Jaffer S, de Koker L (2023) The decline of correspondent banking in Pacific Island countries. Pacific Islands Forum report prepared by the World Bank. https://forumsec.org/sites/default/files/2024-05/CBR%20Report_FINAL.pdf. Accessed 6 Oct 2024

FATF (1998) Annual report 1998–1998. https://www.fatf-gafi.org/content/dam/fatf-gafi/annual-reports/1997%201998%20ENG.pdf. Accessed 27 Feb 2025

FATF (2000) Annual report 1999–2000. https://www.fatf-gafi.org/content/dam/fatf-gafi/annual-reports/1999%202000%20ENG.pdf. Accessed 27 Feb 2025

FATF (2014) Annual report 2013–2014. https://www.fatf-gafi.org/content/dam/fatf-gafi/annual-reports/FATF%20Annual%20report%202013-2014.pdf. Accessed 6 Oct 2024

FATF (2021) High-level synopsis of the stocktake of the unintended consequences of the FATF standards. https://www.fatf-gafi.org/content/dam/fatf-gafi/reports/Unintended-Consequences.pdf. Accessed 6 Oct 2024
FATF (2022) A Report on the state of effectiveness compliance with FATF standards. https://www.fatf-gafi.org/content/dam/fatf-gafi/reports/Report-on-the-State-of-Effectiveness-Compliance-with-FATF-Standards.pdf.coredownload.pdf. Accessed 6 Oct 2024
FATF (2024a) Countries. https://www.fatf-gafi.org/en/countries.html. Accessed 6 Oct 2024
FATF (2024b) Methodology for assessing technical compliance with the FATF Recommendations and the effectiveness of AML/CFT/CPF systems (2022, as amended in August 2024). https://www.fatf-gafi.org/content/dam/fatf-gafi/methodology/FATF-Assessment-Methodology-2022.pdf.coredownload.inline.pdf. Accessed 6 Oct 2024
FATF (2024c) Procedures for the FATF AML/CFT/CPF mutual evaluations, follow-up and ICRG. (updated October 2024). FATF, Paris. http://www.fatf-gafi.org/content/fatf-gafi/en/publications/mutualevaluations/Assessment-Follow-UpICRG-Procedures-2022.html
Global Initiative Against Transnational Organized Crime (2023) Global Organised Crime Index. https://ocindex.net. Accessed 12 June 2025
International Labour Organization (2025) ILOSTAT: statistics on the informal economy. https://ilostat.ilo.org/topics/informality/. Accessed 12 June 2025
Kaufman D, Kraay AC (2024) The worldwide governance indicators: methodology and 2024 update (English). Policy Research working paper;RRR;PROSPERITY. World Bank Group, Washington, D.C. http://documents.worldbank.org/curated/en/099005210162424110. Accessed 12 June 2025
de Koker L, Goldbarsht D (2024) FATF'S risk-based approach: has the pendulum swung too far? In: Goldbarsht D, de Koker L (eds) Financial crime and the law. Ius Gentium: comparative perspectives on law and justice, vol 115. Springer, Cham. span class=ExternalRefspan class=RefSource https://doi.org/10.1007/978-3-031-59543-1_/span/span
de Koker L, Howell J, Morris N (2023) Economic consequences of greylisting by the Financial Action Task Force. Risks 11(5):81. https://doi.org/10.3390/risks11050081
de Koker L, Turkington M (2015) Anti-money laundering measures and the effectiveness question. In: Rider B (ed) Research handbook on international financial crime. Edward Elgar Publishing
de Koker L, Turkington M (2016) Transnational organised crime and the anti-money laundering regime. In: Hauck P, Peterke S (eds) International law and transnational organised crime. Oxford University Press. https://doi.org/10.1093/law/9780198733737.003.0012
Kyriakos-Saad N (2005) Chapter 16. The methodology for assessing compliance with anti-money laundering and combating the financing of terrorism standards. In Current developments in monetary and financial law, 3. Washington, DC: International Monetary Fund. https://www.imf.org/external/np/leg/amlcft/eng/pdf/cdmfl_v3.pdf. Accessed 1 March 2024
LexisNexis Risk Solutions (2023) True cost of financial crime compliance study, 2023
Littrell C (2024) Economic and demographic biases in FATF mutual evaluation results. In: Goldbarsht D, de Koker L (eds) Financial crime and the law. Ius Gentium: comparative perspectives on law and justice, vol 115. Springer, Cham. https://doi.org/10.1007/978-3-031-59543-1_8
Morris N, de Koker L, Nel JY (2026) FATF standards and their impact on sustainable development goals (SDGs) of Global South countries in the Asia-Pacific region. In: Azinge-Egbiri NV, Esoimeme EE, Ryder N (eds) Global anti-money laundering standards: errors in transplantation and unintended consequences for developing countries. Routledge (forthcoming)
Pol RF (2020) Anti-money laundering: the world's least effective policy experiment? Together, we can fix it. Policy Des Pract 3(1):73–94
Van Broekhoven L (2020) Derisking and civil society: drivers, impact and solutions. Human Security Collective. https://www.hscollective.org/news/timeline/article-derisking-and-civil-society-drivers-impact-and-solutions/. Accessed 6 Oct 2024

Dr. Nicholas Morris is an Adjunct Professor at the School of Law of La Trobe University. He has over 45 years' experience advising companies, governments and international agencies, in UK, Australia, Europe, China, SE Asia and the Middle East, on the financing of essential infrastructure and on financial regulation. Nicholas also led a team at Oxford University to examine how the trustworthiness of the financial system could be improved, after the Global Financial Crisis, which led to the book "Capital Failure: Rebuilding Trust in Financial Services" (Oxford University Press, 2014, 2016). Subsequently he published "Management and Regulation of Pension Schemes: Australia: A Cautionary Tale" (Routledge, 2018). He has been working on public finance in Indonesia for over 25 years, assisting the Indonesian government with reforms to its planning and budgeting processes, and previously advised the Chinese government on reforms to the banking system and the development of financial regulations.

Prof. Louis de Koker is a professor of law at La Trobe Law School, Australia, an advisory board member of the Financial Integrity Hub (FIH), and an extraordinary professor in law at the University of the Western Cape, South Africa. His financial crime research focuses on managing the relationship between financial inclusion and anti-money laundering and counter terrorist financing objectives. He has undertaken various university research engagements with the bodies such as the World Bank and the Asian Development Bank and has worked closely with the DC-based Consultative Group to Assist the Poor (CGAP) for nearly two decades. This work extended to a range of developing countries including Ghana, Indonesia, Kenya, Kyrgyzstan, Malaysia, Namibia, Nigeria, Uganda, the Ukraine and Palau. His research has been cited in publications and research papers of international bodies such as the World Bank, the Basel Committee on Banking Supervision, and the FATF.

The Financial War on Crime and Terrorism—Important Research Questions

Louis de Koker, Doron Goldbarsht, and Jamie Ferrill

Abstract The fight against financial crime is often framed in military terms, with compliance officers and law enforcement professionals portrayed as soldiers engaged in battles within a broader war on crime. This collection has examined several facets of that struggle, including the fundamental question of whether the war is, in fact, being won. Yet, in an era of growing geopolitical fragmentation and the increasing deployment of sanctions against nation-states, the boundaries between military conflict and financial crime are becoming increasingly blurred. The overarching strategy—and progress toward it—remains uncertain. Despite significant investment and mounting regulatory pressure, it is still difficult to determine whether current approaches are effectively disrupting criminal activity or merely enhancing compliance metrics. This chapter explores key research questions that emerge from this evolving and complex landscape.

1 Introduction

The combating of financial crime is often couched in military terms. Compliance officers and law enforcement are viewed as soldiers who are fighting battles in the war against crime. This collection highlighted some of the elements of that war,

L. de Koker
La Trobe University and Financial Integrity Hub (FIH), Melbourne, VIC, Australia

University of the Western Cape, Belville, South Africa
e-mail: l.dekoker@latrobe.edu.au

D. Goldbarsht (✉)
Macquarie University and Financial Integrity Hub (FIH), Sydney, NSW, Australia
e-mail: doron.goldbarsht@mq.edu.au

J. Ferrill
Charles Sturt University and Financial Integrity Hub (FIH), Canberra, ACT, Australia
e-mail: jferrill@csu.edu.au

D. Goldbarsht et al. (eds.), *The Financial War on Crime and Terrorism*, European Yearbook of International Economic Law,
https://doi.org/10.1007/978-3-032-06360-1_13

including whether it is being won. It is clear, however, that in light of geopolitical fragmentation and the use of sanctions against nation states, there are increasing overlaps between military warfare and financial crime. What, then, are the key research questions that should be considered in this context?

To this end, we have addressed a number of these outstanding issues in this book—yet there is plenty more to be addressed. Of these outstanding issues, five critical questions that shape the future of anti-money laundering (AML), counter-terrorism financing (CTF), and counter-proliferation financing (CPF) efforts emerge: what is the optimal strategy for AML/CTF/CPF measures, including whether current approaches that displace rather than eliminate criminal activity align with policy intentions and how we can move beyond displacement to genuine prevention?; how do we measure the effectiveness of AML/CTF/CPF measures given the challenges in quantifying "success" in fighting financial crime?; how do we transition from reactive approaches to proactive approaches given the acceleration of criminal innovation?; how do we harness and mitigate the dual role of Artificial Intelligence (AI) as a risk vector and opportunity for detection and prevention?; how do we adapt to shifting geopolitical realities including responses to policy changes, geopolitical fragmentation, and the tension between focusing on small scale vs large scale operations?; and how do we address emerging technological risks, particularly vulnerabilities introduced by financial innovations that outpace regulatory frameworks?

To understand the complexity and urgency of these questions, we can examine the broader context of the ongoing financial war on crime and terrorism, which arguably, has shaped financial crime policy and responses.

2 Wars on Crime and Terrorism

In 1963, J Edgar Hoover, the founding, and long-term, director of the US Federal Bureau of Investigation (FBI), wrote an article in the *DePaul Law Review* entitled "The War on Organised Crime".[1] In that article he used the language of war because he believed that society should be informed, engaged, and enlisted to mitigate the threat of organised crime. The task was too big to be left to law enforcement:

> Only a small portion of American citizens are fighting this sinister threat to law and order and our cherished democratic principles. The public reaction to organized crime must be reversed if we are to stem its growth, much less destroy it. The disinterested, the unconcerned, and the uninformed are the controlling group in this war. And war it must be unless we as a Nation are ready to give in, to surrender more and more of our rights and wealth to a small group of the most vicious, greedy, and unscrupulous thieves, killers, and cheats this country has ever known. [2]

[1] Hoover (1963).

[2] Ibid, p. 195.

He specifically highlighted the criminal wealth of organised crime as its major source of power. He warned that organised crime leaders had gained "vast legitimate holdings" that they operated unscrupulously, posing a growing economic threat to the American nation. Appropriate action was required to reduce their wealth:

> It can be defeated. But it will not be defeated until the American people wake up and take action to stop so much wealth and power from being given into the hands of a few greedy hoodlums. Honest citizens must stop dealing with the gambler, the loan shark, and all other representatives of the underworld. This will greatly reduce organized crime's wealth, its major source of power.[3]

These concerns informed the adoption of laws such as the US Racketeer Influenced and Corrupt Organizations Act (RICO) of 1970[4] that enabled more effective action against crime syndicates that infiltrated legitimate business, and the US Bank Secrecy Act of 1970[5] that enabled bank reporting obligations in the US. Combined, they provided support for what became known as US President Richard Nixon's War on Drugs.[6] Experiences with these in the US[7] informed the international AML measures of the 1988 United Nations Convention against Illicit Drugs and Psychotropic Substances (the Vienna Convention).[8] The AML measures of the Vienna Convention were detailed by the Financial Action Task Force (FATF)—the global inter-governmental standard-setter for AML/CTF/CPF—in 1990 in their 40 Recommendations, that subsequently developed into global standards.[9] This framework was, in turn, leveraged by the 1999 International Convention for the Suppression of the Financing of Terrorism[10] and by US President George W Bush when, following the 9/11 attacks on the US, the Global War on Terrorism was launched. A key component of that war was disrupting financial flows to terrorists, seizing their assets and sealing them out of US and other financial institutions. As President Bush warned on 7 November 2001:

> We put the world's financial institutions on notice: if you do business with terrorists, if you support them or sponsor them, you will not do business with the United States of America.[11]

In response to the 9/11 attacks the United Nations Security Council (UNSC) adopted Resolution 1373 on 28 September 2001 requiring UN Member States to suppress terrorism by implementing targeted financial sanctions in relation to persons

---

[3] Ibid, p. 209.

[4] 18 USC 1961–1968.

[5] 31 USC 5311 et seq (also known as the Financial Recordkeeping and Reporting of Currency and Foreign Transactions Act of 1970).

[6] Johnson et al. (1996); Whitford and Yates (2009); Amicelle (2017).

[7] Blakey and Perry (1990); Rusch (1988).

[8] UN Convention against Illicit Traffic in Narcotic Drugs and Psychotropic Substances (opened for signature 20 December 1988, entered into force 11 November 1990) 1582 UNTS 95.

[9] Financial Action Task Force (1990); Goldbarrsht (2017).

[10] International Convention for the Suppression of the Financing of Terrorism, opened for signature 10 January 2000, 2178, UNTS 197.

[11] US Department of State (2001).

involved in terrorist activities. These sanctions, combined with previously adopted UNSC Resolution 1267 imposing sanctions on the Taliban and creating a framework for related sanctions in 1999, and the impact of the additional terrorist financing standards adopted by the FATF in 2001,[12] embedded sanctions enforcement in financial crime control measures.

This evolution reflects a broader strategic shift, raising the question: How has the framing of combating of trugs, organised crime and terrorism as "wars" influenced the development and effectiveness of financial crime control measures from the 1970s to the post-9/11 era and what are the implications in a fragmented global society?

2.1 Sanctions, Blacklisting and the War on Financial Crime

The FATF standards support UNSC targeted financial sanctions in relation to terrorism and financing of proliferation of weapons of mass destruction. National legislation may broaden the application of UNSC sanctions and countries may impose own, autonomous sanctions that regulated institutions must observe.[13]

While many of the sanctions are imposed on individuals and businesses, in a number of cases they apply directly or indirectly to nation states, including by targeting state officials and state-owned enterprises. Iran and the Democratic People's Republic of Korea (DPRK; North Korea) are important examples. In these cases, the sanctions regimes also overlap with the enforcement processes of the FATF.

The FATF evaluates country compliance with its standards and also the effectiveness with which AML/CTF/CPF measures were implemented. If strategic deficiencies in a country's AML/CTF/CPF measures are identified in this process, the country may be greylisted.[14] Where these deficiencies are serious, countries may be identified as posing a high risk and be blacklisted by the FATF. In principle this requires countries to apply enhanced due diligence measures, and in the most serious cases, countermeasures against these jurisdictions to protect the international financial system from the ongoing money laundering, terrorist financing, and proliferation financing risks emanating from that country.[15] In practice, many regulated institutions will cease doing business with people and businesses linked to such countries.

Iran, North Korea, and Myanmar have spent a number of years on the FATF's High-Risk Jurisdictions Subject to a Call for Action list (i.e. the blacklist) with limited indications that they are committed to actively addressing the identified strategic deficiencies. Apart from technical non-compliance, Iran has also been accused

[12] Financial Action Task Force (2001).

[13] de Koker (2024), pp. 130–131.

[14] de Koker et al. (2023).

[15] Financial Action Task Force (2025).

of funding terrorist groups actively;[16] North Korea has been flouting UNSC sanctions while building its nuclear arsenal; and the world has been left to ponder Iran's nuclear aspirations, with a re-imposition of UNSC sanctions in September 2025.

Banks and other AML/CTF/CPF-regulated institutions are actively enforcing the international and national sanctions regimes in relation to these countries. In that sense, they are in active service on the battlefield. What is, however, not always appreciated by regulators is that these institutions are also under attack in this battle.

In 2013, for example, North Korean malware targeted three large TV broadcasters and three banks in South Korea erasing critical records from an estimated 40,000 computers. This attack disrupted business operations and is estimated to have caused USD 700 million in damage.[17] Importantly, this attack was not aimed at stealing money but rather at causing disruption, loss, and political embarrassment. In many cases, however, ransomware and theft became a feature of such attacks. In 2016 hackers linked to North Korea accessed the computer network of the central bank of Bangladesh to steal approximately USD $81 million from the bank's accounts in the Federal Reserve Bank of New York and to transfer it via SWIFT to controlled accounts in the Philippines, Sri Lanka, and other countries. A typographical error prevented an additional $851 million from being stolen.[18]

In its 2025 virtual asset service provider (VASP) update the FATF noted that:

> … [t]he DPRK continues to be particularly adept at stealing and laundering funds using VAs (virtual assets). Although industry participants had previously pointed to a reduction in the amount of stolen VAs year-over-year due to additional cybersecurity measures, the DPRK conducted the largest single theft of VAs in 2025, stealing $1.46 bn worth of VAs from the VASP ByBit.[19]

The VASP Contact Group of the FATF discussed the methods that enabled the ByBit theft and "highlighted the DPRK's use of unregistered VASPs, including over-the-counter traders and some mixers and bridges, and a large number of wallets in complex transaction pattens (35 bitcoin wallets and 125,000 Ethereum wallets)."[20] Cybercrime is therefore an entrenched part of the response to sanctions and a means to raise finances for nuclear and other national ambitions.

Attacks on financial infrastructure also occur during conventional warfare. During the Israel-Iran war of 2025, Predatory Sparrow, a hacking group with reported links to Israel, claimed responsibility for an attack on Nobitex, the largest cryptocurrency exchange in Iran, that resulted in the theft of nearly USD 90 million,

[16] US Bureau of Counterrorism (2019), p. 2: "In the past, Tehran has spent as much as $700 million per year to support terrorist groups, including Hizballah and Hamas, though its ability to provide financial support in 2019 was constrained by crippling U.S. sanctions." See also US Bureau of Counterrorism (2023) for broader allegations of continuing state sponsorship of terrorism.

[17] Klingner (2021), p. 23; Issuemakerslab (2013).

[18] Hackett (2016); Klingner (2021), p. 29.

[19] Financial Action Task Force (2025a), par 28.

[20] Financial Action Task Force (2025a), par 29.

and for an attack on an Iranian bank (Sepah) that disrupted services and allegedly destroyed data related to the Islamic Revolutionary Guard Corps.[21]

While such thefts and attacks draw attention, there are other less public aspects to this battlefield. The AML/CTF controls of regulated institutions are designed to mitigate the risks of abuse by criminals. Nation-states, on the other hand, have much more capacity to evade controls measures, for example by producing credible customer due diligence documents and data trails over years. Despite stringent sanctions on North Korea they have been able to build a nuclear arsenal and are continuing their efforts to improve their intercontinental ballistic missiles and delivery systems. The sanctions framework clearly has gaps that are being exploited effectively. Countries have been compelling their institutions to adopt CPF measures that are aligned with their AML/CFT measures. Little thought has been given to the fact that the ultimate opposing parties are nation-states, and that controls need to be adapted accordingly to be effective.

North Korean sanctions gaps have often been linked to China.[22] Since the imposition of sanctions on Russia and especially after its full-scale invasion of Ukraine in February 2022, Russia, Iran, North Korea, and China have deepened their collaboration, also financially. Russia and Iran, for example, linked their payment systems to allow for direct transactions that bypass international sanctions.[23] Worryingly, Russia is alleged to be actively supporting North Korea's sanctions evasion.[24] In 2025 the Multilateral Sanctions Monitoring Team issued a report in relation to their evasion of sanctions, stating that:

> Russia and the DPRK have actively engaged in financial transactions using ruble accounts. According to an MSMT participating state, Russia is facilitating North Korea's evasion of UN sanctions and FATF requirements by allowing North Korea to make payments through UN-designated Foreign Trade Bank (a.k.a. FTB, KPe.047) and Korea Kwangson Banking Corporation (a.k.a. KKBC, KPe.025) using ruble accounts it set up in November 2023 at MRB Bank in Georgia's South Ossetia region.[25]

The FATF has noted with concern the growing financial connectivity of Russia with countries subject to FATF countermeasures. Many FATF members are taking proactive measures to protect themselves and the global financial system. The Russian Federation was suspended as a FATF member after its full-scale invasion of Ukraine but still remains accountable for its obligation to implement the FATF Standards.[26]

It is important to bear in mind that the collaboration outlined above may extend beyond such payments and engagements to include leveraging their resources, officials, networks, and professionals to evade financial sanctions controls worldwide.

[21] TRM (2025).

[22] de Koker (2023), pp. 140–141.

[23] Smagin (2025).

[24] Multilateral Sanctions Monitoring Team (2025); Pawlus (2025).

[25] Multilateral Sanctions Monitoring Team (2025), par 40.

[26] Financial Action Task Force (2024).

What can be done to ensure that the systems of the regulated institutions are sufficiently robust against such weapons-grade ML/TF/PF threats?

2.2 *Doubling Down on Combating Proliferation Financing*

In 2012 the FATF's mandate was expanded to include the financing of proliferation of weapons of mass destruction. The FATF's mandate was restricted to enforcing the UNSC's targeted financial sanctions in relation to proliferation. In 2020 the compliance footprint was expanded to require AML/CTF/CPF-regulated institutions to undertake a proliferation financing risk assessment and to adopt enhanced control measures where higher risks were identified. Where lower risks were identified the institutions had to maintain standard control measures to ensure full compliance with the UNSC sanctions.[27]

This new obligation imposed additional knowledge and capacity requirements on all regulated institutions. After pressure from civil society and academia, the FATF allowed countries to exempt institutions from the risk assessment and risk management obligations where it was found that they posed a low proliferation financing risk. This might be true for many rural real estate agents, family lawyers, etc. This exemption is however rarely used by governments.

A host of small AML/CTF/CPF-regulated institutions therefore need to master sufficient knowledge about proliferation risks to undertake a credible, proportionate proliferation financing risk assessment and design appropriate controls. In Australia, an industry survey reported in 2022 found that 28% of the respondents were not concerned about their institutions' exposure to and ability to identify counterproliferation financing and proliferation-related sanctions evasion, while 39% were concerned, but less so about these than about other threats.[28] 57% indicated that their institutions were aware of PF risk indicators and red flags generally.[29] Where institutions are alert to PF threats they may only see a part of the picture. Banks, for example, received export documentation when trade finance is required. Whether the documents correctly reflect the nature of the goods that are being shipped cannot be readily ascertained by banks.[30] This vulnerability is compounded by the use of evasion techniques including the mislabelling of goods, sourcing of components from multiple suppliers and jurisdictions, using transshipment hubs, and employing front and shell companies.[31] Customs and port authorities are in better positions to undertake such checks but they do not have formal AML/CTF/CPF information exchange links with banks.

---

[27] Financial Action Task Force (2021), pp. 47–48; de Koker (2023).

[28] AUSTRAC (2022), p. 23.

[29] AUSTRAC (2022), p. 34.

[30] De Koker (2023), pp. 142–143.

[31] Ibid, p. 22.

While Australia, for example, has established inter-agency coordination involving the Australian Transaction Reports and Analysis Centre (AUSTRAC), the Australian Border Force, the Australian Federal Police, Defence Export Controls, and the Australian Sanctions Office within the Department of Foreign Affairs and Trade, critical gaps remain. Information-sharing arrangements exist between many of the relevant agencies and foreign counterparts, but not all. Slow progress with broadening the scope of AML/CFT/CPF obligations also left vulnerabilities, for example resulting from the historical lack of AML/CTF reporting requirements for crucial professions such as lawyers, accountants, and company service providers who often facilitate the establishment of opaque corporate structures used in proliferation financing.[32]

Furthermore, North Korea often uses open account trading rather than trade finance as it requires less documentation and attracts less bank scrutiny.[33] Australian case studies demonstrate this pattern, where North Korean-linked networks have used Australian-registered companies and complex corporate structures to broker trade in prohibited goods while physically distancing financial services from actual goods movement.[34] This raises an important question: what support and tools do regulated institutions need to be effective in the fight against financial crime?

3 Arming Regulated Institutions

For many years governments have done little to arm regulated institutions in the financial war against other nations. Laws enlisted them in this war on financial crime but they were given sparce information about the enemy and little support by way of intelligence. Even customer due diligence measures were badly supported. There are known vulnerabilities for both small and large financial institutions: smaller banks "could be targeted due to the perception they have weaker due diligence processes, are not aware of their proliferation financing risks and do not have processes in place to identify proliferation financing activity", while large banks may be attractive given their "greater volume of financial transactions handled by these banks, [which] may make it harder for them to identify proliferation financing-related activity, particularly given the complexity of trade financing arrangements that often involves multiple parties and jurisdictions".[35]

---

[32] Of note, from 1 July 2026, AML/CTF obligations will apply to these "Tranche II" entities, following the November 2024 passing of the AML/CTF Amendment Bill 2024 (the Bill), amending the AML/CTF Act.

[33] de Koker (2023), p. 143.

[34] AUSTRAC (2022), p. 25.

[35] Ibid, pp. 22–23.

3.1 Information

With the rise of public-private partnerships,[36] information sharing has improved, but only for those institutions that are members of the partnership. Smaller institutions (relatively speaking) are often not members of these partnerships and that leaves them particularly vulnerable.

The dilemma is that the really useful data is sensitive. As military secrets need to be protected, financial crime intelligence require protection too, especially when measures are aimed at nation-states. Hard intelligence is best restricted to secure channels and a small number of trusted parties. However, how do thousands of regulated institutions effectively identify, assess, and manage their crime risks adequately as soldiers in the broader war on crime, if they are not included in the intelligence-sharing partnership or are included but only receive limited data? Rich data, on the other hand increases the data risks that need to be mitigated, especially when the opposition is skilful at hacking.

Some of these questions were raised by the debates preceding the 2025 revision of the FATF's travel rule for payments and value transfer services in Recommendation 16. This standard was introduced as part of the set of Special Recommendation on Terrorist Financing in 2001 to ensure that originator and beneficiary data accompanied the payment message and was available to the institutions managing the payment and to law enforcement. Advances in payments technology and models and developments in the context of the G20 Priority Action Plan for enhanced cross-border payments required the FATF to revisit this standard.[37]

Among a range of issues, the public consultation on the revision raised the questions whether the FATF should retain the exemption of purchase of goods and services form the full application of Recommendation 16[38] and whether cross-border card-based withdrawals of cash at a different institution should require the institution of the card holder to provide the details of the card holder to the regulated institution managing the cash pay-out, e.g. via an ATM.[39] In such a case, it was proposed that the name of the cardholder should be sent to the acquiring financial institution within 24 h. The proposal also envisaged that information such as the address of the cardholder and the person's date of birth should be provided on request.

The FATF justified these proposals on the strength of observed criminal abuse of payment cards. Examples provided included:[40]

---

[36] See Chapter 3 "FATF and the Conundrum of Public-Private Sector Intelligence and Information Sharing" by Chadderton (2025) in this collection.

[37] Financial Action Task Force (2024a).

[38] Financial Action Task Force (2024b), pp. 1–5.

[39] Financial Action Task Force (2025b).

[40] Financial Action Task Force (2024b), p. 2.

- The use of credit and debit cards and fake merchants to disguise purchases of illicit goods as legitimate purchases.
- The use of shell companies to open offshore bank accounts with merchant acquiring banks to accept credit/debit card charges for illicit goods purchased.
- The use of stolen credit card numbers from black market websites to encode that information onto blank cards, and use of such cards to purchase gift cards or other items that can be quickly sold for cash.

While payment cards are certainly being abused by criminals,[41] it was not clear how additional party data would assist recipient institutions in combating such abuse. Exchange of such data may actually support cybercrime and inform identity fraud. Furthermore, in relation to cash withdrawals it was unclear what a foreign bank would be able to usefully do with the details of a tourist who withdrew USD/EUR 100 at one of its ATMs. If it turned out that the person's name was a partial match for a name on a sanctions list, the bank would have a real compliance dilemma without powers to appropriately investigate that match to determine whether the transaction breached any sanctions.

The proposals also envisaged that enhanced party data would need to be collected and verified, for example the full name, residential address and data of birth of the originator of the payment, where that was a natural person and the payment value was above a de minimis threshold, if any. Concern was expressed in the public consultation period that such information would form access barriers for many users in developing countries and would therefore increase financial exclusion risks to the FATF's financial integrity objectives.[42]

In June 2025 the FATF adopted a revised Recommendation 16. The party data required to be collected and verified was revised to prevent financial exclusion of those without formalised postal address information or without full date of birth information.[43] With respect to any card-based payments for the purchase of goods or services, the credit or debit or prepaid card number should accompany all transfers flowing from the transaction and the name and location of the card issuing and merchant acquiring financial institutions should be made available upon request.[44] With respect to cross-border card-based cash withdrawals, the card number should accompany cash withdrawal and the name of the cardholder should be sent to the acquiring financial institution upon request, within three business days of receiving the request.[45]

Time will tell whether the right balance was struck but the design of the revised Recommendation 16 reflects the tension between ensuring that regulated institutions have appropriate information to mitigate crime risks and the protecting

[41] Goldbarsht (2020), pp. 126–8.

[42] de Koker et al. (2025).

[43] Financial Action Task Force (2012–2025), INR16.9.

[44] Financial Action Task Force (2012–2025), INR16.16.

[45] Financial Action Task Force (2012–2025), INR16.19.

personal data from criminal abuse. That protection is especially important where systems are targets of national states subject to financial sanctions.

3.2 Customer Due Diligence Support

Regulated institutions enjoy limited support to undertake customer due diligence measures effectively and efficiently. Regulated institutions must for example verify the identities of their customers. Many countries do not have national identity systems and even fewer have digital identity systems and frameworks. This increases the costs of due diligence measures but also limits their effectiveness, especially when false identity documents are well-prepared and can pass reasonable human scrutiny.

Similarly, regulated institutions have to identify the natural persons who ultimately control legal entities and arrangements as beneficial owners. Yet, in 2022 in Australia it was still reported that "[t]here is no requirement to provide ultimate beneficial ownership information for corporate registration, with nominees permitted to register as company directors and non-beneficial shareholders".[46] Nineteen percent of industry survey respondents at that time reported that they cannot access sufficient ultimate beneficial ownership information to effectively assess potential exposure to sanctioned entities or other illicit activity.[47] Laws in Australia and elsewhere continue to enable overly opaque and complex corporate structures and arrangements. The FATF amended its standards on the creation and maintenance of beneficial ownership registers in 2022. The data in such registers is however still not necessarily available to support institutional customer due diligence processes, and in turn, has limited utility as it stands.[48] While governments continue to provide weak support for institutions to identify beneficial owners, laws continue to allow overly complex corporate and other legal structures that can obscure control and beneficial ownership. How can these enabling corporate and trust laws be amended to prevent the creation of unnecessarily complex, opaque structures?[49]

3.3 Toward a Financial Integrity Harm Index

Like many developments in the field of crime prevention, the architecture of AML/CTF measures evolved without clearly defined metrics to measure effectiveness or efficiency. Political momentum behind these initiatives was largely driven by the

---

[46] AUSTRAC (2022), p. 32.

[47] Ibid, p. 33.

[48] Leuprecht et al. (2025), pp. 264–286.

[49] de Koker (2023).

assumption that targeting financial crime was inherently beneficial, a public good in itself. As such, detailed assessments of harm reduction or cost effectiveness were secondary, if considered at all. Over a decade after the FATF's establishment, those drafting the Recommendations were reportedly advised not to account for the systemic or financial costs of the proposed framework.[50] It has largely been presumed that efforts to counter money laundering and terrorism financing generate positive net social outcomes.

In a 1998 address to the FATF, the then IMF Managing Director, drawing on Vito Tanzi's work, introduced the estimate that money laundering accounted for "2 to 5 percent of global GDP". However, the methodology underpinning this claim was never fully documented, and even IMF researchers were later unable to verify its basis.[51] The estimate, while influential, appears to have been more illustrative than empirical.

Nearly four decades years after global concern around money laundering first gained prominence, there are still no authoritative estimates of the total volume of funds laundered annually. More critically, we lack meaningful national or international measures of the specific harms that AML/CTF regimes are designed to prevent. The FATF's current mandate articulates its objectives as protecting financial systems from the threats of money laundering, terrorism financing, and proliferation, thereby strengthening integrity and contributing to broader security.[52] Yet these goals remain difficult to quantify or track with precision.

Although there is broad consensus that money laundering and terrorist financing cause significant harm, one of the central challenges remains our limited ability to estimate the scale of illicit financial activity. As stated in the chapter "Financial Crime Prevention in an Age of Paradox", "This systemic paradox is amplified by our fundamental uncertainty about the problem's scope".[53] Estimates of total laundered funds remain elusive, and robust evaluation of actual harm is rare. The nature of harm caused by financial crime is complex and multifaceted ranging from economic distortions, harm to public trust, to specific societal consequences. Yet existing metrics often lack precision or credibility.[54]

Domestically, similar difficulties persist. In Australia, the Australian Institute of Criminology (AIC), have identified major methodological gaps in tracking the effects of money laundering and terrorism financing.[55] Recognising these limitations, the Basel Institute on Governance launched the *Basel AML Index* in 2012 to help assess country level money laundering risks. This tool ranks jurisdictions based on available data and relies significantly on data relevant to FATF-related compliance and effectiveness levels and less on data relating to actual criminal threats and

---

[50] Levi et al. (2018), pp. 307, 308.

[51] Walker and Unger (2013), p. 159.

[52] Financial Action Task Force (2019) *Mandate*, p. 4.

[53] Ferrill et al. (2025).

[54] See Levi (2018) and references therein.

[55] Schmidt (2024): AIC report.

risks.[56] In Australia, AUSTRAC has commissioned the AIC to conduct a scoping and feasibility study aimed at measuring the broader impact of money laundering and terrorism financing on government, business, and the community. While valuable, this research does not attempt to determine whether AML/CTF efforts are reducing predicate crimes.

To fill this gap, the Financial Integrity Hub (FIH) is developing a model to assess the harms caused by financial crime in Australia, particularly in relation to money laundering and terrorism financing. Drawing on AUSTRAC's (2024) *National Risk Assessment*,[57] the FIH project prioritises three predicate offences: Illicit drug trafficking—identified as the top money laundering threat, with high proceeds and prevalent cash-based laundering; fraud—especially cyber-enabled scams and identity theft, the most commonly reported predicate offence; and tax evasion—often facilitated through professional services and complex financial structures. The objective is to assess whether AML/CTF efforts in Australia effectively reduce, have no effect on, or inadvertently support these predicate crimes. This focus on outcome—actual harm disrupted—extends beyond the current scope of the AIC's study and complements broader policy needs. Building on this foundation, future research could explore broader questions such as: What are the social and economic harms associated with money laundering and terrorism financing, and how can they be effectively measured? How is such an index best developed, tested and applied? How can it best respond to new, emerging risks and to significant risks that are reasonably rare, such as proliferation financing risks? What may be the beneficial and the unintended negative consequences of such an index? Such inquiries could also extend to examining the impact of emerging threats, including scams and cyber-enabled fraud.

4 Conclusion

The combating of financial crime has become more complex. The assumption-based measures of the 1980s need to be tested and informed by appropriate evidence to guide important design and policy measures. The twentieth century framework succeeded in ensuring global application of standardised, risk-based AML/CFT/CPF measures. However, many gaps remain, and these allow for the development of new threats. If we are in a war, it is crucial that policy leaders are sufficiently informed to devise strategic approaches that advance the cause of integrity. In the fog of uncertainty troop movements are taking place but have those actions increased the chances of a successful outcome? Where have they been out-manoeuvred and what are the new weapons that they may face or employ? An improved alignments between researchers, policymakers, compliance officers and law enforcement may improve the outcomes while building an resilient, effective and efficient AML/CTF/CPF framework.

[56] Basel AML Index (2024).

[57] AUSTRAC's (2024) *National Risk Assessment.*

References

Amicelle A (2017) When finance met security: Back to the war on drugs and the problem of dirty money. Finance Soc 3(2):106–123. https://doi.org/10.2218/finsoc.v3i2.2572

AUSTRAC (2024) Proliferation financing in Australia: national risk assessment. https://www.austrac.gov.au/sites/default/files/2022-12/AUSTRAC_Proliferation_Financing_in_Australia-National_Risk_%20Assessment_Web.pdf; https://www.austrac.gov.au/sites/default/files/2025-03/AUSTRAC%20Proliferation%20Financing%20in%20Australia-National%20Risk%20Assessment.pdf

Basel Institute on Governance (2024) Basel AML index. https://baselgovernance.org/publications/basel-aml-index-2024

Blakey GR, Perry TA (1990) An analysis of the myths that bolster efforts to rewrite RICO and the various proposals for reform: 'Mother of God - is this the end of RICO?' Vanderbilt Law Rev 43:851–1101

Chadderton P (2025) FATF and the conundrum of public-private sector intelligence and information sharing. In Goldbarsht D, de Koker L, Ferrill J (eds) The financial war on crime and terrorism: opportunities and challenges. Springer, Cham

Ferrill J, de Koker L, Goldbarsht D (2025) Financial crime prevention in an age of paradox. In: Goldbarsht D, de Koker L, Ferrill J (eds) The financial war on crime and terrorism: opportunities and challenges. Springer, Cham

Financial Action Task Force (2001) Eight Special Recommendations on Terrorist Financing. https://www.fatf-gafi.org/content/dam/fatf-gafi/annual-reports/2001%202002%20ENG.pdf

Financial Action Task Force (2012–2025) International standards on combating money laundering and the financing of terrorism & proliferation. https://www.fatf-gafi.org/en/publications/Fatfrecommendations/Fatf-recommendations.html

Financial Action Task Force (2019) Mandate. https://www.fatf-gafi.org/en/publications/Fatfgeneral/Fatf-mandate.html

Financial Action Task Force (2021) Guidance on proliferation financing risk assessment and mitigation. https://www.fatf-gafi.org/publications/financingofproliferation/documents/proliferation-financing-riskassessment-mitigation.html

Financial Action Task Force (2024) FATF statement on the Russian Federation. https://www.fatf-gafi.org/en/publications/Fatfgeneral/fatf-statement-russian-federation-feb-2024.html

Financial Action Task Force (2024a) Public consultation on Recommendation 16 on payment transparency. https://www.fatf-gafi.org/en/publications/Fatfrecommendations/R16-public-consultation-Feb24.html

Financial Action Task Force (2024b) Explanatory memorandum and draft revisions to Recommendation 16. https://www.fatf-gafi.org/en/publications/Fatfrecommendations/R16-public-consultation-Feb24.html

Financial Action Task Force (13 June 2025) High-risk jurisdictions subject to a call for action. https://www.fatf-gafi.org/en/publications/High-risk-and-other-monitored-jurisdictions/Call-for-action-june-2025.html

Financial Action Task Force (2025a) Targeted update on implementation of the FATF standards on virtual assets/VASPs. https://www.fatf-gafi.org/content/fatf-gafi/en/publications/Fatfrecommendations/targeted-update-virtualassets-vasps-2025.html

Financial Action Task Force (2025b) Second public consultation on payment transparency: proposed revisions to R.16. https://www.fatf-gafi.org/en/publications/Fatfrecommendations/R16-public-consultation-February-2025.html

Goldbarsht D (2017) Who's the legislator anyway? How the FATF's global norms reshape Australian counter terrorist financing laws. Fed Law Rev 45:127–151

Goldbarsht D (2020) New payment systems: potential counter-terrorist financing risks and the legal response in the United Kingdom. In: Assets, crimes and the state. Routledge, pp 125–139

Hackett R (2016) Everything you need to know about North Korea's suspected bank blitzkrieg. Fortune. https://fortune.com/2016/06/23/north-korea-hackers-banks
Hoover JE (1963) The war on organized crime. DePaul L Rev 13:195–209
Issuemakerslab (2013) South Korea identified who's behind the massive cyber attack on March 20th. http://www.issuemakerslab.com/research1/index.html
Johnson TJ, Wanta W, Boudreau T, Blank-Libra J, Schaffer K, Turner S (1996) Influence dealers: a path analysis model of agenda building during Richard Nixon's war on drugs. Journal Mass Commun Q 73(1):181–194. https://doi.org/10.1177/107769909607300116
Klingner B (2021) North Korean cyberattacks: a dangerous and evolving threat. The Heritage Foundation. https://www.heritage.org/sites/default/files/2021-09/SR247.pdf
de Koker L (2023) FATF measures and the combating of corruption in developing countries. In: Rider BAK (ed) A research agenda for economic crime and development. Edward Elgar Publishing, pp 175–204
de Koker L (2024) The FATF's combating of financing of proliferation standards: private sector implementation challenges. In: Goldbarsht D, de Koker L (eds) Financial crime and the law. Ius Gentium: comparative perspectives on law and justice, vol 115. Springer, Cham. https://doi.org/10.1007/978-3-031-59543-1_6
de Koker L, Kerse M, Jeník I (2025) Public consultation on FATF's guidance on AML/CFT measures and financial inclusion. CGAP Briefing Note
de Koker L, Morris NC, Howell J (2023) Economic consequences of greylisting by the Financial Action Task Force. Risks 11(5):81. https://doi.org/10.3390/risks11050081
Leuprecht C, Ferrill J, Ozga M, Tiwari M, Karunakaran J (2025) Detecting, disrupting and deterring sexual exploitation of trafficked persons: leveraging beneficial ownership registries to reduce criminogenic information asymmetry and raise public expectations. Curr Issues Crim Just 37(2):264–286
Levi M, Reuter P, Halliday T (2018) Can the AML system be evaluated without better data? Crime Law Soc Chang 69:307–328
Multilateral Sanctions Monitoring Team (2025) Unlawful Military cooperation including arms transfers between North Korea and Russia. https://msmt.info/Publications/detail/MSMT%20Report/4195
Pawlus W (2025) Russia is now actively funding North Korea's nuclear programme. RUSI. https://www.rusi.org/explore-our-research/publications/commentary/russia-now-actively-funding-north-koreas-nuclear-programme
Rusch JJ (1988) Hue and cry in the counting-house: some observations on the Bank Secrecy Act. Cathol Univ Law Rev 37(2):465–488
Schmidt A (2024) Impacts of money laundering and terrorism financing: final report. Special reports. Australian Institute of Criminology, Canberra. https://doi.org/10.52922/sp77543
Smagin N (2025) New Russia-Iran treaty reveals the limits of their partnership. Carnegie Politika. https://carnegieendowment.org/russia-eurasia/politika/2025/01/russia-iran-strategic-agreement?lang=en
TRM (18 June 2025) Iran's largest crypto exchange targeted in $90M hack. TRM Blog. https://www.trmlabs.com/resources/blog/irans-largest-crypto-exchange-targeted-in-90m-hack
US Bureau of Counterrorism (2019) Country reports on terrorism 2019. https://www.state.gov/reports/country-reports-on-terrorism-2019/#:~:text=Iran's%20annual%20financial%20backing%20to,pose%20a%20threat%20to%20Israel
US Bureau of Counterrorism (2023) Country reports on terrorism 2023. https://www.state.gov/reports/country-reports-on-terrorism-2023/
US Department of State (2001) The global war on terrorism: the first 100 days. https://2001-2009.state.gov/s/ct/rls/wh/6947.htm
Walker J, Unger B (2013) Measuring global money laundering: the 'Walker gravity model'. In: Research handbook on money laundering. Edward Elgar Publishing
Whitford AB, Yates J (2009) Presidential rhetoric and the public agenda: constructing the war on drugs. JHU Press

Prof. Louis de Koker is a Professor of Law at La Trobe Law School, Australia, an Extraordinary Professor of Law at the University of the Western Cape, South Africa, and an advisory board member of the Financial Integrity Hub (FIH). His financial crime research focuses on managing the relationship between financial inclusion and anti-money laundering and counter terrorist financing objectives. He has undertaken various university research engagements with the bodies such as the World Bank and the Asian Development Bank and has worked closely with the DC-based Consultative Group to Assist the Poor (CGAP) and with the Financial Integrity Working Group of the Alliance for Financial Inclusion (AFI). This work extended to a range of developing countries including Ghana, Indonesia, Kenya, Kyrgyzstan, Malaysia, Namibia, Nigeria, Uganda, the Ukraine and Palau. His publications have been cited in publications and research papers of international bodies such as the World Bank, the Basel Committee on Banking Supervision, the International Labour Organization.

Dr. Doron Goldbarsht LLB, LLM (HUJI), PHD (UNSW) is an Associate Professor at Macquarie Law School, the Academic Head of the Graduate Certificate in Financial Integrity Law and the Founder and Director of the Financial Integrity Hub (FIH). With over 20 years of expertise in anti-money laundering (AML) and counterterrorist financing (CTF), he has co-edited several books on financial crime and compliance, including Financial Crime and the Law: Identifying and Mitigating Risks (Springer 2024) and Financial Technology and the Law: Combating Financial Crime (Springer, 2022). Certified as a lawyer in both Israel and Australia, Doron also provides expert opinions to government and private sector in litigation, advising on financial crime and regulatory matters.

Dr. Jamie Ferrill is a Senior Lecturer of Financial Crime Studies at the Australian Graduate School of Policing and Security, Charles Sturt University and a research fellow with the Financial Integrity Hub (FIH). Before transitioning to academia, she gained nearly a decade of experience in law enforcement, serving with the Canadian federal government. Jamie's research addresses threats to national and economic security, with a particular interest in the intersection of financial crime with border governance frameworks, international cooperation, and organisational effectiveness. Jamie has been a visiting fellow at the Academy of International Affairs NRW and the Border Policy Research Institute, and she is a fellow of the Financial Integrity Hub, the Institute of Intergovernmental Relations at Queen's University, and Borders in Globalization at the University of Victoria. Her latest book is titled Dirty Money: Financial Crime in Canada (McGill-Queen's University Press).

Correction to: Geopolitics of State Capture: Systemic Corruption as a Professional Service

Nicholas Donaldson and Christian Leuprecht

Correction to:
Chapter 8 in: D. Goldbarsht et al. (eds.), *The Financial War on Crime and Terrorism*, European Yearbook of International Economic Law, https://doi.org/10.1007/978-3-032-06360-1_8

Inadvertently, Figs. 1, 2, and 3 in this chapter were initially published with errors. The correct presentation is given here.

The updated version of this chapter can be found at
https://doi.org/10.1007/978-3-032-06360-1_8

D. Goldbarsht et al. (eds.), *The Financial War on Crime and Terrorism*,
European Yearbook of International Economic Law,
https://doi.org/10.1007/978-3-032-06360-1_14

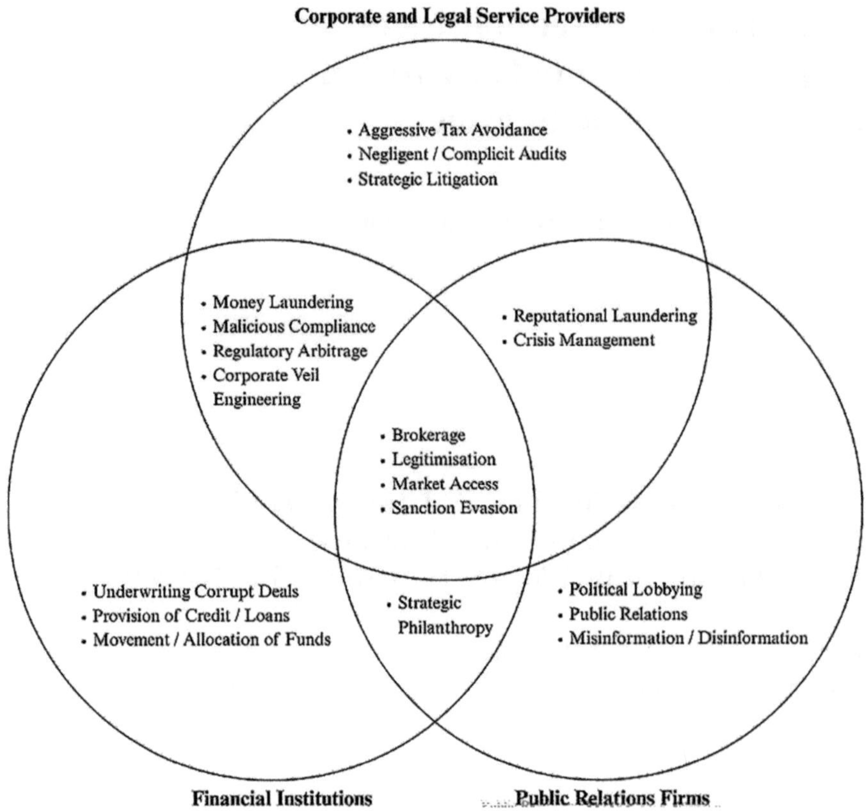

Fig. 1 Venn diagram of overlapping services provided by professional intermediaries

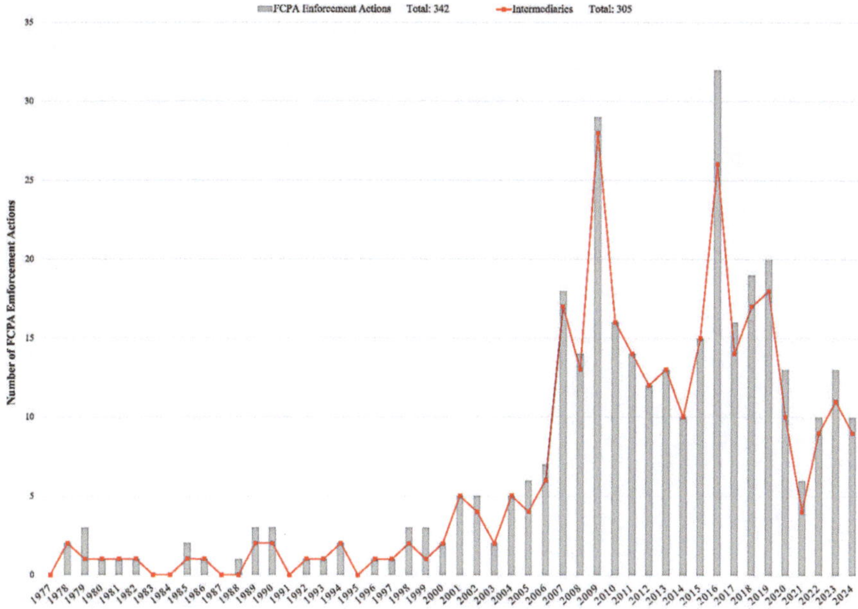

Fig. 2 FCPA enforcement data (1977–2025) by third-party intermediaries

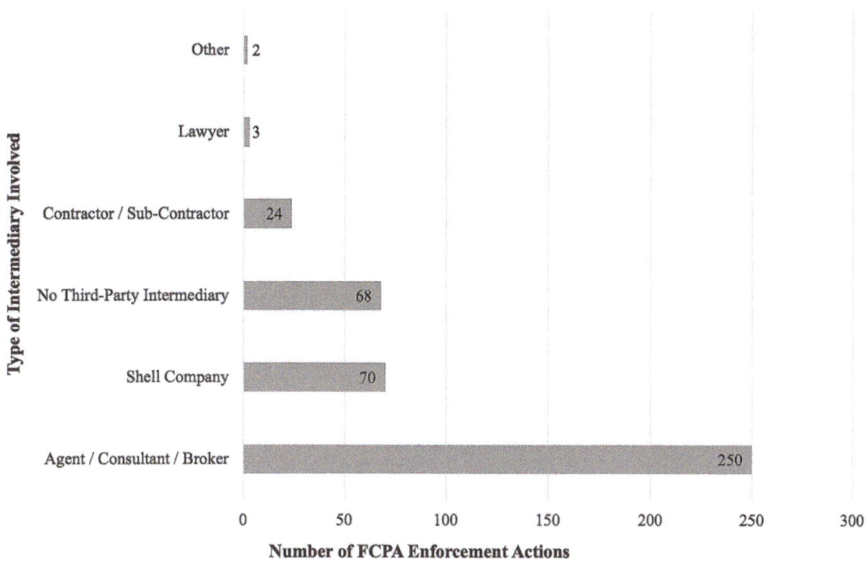

Fig. 3 FCPA enforcement data (1977–2025) by type of intermediary

MIX
Papier aus verantwortungsvollen Quellen
Paper from responsible sources
FSC® C105338

If you have any concerns about our products,
you can contact us on
ProductSafety@springernature.com

In case Publisher is established outside the EU,
the EU authorized representative is:
Springer Nature Customer Service Center GmbH
Europaplatz 3, 69115 Heidelberg, Germany

Printed by Libri Plureos GmbH
in Hamburg, Germany